3 YEAR BIBLE CHRONOLOGICAL DAILY DEVOTIONAL

BIBLE CHAT

YEAR ONE

A Chronological Devotional Journey through the entire Bible, featuring shorter 3-year Old Testament Readings, yearly New Testament Readings, Daily Proverbs, and a Christmas Reflection... suitable for all ages!

CYRIL OPOKU

© 2025 *Cyril Opoku*. Bible Chat Devotional. All rights reserved.

No part of this book may be reproduced, stored in a retrieval system, or transmitted in any form or by any means—electronic, mechanical, photocopying, recording, or otherwise—without the prior written permission of the publisher, except for brief quotations used in critical reviews or articles.

Unless otherwise indicated, the Scripture quotations in this book are from the ESV® Bible (The Holy Bible, English Standard Version®), © 2001 by Crossway, a publishing ministry of Good News Publishers. ESV Text Edition: 2025. The ESV text may not be quoted in any publication made available to the public by a Creative Commons license. The ESV may not be translated in whole or in part into any other language. Used by permission. All rights reserved.

The bible reading plan used in this devotional is based on the *3 Year Bible plan*, created by Dr. Ted Williams as a way to engage with the entire Bible in a meaningful and sustainable way that focused primarily on the New Testament while still incorporating the Old Testament, Psalms, and Proverbs.

Published by *Quest Publications*.

Email: questpublications@outlook.com

ISBN-13: 978-1-988439-47-1 (Hardcover)

ISBN-13: 978-1-988439-48-8 (Paperback)

Printed in U.S.A. & Canada.

INTRODUCTION

Welcome to the *3-Year Bible Chronological Daily Devotional* (Year One)—your daily companion for a manageable and meaningful journey through God's Word.

Each devotional features short, reflective readings—perfect for your morning routine or quiet time. Based on the unique 3 Year Bible reading plan created by Dr. Ted Williams, you'll walk through the entire Old Testament in manageable segments over three years, while the New Testament, Psalms, and Proverbs are revisited each year.

The devotional features:

- **Shorter Readings:** Designed to be easily incorporated into your daily routine, even on busy days. The shorter readings also allow for deeper reflection and meditation.
- **3-year Old Testament Plan:** The 3-Year Old Testament Plan offers shorter daily readings, covering Genesis to Judges in year one, Job to Solomon in year two, and the kings to Malachi in year three.
- **New Testament Focus:** Spend more time in the New Testament, immersing yourself in the teachings of Jesus and the early church.
- **Daily Proverbs:** One to two carefully selected proverbs each day provide bite-sized wisdom for daily living.
- **Chronological Arrangement:** Experience the unfolding narrative of Scripture by reading biblical stories and prophecies in their historical context. Discover fascinating connections, like reading the Psalm David wrote after hiding from Saul in a cave.
- **December's Christmas Devotional:** Journey through the anticipation of Christ's coming with readings that highlight God's plan of redemption throughout history.

At the end of each day's devotional message, you will find *Think About It*, thoughtfully designed to deepen your engagement with the Scripture and the devotional message. These questions are an invitation to pause and reflect, helping you connect personally with God's Word and apply its timeless truths to your daily life. Whether used individually or in a group setting, these questions encourage you to examine your thoughts, actions, and faith journey, fostering spiritual growth and transformation.

Each day's devotion also includes a *Devotional Prayer*, inviting you to bring your reflections before God in a personal and heartfelt way. These prayers serve as a guide, helping you express your thoughts, desires, and concerns to God while aligning your heart with His will. They offer a powerful moment of connection with God, strengthening your faith and providing peace as you close each day in prayer.

Supplemented by the acclaimed Bible Chat Devotional Podcast, the *3-Year Bible Chronological Daily Devotional* prioritizes a conversational and contemplative experience that fosters a deeper understanding of Scripture and its relevance to your life today.

Contents

Introduction iii	February 13 44	March 30 89
Contents iv	February 14 45	March 31 90
January 1 1	February 15 46	April 1 91
January 2 2	February 16 47	April 2 92
January 3 3	February 17 48	April 3 93
January 4 4	February 18 49	April 4 94
January 5 5	February 19 50	April 5 95
January 6 6	February 20 51	April 6 96
January 7 7	February 21 52	April 7 97
January 8 8	February 22 53	April 8 98
January 9 9	February 23 54	April 9 99
January 10 10	February 24 55	April 10 100
January 11 11	February 25 56	April 11 101
January 12 12	February 26 57	April 12 102
January 13 13	February 27 58	April 13 103
January 14 14	February 28 59	April 14 104
January 15 15	March 1 60	April 15 105
January 16 16	March 2 61	April 16 106
January 17 17	March 3 62	April 17 107
January 18 18	March 4 63	April 18 108
January 19 19	March 5 64	April 19 109
January 20 20	March 6 65	April 20 110
January 21 21	March 7 66	April 21 111
January 22 22	March 8 67	April 22 112
January 23 23	March 9 68	April 23 113
January 24 24	March 10 69	April 24 114
January 25 25	March 11 70	April 25 115
January 26 26	March 12 71	April 26 116
January 27 27	March 13 72	April 27 117
January 28 28	March 14 73	April 28 118
January 29 29	March 15 74	April 29 119
January 30 30	March 16 75	April 30 120
January 31 31	March 17 76	May 1 121
February 1 32	March 18 77	May 2 122
February 2 33	March 19 78	May 3 123
February 3 34	March 20 79	May 4 125
February 4 35	March 21 80	May 5 126
February 5 36	March 22 81	May 6 128
February 6 37	March 23 82	May 7 129
February 7 38	March 24 83	May 8 130
February 8 39	March 25 84	May 9 131
February 9 40	March 26 85	May 10 132
February 10 41	March 27 86	May 11 133
February 11 42	March 28 87	May 12 135
February 12 43	March 29 88	May 13 136

May 14 137	July 1 187	August 18 236
May 15 138	July 2 188	August 19 237
May 16 139	July 3 189	August 20 238
May 17 140	July 4 190	August 21 239
May 18 141	July 5 191	August 22 240
May 19 142	July 6 192	August 23 241
May 20 143	July 7 193	August 24 242
May 21 144	July 8 194	August 25 243
May 22 145	July 9 195	August 26 244
May 23 146	July 10 196	August 27 245
May 24 147	July 11 197	August 28 246
May 25 148	July 12 198	August 29 247
May 26 149	July 13 199	August 30 248
May 27 150	July 14 200	August 31 249
May 28 151	July 15 201	September 1 250
May 29 152	July 16 202	September 2 251
May 30 153	July 17 203	September 3 252
May 31 154	July 18 204	September 4 253
June 1 155	July 19 206	September 5 254
June 2 156	July 20 207	September 6 255
June 3 157	July 21 208	September 7 256
June 4 158	July 22 209	September 8 257
June 5 159	July 23 210	September 9 258
June 6 160	July 24 211	September 10 259
June 7 162	July 25 212	September 11 260
June 8 163	July 26 213	September 12 261
June 9 164	July 27 214	September 13 262
June 10 165	July 28 215	September 14 263
June 11 166	July 29 216	September 15 264
June 12 167	July 30 217	September 16 265
June 13 168	July 31 218	September 17 266
June 14 169	August 1 219	September 18 267
June 15 170	August 2 220	September 19 268
June 16 171	August 3 221	September 20 269
June 17 172	August 4 222	September 21 270
June 18 173	August 5 223	September 22 271
June 19 174	August 6 224	September 23 272
June 20 175	August 7 225	September 24 273
June 21 176	August 8 226	September 25 274
June 22 177	August 9 227	September 26 275
June 23 178	August 10 228	September 27 276
June 24 179	August 11 229	September 28 277
June 25 180	August 12 230	September 29 278
June 26 181	August 13 231	September 30 279
June 27 183	August 14 232	October 1 280
June 28 184	August 15 233	October 2 281
June 29 185	August 16 234	October 3 282
June 30 186	August 17 235	October 4 283

October 5 284	November 5 315	December 6 346
October 6 285	November 6 316	December 7 347
October 7 286	November 7 317	December 8 348
October 8 287	November 8 318	December 9 349
October 9 288	November 9 319	December 10 350
October 10 289	November 10 320	December 11 351
October 11 290	November 11 321	December 12 352
October 12 291	November 12 322	December 13 353
October 13 292	November 13 323	December 14 354
October 14 293	November 14 324	December 15 355
October 15 294	November 15 325	December 16 356
October 16 295	November 16 326	December 17 357
October 17 296	November 17 327	December 18 358
October 18 297	November 18 328	December 19 359
October 19 298	November 19 329	December 20 360
October 20 299	November 20 330	December 21 361
October 21 300	November 21 331	December 22 363
October 22 301	November 22 332	December 23 365
October 23 302	November 23 333	December 24 366
October 24 303	November 24 334	December 25 367
October 25 304	November 25 335	December 26 368
October 26 305	November 26 336	December 27 369
October 27 306	November 27 337	December 28 370
October 28 307	November 28 338	December 29 371
October 29 308	November 29 339	December 30 372
October 30 309	November 30 340	December 31 373
October 31 310	December 1 341	***Continue the Journey: Year Two Awaits*** *374*
November 1 311	December 2 342	
November 2 312	December 3 343	
November 3 313	December 4 344	
November 4 314	December 5 345	

January 1

Wise Roots

3-Year-Bible Reading: Proverbs 1:1–7; Psalm 1

"The fear of the Lord is the beginning of knowledge; fools despise wisdom and instruction."
— Proverbs 1:7

"Blessed is the man who walks not in the counsel of the wicked…but his delight is in the law of the Lord, and on his law he meditates day and night."
— Psalm 1:1–2

Have you ever felt overwhelmed by all the choices you have to make—school, friends, future plans? Life can feel like standing at a hundred crossroads, each with its own flashing signs and voices pulling you in different directions. Proverbs and Psalms remind us there *is* a clear path—a wise path.

According to **Proverbs 1:7**, wisdom begins with honoring and trusting God. And **Psalm 1** paints a vivid picture of a person who is rooted in God's Word, growing strong and steady like a tree by a stream. The more time we spend learning from God, the clearer our decisions become and the stronger we grow.

Think About It

1. **Wisdom Starts With God:** Who are you listening to the most—your friends, social media, or God? Real wisdom begins by putting God first and trusting that His way is best.

2. **What Are You Rooted In?** Psalm 1 says those who meditate on God's Word are like trees planted by water. Are you giving God space in your day to grow your faith, or are you just squeezing Him in when it's convenient?

3. **Watch Your Walk:** The Psalm warns about walking with the wicked. Who you spend time with shapes your future. Are your friendships helping you grow closer to God or pulling you away?

Bottom Line

Living wisely doesn't mean having all the answers—it means choosing to trust God and stay rooted in His truth. When you build your life on Him, you won't be easily shaken.

Prayer

Heavenly Father, thank You for being the source of all wisdom. Help me to put You first in everything I do and to find joy in Your Word. Show me how to make wise choices, even when it's hard, and surround me with people who will help me grow in my faith. Plant me deep in Your truth so I can stand strong every day. In Jesus' Name, Amen.

January 2

Choose Wisdom Before It's Too Late

3-Year-Bible Reading: Proverbs 1:8–33; Psalm 2

"The fear of the Lord is the beginning of knowledge; fools despise wisdom and instruction." — Proverbs 1:7

"Because I have called and you refused to listen, have stretched out my hand and no one has heeded…" — Proverbs 1:24

"Blessed are all who take refuge in him." — Psalm 2:12

Let's be real—no one likes being told what to do. Whether it's a parent's advice or a teacher's warning, it's easy to brush it off and think, *"I've got this."* But in **Proverbs 1**, wisdom is like a person calling out in the streets, trying to get our attention before it's too late. And in **Psalm 2**, we see a powerful reminder that God is in charge no matter what the world thinks. Both passages point to a truth we can't ignore: choosing to listen to God leads to blessing, while ignoring Him brings consequences.

THINK ABOUT IT

1. **Who's Talking?** Wisdom is described like a person shouting in public, trying to warn people. Are there people in your life—maybe parents, mentors, or friends—who speak godly wisdom to you? Are you listening?

2. **What Happens If We Ignore God?** Proverbs warns that ignoring wisdom leads to regret. Psalm 2 shows that rebellion against God leads to judgment. Do you ever delay obeying God, thinking you'll "get serious later"? What might you be risking?

3. **Where's Your Refuge?** Psalm 2 ends with a promise: *"Blessed are all who take refuge in him."* In tough times, where do you go for comfort or strength? Are you leaning into God—or escaping to distractions?

BOTTOM LINE

God offers wisdom freely, but we have to choose to listen. Taking Him seriously now leads to peace, protection, and purpose—while ignoring His voice can leave us stuck with consequences we never wanted.

PRAYER

Heavenly Father, help me to recognize Your voice and choose wisdom over foolishness. Give me a heart that listens and obeys, even when it's hard or unpopular. Remind me that true blessing comes from taking refuge in You. I don't want to learn the hard way—teach me to walk in Your ways now. In Jesus' Name, Amen.

January 3

Guardrails for the Journey

3-Year-Bible Reading: Proverbs 2:1–22; Psalm 3

"Then you will understand the fear of the Lord and find the knowledge of God." — Proverbs 2:5

"You, O Lord, are a shield about me, my glory, and the lifter of my head." — Psalm 3:3

Life can feel like a confusing maze sometimes. There are so many voices telling us what to do, where to go, and who to be. It's easy to get overwhelmed and wonder if you're making the right choices. But **Proverbs 2** reminds us that God offers something powerful when we pursue Him—wisdom.

This kind of wisdom isn't just about knowing facts; it's about learning how to live well, avoid traps, and stay safe on the path of life. And when things get tough, like David in **Psalm 3**, we can be confident that God is our shield, our protector, and the one who helps us lift our heads high even when life tries to knock us down.

Think About It

1. **Chasing Wisdom:** Are you actively seeking God's wisdom like treasure? Proverbs 2 says we should search for it like silver—something valuable and worth effort.

2. **God's Protection:** Psalm 3 shows David in a tough situation, surrounded by enemies, but he still declares God as his shield. Do you believe God is protecting you even when you feel scared or surrounded by problems?

3. **The Right Path:** Proverbs talks about wisdom saving us from people with bad intentions and helping us stay on the right track. What "paths" are you walking right now, and are they leading you toward or away from God?

Bottom Line

God's wisdom is like a guardrail on the road of life—it doesn't restrict you, it protects you. When you trust God and follow His wisdom, He not only leads you safely, but He also stands as your shield when life gets hard.

Prayer

Heavenly Father, thank You for offering wisdom to anyone who seeks it. Help me to value Your truth more than anything this world promises. Guide my steps, protect my heart, and remind me that You are always with me—even when things are scary or confusing. Be the lifter of my head and the guard of my path. In Jesus' Name, Amen.

January 4

Stay True, Shine Bright

3-Year-Bible Reading: Proverbs 3:1–4; Matthew 1

"Let not steadfast love and faithfulness forsake you; bind them around your neck; write them on the tablet of your heart. So you will find favor and good success in the sight of God and man." — Proverbs 3:3–4

"She will bear a son, and you shall call his name Jesus, for he will save his people from their sins." — Matthew 1:21

Ever feel like life is pulling you in a million directions? Maybe it's the pressure to fit in, do well in school, or figure out who you're even supposed to be. In moments like that, **Proverbs 3:1–4** reminds us to hold on tight to love and faithfulness—not just in what we say, but in how we live.

And **Matthew 1** zooms in on Joseph, a regular guy who chose to trust and obey God, even when it was hard. His part in Jesus' story wasn't flashy, but it was faithful. That's big. It tells us that our choices, even quiet ones, matter more than we think.

Think About It

1. **What's written on your heart?** Proverbs talks about writing love and faithfulness on the "tablet of your heart." What are you letting shape your thoughts and actions—God's truth or the world's trends?

2. **Faith over fear:** Joseph had every reason to walk away from Mary's pregnancy, but he chose to believe God's bigger plan. Are you willing to follow God, even when it's confusing or unpopular?

3. **Favor that lasts:** True success comes not from popularity, likes, or achievements, but from living a life that honors God. Are you chasing favor with people, or with God?

Bottom Line

When you choose love, faithfulness, and trust in God—even in the small stuff—you'll shine in ways that really matter. Like Joseph, your quiet obedience could be part of something way bigger than you can see right now.

Prayer

Heavenly Father, thank You for reminding me that faithfulness matters. Help me to hold on to Your love and truth, even when life feels confusing. Give me the courage to follow You like Joseph did, trusting that Your plans are always good. Help me live in a way that honors You and points others to Jesus. In Jesus' Name, Amen.

January 5

Trust the Guide

3-Year-Bible Reading: Proverbs 3:5-6; Matthew 2

"Trust in the Lord with all your heart, and do not lean on your own understanding. In all your ways acknowledge him, and he will make straight your paths." — Proverbs 3:5–6

"And being warned in a dream not to return to Herod, they departed to their own country by another way." — Matthew 2:12

Have you ever used GPS and still ended up lost? You followed every direction, but something didn't feel right—and sure enough, you ended up at a dead end or the wrong address. Life is kind of like that sometimes. We try to figure out our next move based on what *seems* right to us, but things don't always go as planned.

That's why **Proverbs 3:5–6** encourages us to trust God more than we trust our own understanding. In **Matthew 2**, the wise men didn't go back to Herod like they originally planned—they followed God's warning instead. When God guides, it's always the right way, even if it doesn't make total sense in the moment.

Think About It

1. **God's GPS:** Are you trusting God with all your heart, or are you relying on your own understanding? What might it look like to "acknowledge Him" in your everyday decisions—like school, friendships, or your future?

2. **When Plans Change:** The wise men had to change their route because of God's warning. How do you react when God redirects your plans? Are you willing to follow, even when it's inconvenient or confusing?

3. **God Sees the Bigger Picture:** Sometimes we only see part of the story, but God sees it all. How does knowing that help you trust Him more deeply?

Bottom Line

God always knows the best path—even when we don't. Trusting Him with your whole heart leads to a life that's guided by His wisdom and purpose.

Prayer

Heavenly Father, thank You for being the perfect guide. Help me to trust You, especially when I don't understand what's happening. Teach me to listen for Your voice and follow Your direction, just like the wise men did. Make my path straight, and help me live a life that honors You. In Jesus' Name, Amen.

January 6

Wiser Than You Think

3-Year-Bible Reading: Proverbs 3:7–8; Psalm 4; Matthew 3

"Be not wise in your own eyes; fear the Lord, and turn away from evil. It will be healing to your flesh and refreshment to your bones." — Proverbs 3:7–8

"In peace I will both lie down and sleep; for you alone, O Lord, make me dwell in safety." — Psalm 4:8

"Repent, for the kingdom of heaven is at hand." — Matthew 3:2

Sometimes, we like to think we've got life figured out—especially when things seem to be going well. But the Bible reminds us that being "wise in your own eyes" isn't real wisdom at all **(Proverbs 3:7)**. True wisdom starts with fearing the Lord and turning away from sin. That might not sound exciting, but when we live that way, it actually brings peace, healing, and rest—exactly what our souls need.

Whether we're dealing with stress from school, friendships, or trying to figure out who we are, God's Word gives us a better way. And in **Matthew 3**, John the Baptist reminds us to turn our lives around—because God's kingdom isn't just some far-off idea. It's here. It's now. And we get to be part of it.

Think About It

1. **Who's Really in Control?** When you face tough decisions, do you rely more on your own thoughts or God's guidance? Proverbs tells us not to lean on our own understanding, but to fear the Lord instead.

2. **Finding Real Peace:** Psalm 4 shows us that true peace doesn't come from having everything figured out—it comes from trusting that God is keeping us safe, even when life feels uncertain.

3. **Time to Turn Around?** John's call to repent isn't about being perfect—it's about being real. Are there areas in your life where you need to turn back to God and let Him lead?

Bottom Line

Wisdom isn't about having all the answers—it's about trusting God enough to follow His. When we let Him guide our lives, we find peace, healing, and purpose.

Prayer

Heavenly Father, thank You for being the source of true wisdom and peace. Help me not to rely on myself, but to trust You in everything I face. Show me where I need to turn back to You, and give me the courage to follow Your ways. Fill me with Your peace, and remind me that I'm never alone. In Jesus' Name, Amen.

January 7

Give God Your Best

3-Year-Bible Reading: Proverbs 3:9–10; Psalm 5; Matthew 4

"Honor the Lord with your wealth and with the firstfruits of all your produce; then your barns will be filled with plenty, and your vats will be bursting with wine." — Proverbs 3:9–10

"But I, through the abundance of your steadfast love, will enter your house. I will bow down toward your holy temple in the fear of you." — Psalm 5:7

"Then Jesus said to him, 'Be gone, Satan! For it is written, "You shall worship the Lord your God and him only shall you serve."'" — Matthew 4:10

Ever try to do a hundred things at once and realize none of them are really getting your best effort? Between school, sports, friends, and everything else, it's easy to let God get whatever's left over. But these verses remind us of something important: God deserves more than just the leftovers.

In **Proverbs 3:9–10**, we're challenged to give God our "firstfruits"—the best and first parts of what we have. **Psalm 5** shows us the heart of someone who chooses to approach God with awe and love first thing in the day. And in **Matthew 4**, even when Jesus is tempted in the wilderness, He chooses to worship and serve only God. These passages together remind us that when we give God our best—our time, our focus, our love—He fills our lives with what we truly need.

Think About It

1. **What Are Your "Firstfruits"?** Think about how you start your day. Is God part of your morning, or do you rush through it without even checking in with Him?

2. **Worship Isn't Just Music:** Jesus reminds us in **Matthew 4:10** that worship is about who we serve. Are you putting other things—like popularity, success, or comfort—above God?

3. **God Fills What You Give Him:** Proverbs 3:10 says that when we honor God first, He fills us up. That doesn't always mean more stuff—but it does mean more peace, more purpose, and more of His presence.

Bottom Line

When you give God your first and best, He blesses the rest.

Prayer

Heavenly Father, help me to give You the first and best parts of my day, my energy, and my heart. Teach me to worship You not just in songs, but in every choice I make. Thank You for loving me and filling my life with Your presence. In Jesus' Name, Amen.

January 8

Corrected by Love

3-Year-Bible Reading: Proverbs 3:11–12; Matthew 5

"My son, do not despise the Lord's discipline or be weary of his reproof, for the Lord reproves him whom he loves, as a father the son in whom he delights." — Proverbs 3:11–12

"Blessed are those who mourn, for they shall be comforted… Blessed are those who are persecuted for righteousness' sake, for theirs is the kingdom of heaven." — Matthew 5:4,10

Let's be real—being corrected or going through tough times isn't exactly on anyone's wishlist. Whether it's a coach pointing out your mistakes, a parent calling you out, or a season of life that just feels unfair, it can feel like you're being picked on.

But **Proverbs 3:11–12** and **Matthew 5** tell a different story: one where God's correction isn't punishment, but proof of His love. Jesus even says that people who are struggling—mourning, persecuted, or just trying to live right—are *blessed*. That's a whole shift in perspective.

Think About It

1. **Discipline = Love:** When God corrects you, it's not to shame you—it's to shape you. Can you think of a time you felt challenged but grew stronger or wiser because of it?

2. **Blessings in the Broken:** Jesus says those who mourn or are persecuted are *blessed*. What if the hard things you're facing are actually helping you grow closer to God?

3. **God's Got a Plan:** You may not see the purpose behind your pain right now, but trust that God is using it to build something better in you.

Bottom Line

God's discipline and your struggles aren't signs He's against you—they're proof that He's right there with you, helping you grow into who He made you to be.

Prayer

Heavenly Father, thank You for loving me enough to correct me and guide me, even when it's uncomfortable. Help me to see my struggles through Your eyes and to trust that You're working for my good. Give me the strength to keep going and the faith to grow through it. In Jesus' Name, Amen.

January 9

More Than Gold

3-Year-Bible Reading: Proverbs 3:13–20; Matthew 6

"Blessed is the one who finds wisdom, and the one who gets understanding, for the gain from her is better than gain from silver and her profit better than gold." — Proverbs 3:13–14

"But seek first the kingdom of God and his righteousness, and all these things will be added to you." — Matthew 6:33

What do you think would make your life better right now? A new phone? More friends? Better grades? It's easy to get caught up in chasing after things that seem important. Jesus gets it—**Matthew 6** is full of reminders not to stress about stuff like clothes, food, or even tomorrow. But instead of worrying, He tells us to focus on God first.

Similarly, **Proverbs 3** tells us that wisdom—seeing life from God's perspective—is more valuable than anything money can buy. When we put God's truth and His way of living first, everything else falls into place.

Think About It

1. **What Are You Seeking?** Jesus tells us to "seek first the kingdom of God." What are you spending the most time thinking about or chasing after right now?

2. **Wisdom Over Wealth:** Proverbs compares wisdom to treasure. Do you treat God's wisdom—His Word, His truth, His guidance—as something truly valuable in your daily life?

3. **Trust God's Order:** Both passages remind us that when we prioritize God, we can trust Him to handle the rest. What's one area of your life you need to let God take the lead in?

Bottom Line

Chasing after stuff won't fill you up, but seeking God and His wisdom will lead you to a life that's full, steady, and truly blessed.

Prayer

Heavenly Father, thank You for reminding me that Your wisdom is worth more than anything else I could want. Help me to seek You first—above all the distractions, stress, and things that try to grab my attention. Teach me to trust that when I put You first, everything else will fall into place. In Jesus' Name, Amen.

January 10

Walk in Confidence

3-Year-Bible Reading: Proverbs 3:21–26; Matthew 7

"My son, do not lose sight of these—keep sound wisdom and discretion, and they will be life for your soul and adornment for your neck. Then you will walk on your way securely, and your foot will not stumble." — Proverbs 3:21–23

"Everyone then who hears these words of mine and does them will be like a wise man who built his house on the rock." — Matthew 7:24

Life can feel like a whirlwind sometimes — school pressure, friendships changing, making big decisions about your future. You might feel unsure, like you're walking through a fog. But God doesn't want you to live in fear or confusion.

In **Proverbs 3**, He promises that if you hold tightly to wisdom and discretion, you'll walk securely, without stumbling. And in **Matthew 7**, Jesus gives us a visual: build your life on His teachings and you'll be unshakable, like a house on solid rock—even when storms come.

Think About It

1. **Build on the Rock:** What are you building your life on right now—God's truth, or opinions, trends, or feelings? Only God's Word gives a strong enough foundation to withstand life's ups and downs.

2. **Wisdom is Protection:** Proverbs reminds us that wisdom isn't just smart thinking—it's a spiritual safeguard. Are you spending time in Scripture, seeking God's perspective when you make decisions?

3. **Don't Panic in the Storm:** Life's storms will come—stress, change, conflict. But Jesus says the wise builder doesn't panic because their foundation is firm. How can you practice trusting God in small challenges so you're ready for the big ones?

Bottom Line

God wants you to walk through life with confidence, not fear. When you build your life on His Word and hold tightly to wisdom, you'll stand strong no matter what comes your way.

Prayer

Heavenly Father, thank You for offering wisdom and guidance through Your Word. Help me to listen to Jesus' words and live them out, so I can be like the wise builder. When I feel overwhelmed or unsure, remind me that You are my foundation and I don't have to walk in fear. In Jesus' Name, Amen.

January 11

Choose Kindness Anyway

3-Year-Bible Reading: Proverbs 3:27–30; Psalm 6; Matthew 8

Do not withhold good from those to whom it is due, when it is in your power to do it. —Proverbs 3:27

Be gracious to me, O Lord, for I am languishing; heal me, O Lord, for my bones are troubled. —Psalm 6:2

And Jesus stretched out his hand and touched him, saying, "I will; be clean." And immediately his leprosy was cleansed. —Matthew 8:3

Have you ever been in a situation where you knew you could help someone, but something held you back? Maybe you were afraid of what others might think, or you felt like the person didn't deserve it.

In **Proverbs 3:27–30**, we're reminded not to hold back doing good when we're able. **Psalm 6** gives us a look into someone crying out to God in pain, asking for grace and healing. Then, in **Matthew 8**, Jesus doesn't hesitate—He reaches out to touch and heal a man everyone else avoided. These three passages come together with one powerful message: When you have the chance to help, heal, or show love, do it—because that's what Jesus did.

Think About It

1. **Why Wait?** Are you holding back from helping someone when you know it's within your power to act? God calls us to respond to others with compassion, not excuses.

2. **See the Hurt:** Psalm 6 shows us that people may be dealing with deep pain we can't always see. Do you take time to notice when someone's struggling, even if they're hiding it?

3. **Jesus Touched the Untouchable:** In Matthew 8, Jesus didn't just say words—He touched the man with leprosy. How can you step out of your comfort zone to love someone others overlook?

Bottom Line

God calls us to reflect His compassion. When you see someone hurting or in need, don't hold back. Be bold, be kind, and be the one who chooses love—even when it's hard or uncomfortable.

Prayer

Heavenly Father, thank You for always seeing us, even in our lowest moments. Help us to be more like Jesus, willing to reach out and love others boldly. Give us courage to do good when we have the chance and hearts that see the pain others are going through. Make us people who respond with kindness, not judgment. In Jesus' Name, Amen.

January 12

Don't Follow the Crowd

3-Year-Bible Reading: Proverbs 3:31–33; Matthew 9

Do not envy a man of violence and do not choose any of his ways, for the devious person is an abomination to the Lord, but the upright are in his confidence. The Lord's curse is on the house of the wicked, but he blesses the dwelling of the righteous. — Proverbs 3:31–33

And as Jesus reclined at table in the house, behold, many tax collectors and sinners came and were reclining with Jesus and his disciples. And when the Pharisees saw this, they said to his disciples, "Why does your teacher eat with tax collectors and sinners?" But when he heard it, he said, "Those who are well have no need of a physician, but those who are sick." — Matthew 9:10–12

Have you ever felt pressure to go along with what everyone else is doing, even when you know it's not right? Maybe it's a trend, a joke, a group chat, or even just the way people talk about others at school. Proverbs reminds us not to envy people who seem powerful or popular for doing the wrong thing.

At the same time, in **Matthew 9**, we see Jesus doing something radical: hanging out with people the "cool" religious leaders avoided. He didn't choose the crowd-pleasers. He chose the ones who needed Him most. Jesus invites us to see people through His eyes, not the world's.

Think About It

1. **Who Are You Watching?** Are there people you look up to who act in ways that don't line up with God's truth? What draws you to them?

2. **Jesus' Example:** Jesus didn't chase popularity—He loved the rejected and broken. How can you follow His example at school, home, or online?

3. **What Does God Value?** Proverbs says God blesses the righteous. How can you focus more on what matters to God than what's trending?

Bottom Line

Don't let the world define what's worth following. Choose God's way—even when it's not popular—because His approval matters most.

Prayer

Heavenly Father, help me not to envy people who seem to have it all but live far from You. Give me the courage to follow Your way, even when it's hard or unpopular. Teach me to see others like Jesus does and love them with compassion and truth. In Jesus' Name, Amen.

JANUARY 13

Grace for the Humble

3-Year-Bible Reading: Proverbs 3:34; Matthew 10

"Toward the scorners he is scornful, but to the humble he gives favor." — Proverbs 3:34

"And do not fear those who kill the body but cannot kill the soul. Rather fear him who can destroy both soul and body in hell... So everyone who acknowledges me before men, I also will acknowledge before my Father who is in heaven." — Matthew 10:28, 32

Have you ever felt like being a Christian puts a target on your back? Maybe you've been laughed at for what you believe or felt like the only one standing up for your faith. Jesus knew this would happen, and in **Matthew 10**, He doesn't sugarcoat it—following Him comes with challenges. But He also gives us something huge to hold onto: *grace and favor for those who stay humble and faithful.*

Just like **Proverbs 3:34** says, God gives grace to the humble—even when the world pushes back. Being bold in faith doesn't mean being loud or arrogant; it means being real, courageous, and trusting God no matter what.

THINK ABOUT IT

1. **Who do you fear?** Jesus tells us not to fear people who can only hurt our bodies, but to focus on what really matters—our souls. Are you more worried about what people think or about living in a way that honors God?

2. **Speak up or stay silent?** Jesus promises to acknowledge those who acknowledge Him. That could be as simple as standing up for what's right, praying at lunch, or not hiding your faith. What's one way you can acknowledge Jesus this week?

3. **God's grace is worth it:** Humility isn't weakness—it's strength under control. God lifts up those who don't chase attention but chase after Him. What area of your life needs more humility?

BOTTOM LINE

Following Jesus isn't always easy, but His favor is always worth it. Stay humble, stay faithful, and don't be afraid to stand out for Him.

PRAYER

Heavenly Father, thank You for loving me and giving me courage to follow You even when it's hard. Help me stay humble and bold at the same time. Remind me that Your opinion matters more than the world's. Let me be someone who lives and speaks in a way that points others to You. In Jesus' Name, Amen.

January 14

Wise or Foolish?

3-Year-Bible Reading: Proverbs 3:35; Psalm 7; Matthew 11

The wise will inherit honor, but fools get disgrace. — Proverbs 3:35

Oh, let the evil of the wicked come to an end, and may you establish the righteous— you who test the minds and hearts, O righteous God! — Psalm 7:9

Come to me, all who labor and are heavy laden, and I will give you rest. — Matthew 11:28

Have you ever made a choice you instantly regretted—like snapping at a friend, cheating on a quiz, or ignoring someone who needed help? We've all been there. The Bible doesn't hide from those moments. In fact, **Proverbs 3:35** makes a bold statement: wise people receive honor, while foolish choices lead to disgrace.

But here's the good news—God sees our hearts, like in **Psalm 7**, and offers us grace and rest, like in **Matthew 11:28**. Even when we mess up, God doesn't give up on us. He invites us to come to Him, learn from Him, and grow wiser day by day.

Think About It

1. **What does it mean to be wise?** Wisdom isn't just about getting good grades or saying the right things. It's about knowing God's truth and applying it in everyday situations— especially when it's hard.

2. **Check your heart:** God tests the *minds and hearts* (Psalm 7:9). That means He sees beyond your words and actions to your real intentions. Are you trying to do what's right, or are you just going through the motions?

3. **You don't have to carry it all:** Jesus says, "Come to me… and I will give you rest." (Matthew 11:28). Whether you're stressed from school, friendships, or just trying to live right, Jesus offers peace when you lean on Him.

Bottom Line

Wisdom starts with trusting God, not being perfect. When you mess up, turn to Him. He gives honor to those who seek Him and rest to those who are worn out from trying to do it all on their own.

Prayer

Heavenly Father, thank You for offering wisdom, rest, and grace when I need it most. Help me to make choices that honor You, even when it's not easy. Search my heart, guide my steps, and teach me to lean on You instead of trying to do life alone. In Jesus' Name, Amen.

January 15

Wise Up

3-Year-Bible Reading: Proverbs 4:1–9; Matthew 12

"Get wisdom; get insight; do not forget, and do not turn away from the words of my mouth… The beginning of wisdom is this: Get wisdom, and whatever you get, get insight." — Proverbs 4:5,7

"For whoever does the will of my Father in heaven is my brother and sister and mother." — Matthew 12:50

Have you ever tried to build something without the instructions? Maybe a LEGO set or a piece of furniture? At first, it seems doable, but soon enough, you're confused, frustrated, and probably ready to give up. That's a lot like life without wisdom.

In **Proverbs 4:1–9**, Solomon tells us to chase wisdom like it's the most valuable treasure. Why? Because it actually is. In **Matthew 12**, Jesus reminds us that being close to God isn't just about saying we believe—it's about living like it. Those who listen to God and live out His will are truly part of His family. When we seek wisdom and walk in it, we grow closer to Him.

Think About It

1. **What is wisdom, really?** Wisdom isn't just being smart or getting good grades. It's about knowing what's right and having the courage to live it out—especially when it's hard.

2. **Your choices matter:** Proverbs talks about guarding what you hear, say, and think. Are your decisions helping you grow in wisdom or pulling you away from it?

3. **Family of faith:** In **Matthew 12:50**, Jesus says obedience makes us His family. Are your actions showing that you belong to Him?

Bottom Line

Wisdom is more than knowledge—it's choosing to live God's way every day. When we do that, we're not just learning; we're living as part of God's family.

Prayer

Heavenly Father, thank You for the gift of wisdom and for inviting me to be part of Your family. Help me to listen to Your Word, make wise choices, and walk closely with You even when it's tough. Give me insight to see what really matters and the strength to live it out. In Jesus' Name, Amen.

January 16

Light Up the Path

3-Year-Bible Reading: Proverbs 4:10–19; Matthew 13

"The path of the righteous is like the light of dawn, which shines brighter and brighter until full day."
— Proverbs 4:18

"For to the one who has, more will be given, and he will have an abundance." — Matthew 13:12

"But the one who received the seed on the good soil is the one who hears the word and understands it."
— Matthew 13:23

Have you ever tried walking through your house in total darkness? You bump into furniture, stub your toe, maybe even trip over the dog. Life without direction feels the same. **Proverbs 4** paints a picture of two paths—one lit by righteousness and another lost in darkness.

Jesus, in **Matthew 13**, uses parables to help people see that the Word of God is like a seed—only when it lands in open, willing hearts will it grow and bring clarity and purpose. God isn't just calling us to hear His truth; He wants us to live by it, step by step, in the light of His wisdom.

Think About It

1. **Two Roads, One Choice:** Are you walking on the path that gets brighter or stumbling in the dark? God offers you a way that leads to life, peace, and growth. Which direction are your choices leading you today?

2. **Soil Check:** Jesus talks about hearts being like soil. Is your heart ready to receive what God is planting? Think about what might be blocking His Word from taking root—distractions, fear, or even doubt.

3. **Grow with the Light:** When you choose to follow Jesus, it's not instant perfection—it's a journey. Like the morning sun, His light grows in your life as you keep walking with Him. Are you letting Him light the way each day?

Bottom Line

God's Word lights up your path and grows your life when you let it sink deep into your heart and guide your steps.

Prayer

Heavenly Father, thank You for giving me a path that leads to life. Help me to choose Your way, even when it's hard or unclear. Make my heart like good soil—ready to receive Your Word and grow. Keep me walking in Your light every day. In Jesus' Name, Amen.

January 17

Guard Your Heart, Step in Faith

3-Year-Bible Reading: Proverbs 4:20–23; Matthew 14

"Keep your heart with all vigilance, for from it flow the springs of life." — Proverbs 4:23

"But immediately Jesus spoke to them, saying, 'Take heart; it is I. Do not be afraid.' Peter answered him, 'Lord, if it is you, command me to come to you on the water.' He said, 'Come.' So Peter got out of the boat and walked on the water and came to Jesus." — Matthew 14:27–29

We all have moments when life feels like a storm—confusing, overwhelming, and just plain scary. Whether it's a tough day at school, drama with friends, or fears about the future, it's easy to let anxiety take over. In **Matthew 14**, Peter stepped out of the boat into a literal storm, simply because Jesus told him to come. It took major faith. But before that moment, his heart had to be in the right place—focused on Jesus.

That's where **Proverbs 4** comes in. Guarding your heart doesn't just mean avoiding bad stuff—it means choosing to focus on what matters most. When your heart is anchored in Jesus, you can step out even when the waves are high.

Think About It

1. **Guard Your Heart:** What are you letting into your heart—through your music, your shows, your social media? Proverbs says everything flows from the heart. What kind of life do you want flowing from yours?

2. **Eyes on Jesus:** Peter only started sinking when he looked at the wind instead of Jesus. Where are your eyes when life gets stressful—on the problem or on the One who has power over it?

3. **Step Out:** What is one way you can trust Jesus today, even if it feels a little risky? Maybe it's standing up for someone, sharing your faith, or choosing peace over drama.

Bottom Line

When your heart is guarded by God's truth, and your eyes are fixed on Jesus, you'll find the courage to step out of the boat—even in the middle of life's storms.

Prayer

Heavenly Father, thank You for being with me in every storm. Help me guard my heart and keep my focus on You, even when everything around me feels uncertain. Give me the courage to step out in faith, trusting that You've got me. In Jesus' Name, Amen.

January 18

Stay in Your Lane

3-Year-Bible Reading: Proverbs 4:24–27; Psalm 8; Matthew 15

"Put away from you crooked speech, and put devious talk far from you. Let your eyes look directly forward… Ponder the path of your feet; then all your ways will be sure." — Proverbs 4:24–26

"When I look at your heavens, the work of your fingers… what is man that you are mindful of him?" — Psalm 8:3–4

"But what comes out of the mouth proceeds from the heart, and this defiles a person." — Matthew 15:18

Have you ever been running or biking on a narrow path, and someone yells, "Stay in your lane!" It's not always meant to be rude—it's actually for your safety. Staying in your lane keeps you from crashing, veering off course, or hurting someone else. In **Proverbs 4**, we're reminded to "ponder the path" of our feet and focus straight ahead. **Psalm 8** zooms out to remind us how small we are in this big universe, yet God deeply cares for us.

Then in **Matthew 15**, Jesus makes it personal—what comes from our mouths reveals what's in our hearts. Put all these together, and you get a challenge: walk wisely, speak truthfully, and stay close to the heart of God. The world will try to pull you in different directions, but God's path is the one that leads to life.

Think About It

1. **Guard Your Speech:** Are your words building people up or tearing them down? Jesus said our words show what's in our hearts. What does your speech reveal about your inner life?

2. **Mind the Path:** Are you walking with purpose, or just going with the flow? Proverbs tells us to think carefully about our steps. What are some distractions or habits that are making you veer off God's path?

3. **Remember Your Worth:** Psalm 8 reminds us that even though we're small compared to the universe, God still crowns us with glory and purpose. How does that change the way you see yourself?

Bottom Line

God has given you a path that leads to life, truth, and purpose—keep your eyes on Him, guard your heart, and stay in your lane.

Prayer

Heavenly Father, thank You for guiding my steps and caring for me even when I feel small or lost. Help me speak words that reflect a heart that loves You. Show me when I start to drift off course and give me the strength to stay on Your path. Thank You for creating me with purpose and calling me to live it out. In Jesus' Name, Amen.

January 19

Choose Wisdom, Follow Christ

3-Year-Bible Reading: Proverbs 5:1–23; Matthew 16

"For a man's ways are before the eyes of the Lord, and he ponders all his paths." — Proverbs 5:21

"Then Jesus told his disciples, 'If anyone would come after me, let him deny himself and take up his cross and follow me.'" — Matthew 16:24

We all crave freedom—to make our own choices, go our own way, and live how we want. But in **Proverbs 5**, Solomon warns us that chasing temporary pleasure without wisdom can lead to regret and destruction.

At the same time, **Matthew 16** challenges us with something even deeper: real freedom comes through surrender—denying ourselves and following Jesus, even when it's hard. Both passages remind us that the decisions we make today shape who we become tomorrow.

Think About It

1. **Your Life is Under God's Gaze:** Proverbs 5:21 reminds us that God sees every choice we make. That's not meant to scare us—it's meant to protect us. Are you living like your decisions matter to Him?

2. **Short-Term Pleasure vs. Long-Term Purpose:** Proverbs warns against being pulled in by temptation that looks good in the moment. Think: are there choices you're facing right now where it's hard to say no, even though you know it's not wise?

3. **Following Jesus Isn't Always Easy:** In Matthew 16, Jesus says we must take up our cross. That means choosing His way over our own—sacrificing comfort, popularity, or control. Are you willing to follow Him even when it costs you something?

Bottom Line

Choosing wisdom means seeing beyond the moment. Following Jesus means trusting that His way leads to real life—even when it's hard. God sees your path, walks with you, and calls you to something greater.

Prayer

Heavenly Father, thank You for seeing every part of my life and still loving me. Help me make wise choices, even when it's hard. Teach me to deny myself and follow Jesus fully. I want to live for You and walk the path You've laid out for me. In Jesus' Name, Amen.

January 20

Tangled, But Not Trapped

3-Year-Bible Reading: Proverbs 6:1–5; Psalm 9; Matthew 17

"If you have struck your hands in pledge for a stranger…save yourself, for you have come into the hand of your neighbor; go, hasten, and plead urgently with your neighbor." — Proverbs 6:1, 3

"The Lord is a stronghold for the oppressed, a stronghold in times of trouble." — Psalm 9:9

"Then the disciples came to Jesus privately and said, 'Why could we not cast it out?' He said to them, 'Because of your little faith.'" — Matthew 17:19–20

Have you ever made a quick decision that got you in over your head? Maybe you promised to do something you couldn't handle, or got caught up in a mess because you didn't think it through. **Proverbs 6** warns about making hasty promises—especially ones that could trap us. **Psalm 9** reminds us that even in the worst situations, God is our safe place.

And in **Matthew 17**, Jesus tells His disciples that their struggle came from their lack of faith. But He doesn't leave them there—He calls them to trust bigger and go deeper.

Think About It

1. **Watch What You Promise:** Proverbs 6 teaches us that being careless with our words can land us in tough spots. Have you ever said "yes" to something too fast and regretted it?

2. **God Is a Refuge:** Psalm 9 reminds us that no matter how deep we get into trouble—whether it's from our own choices or not—God is still our refuge. He doesn't expect us to fix everything alone. When things feel too big, run to Him.

3. **Faith That Moves Mountains:** In Matthew 17, Jesus tells His disciples that even a little real faith can move mountains. It's not about being perfect—it's about trusting Him. When you feel like you've failed or fallen short, Jesus is still there, calling you to believe again.

Bottom Line

Even when we get ourselves tangled up in tough situations, God is always ready to help us out. He gives us wisdom to make better choices, grace when we mess up, and strength to trust Him more.

Prayer

Heavenly Father, Thank You for being a stronghold when I feel overwhelmed or stuck. Help me think before I act or speak, and give me wisdom in my choices. Strengthen my faith, even when it feels small, and remind me that You are always near. Teach me to trust You more every day. In Jesus' Name, Amen.

January 21

Wake Up and Step Up

3-Year-Bible Reading: Proverbs 6:6–11; Matthew 18

"Go to the ant, O sluggard; consider her ways, and be wise. Without having any chief, officer, or ruler, she prepares her bread in summer and gathers her food in harvest." — Proverbs 6:6–8

"A little sleep, a little slumber, a little folding of the hands to rest, and poverty will come upon you like a robber, and want like an armed man." — Proverbs 6:10–11

"Whoever humbles himself like this child is the greatest in the kingdom of heaven." — Matthew 18:4

Have you ever hit snooze a few too many times, only to rush out the door feeling behind and unprepared? Or maybe you've procrastinated so long on a school project that panic finally kicked in the night before. We all face moments where it's easier to chill than to act, but **Proverbs 6:6–11** reminds us that laziness leads to more than just missed homework—it can impact our whole future.

And in **Matthew 18**, Jesus shifts our focus again, showing that the greatest in God's Kingdom are those who are humble like children. These two passages may seem unrelated, but they both challenge us to wake up—literally and spiritually—and live with intentionality and humility.

Think About It

1. **Learn from the Ant:** Ants work hard, even when no one is watching. What motivates you when no one's pushing you? How can you build good habits that help you grow?

2. **Be Alert, Not Asleep:** Laziness doesn't just waste time—it wastes potential. Where might you be "asleep" in your spiritual life or daily responsibilities?

3. **Stay Humble, Stay Great:** Jesus says greatness in the Kingdom starts with humility. What does it look like to be both humble and hardworking in your daily life?

Bottom Line

God calls us to live awake—physically, mentally, and spiritually. When we combine diligence with a humble heart, we step into the kind of life He created us for.

Prayer

Heavenly Father, thank You for the reminders in Your Word to be wise, diligent, and humble. Help me not to waste the opportunities You've given me. Teach me to live with purpose and to serve others with a heart like Jesus'. Wake me up where I've been spiritually asleep and help me live each day for Your glory. In Jesus' Name, Amen.

JANUARY 22

The Danger of the Wink and the Whisper

3-Year-Bible Reading: Proverbs 6:12–15; Psalm 10; Matthew 19

"A worthless person, a wicked man, goes about with crooked speech, winks with his eyes, signals with his feet, points with his finger, with perverted heart devises evil, continually sowing discord…" — Proverbs 6:12–14

"He says in his heart, 'God has forgotten, he has hidden his face, he will never see it.'" — Psalm 10:11

"Jesus said, 'If you would be perfect, go, sell what you possess and give to the poor, and you will have treasure in heaven; and come, follow me.'" — Matthew 19:21

Have you ever known someone who seemed to always be stirring up trouble—but did it with a smile, a wink, or a smooth word? In **Proverbs 6**, we're warned about that kind of person—the one who uses subtle actions and sneaky words to cause drama and division. It's not just obvious wrongdoing that God sees; He also sees what's going on in our hearts. **Psalm 10** talks about people who think God's not watching or doesn't care. But the truth is, God sees *everything*.

Then in **Matthew 19**, Jesus has a conversation with a rich young man who seemed to have it all together—he followed the rules—but Jesus pointed out that following Him meant surrendering the *heart*, not just checking boxes. All three passages remind us that the condition of our hearts—and the choices that flow from it—matter deeply to God.

THINK ABOUT IT

1. **What's your heart saying?** It's easy to say or do the "right" things on the outside, but what's really going on in your thoughts and intentions?
2. **Are you living like God sees?** Psalm 10 shows us how easy it is to think, *"No one's watching."* But God is always present. How would your choices change if you lived every moment knowing He sees and loves you?
3. **Following or Faking?** The rich young man in Matthew 19 thought he was doing everything right, but Jesus challenged him to go deeper. What's one thing you might be holding back from God?

BOTTOM LINE

God cares more about our hearts than our appearances. Don't just look good—*be* good by staying honest, humble, and fully committed to following Jesus.

PRAYER

Heavenly Father, thank You for seeing my heart and loving me anyway. Help me to live in a way that honors You not just in my actions, but in my thoughts, words, and choices. Teach me to follow You fully, even when it's hard. I don't want to fake it—I want to be real with You. In Jesus' Name, Amen.

JANUARY 23

Watch What You're Building

3-Year-Bible Reading: Proverbs 6:16–19; Matthew 20

"There are six things that the Lord hates, seven that are an abomination to him: haughty eyes, a lying tongue, and hands that shed innocent blood…"— Proverbs 6:16–17

"…whoever would be great among you must be your servant, and whoever would be first among you must be your slave, even as the Son of Man came not to be served but to serve…"— Matthew 20:26–28

Ever played Jenga? You build a tower, piece by piece, carefully balancing each block. But one wrong move and it all comes crashing down. Life's kind of like that. Every action, every word, every attitude is a block you add to your character.

In **Proverbs 6**, we're warned about behaviors that tear down rather than build up—things God hates because they destroy community and trust. In **Matthew 20**, Jesus flips our idea of greatness: the best leaders aren't those who get the spotlight, but those who humbly serve. That's a tower worth building.

Think About It

1. **Check Your Blocks:** What kind of "blocks" are you building with—pride, lies, anger… or kindness, truth, and humility? Proverbs 6 lists behaviors that God sees as harmful. Which ones do you notice in your own life or friend group?

2. **Flip the Script:** In Matthew 20, Jesus redefines greatness. Do you chase recognition or look for ways to serve quietly? How could you lead like Jesus in your school, home, or team?

3. **Heart Check:** Why do you think God cares so deeply about things like lying or stirring up conflict? How do those actions impact others—and you?

Bottom Line

God isn't just looking at what you do—He's looking at who you're becoming. Build a life that honors Him by choosing humility, truth, and love.

Prayer

Heavenly Father, help me to recognize the attitudes and actions that tear others down and replace them with things that reflect Your heart. Teach me to serve like Jesus and build my life with integrity and love. In Jesus' Name, Amen.

January 24

Guardrails for Your Heart

3-Year-Bible Reading: Proverbs 6:20–35; Matthew 21

"My son, keep your father's commandment, and forsake not your mother's teaching. Bind them on your heart always; tie them around your neck."—Proverbs 6:20–21

"Whoever falls on this stone will be broken to pieces; and when it falls on anyone, it will crush him."—Matthew 21:44

Have you ever been at a skate park or driving down the road and noticed the safety rails or warning signs? They're not there to ruin your fun—they're there to protect you. In **Proverbs 6**, God gives us some serious warnings about temptation, especially sexual temptation, and urges us to value the wisdom of our parents and God's commands.

And in **Matthew 21**, Jesus shares parables that show the danger of rejecting God's authority. Both passages remind us that when we ignore God's boundaries, we're headed for a crash—but when we listen and obey, we stay safe and strong.

Think About It

1. **Who's Leading Your Heart?** Are you paying attention to the wisdom and instruction God has placed in your life—like Scripture, parents, mentors, and youth leaders?

2. **Danger Ahead:** Proverbs warns about being lured into temptation by things that *look* good but lead to destruction. What are some temptations in your world that seem harmless but could hurt you spiritually or emotionally?

3. **Jesus Is the Cornerstone:** In Matthew 21, Jesus is the stone that either becomes your foundation or your downfall. Are you building your life on Him, or resisting His direction?

Bottom Line

God's Word is like guardrails for your heart. His boundaries aren't about restriction—they're about protection. When you follow His wisdom, you stay on the path that leads to life, not regret.

Prayer

Heavenly Father, thank You for loving me enough to set boundaries that protect my heart. Help me to listen to Your voice, honor the wisdom You've given through my family and leaders, and resist temptations that pull me away from You. Teach me to build my life on Jesus, the true foundation. In Jesus' Name, Amen.

January 25

Guard Your Heart, Follow the King

3-Year-Bible Reading: Proverbs 7:1–27; Psalm 110:1; Matthew 22

"My son, keep my words and treasure up my commandments with you; keep my commandments and live; keep my teaching as the apple of your eye." — Proverbs 7:1–2

"The Lord says to my Lord: 'Sit at my right hand, until I make your enemies your footstool.'" — Psalm 110:1

"Jesus said to them, 'How is it then that David, in the Spirit, calls him Lord, saying, "The Lord said to my Lord, Sit at my right hand, until I put your enemies under your feet"?'" — Matthew 22:43–44

Have you ever made a choice you knew wasn't great but did it anyway because it looked good in the moment? Proverbs 7 paints a vivid picture of a young person getting pulled into temptation—not because they wanted to wreck their life, but because they weren't paying attention to wisdom. Meanwhile, **Psalm 110** and **Matthew 22** remind us who truly sits on the throne: Jesus, the King with ultimate power and authority.

In a world full of distractions, temptations, and half-truths, God calls us to treasure His Word and recognize that Jesus is more than just a wise teacher—He's the Lord over everything, including the battle for your heart.

Think About It

1. **Protect What Matters:** Proverbs 7 warns against the dangers of ignoring God's commands. Are you making space in your life for God's Word, or is it being drowned out by other voices?

2. **Who's on the Throne?** Psalm 110 and Matthew 22 show Jesus as the one sitting at God's right hand. Do you treat Him as Lord in your life, or more like a backup plan when things go wrong?

3. **Know Before You Go:** The person in Proverbs 7 didn't fall into sin by accident—it was a slow slide. What steps can you take to walk in wisdom and stay alert to what's really going on?

Bottom Line

God calls you to guard your heart with His truth and recognize Jesus as the true King who leads you in wisdom and victory.

Prayer

Heavenly Father, help me to treasure Your Word and keep it close so I won't be easily led astray. Remind me daily that Jesus is not just a good teacher, but my King and my Savior. Give me the strength to follow Him, even when temptations try to pull me in another direction. Help me to choose wisdom over what feels good in the moment. In Jesus' Name, Amen.

January 26

Wisdom That Speaks Louder Than Words

3-Year-Bible Reading: Proverbs 8:1–36; Matthew 23

"Does not wisdom call? Does not understanding raise her voice?" — Proverbs 8:1

"Whoever finds me finds life and obtains favor from the Lord, but he who fails to find me injures himself; all who hate me love death." — Proverbs 8:35–36

"They preach, but do not practice." — Matthew 23:3

Have you ever met someone who *talks* a big game but doesn't actually live it out? Maybe they preach kindness but treat others poorly, or claim to be wise but make reckless choices. In **Matthew 23**, Jesus calls out the religious leaders for doing just that—sounding holy but missing the heart of God.

Contrast that with **Proverbs 8**, where wisdom is personified as a woman calling out, longing to be heard and followed. She isn't quiet or hidden—she's loud, clear, and available to anyone willing to listen. The difference? Wisdom isn't about fancy words or religious performance. It's about aligning your life with God's truth.

Think About It

1. **What voice are you listening to?** Wisdom in **Proverbs 8** is calling out to us, but so are a million other voices—social media, peer pressure, insecurity. Are you making space to hear the voice of wisdom?

2. **Talk vs. Walk:** In **Matthew 23**, Jesus warns against people who say the right things but don't live them out. Are you living what you believe? Do your actions match your faith?

3. **Life or Regret:** Proverbs says those who find wisdom "find life," but those who ignore it hurt themselves. What choices are you making today that show you're choosing life and God's favor?

Bottom Line

Wisdom isn't just about knowing the right things—it's about living them. Jesus wants our hearts, not just our words. Listen to wisdom. Live it out.

Prayer

Heavenly Father, help me to not just hear wisdom but to follow it. Keep me from being someone who talks about You without actually living for You. Give me courage to listen to Your voice above all others and to live in a way that reflects Your heart. In Jesus' Name, Amen.

January 27

Unshaken in the Storm

3-Year-Bible Reading: Psalms 11; Matthew 24

"The Lord is in his holy temple; the Lord's throne is in heaven; his eyes see, his eyelids test the children of man." — Psalm 11:4

"But the one who endures to the end will be saved." — Matthew 24:13

Have you ever felt like the world is falling apart around you? Maybe it's a chaotic day at school, stress at home, or just scrolling through the news and seeing nothing but bad stories. It can feel overwhelming, even scary. In **Psalm 11**, David talks about how people were telling him to run and hide because everything seemed broken. But instead of panicking, David says something powerful: "The Lord is on His throne." No matter how shaky life gets, God is still steady.

And in **Matthew 24**, Jesus warns His followers that tough times will come—wars, lies, betrayal, and even hate—but He encourages them to *endure*. Why? Because those who stay faithful are not forgotten—they're saved. That's hope you can hold onto.

Think About It

1. **God is still in control:** When the world feels crazy, do you remember that God is still on His throne, watching and caring for you?
2. **Endurance isn't easy—but it's worth it:** Jesus never promised us a perfect life, but He did promise His presence. What helps you keep going when things get tough?
3. **Faith over fear:** Are there areas in your life where you're tempted to run away or give up instead of trusting God?

Bottom Line

Even when the world feels like it's falling apart, you don't have to. God is on His throne, and if you stick with Him, He'll get you through anything.

Prayer

Heavenly Father, thank You for being steady when life feels unstable. Remind me that You are always in control, even when I can't see it. Help me to stand strong, to keep my eyes on You, and to not give up when things get hard. I want to trust You more every day. In Jesus' Name, Amen.

January 28

Wisdom at the Door

3-Year-Bible Reading: Proverbs 9:1–12; Psalm 12; Matthew 25

"The fear of the Lord is the beginning of wisdom, and the knowledge of the Holy One is insight." — Proverbs 9:10

"On every side the wicked prowl, as vileness is exalted among the children of man." — Psalm 12:8

"Watch therefore, for you know neither the day nor the hour." — Matthew 25:13

We live in a world full of choices—and not all of them are easy. Some seem harmless at first, but they lead us away from God's wisdom. Whether it's what we watch, who we follow online, or how we treat others, we're constantly choosing between following what's popular or following what's wise.

In **Proverbs 9**, wisdom is pictured as a woman inviting us to a feast—a life of understanding and truth. But **Psalm 12** reminds us that the world often lifts up lies, and **Matthew 25** warns us to be ready for Jesus at any moment. The big question is: are we living wisely or just going with the flow?

Think About It

1. **What are you feeding on?** Wisdom invites us to a feast, but so does foolishness (read all of **Proverbs 9** for both invitations). What are you putting into your heart and mind every day—truth or junk?

2. **Who's shaping your worldview?** Psalm 12 talks about how lies and flattery rule in a broken world. Are you letting the world's standards shape you, or are you standing on what God says?

3. **Are you ready?** Jesus tells the story of the ten virgins in **Matthew 25** to remind us that we won't get a heads-up before He returns. Are you living like someone who's prepared to meet Him today?

Bottom Line

Wisdom doesn't shout like the world does, but it's always calling. Following Jesus means listening to His voice, living ready, and choosing truth—even when it's hard.

Prayer

Heavenly Father, help me to tune out the noise of the world and listen for Your voice. Give me a heart that loves wisdom and a life that reflects Your truth. Help me be ready for whatever You call me to, today and every day. In Jesus' Name, Amen.

January 29

Betrayed But Not Broken

3-Year-Bible Reading: Matthew 26

"Watch and pray that you may not enter into temptation. The spirit indeed is willing, but the flesh is weak." — Matthew 26:41

"Then all the disciples left him and fled." — Matthew 26:56b

"Then Peter remembered the saying of Jesus, 'Before the rooster crows, you will deny me three times.' And he went out and wept bitterly." — Matthew 26:75

Jesus knew what was coming. He saw betrayal in Judas's kiss, fear in Peter's eyes, and weakness in His closest friends who couldn't stay awake to pray. Still, He chose to press on. In **Matthew 26**, we watch Jesus move through some of His darkest moments—not with panic, but with purpose. Even when people failed Him, He stayed faithful.

For young people today, this chapter speaks volumes. Whether it's pressure from friends, fear of rejection, or feeling let down by those we trust, we're reminded that Jesus understands. He lived it. And He shows us how to respond—with prayer, with honesty, and with unwavering commitment to God's will.

Think About It

1. **Jesus understands your pain:** Have you ever felt betrayed or let down by someone close? Jesus knows that pain deeply. He invites you to bring that hurt to Him.

2. **Your spirit is willing:** Jesus didn't shame the disciples for being weak—He encouraged them to pray. When you feel like you're falling short, turn to Him instead of giving up.

3. **Failure isn't the end:** Peter denied Jesus, yet Jesus still had a plan for him. Your worst moment doesn't cancel God's purpose for your life.

Bottom Line

Even when people fail us or we fail ourselves, Jesus remains faithful—and invites us to rise again with Him.

Prayer

Heavenly Father, thank You for showing us, through Jesus, how to stay strong even when life gets tough. Help me to stay close to You when I feel weak, afraid, or hurt by others. Remind me that You understand and never give up on me. Give me courage to follow You, even when it's hard. In Jesus' Name, Amen.

January 30

Forsaken but Not Forgotten

3-Year-Bible Reading: Psalms 22; Matthew 27

"My God, my God, why have you forsaken me? Why are you so far from saving me, from the words of my groaning?" — Psalm 22:1

"And about the ninth hour Jesus cried out with a loud voice, saying, 'Eli, Eli, lema sabachthani?' that is, 'My God, my God, why have you forsaken me?'" — Matthew 27:46

Ever felt abandoned by God? Maybe during a tough exam, a broken friendship, or when life just feels too heavy. You're not alone—literally. In **Psalm 22**, David cries out from a place of deep pain, and centuries later, Jesus echoes those same words from the cross in **Matthew 27**.

Jesus—the Son of God—knows what it's like to feel totally alone. But even in that moment of forsakenness, He was fulfilling a purpose bigger than the pain. And that's something we can hold onto too.

Think About It

1. **God Understands Your Pain:** Jesus quoting **Psalm 22** on the cross shows that He fully entered our human experience. Have you ever cried out like David or Jesus? Know that God isn't offended by your honesty—He welcomes it.

2. **It's Okay to Ask "Why?":** Feeling confused or hurt doesn't mean you're weak in faith. Even Jesus asked why. The important thing is to bring those questions to God, not hide them.

3. **Pain with a Purpose:** The suffering in **Matthew 27** wasn't the end—it led to the resurrection. What hard thing might God be using in your life to shape you or bring hope to others?

Bottom Line

God may feel distant in your hardest moments, but He is never absent. Jesus knows your pain and promises that you are never alone.

Prayer

Heavenly Father, thank You for understanding what it feels like to be alone and in pain. When life gets hard and I don't understand what You're doing, help me remember that You never leave me. Teach me to trust You even in the silence. In Jesus' Name, Amen.

January 31

Whispers and Warnings

3-Year-Bible Reading: Proverbs 9:13–18; Psalm 13; Matthew 28

"The woman Folly is loud; she is seductive and knows nothing… But he does not know that the dead are there, that her guests are in the depths of Sheol." — Proverbs 9:13, 18

"How long, O Lord? Will you forget me forever? How long will you hide your face from me?" — Psalm 13:1

"And Jesus came and said to them, 'All authority in heaven and on earth has been given to me. Go therefore and make disciples of all nations… And behold, I am with you always, to the end of the age.'" — Matthew 28:18–20

Sometimes life feels like a tug-of-war between two voices. One is loud and tempting, promising excitement and freedom — but it never mentions the cost. The other speaks hope in whispers, sometimes hard to hear when you're overwhelmed, confused, or doubting God's presence. In **Proverbs 9**, "Folly" is portrayed as loud and flashy but leading straight to destruction.

Psalm 13 shows us David crying out, feeling forgotten by God — a feeling you might know too well. And yet, in **Matthew 28**, Jesus reminds us that He is always with us and has all authority — meaning nothing is out of His control. Even when the world's noise drowns out God's voice, He's still speaking. And His way leads to life.

Think About It

1. **What voices are you listening to?** Are there influences in your life — media, people, thoughts — that are loud but empty?

2. **God can handle your questions:** David poured out his raw emotions in Psalm 13. You don't have to pretend with God. Bring your doubts, your frustration, and your confusion to Him — He wants your honesty.

3. **Jesus sends and stays:** The Great Commission in Matthew 28 isn't just about mission — it's about *presence*. When you follow Jesus, He doesn't send you out alone. He promises to be with you always.

Bottom Line

Even when life is noisy, confusing, or feels like God is distant, Jesus is still near — guiding you with truth and giving you strength to choose the path that leads to life.

Prayer

Heavenly Father, sometimes it's hard to tell what's right when everything around me is loud and distracting. Help me recognize the voice of wisdom and follow Your lead. Thank You that I can come to You with all my thoughts — even the messy ones — and that You never leave me, even when I can't feel You. Give me courage to live out Your truth and trust Your presence every step of the way. In Jesus' Name, Amen.

February 1

Wise Moves and Bold Faith

3-Year-Bible Reading: Proverbs 10:1; Acts 1

"A wise son makes a glad father, but a foolish son is a sorrow to his mother." — Proverbs 10:1

"But you will receive power when the Holy Spirit has come upon you, and you will be my witnesses in Jerusalem and in all Judea and Samaria, and to the end of the earth." — Acts 1:8

Sometimes it feels like being a teenager means standing at a thousand crossroads every day. Do I speak up or stay quiet? Do I follow the crowd or stand alone? Do I scroll another hour or open my Bible instead? In **Proverbs 10:1**, we're reminded that our choices matter—wise choices bring joy, but foolish ones hurt the people who care about us most.

Meanwhile, **Acts 1** introduces us to a moment right before Jesus goes back to heaven. He tells His followers that the Holy Spirit is coming to give them power—not for popularity or comfort, but so they can be bold and live out their faith wherever they go. Wisdom and boldness go hand-in-hand, especially when you're trying to follow Jesus in a world full of distractions and pressure.

Think About It

1. **Wise Choices Matter:** Are there areas in your life where you've seen how your choices affect others—especially your parents or friends? What does it mean to be "wise" in those moments?

2. **Holy Spirit Power:** Jesus promised His followers they would receive *power*. That same Spirit lives in you today if you follow Him. How can knowing this help you be more confident in living out your faith?

3. **Your Mission Starts Now:** You don't have to wait to be older to make a difference. Jesus didn't say to wait until everything's perfect—He said *go*. What's one way you can be a witness for Jesus at school, in your friend group, or online?

Bottom Line

Living wisely and boldly for Jesus isn't just for adults or church leaders—it's for *you*. With God's Spirit in you, every choice you make can reflect Him and make a real impact.

Prayer

Heavenly Father, help me to choose wisdom even when it's hard or unpopular. Thank You for giving me the Holy Spirit to guide and strengthen me. Teach me to be bold in my faith and to live in a way that brings You joy. Use my life to reflect Your love and truth to those around me. In Jesus' Name, Amen.

FEBRUARY 2

Chasing What Lasts

3-Year-Bible Reading: Proverbs 10:2; Psalm 16; Acts 2

"Treasures gained by wickedness do not profit, but righteousness delivers from death." — Proverbs 10:2

"You make known to me the path of life; in your presence there is fullness of joy; at your right hand are pleasures forevermore." — Psalm 16:11

"And it shall come to pass that everyone who calls upon the name of the Lord shall be saved." — Acts 2:21

We live in a world where everyone's chasing something—money, likes, popularity, success. It's easy to feel like we need to do whatever it takes to get ahead. But **Proverbs 10:2** warns that even if we "win" by doing the wrong thing, it won't be worth it. Real life—the kind that fills you with joy and lasts forever—comes from God, not from shortcuts or sketchy choices.

Psalm 16 reminds us that God's presence is where true happiness is found. And **Acts 2** delivers the best news of all: no matter where we've been or what we've done, calling on Jesus brings salvation. That's a promise worth holding onto.

THINK ABOUT IT

1. **What Are You Chasing?** Are you trying to find your worth in things that won't last—like popularity or possessions? Proverbs 10:2 challenges us to think about what really matters and what actually leads to life.

2. **Where's Your Joy Coming From?** Psalm 16 says fullness of joy is found in God's presence. If you're feeling empty or lost, maybe it's time to check your spiritual GPS. Are you looking to God or to stuff that fades?

3. **Have You Called on Jesus?** Acts 2:21 is clear—*everyone* who calls on the Lord will be saved. It's not about being perfect; it's about reaching out. If you've never done that, today could be the day.

BOTTOM LINE

A life built on God is a life that lasts. Joy, purpose, and salvation don't come from chasing the world—they come from walking with Jesus.

PRAYER

Heavenly Father, Help me not to chase things that don't last. Show me what it means to live in Your presence and find real joy in You. Thank You for the promise that anyone who calls on You will be saved. I want to follow the path of life You've laid out for me. In Jesus' Name, Amen.

FEBRUARY 3

Fully Satisfied

3-Year-Bible Reading: Proverbs 10:3; Acts 3

"The Lord does not let the righteous go hungry, but he thwarts the craving of the wicked." — Proverbs 10:3

"But Peter said, 'I have no silver and gold, but what I do have I give to you. In the name of Jesus Christ of Nazareth, rise up and walk!'" — Acts 3:6

"And leaping up he stood and began to walk, and entered the temple with them, walking and leaping and praising God." — Acts 3:8

Have you ever wanted something so badly you couldn't think about anything else? Maybe it's the latest phone, more followers, or even just to feel like you *matter*. Our culture constantly tells us that we need *more* to be happy. But **Proverbs 10:3** reminds us that the Lord doesn't let His people go hungry—not just physically, but spiritually too.

In **Acts 3**, a man who couldn't walk asked Peter and John for money. But what he got instead was healing—something far greater. Sometimes we chase what we *think* we need, but God is offering us something way better: Himself.

THINK ABOUT IT

1. **What are you hungry for?** Is it popularity, approval, success, or love? What if those cravings are just signs pointing you to your deeper need for God?

2. **God gives what we *really* need:** The lame man thought money would fix his problem, but Jesus gave him healing and joy. Are you open to God's better plan, even if it looks different from what you asked for?

3. **You have something to give:** Peter had no money, but he gave what he *did* have—Jesus. Even as a teen, you can make a real impact just by sharing hope, encouragement, and truth with others.

BOTTOM LINE

God doesn't just give us what we *want*—He gives us what we *truly need*. When we trust Him, He fills us with joy, strength, and purpose that no earthly thing can offer.

PRAYER

Heavenly Father, Thank You for always seeing what I really need, even when I don't. Help me to trust You more and to be satisfied in what You give. Open my eyes to see the people around me who need hope, and give me the courage to share Your love with them. I want to live each day walking and leaping and praising You. In Jesus' Name, Amen.

FEBRUARY 4

Stay Awake, Stay Wise

3-Year-Bible Reading: Proverbs 10:4–5; Psalm 14; Acts 4

"A slack hand causes poverty, but the hand of the diligent makes rich. He who gathers in summer is a prudent son, but he who sleeps in harvest is a son who brings shame." — Proverbs 10:4–5

"The fool says in his heart, 'There is no God.' They are corrupt, they do abominable deeds; there is none who does good." — Psalm 14:1

"And there is salvation in no one else, for there is no other name under heaven given among men by which we must be saved." — Acts 4:12

Ever feel like everything's moving fast—school, friends, sports, social media—and you're just trying to keep up? It's easy to get distracted or even lazy when life feels overwhelming. But in **Proverbs 10**, we're reminded that staying diligent—doing the work, even when it's hard—is what leads to growth. Meanwhile, **Psalm 14** warns against ignoring God and choosing our own path, calling it foolish.

And in **Acts 4**, Peter boldly says that Jesus is the only way to salvation, no matter how many other voices we hear. Together, these verses point to a truth we can't ignore: we need to wake up to what matters most—faith in Jesus and living like it counts.

THINK ABOUT IT

1. **Diligence Matters:** What areas of your life are you "sleeping through"? Is it your relationship with God, school, or friendships? God honors effort that comes from the heart.

2. **Don't Be Fooled:** Psalm 14 calls out the lie that God doesn't matter. What influences (TikTok, music, friends, etc.) make it harder to believe or live out your faith?

3. **Jesus is the Only Way:** Acts 4:12 makes it clear—salvation isn't found in being "good enough" or fitting in. Have you made Jesus the center of your life, or just a part of your Sunday routine?

BOTTOM LINE

Don't sleep through the moments that matter. Live with purpose, stay close to Jesus, and don't let the world fool you into thinking anything else will save you.

PRAYER

Heavenly Father, help me stay awake to what really matters. Give me a heart that works hard, a mind that stays sharp in truth, and a soul that's anchored in Jesus. Keep me from drifting and draw me closer to You every day. In Jesus' Name, Amen.

FEBRUARY 5

Legacy in the Light

3-Year-Bible Reading: Proverbs 10:6–7; Acts 5

"Blessings are on the head of the righteous, but the mouth of the wicked conceals violence. The memory of the righteous is a blessing, but the name of the wicked will rot." — Proverbs 10:6–7

"But Peter said, 'Ananias, why has Satan filled your heart to lie to the Holy Spirit… You have not lied to man but to God.'" — Acts 5:3–4

"And great fear came upon the whole church and upon all who heard of these things." — Acts 5:11

Have you ever thought about how you'll be remembered? It might sound kind of deep, but the choices you make now are shaping your reputation and legacy. In **Proverbs 10:6–7**, Solomon talks about how the righteous are remembered with honor, but the wicked leave behind regret.

We see this played out dramatically in **Acts 5** with Ananias and Sapphira. They tried to lie and act like they were more generous than they really were—and it didn't end well. Their names became a warning story instead of a legacy of faith.

THINK ABOUT IT

1. **What Story Are You Writing?** Every decision you make builds your story. Are your words and actions leading people to see Jesus in you, or something else?

2. **Integrity Matters:** Ananias and Sapphira's mistake wasn't just holding back money—it was pretending to be something they weren't. Honesty with God and others is key to a lasting, God-honoring life.

3. **Fear of God—Not in a Scary Way:** The church's reaction to their story wasn't just fear—it was awe. It reminded them (and us) that God takes our hearts seriously. Respecting Him leads to wisdom and real blessing.

BOTTOM LINE

How you live today matters for how you'll be remembered tomorrow. Live with integrity and honor God with every choice.

PRAYER

Heavenly Father, help me to live a life that honors You in both big and small decisions. Give me the courage to be real, the wisdom to make good choices, and the strength to walk in integrity. Let my life be a light and my memory be a blessing to others. In Jesus' Name, Amen.

FEBRUARY 6

Choose Wisdom Over Noise

3-Year-Bible Reading: Proverbs 10:8; Psalm 15; Acts 6

"The wise of heart will receive commandments, but a babbling fool will come to ruin." — Proverbs 10:8

"He who walks blamelessly and does what is right and speaks truth in his heart... shall never be moved." — Psalm 15:2,5

"And they chose Stephen, a man full of faith and of the Holy Spirit..." — Acts 6:5

Have you ever been in a group chat where everyone's talking, but no one's really listening? In our loud world—online and offline—it's easy to feel like we have to speak up constantly just to be noticed. But the Bible reminds us that real wisdom often comes from quiet strength, faithful action, and listening first.

In **Proverbs 10:8**, we see the contrast between someone who listens and obeys versus someone who just runs their mouth and ends up in trouble. **Psalm 15** shows us what it looks like to live with integrity, and **Acts 6** introduces us to Stephen—a young man whose quiet, Spirit-filled life spoke louder than any argument.

THINK ABOUT IT

1. **Listen First:** Are you quick to talk or quick to listen? Proverbs 10:8 reminds us that wise people are teachable. When someone gives you advice or correction, do you push back—or do you take it to heart?

2. **Character Over Clout:** Psalm 15 paints a picture of someone who lives with integrity even when no one's watching. What does your private life say about your character?

3. **Full of Faith:** Stephen wasn't famous, but he was faithful. Acts 6 tells us he was chosen because of his faith and the Spirit in him. Are you letting God shape your inside world, even if others don't notice right away?

BOTTOM LINE

Being wise doesn't mean being the loudest voice—it means being the one who listens, lives with integrity, and lets God's Spirit lead. In a world full of noise, let your life speak through quiet strength and faithful choices.

PRAYER

Heavenly Father, help me to be someone who listens more than I speak. Teach me to walk in wisdom and integrity, even when it's not popular. Fill me with Your Spirit like You did with Stephen, so that I can live boldly and humbly for You. Let my life reflect Your truth, not just in what I say but in what I do. In Jesus' Name, Amen.

February 7

Walk the Talk

3-Year-Bible Reading: Proverbs 10:9–10; Acts 7

"Whoever walks in integrity walks securely, but he who makes his ways crooked will be found out. Whoever winks the eye causes trouble, and a babbling fool will come to ruin." — Proverbs 10:9–10

"And as they were stoning Stephen, he called out, 'Lord Jesus, receive my spirit.' And falling to his knees he cried out with a loud voice, 'Lord, do not hold this sin against them.'" — Acts 7:59–60

Have you ever tried to cut corners—maybe cheated just a little on a test or kept quiet when you saw something wrong—thinking it wouldn't matter much? It's tempting to take the easy way out, but the Bible reminds us that real strength comes from walking in truth, even when it costs us something. In **Proverbs 10:9–10**, we're told that people with integrity can walk securely, while those who try to hide or fake it will eventually be exposed.

Then we see a powerful example of this in **Acts 7**, where Stephen stands boldly for his faith, even though it leads to his death. He doesn't lie, twist the truth, or back down. He walks with integrity, and even in his final breath, he chooses to forgive. That's powerful—and it challenges us to think about how we're walking today.

Think About It

1. **What does integrity look like?** Integrity isn't about being perfect—it's about being real. Are you honest in your words and actions, even when no one's watching?

2. **Stephen's courage:** Stephen stood firm in his faith even when it was dangerous. Would you be willing to speak the truth about what you believe, even if it costs you popularity or comfort?

3. **Ripple effect:** People notice how you live. Are your actions pointing others toward Jesus, or away from Him?

Bottom Line

Walking with integrity might not always be easy, but it brings security, peace, and a witness that can change lives—just like Stephen's.

Prayer

Heavenly Father, thank You for the example of integrity and courage in Your Word. Help me to walk in truth and stand firm in my faith, even when it's hard. Give me the strength to do what's right and the heart to forgive others like Stephen did. Let my life reflect Your light in every situation. In Jesus' Name, Amen.

FEBRUARY 8

Love That Sticks

3-Year-Bible Reading: Proverbs 10:11–12; Acts 8

"The mouth of the righteous is a fountain of life, but the mouth of the wicked conceals violence. Hatred stirs up strife, but love covers all offenses."
— Proverbs 10:11–12

"And the crowds with one accord paid attention to what was being said by Philip when they heard him and saw the signs that he did." — Acts 8:6

"But Peter said to him, 'May your silver perish with you, because you thought you could obtain the gift of God with money!'" — Acts 8:20

You don't have to scroll long on social media to find someone arguing, canceling, or calling someone out. The world can be loud with hate, but **Proverbs 10** says that love *covers* offense. That doesn't mean love ignores problems—it means it doesn't add fuel to the fire. It looks for healing, not drama.

In **Acts 8**, we see two very different reactions to the good news of Jesus. The crowd listens to Philip and sees miracles—because love and truth are at work. But then Simon tries to buy the Holy Spirit like it's a video game upgrade. Peter calls him out because God's gifts are just that: gifts. Real love can't be bought, forced, or faked.

THINK ABOUT IT

1. **Your Words Matter:** Are your words a fountain of life like **Proverbs 10:11** says? Do they build people up or tear them down? Your mouth is powerful—use it for love.

2. **Check Your Motives:** Simon wanted the power of God, but for the wrong reasons. Why do you follow Jesus? For what He gives—or for who He is?

3. **Love Covers Offense:** When someone offends or hurts you, is your first move to fire back or to forgive? Love doesn't mean pretending nothing happened—it means choosing peace over payback.

BOTTOM LINE

God's love transforms how we speak, act, and respond. When love leads the way, everything changes—for us and the people around us.

PRAYER

Heavenly Father, thank You for showing us what real love looks like—love that forgives, restores, and gives freely. Help me use my words to bring life, not hurt. Teach me to follow You with pure motives and to reflect Your love even when it's hard. Fill me with Your Spirit so I can love like Jesus. In Jesus' Name, Amen.

FEBRUARY 9

Wise Words and a Willing Heart

3-Year-Bible Reading: Proverbs 10:13–14; Acts 9

"On the lips of him who has understanding, wisdom is found… The wise lay up knowledge, but the mouth of a fool brings ruin near." — Proverbs 10:13–14

"But the Lord said to him, 'Go, for he is a chosen instrument of mine to carry my name before the Gentiles and kings and the children of Israel.'" — Acts 9:15

Have you ever said something and immediately regretted it? Maybe it was something harsh, sarcastic, or just completely wrong. Words are powerful—and so is the heart behind them. In **Proverbs 10**, we see that wise people are careful with their words, but foolish words can lead to destruction.

In **Acts 9**, we meet Saul (who becomes Paul), a guy whose words and actions were destroying lives—literally—until God changed his heart. God saw something in Saul that no one else did: a heart that could be used for His glory. It's a powerful reminder that God isn't just listening to our words—He's also shaping our hearts to match His mission.

Think About It

1. **Wise Words Matter:** What kind of words are coming out of your mouth? Are they helpful, kind, or encouraging? Proverbs says wisdom shows up in what we say.

2. **God Can Use Anyone:** Saul was the last person people expected God to use. But God sees potential in people the world might overlook. Who do you think God might be calling you to become?

3. **Be Willing to Change:** Saul had a dramatic encounter with Jesus that completely changed his life. You may not have a blinding-light moment, but are you open to God shaping your story?

Bottom Line

God values both wise words and willing hearts. When we speak with wisdom and let God lead our lives—even if we've messed up—He can use us for incredible things.

Prayer

Heavenly Father, thank You for giving us wisdom through Your Word and for seeing the potential in us even when others don't. Help me to speak with love and live with a heart that's open to Your calling. Change me where I need to grow, and use me for Your purpose. In Jesus' Name, Amen.

February 10

Built to Last

3-Year-Bible Reading: Proverbs 10:15–16; Psalm 17; Acts 10

"A rich man's wealth is his strong city; the poverty of the poor is their ruin. The wage of the righteous leads to life, the gain of the wicked to sin." — Proverbs 10:15–16

"Keep me as the apple of your eye; hide me in the shadow of your wings." — Psalm 17:8

"So Peter opened his mouth and said: 'Truly I understand that God shows no partiality, but in every nation anyone who fears him and does what is right is acceptable to him.'" — Acts 10:34–35

We live in a world where popularity, wealth, and followers can seem like everything. Social media screams that status is what makes you matter. But what happens when the likes stop? What lasts when money fades or people move on? The readings today remind us that our real value isn't in what we have or how we look, but in living a life rooted in God.

Proverbs 10 shows that doing what's right leads to life, while chasing the wrong things leads us nowhere. In **Psalm 17**, David cries out to God for protection, confident that he's precious in God's sight. And in **Acts 10**, Peter realizes that God welcomes *everyone* who honors Him—no matter their background, culture, or past.

Think About It

1. **What Are You Building On?** Are you building your confidence on things that can disappear—like popularity, money, or appearance? Proverbs reminds us that only the choices rooted in righteousness last.

2. **God Sees You:** Psalm 17 says God keeps you as the "apple of His eye." That means you are deeply loved and protected by Him. When you feel overlooked, remember—you're seen by the One who matters most.

3. **No Favorites:** In Acts, Peter learns that God doesn't play favorites. No matter your past or where you come from, God invites *you* to know Him and walk in His truth. Are you making room in your heart and life for others like God does?

Bottom Line

What we chase in life shows what we value. True life doesn't come from wealth, status, or being popular—it comes from living right with God, knowing you're loved by Him, and following His lead.

Prayer

Heavenly Father, thank You for seeing me, loving me, and calling me into a life that matters. Help me not to chase things that fade, but to build my life on what's true and lasting. Teach me to live righteously and to welcome others like You welcome me. In Jesus' Name, Amen.

FEBRUARY 11

Stay on the Path

3-Year-Bible Reading: Proverbs 10:17; Acts 11

"Whoever heeds instruction is on the path to life, but he who rejects reproof leads others astray." — Proverbs 10:17

"And when he had found him, he brought him to Antioch. For a whole year they met with the church and taught a great many people. And in Antioch the disciples were first called Christians." — Acts 11:26

Ever feel like you're just trying to figure out who you are and where you're going? Maybe you've wondered, *"What does it even mean to be a Christian, and how do I know I'm doing it right?"* In **Proverbs 10:17**, we're reminded that listening to wise advice keeps us on the right path.

In **Acts 11**, we get a glimpse of early believers in Antioch who were *first* called Christians—not because they had a label, but because their lives reflected Jesus. They were known for living out their faith, listening to God, and sticking together. You don't have to have all the answers right now, but you *do* need to pay attention to the voices that lead you toward life.

THINK ABOUT IT

1. **Check Your GPS:** Who are you listening to? Are your friends, mentors, and media influences helping you follow Jesus—or pulling you off course?

2. **Live the Label:** Being called a Christian isn't about a title. It's about showing Jesus through how you treat others, what you stand for, and how you love.

3. **Growth Happens Together:** The believers in Antioch didn't grow in isolation—they met together, learned together, and followed Jesus as a community. Are you staying connected to people who help you grow in your faith?

BOTTOM LINE

Listening to godly instruction and surrounding yourself with the right people keeps you on the path of life—and helps you live out your identity in Christ.

PRAYER

Heavenly Father, thank You for giving me people who speak truth into my life. Help me to listen to Your Word, follow the right path, and reflect Jesus in the way I live. Surround me with a community that helps me grow closer to You. In Jesus' Name, Amen.

FEBRUARY 12

Watch Your Words, Trust His Power

3-Year-Bible Reading: Proverbs 10:18–19; Psalm 18; Acts 12

"The one who conceals hatred has lying lips, and whoever utters slander is a fool. When words are many, transgression is not lacking, but whoever restrains his lips is prudent." — Proverbs 10:18–19

"The LORD is my rock and my fortress and my deliverer… I call upon the LORD, who is worthy to be praised, and I am saved from my enemies." — Psalm 18:2–3

"So Peter was kept in prison, but earnest prayer for him was made to God by the church." — Acts 12:5

Words can build up or tear down. That's not just something your parents say—it's straight from Scripture (**Proverbs 10:18–19**). Whether it's texting in a group chat, snapping back during an argument, or just talking without thinking, our words reveal what's going on in our hearts.

At the same time, life can feel like a constant battle—like Peter in **Acts 12**, stuck in a prison with no way out. But here's the amazing thing: when God's people prayed, God moved. **Psalm 18** reminds us that He's our Rock and Rescuer. When we control our words and trust in His power, we step into a life that reflects who He is.

Think About It

1. **What Are You Saying?** Are your words encouraging others or tearing them down? Think about your last few conversations—what do they say about your heart?

2. **Silent Strength:** Proverbs tells us that too many words often lead to sin. What would it look like for you to pause and listen more before speaking?

3. **God Can Still Move:** Just like Peter's friends prayed and God showed up big time, don't forget how powerful prayer is. Who do you need to pray for right now?

Bottom Line

Your words have power, and so does your God. Use both wisely. Choose silence when needed, speak with kindness, and never stop praying—God is always ready to show up.

Prayer

Heavenly Father, thank You for being my Rock and my Deliverer. Help me to use my words to bring life, not hurt. Teach me to listen more and speak wisely. And when things feel impossible, remind me that You still move through prayer. In Jesus' Name, Amen.

FEBRUARY 13

The Power of Words

3-Year-Bible Reading: Proverbs 10:20–21; Acts 13

"The tongue of the righteous is choice silver; the heart of the wicked is of little worth. The lips of the righteous feed many, but fools die for lack of sense." — Proverbs 10:20–21

"And when they had carried out all that was written of him, they took him down from the tree and laid him in a tomb. But God raised him from the dead." — Acts 13:29–30

Words are powerful. Whether it's the encouragement of a friend or a quick text that totally deflates your day, what people say matters—and what *you* say matters even more. In **Proverbs 10:20–21**, we see that the words of the righteous are like "choice silver" and have the power to *feed many*. That's a pretty cool image: words that give life and strength like a good meal.

Then in **Acts 13**, we see Paul preaching truth boldly, not holding back from declaring the good news of Jesus—even when it wasn't popular. His words weren't just talk; they were rooted in truth and changed lives. So, what kind of impact are *your* words having?

THINK ABOUT IT

1. **What are your words worth?** If your words were like money, would they be "choice silver" or cheap coins? Do your texts, comments, and convos lift people up or tear them down?

2. **Are you speaking truth?** Paul spoke the truth about Jesus, even when it wasn't easy. Do you stand up for what's right, or stay silent to fit in?

3. **Feed others with your speech:** Proverbs says righteous lips *feed many*. Who can you encourage or speak life into today—maybe a classmate, sibling, or even someone who's hard to love?

BOTTOM LINE

Your words have the power to hurt or heal. Choose to speak with love, truth, and boldness—just like Jesus did, and just like Paul did in Acts.

PRAYER

Heavenly Father, thank You for showing me that my words matter. Help me use my voice to speak truth, encourage others, and reflect who You are. Give me courage to be bold like Paul and kind like Jesus. Teach me to feed others with my words, not tear them down. In Jesus' Name, Amen.

FEBRUARY 14

Blessings Without the Burden

3-Year-Bible Reading: Proverbs 10:22; Psalm 19; Acts 14

"The blessing of the Lord makes rich, and he adds no sorrow with it." — Proverbs 10:22

"Let the words of my mouth and the meditation of my heart be acceptable in your sight, O Lord, my rock and my redeemer." — Psalm 19:14

"Yet he did not leave himself without witness, for he did good by giving you rains from heaven and fruitful seasons, satisfying your hearts with food and gladness." — Acts 14:17

Have you ever gotten something you really wanted, only to find out it came with a lot of stress? Maybe it was a spot on the team, a new phone, or even a leadership role at school. Sometimes blessings can feel heavy—unless they're from God. **Proverbs 10:22** reminds us that when God blesses us, it comes without the extra baggage of sorrow.

In **Psalm 19**, David prays for his heart and words to stay right with God, showing that staying close to Him is the key to real joy. Then in **Acts 14**, Paul points out that even simple things—like good food and rainy seasons—are signs of God's kindness to us. God's blessings aren't just "stuff"; they're His way of showing love and filling our hearts with true happiness.

Think About It

1. **What Kind of Riches?** Are you chasing blessings that are "rich" in God's eyes, or just in the world's? God's riches bring peace, not pressure.

2. **Heart Check:** Are the thoughts you meditate on and the words you speak pleasing to God, like David prayed in Psalm 19?

3. **Recognizing God's Goodness:** Can you see God's kindness in your everyday life—like through a good meal, a sunny day, or laughter with friends?

Bottom Line

God's blessings are good, pure, and bring joy without regret. When we seek Him first, we'll experience His gifts in ways that satisfy our souls, not just our wants.

Prayer

Heavenly Father, Thank You for blessing us with good things that bring real joy, not just temporary happiness. Help us to stay focused on You and recognize Your kindness all around us. Teach us to trust Your timing and Your way, knowing that everything You give is for our good. Let our hearts and words be pleasing to You today and every day. In Jesus' Name, Amen.

FEBRUARY 15

Choose Your Fun Wisely

3-Year-Bible Reading: Proverbs 10:23, 26; Acts 15

"Doing wrong is like a joke to a fool, but wisdom is pleasure to a man of understanding." — Proverbs 10:23

"Like vinegar to the teeth and smoke to the eyes, so is the sluggard to those who send him." — Proverbs 10:26

"It has seemed good to the Holy Spirit and to us to lay on you no greater burden than these requirements." — Acts 15:28

Let's be honest—some things that seem fun in the moment can leave you with serious regret later. Proverbs warns us that fools treat sin like a joke (**Proverbs 10:23**), and that being lazy or careless affects more than just you—it impacts the people who count on you (**Proverbs 10:26**).

In **Acts 15**, we see how early church leaders made careful decisions, guided by the Holy Spirit, to help people follow Jesus without adding unnecessary burdens. They weren't careless; they were thoughtful, wise, and intentional. That's a big contrast to how many people approach life—living for laughs without thinking long-term.

THINK ABOUT IT

1. **What's your definition of fun?** Are the things you enjoy building you up or pulling you away from God's best? Proverbs warns that making light of sin is foolish, even if it seems fun in the moment.

2. **How do your actions affect others?** Proverbs 10:26 compares a lazy person to vinegar on teeth—basically annoying and painful. Are you someone others can count on?

3. **Seek God's guidance:** The church in Acts 15 didn't make decisions based on pressure or popular opinion. They prayed, listened, and followed the Holy Spirit's lead. What would it look like for you to do the same?

BOTTOM LINE

Fun isn't bad—but fun that dishonors God or hurts others isn't worth it. Choose wisdom, live intentionally, and let the Holy Spirit guide your decisions.

PRAYER

Heavenly Father, thank You for giving us Your Word and the Holy Spirit to guide us. Help me to be someone who chooses wisdom over cheap laughs, and to live in a way that honors You and blesses others. Teach me to be reliable, thoughtful, and strong in my faith. In Jesus' Name, Amen.

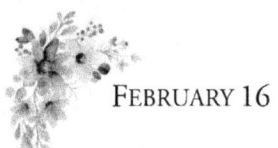

FEBRUARY 16

Storm-Proof Faith

3-Year-Bible Reading: Proverbs 10:24–25; Acts 16

"What the wicked dreads will come upon him, but the desire of the righteous will be granted. When the tempest passes, the wicked is no more, but the righteous is established forever." — Proverbs 10:24–25

"About midnight Paul and Silas were praying and singing hymns to God, and the prisoners were listening to them." — Acts 16:25

Life can sometimes feel like a roller coaster you didn't sign up for. One minute you're on top of the world, and the next you're facing stress, fear, or pain. In **Acts 16**, Paul and Silas were literally thrown into prison for doing what was right—sharing the gospel.

But instead of complaining or panicking, they started *singing*. That's the kind of storm-proof faith God calls us to. And **Proverbs 10** reminds us that even when life gets wild, those who trust in God will stand firm when the storm is over.

THINK ABOUT IT

1. **What do you do in the storm?** When Paul and Silas were locked up, they didn't wait until they were free to worship—they did it in the middle of the chaos. What's your first response when things go wrong? Prayer and worship change our perspective.

2. **Built to Last:** Proverbs 10 tells us that the righteous are "established forever." That doesn't mean life is always easy—but it does mean that with God, we're anchored in something solid. Are you building your life on God's truth?

3. **Who's listening?** Other prisoners heard Paul and Silas worship. Your faith in tough times might be someone else's turning point. How you handle pressure can show others the power of a relationship with Jesus.

BOTTOM LINE

Storms will come—but when you trust in God, you don't have to be shaken. Your faith can not only carry you through, but also impact everyone around you.

PRAYER

Heavenly Father, thank You for being my strength when life gets hard. Help me to turn to You first, to worship even when I don't feel like it, and to be a light to others when storms hit. I want a faith that stands strong, no matter what comes. In Jesus' Name, Amen.

FEBRUARY 17

Living with Purpose

3-Year-Bible Reading: Proverbs 10:27–28; Acts 17

"The fear of the Lord prolongs life, but the years of the wicked will be short. The hope of the righteous brings joy, but the expectation of the wicked will perish."— Proverbs 10:27–28

"Yet he is actually not far from each one of us, for 'In him we live and move and have our being'; as even some of your own poets have said, 'For we are indeed his offspring.'"— Acts 17:27b–28

Let's be real—life can feel confusing sometimes. There's school stress, friendships that shift, family stuff, and all the pressure to figure out who you're supposed to be. In all the noise, it's easy to wonder if your life really has a purpose. That's why **Acts 17** is so powerful. Paul reminds us that we're not here by accident—God created us, and He's closer than we think.

Pair that with **Proverbs 10,** which shows that a life rooted in awe and respect for God is not only meaningful but full of real joy and lasting hope. When we live with God in focus, we don't just survive—we thrive with purpose.

Think About It

1. **What does it mean to "fear the Lord"?** It's not about being scared—it's about having deep respect, trust, and awe for who God is. This kind of mindset shapes how we live, choose, and treat others.

2. **God is near:** Paul says we "live and move and have our being" in Him. That means your whole life—your breath, your dreams, your struggles—is connected to God. He's not distant; He's present in every part of your day.

3. **Hope that lasts:** According to **Proverbs 10:28**, the hope of those who follow God brings joy. Unlike the temporary highs the world offers, God gives us peace that sticks even when life gets tough.

Bottom Line

You were made by God, for God. When you live with Him at the center, you'll find purpose, joy, and a hope that doesn't fade.

Prayer

Heavenly Father, thank You for being close to me—even when I don't always feel it. Help me to live each day with a heart that respects and trusts You. Teach me to find my identity and purpose in You alone. Let my life reflect the hope and joy You give. In Jesus' Name, Amen.

FEBRUARY 18

The Road You Choose

3-Year-Bible Reading: Proverbs 10:29–32; Psalm 20; Acts 18

"The way of the Lord is a stronghold to the blameless, but destruction to evildoers." — Proverbs 10:29

"Some trust in chariots and some in horses, but we trust in the name of the Lord our God." — Psalm 20:7

"And the Lord said to Paul one night in a vision, 'Do not be afraid, but go on speaking and do not be silent, for I am with you...'" — Acts 18:9–10

Life is full of choices—what to say, who to hang out with, how to react when things go sideways. Sometimes doing the right thing feels like the hard thing, and trusting God can seem risky when you can't see the outcome. But today's verses remind us that the way of the Lord isn't just right—it's *safe*. **Proverbs 10:29** says it's a stronghold, a place of strength and protection.

Psalm 20 reminds us that while others trust in their own power, we put our hope in God's name. And in **Acts 18**, God personally encourages Paul to keep going, promising, "I am with you." Whether you're speaking up for your faith or walking through something tough, you're not alone.

THINK ABOUT IT

1. **God's way is a stronghold:** What does it mean for God's path to be a "stronghold"? How might following Him give you strength in situations where you feel weak or uncertain?

2. **Where is your trust?** It's easy to trust in what we can see—grades, talents, popularity. But what does it look like to trust in God's name instead?

3. **Boldness comes from presence:** God told Paul not to be afraid because *He* was with him. Are there areas in your life where fear is holding you back from being who God's called you to be?

BOTTOM LINE

Choosing to follow God's way may not always be easy, but it leads to strength, security, and purpose—because God walks with you every step of the way.

PRAYER

Heavenly Father, thank You for being a stronghold I can trust. Help me to choose Your way, even when it's hard or I feel afraid. Remind me that You are always with me, just like You were with Paul. Give me boldness to live for You and confidence that Your way is the best way. In Jesus' Name, Amen.

FEBRUARY 19

Honest to God

3-Year-Bible Reading: Proverbs 11:1; Acts 19

"A false balance is an abomination to the Lord, but a just weight is his delight." — Proverbs 11:1

"And this became known to all the residents of Ephesus, both Jews and Greeks. And fear fell upon them all, and the name of the Lord Jesus was extolled." — Acts 19:17

We've all been tempted to cut corners—maybe copying a friend's homework or saying "just a little lie" to get out of trouble. But in **Proverbs 11:1**, God makes it clear: dishonesty isn't just "not great"—it's an *abomination*. That's a strong word!

In **Acts 19**, we see what happens when people encounter the real power of Jesus. They're so impacted that they confess their wrongdoing and even burn the stuff they used for magic—worth tons of money! That's some serious life change. When people really meet Jesus, honesty and integrity aren't optional—they're evidence that something real has happened in their hearts.

THINK ABOUT IT

1. **God Cares About Integrity:** Proverbs 11:1 reminds us that our character matters to God, even in the small stuff. Are you being honest in school, friendships, and online?

2. **Power of Real Change:** In Acts 19, people were so transformed by Jesus that they got rid of anything that didn't honor Him. What might God be asking you to let go of so you can live more honestly?

3. **What Are You Known For?** The people in Ephesus were gripped with respect for Jesus because of the way His followers lived. If people looked at your life, would they see Jesus in how you speak and act?

BOTTOM LINE

God delights in honesty. When we live with integrity, especially when it's hard, we reflect the character of Jesus and show the world what He's really like.

PRAYER

Heavenly Father, help me to be honest in every part of my life—even when no one is watching. Teach me to value what You value and give me the courage to make things right when I mess up. Let my life be a reflection of Your truth and love. In Jesus' Name, Amen.

February 20

Humble Wins

3-Year-Bible Reading: Proverbs 11:2; Psalm 21; Acts 20

"When pride comes, then comes disgrace, but with the humble is wisdom." — Proverbs 11:2

"For you meet him with rich blessings; you set a crown of fine gold upon his head." — Psalm 21:3

"In all things I have shown you that by working hard in this way we must help the weak and remember the words of the Lord Jesus, how he himself said, 'It is more blessed to give than to receive.'" — Acts 20:35

We live in a world that says, "Be the best. Show off. Climb to the top." But God's Word flips that script. **Proverbs 11:2** warns us that pride leads to downfall, while humility leads to wisdom. **Psalm 21** celebrates how God honors those He chooses, but it's clear that the blessings come from God, not from our own greatness.

And in **Acts 20**, Paul reminds us that a life poured out for others is the life that truly matters. That's not always easy to accept when everything around us says to look out for ourselves first. But when we live humbly and give freely, we find something deeper than success—we find purpose.

Think About It

1. **Humility is Strength:** What does it really mean to be humble? Being humble doesn't mean thinking less of yourself; it means thinking of yourself less. How can you practice humility in your daily life?

2. **Giving is Greater:** Paul quotes Jesus saying, "It is more blessed to give than to receive." Why do you think giving brings more blessing than getting? Can you think of a time when helping someone else made you feel full inside?

3. **Where's Your Crown Coming From?** Psalm 21 speaks of blessings and honor. But those good things came from God, not from trying to prove something. Are you chasing recognition from others, or are you living for God's approval?

Bottom Line

True greatness isn't found in being first—it's found in serving others, staying humble, and trusting God to lift you up in His timing.

Prayer

Heavenly Father, Thank You for reminding me that pride only leads to trouble, but humility brings wisdom and joy. Help me not to chase attention or praise, but to live a life that honors You. Teach me to give freely, love deeply, and stay grounded in Your truth. May I always remember that what You give is better than anything I can gain on my own. In Jesus' Name, Amen.

February 21

Straight Paths & Strong Convictions

3-Year-Bible Reading: Proverbs 11:3–4; Acts 21–22

The integrity of the upright guides them, but the crookedness of the treacherous destroys them. Riches do not profit in the day of wrath, but righteousness delivers from death — Proverbs 11:3–4

"Then Paul answered, 'What are you doing, weeping and breaking my heart? For I am ready not only to be imprisoned but even to die in Jerusalem for the name of the Lord Jesus.'" — Acts 21:13

"'I am a Jew, born in Tarsus in Cilicia, but brought up in this city, educated at the feet of Gamaliel…being zealous for God as all of you are this day.'" — Acts 22:3

It's not always easy to stand for what's right—especially when no one else seems to be. Whether it's pressure at school, online, or even among friends, choosing integrity over popularity can feel like walking against the current. But **Proverbs 11:3–4** reminds us that integrity acts like a GPS for life—it guides us when everything else feels uncertain.

And when we look at **Acts 21–22**, we see Paul living this out. Even when warned of danger, he stayed on God's path. He wasn't reckless—he was convicted. He knew who he was, who God was, and why that mattered more than his comfort or safety.

Think About It

1. **What guides your decisions?** Are your choices shaped by what's easy or what's right? Proverbs says integrity *guides* us—meaning it helps us decide which way to go even when things are confusing.

2. **Courage through conviction:** Paul wasn't afraid because he had clarity about his mission. What convictions or truths about God give you courage when life is scary or uncertain?

3. **Own your story:** In Acts 22, Paul shares his background with boldness. Your testimony—how God is working in your life—is powerful. How can you share it with others, even if it's still in progress?

Bottom Line

Integrity isn't about being perfect—it's about consistently choosing what honors God, even when it's hard. Like Paul, you can walk boldly when you let God's truth guide you.

Prayer

Heavenly Father, thank You for being a steady guide when life feels confusing or scary. Help me to choose integrity over convenience and boldness over fear. Teach me to stand strong in my faith like Paul, and to live in a way that reflects who You are. In Jesus' Name, Amen.

FEBRUARY 22

Straight Paths and Steady Hearts

3-Year-Bible Reading: Proverbs 11:5–6; Psalm 22

"The righteousness of the blameless keeps his way straight, but the wicked falls by his own wickedness. The righteousness of the upright delivers them, but the treacherous are taken captive by their lust." — Proverbs 11:5–6

"My God, my God, why have you forsaken me? Why are you so far from saving me, from the words of my groaning?... Yet you are holy, enthroned on the praises of Israel." — Psalm 22:1, 3

Ever feel like you're doing the right thing, but life still feels unfair or confusing? Maybe you're trying to stay honest, keep your word, or walk away from drama—and yet, it feels like others who take shortcuts are winning. **Proverbs 11:5–6** reminds us that choosing righteousness (aka, living in a way that pleases God) keeps our path straight and our hearts steady, even when things around us are chaotic.

And **Psalm 22** gives us a raw look at someone feeling abandoned and unheard—but still choosing to trust in God's goodness. Even when life feels like a mess, God is still on the throne, still holy, and still with us.

Think About It

1. **The Power of Choices:** What does it mean to be "blameless" or "upright" in your world—at school, online, or with friends? How can choosing what's right help keep your path straight?

2. **Feeling Forsaken:** Psalm 22 shows us that even faithful people can feel far from God. What should we do when God feels silent? How can we remind ourselves that He's still there?

3. **God Sees the Heart:** The world might celebrate people who cheat, lie, or fake it to get ahead. But God celebrates hearts that seek Him. Are there areas in your life where you're tempted to cut corners instead of walking the path God laid out?

Bottom Line

God sees the choices we make. Even when doing the right thing feels hard or unnoticed, He honors righteousness and walks with us—even in our hardest moments.

Prayer

Heavenly Father, thank You for being with me on the good days and the tough ones. Help me to choose what's right, even when it's not easy. Remind me that You see my heart and guide my steps when I follow You. When I feel alone or overlooked, draw me close and fill me with Your peace. In Jesus' Name, Amen.

FEBRUARY 23

What Are You Living For?

3-Year-Bible Reading: Proverbs 11:7–8; Acts 23

"When the wicked dies, his hope will perish, and the expectation of wealth perishes too. The righteous is delivered from trouble, and the wicked walks into it instead." — Proverbs 11:7–8

"And looking intently at the council, Paul said, 'Brothers, I have lived my life before God in all good conscience up to this day.'" — Acts 23:1

Imagine putting your whole life into something—popularity, money, being liked—and then one day realizing it doesn't last. That's what **Proverbs 11:7** is getting at. If your life is only about chasing stuff that fades, then what happens when it all disappears?

But when you live for God, like Paul talks about in **Acts 23:1**, your life has purpose beyond just the now. Even when things get messy or unfair (and they did for Paul, big time), God's with you, guiding your steps and even using the hard moments for something bigger.

THINK ABOUT IT

1. **What Are You Hoping In?** Are your hopes tied to things like likes on social media, getting into a certain school, or looking a certain way? Those aren't bad things, but if they're your *everything*, you're building on shaky ground.

2. **Living with a Clear Conscience:** Paul could stand in front of people trying to bring him down and say, "I've lived with a good conscience." Could you say the same about how you treat others, how you talk online, or what you do when no one's watching?

3. **God Delivers the Righteous:** Even though Paul went through some scary and unfair stuff, God was still at work. Proverbs reminds us that God watches over those who follow Him. That doesn't mean life's always easy, but it does mean we're never alone in it.

BOTTOM LINE

Living for God gives your life direction and purpose that lasts—even when everything else feels uncertain or temporary.

PRAYER

Heavenly Father, help me to live for something that matters. Remind me when I'm tempted to chase things that don't last. Like Paul, I want to live with a clear conscience and stay close to You, even when life is hard. Help me trust You to deliver me and guide me. In Jesus' Name, Amen.

FEBRUARY 24

True Talk

3-Year-Bible Reading: Proverbs 11:9; Acts 24

With his mouth the godless man would destroy his neighbor, but by knowledge the righteous are delivered. — Proverbs 11:9

So I always take pains to have a clear conscience toward both God and man. — Acts 24:16

Have you ever been misunderstood—or worse, misjudged—just because someone twisted the truth? It hurts, right? In **Proverbs 11:9**, we see how destructive words can be when someone uses them carelessly or with bad intentions. But we also see the power of truth and wisdom to bring freedom.

Then in **Acts 24**, we find Paul standing trial, falsely accused, but still speaking with clarity and calmness because he knows his conscience is clean before God. Even when others didn't believe him, Paul didn't freak out. He trusted God with the outcome and kept speaking the truth.

THINK ABOUT IT

1. **The Power of Words:** What kind of impact are your words having on the people around you? Are they tearing down or building up?

2. **Living with a Clear Conscience:** Paul made it his goal to keep a clear conscience before God and people. What does that look like for you at school, with friends, or online?

3. **Stay True Even When Misunderstood:** Paul didn't stop standing for the truth even when people didn't believe him. How can you stay bold in your faith when others question or challenge it?

BOTTOM LINE

Truth may not always be popular, but it always matters. Stay faithful, speak life, and let your integrity speak louder than lies.

PRAYER

Heavenly Father, help me to use my words wisely and to live in a way that honors You. When others misunderstand me or speak falsely, give me the courage to stay calm, stand firm, and trust You with the outcome. Make my heart clean, my conscience clear, and my voice strong for truth. In Jesus' Name, Amen.

FEBRUARY 25

When Goodness Goes Viral

3-Year-Bible Reading: Proverbs 11:10–11; Acts 25

"When it goes well with the righteous, the city rejoices, and when the wicked perish there are shouts of gladness. By the blessing of the upright a city is exalted, but by the mouth of the wicked it is overthrown." — Proverbs 11:10–11

"But Festus, wishing to do the Jews a favor, said to Paul, 'Do you wish to go up to Jerusalem and there be tried on these charges before me?' But Paul said, 'I am standing before Caesar's tribunal, where I ought to be tried. To the Jews I have done no wrong, as you yourself know very well.'" — Acts 25:9–10

Have you ever noticed how one person's integrity can change the vibe of a whole group? In **Proverbs 11:10–11**, we see a picture of a community rejoicing not just because someone is doing well, but because that someone is righteous—living with honesty and godly character.

Meanwhile, in **Acts 25**, Paul faces serious accusations, yet stays bold and faithful, refusing to let pressure make him compromise. In both passages, there's this clear message: righteousness isn't just a personal win—it blesses everyone around you.

THINK ABOUT IT

1. **Goodness Impacts Everyone:** Proverbs shows us that when people live rightly, entire communities benefit. Your choices—kindness, truth, courage—can make school, home, or even your friend group a better place.

2. **Stand Firm Like Paul:** Paul was under intense pressure, yet he didn't back down or try to please people over God. What would it look like for you to stand up for what's right even when it's unpopular?

3. **Words Build Up or Tear Down:** Proverbs warns that the words of the wicked can destroy. Are your words helping lift others up, or are they tearing others down?

BOTTOM LINE

When you choose to live with integrity, it's not just your life that changes—your whole community can feel the impact. Stand firm in your faith, speak life with your words, and don't underestimate how your character can influence the world around you.

PRAYER

Heavenly Father, thank You for reminding me that my life matters beyond just me. Help me to live in a way that honors You and blesses others. Give me the courage to stand strong like Paul and the wisdom to speak words that build up, not tear down. Let my life be a light in my school, home, and friendships. In Jesus' Name, Amen.

February 26

Words That Stick

3-Year-Bible Reading: Proverbs 11:12–13; Psalm 23; Acts 26

"Whoever belittles his neighbor lacks sense, but a man of understanding remains silent. Whoever goes about slandering reveals secrets, but he who is trustworthy in spirit keeps a thing covered." — Proverbs 11:12–13

"Even though I walk through the valley of the shadow of death, I will fear no evil, for you are with me; your rod and your staff, they comfort me." — Psalm 23:4

"To this day I have had the help that comes from God, and so I stand here testifying both to small and great." — Acts 26:22

You've probably heard the phrase, "sticks and stones may break my bones, but words will never hurt me." Truth is, words can cut deep—and they often stick longer than we expect. In **Proverbs 11:12–13**, we're warned about gossip and tearing others down. It might feel harmless in the moment, but those careless words have weight. Meanwhile, **Psalm 23** reminds us that even when we feel like we're walking through the darkest parts of life, God's comfort and presence are with us.

And in **Acts 26**, Paul stands strong in his testimony because of God's help, sharing boldly even when it's not popular. What do these all have in common? Whether we're speaking, listening, or walking through tough times, how we use our words—and whose voice we listen to—matters deeply.

Think About It

1. **Words Have Power:** Are your words building others up or breaking them down? Ask yourself: Would I say this if the person were standing right next to me?

2. **God Walks With You:** Psalm 23 is a reminder that you're never alone—not in school, not at home, not even in your lowest moments. God is with you through every valley. How might that truth help you speak and act with more confidence and compassion?

3. **Speak Boldly, Like Paul:** In Acts, Paul didn't back down. He shared his story and what God had done in his life, even in front of powerful people. What's one way you can share your faith—through words, kindness, or actions—this week?

Bottom Line

Your words reflect your heart. Use them wisely to lift others up, speak truth with love, and trust God to guide you through every conversation and challenge.

Prayer

Heavenly Father, thank You for always being with me, even in the tough times. Help me to guard my words, to choose kindness over gossip, and to speak with courage like Paul. Let my words reflect Your love and truth to everyone around me. In Jesus' Name, Amen.

FEBRUARY 27

Storm-Ready Wisdom

3-Year-Bible Reading: Proverbs 11:14–15; Acts 27

Where there is no guidance, a people falls, but in an abundance of counselors there is safety. Whoever puts up security for a stranger will surely suffer harm, but he who hates striking hands in pledge is secure. — Proverbs 11:14–15

Since they had been without food for a long time, Paul stood up among them and said, "Men, you should have listened to me… Yet now I urge you to take heart, for there will be no loss of life among you, but only of the ship." — Acts 27:21–22

Have you ever been warned not to do something, ignored the advice, and then regretted it later? Maybe a friend told you not to text someone, or your parents told you to study more for a test. When we ignore good advice, we often end up in situations we could've avoided. In **Proverbs 11**, we're reminded how important wise counsel is—it literally keeps us safe.

And in **Acts 27**, Paul gives a real-life example. He warned the ship's crew not to set sail, but they didn't listen. The result? A brutal storm and a shipwreck. Still, God's grace showed up—even in the middle of the mess.

THINK ABOUT IT

1. **Who's in your circle?** Are you surrounded by people who give wise, godly advice—or just people who tell you what you want to hear? The right voices matter.

2. **Don't wait for the storm:** Paul wasn't trying to be a know-it-all; he had spiritual insight. God often gives us warnings through His Word and through others—are you paying attention before things go off course?

3. **God shows up in the storm:** Even when we make bad choices or ignore wisdom, God doesn't abandon us. Like Paul told the crew, take heart—God is still in control and can bring hope from wreckage.

BOTTOM LINE

Listening to wise counsel can protect you from unnecessary pain—but even when you mess up, God's presence is your anchor in any storm.

PRAYER

Heavenly Father, thank You for placing wise people in my life and for always guiding me through Your Word. Help me to listen before I leap, and to trust You even when I find myself in storms of my own making. Teach me to value Your voice above all others and to find hope in Your promises, no matter what I'm facing. In Jesus' Name, Amen.

February 28

Kindness That Stands Out

3-Year-Bible Reading: Proverbs 11:16–17; Psalm 24; Acts 28

"A gracious woman gets honor, and violent men get riches. A man who is kind benefits himself, but a cruel man hurts himself." — Proverbs 11:16–17

"Who shall ascend the hill of the Lord? And who shall stand in his holy place? He who has clean hands and a pure heart." — Psalm 24:3–4

"He welcomed us and entertained us hospitably for three days." — Acts 28:7

Imagine showing up somewhere completely unexpected, maybe not dressed right, not sure if you even belong—and someone welcomes you like you're family. That's what happened to Paul and his companions in **Acts 28** when they were shipwrecked on the island of Malta. Instead of being ignored or turned away, they were treated with kindness. That moment of unexpected hospitality mirrors what **Proverbs 11** talks about: the power of kindness and grace.

And when we think about standing in God's presence like **Psalm 24** describes, having a pure heart isn't just about avoiding sin—it's about living with love, compassion, and generosity. In a world where people often look out for themselves, kindness makes you stand out—and points others to Jesus.

Think About It

1. **Kindness Benefits You Too:** Proverbs 11 says being kind helps you, not just others. When have you seen kindness come full circle in your life?

2. **A Pure Heart Matters:** Psalm 24 talks about clean hands and a pure heart. How can kindness reflect a heart that wants to honor God?

3. **Unexpected Moments to Shine:** The people of Malta had no idea Paul was coming but they still welcomed him. What does it look like to be ready to show hospitality or kindness even when it's not convenient?

Bottom Line

Kindness isn't weakness—it's a strength that honors God, blesses others, and reflects a heart that's close to Him.

Prayer

Heavenly Father, thank You for showing us what true kindness looks like through Jesus. Help me to live with a heart that's open, generous, and ready to love people—even when it's inconvenient. Give me clean hands, a pure heart, and the courage to stand out by choosing grace in every situation. In Jesus' Name, Amen.

MARCH 1

Rooted in What's Right

3-Year-Bible Reading: Proverbs 11:18–19; Genesis 1–2

"The wicked earns deceptive wages, but one who sows righteousness gets a sure reward. Whoever is steadfast in righteousness will live, but he who pursues evil will die." — Proverbs 11:18–19

"In the beginning, God created the heavens and the earth." — Genesis 1:1

"So God created man in his own image, in the image of God he created him; male and female he created them." — Genesis 1:27

Have you ever been promised something that didn't turn out like you thought? Maybe a product didn't deliver, a friendship failed, or a shortcut backfired. In **Proverbs 11:18–19**, we're warned about the difference between doing what's right and chasing what looks good in the moment. Righteousness—living in a way that honors God—isn't just about "being good." It's about being *rooted* in something real and lasting.

And if we go all the way back to the beginning in **Genesis 1–2**, we see God creating everything with care, purpose, and goodness. We weren't made for fake rewards or shortcuts. We were created in God's image—for truth, life, and relationship with Him.

THINK ABOUT IT

1. **What Are You Chasing?** Are you after things that feel good for a second but leave you empty? Proverbs says deceptive rewards don't last, but doing what's right brings life.

2. **Your Identity Matters:** Genesis reminds us that you were created in the image of God. That means you have worth, purpose, and the ability to reflect His goodness.

3. **Righteousness Is a Journey:** Being steadfast in righteousness isn't about perfection—it's about direction. Are you moving toward God or away from Him in your daily choices?

BOTTOM LINE

God designed you with purpose, made you in His image, and invites you to walk in what is right—not because it's easy, but because it leads to real life.

PRAYER

Heavenly Father, thank You for creating me with purpose and calling me to something greater than empty rewards. Help me to stay rooted in You and to walk in righteousness, even when it's hard. Remind me of who I am in You, and help me reflect Your goodness in everything I do. In Jesus' Name, Amen.

March 2

Broken but Not Forsaken

3-Year-Bible Reading: Proverbs 11:20–21; Genesis 3

"Those of crooked heart are an abomination to the Lord, but those of blameless ways are his delight. Be assured, an evil person will not go unpunished, but the offspring of the righteous will be delivered." — Proverbs 11:20–21

"So when the woman saw that the tree was good for food... she took of its fruit and ate, and she also gave some to her husband who was with her, and he ate." — Genesis 3:6

"And they heard the sound of the Lord God walking in the garden... and the man and his wife hid themselves from the presence of the Lord God." — Genesis 3:8

Have you ever messed up and felt like hiding? Maybe you said something hurtful, crossed a line, or broke someone's trust. That gut-wrenching feeling of guilt—that's what Adam and Eve felt after eating the forbidden fruit. In **Genesis 3**, their choice to disobey God didn't just change their day; it changed the whole world. They went from walking freely with God to hiding in shame. And yet, even in their failure, God didn't walk away. He called out to them. He covered them. There were consequences, but there was also care.

Proverbs 11:20–21 reminds us that while God takes sin seriously, He also delights in those who walk in honesty and repentance. Even when we fall, God wants to restore us.

Think About It

1. **God Sees It All:** How do you usually respond when you mess up—do you hide, make excuses, or come clean? Remember, God already knows, and He still invites you to come to Him.

2. **Sin Has Consequences:** What were the results of Adam and Eve's sin in **Genesis 3**? What does that show us about how serious disobedience is—and how it affects more than just us?

3. **Grace in the Garden:** Even after they sinned, God covered Adam and Eve with garments. How does this reflect God's heart toward us when we fail?

Bottom Line

Even when we mess up, God doesn't walk away. He sees our brokenness, calls us out of hiding, and offers grace when we turn back to Him.

Prayer

Heavenly Father, thank You for seeing me fully and loving me still. When I fall short or make wrong choices, help me not to hide but to come to You. Thank You for your forgiveness and grace. Teach me to walk in honesty and humility. I want to follow You with a heart that delights You. In Jesus' Name, Amen.

March 3

More Than Skin Deep

3-Year-Bible Reading: Proverbs 11:22–23; Psalm 25; Genesis 4

"Like a gold ring in a pig's snout is a beautiful woman without discretion." — Proverbs 11:22

"Make me to know your ways, O Lord; teach me your paths." — Psalm 25:4

"The Lord said to Cain, 'Why are you angry, and why has your face fallen? If you do well, will you not be accepted?'" — Genesis 4:6–7

We live in a world that puts a lot of focus on outward appearances—how you look, dress, or perform on social media. But **Proverbs 11:22** makes it clear that beauty without wisdom is like putting expensive jewelry on a pig—it doesn't change what's underneath. Real value comes from character. In **Genesis 4**, Cain's story reminds us that when jealousy and anger take over our hearts, it leads to destructive choices.

Meanwhile, **Psalm 25** gives us a better way: asking God to lead us and teach us how to live. When we let God shape our character, we find purpose, peace, and direction, no matter what the world says is impressive.

Think About It

1. **Character Over Looks:** Do you spend more time caring about how you appear to others or how you appear before God? Why does Proverbs compare beauty without wisdom to a gold ring in a pig's nose?

2. **Check Your Heart:** Cain's anger came from comparison and rejection. What are some areas in your life where jealousy or hurt could be turning into something toxic?

3. **Choose God's Path:** Psalm 25 is a prayer for guidance. Are you asking God to teach you His way—or trying to figure life out on your own?

Bottom Line

Who you are on the inside matters way more than how you look on the outside. Let God shape your heart, and your life will reflect something truly beautiful—wisdom, grace, and love.

Prayer

Heavenly Father, help me not to focus only on what others see but on who I am becoming. Teach me Your ways so I can walk in wisdom, not pride or jealousy. Guard my heart and guide my steps. I want to reflect You in my words, actions, and choices. In Jesus' Name, Amen.

March 4

Living Wide-Open

3-Year-Bible Reading: Proverbs 11:24–26; Psalm 26; Genesis 5

"One gives freely, yet grows all the richer; another withholds what he should give, and only suffers want. Whoever brings blessing will be enriched, and one who waters will himself be watered." — Proverbs 11:24–25

"Prove me, O Lord, and try me; test my heart and my mind." — Psalm 26:2

"Thus all the days of Enoch were 365 years. Enoch walked with God, and he was not, for God took him." — Genesis 5:23–24

Sometimes we're told the way to get ahead is to look out for ourselves—to hoard time, money, energy, or attention. But in **Proverbs 11**, God flips that thinking on its head. The one who *gives* actually becomes *richer*, and the one who *blesses* others ends up being *blessed*. This same heart shows up in **Psalm 26**, where David invites God to test him—he wants to live with a pure heart, walking in integrity.

And in **Genesis 5**, we see Enoch, a man who didn't just believe in God from a distance, but walked closely with Him every day. That kind of life—generous, pure-hearted, and close to God—is what we're called to live too. It's not always flashy, but it's powerful.

Think About It

1. **Generosity Grows You:** Are you living with open hands or closed fists? God's Word says generosity doesn't drain you—it grows you. In what ways can you "water" others today?

2. **Heart Check:** When was the last time you asked God to test your motives like David did? It might feel scary, but letting Him search your heart helps you grow into who you're meant to be.

3. **Walk Like Enoch:** Enoch didn't just know *about* God—he *walked* with Him. What would it look like for you to walk with God this week—at school, online, or with friends?

Bottom Line

Living wide-open to God—through generosity, integrity, and closeness—leads to a life that's truly rich, even if the world doesn't always see it that way.

Prayer

Heavenly Father, Help me to live with open hands and an open heart. Teach me to be generous, not just with stuff, but with kindness, time, and encouragement. Search my heart and shape it to be more like Yours. Like Enoch, help me to walk closely with You every day, no matter where I am or what I face. In Jesus' Name, Amen.

MARCH 5

Searchlight Living

3-Year-Bible Reading: Proverbs 11:27; Genesis 6–9

"Whoever diligently seeks good seeks favor, but evil comes to him who searches for it." — Proverbs 11:27

"But Noah found favor in the eyes of the Lord." — Genesis 6:8

"Then God said, 'I establish my covenant with you, that never again shall all flesh be cut off by the waters of the flood.'" — Genesis 9:11

Have you ever walked into a dark room with a flashlight? Wherever you point the light, that's what you see—whether it's something beautiful or something messy. Life is like that too. What we *look for* often shapes what we *find*. **Proverbs 11:27** says that seeking good brings favor, while chasing after evil brings trouble.

That was true for Noah. In a world full of evil, Noah chose to live differently. He was the one person who sought good, and because of that, he found favor with God (**Genesis 6:8**). His story—surviving the flood, building the ark, and receiving God's promise—shows us the power of living a life that searches for God's best, even when the world seems to go the opposite direction.

THINK ABOUT IT

1. **What Are You Looking For?** Are you focused on the good in people and situations, or do you tend to expect the worst? Like Noah, we can choose to live with hope and integrity, even if it feels like we're the only one.

2. **Living Set Apart:** Noah stood out in a world that was falling apart. He wasn't perfect, but he was obedient. How can you stand strong for God when everyone else seems to ignore Him?

3. **God Keeps His Promises:** The rainbow is a reminder of God's faithfulness. What promises has God made in His Word that you can hold onto today?

BOTTOM LINE

Choosing to seek good, like Noah did, opens the door to God's favor and faithfulness—even when it's not popular or easy.

PRAYER

Heavenly Father, help me be like Noah—someone who chooses to seek good, even when the world around me isn't. Give me the courage to live differently and trust that You see and honor that. Thank You for being faithful and keeping Your promises. Teach me to walk in obedience and shine Your light in the darkness. In Jesus' Name, Amen.

March 6

Rooted or Ruined?

3-Year-Bible Reading: Proverbs 11:28; Genesis 10–11

"Whoever trusts in his riches will fall, but the righteous will flourish like a green leaf." — Proverbs 11:28

"These are the clans of the sons of Noah, according to their genealogies, in their nations, and from these the nations spread abroad on the earth after the flood." — Genesis 10:32

"Come, let us build ourselves a city and a tower with its top in the heavens, and let us make a name for ourselves…" — Genesis 11:4

Ever tried stacking cards into a tall tower? At first, it seems like it's going great—until a shaky hand or sudden breath knocks it all down. That's a lot like what happened in **Genesis 11**, when people decided to build a tower to heaven. Their goal? "Make a name for ourselves." But they were missing one huge thing: God. Instead of rooting their lives in Him, they trusted in themselves and their own "tower."

Proverbs 11:28 reminds us that trusting in anything besides God—especially riches, popularity, or power—leads to a fall. But those who live right and trust in Him? They flourish.

Think About It

1. **What Are You Building On?** Are you building your life on your talents, appearance, or popularity—or are you building on God's truth? A shaky foundation won't last.

2. **Chasing a Name vs. Living with Purpose:** The people in Babel wanted to "make a name." But God offers something better: purpose, identity, and eternal value. Where are you finding your worth?

3. **Flourishing Faith:** The righteous are compared to "a green leaf." That's a picture of life, growth, and strength. Are you staying connected to God so your faith can flourish?

Bottom Line

Building your life without God may look impressive for a while, but it never lasts. True success and growth come when you root your life in Him.

Prayer

Heavenly Father, help me not to chase success or identity in things that don't last. Remind me that You are the only foundation worth building my life on. Teach me to trust You more every day, and help my faith to grow strong and rooted in Your truth. In Jesus' Name, Amen.

March 7

When the Future Feels Uncertain

3-Year-Bible Reading: Proverbs 11; Psalm 27; Genesis 12

"Whoever troubles his own household will inherit the wind, and the fool will be servant to the wise of heart." —Proverbs 11:29

"Wait for the Lord; be strong, and let your heart take courage; wait for the Lord!" —Psalm 27:14

"Now the Lord said to Abram, 'Go from your country and your kindred and your father's house to the land that I will show you.'" —Genesis 12:1

Sometimes, it feels like life throws more questions than answers. Maybe you're unsure of your next step—what to do after high school, how to deal with drama at home, or whether you'll ever feel close to God again. In **Genesis 12**, Abram (later Abraham) was told to leave everything familiar and step into a future that hadn't been fully revealed yet. That takes courage.

Psalm 27 reminds us that waiting on God doesn't mean doing nothing—it means trusting Him when the path ahead is foggy. And **Proverbs 11:29** gives us a glimpse into how our choices affect others—our families, friends, and futures. Even in uncertainty, our trust in God shapes not only where we go, but who we become.

THINK ABOUT IT

1. **Trust the Unknown:** Abram followed God without knowing exactly where he was going. Are you willing to trust God even when the details aren't clear?

2. **Choose Peace at Home:** Proverbs reminds us that our actions can stir up or settle down our households. Are you bringing peace or pressure into your relationships?

3. **Wait with Courage:** Waiting isn't weakness—it's strength wrapped in trust. Psalm 27 encourages us to be brave while we wait. How can you show courage while trusting God's timing?

BOTTOM LINE

God often calls us into the unknown—not to confuse us, but to grow our trust in Him. Even when the future feels uncertain, His promises are sure.

PRAYER

Heavenly Father, Sometimes I feel unsure of what's next or afraid to take that first step. Help me trust You like Abram did, even when I don't have all the answers. Teach me to be patient and courageous as I wait on You, and guide my choices so I can bring peace and love to those around me. In Jesus' Name, Amen.

March 8

Roots That Reach Others

3-Year-Bible Reading: Proverbs 11:30–31; Genesis 13–14

"The fruit of the righteous is a tree of life, and whoever captures souls is wise. If the righteous is repaid on earth, how much more the wicked and the sinner!" — Proverbs 11:30–31

"Then Abram said to Lot, 'Let there be no strife between you and me...for we are kinsmen.'" — Genesis 13:8

"And he brought back all the possessions, and also brought back his kinsman Lot with his possessions, and the women and the people." — Genesis 14:16

Sometimes the choices we make in relationships—especially family or close friendships—can either build peace or stir up drama. In **Genesis 13**, Abraham (then called Abram) had a real chance to fight over land and power with his nephew Lot. But instead, he chose peace and trusted God with the outcome.

Later, when Lot got into serious trouble (he literally got captured in a war), Abraham risked everything to rescue him (**Genesis 14**). This story shows how living righteously—being kind, peaceful, and selfless—bears fruit, just like **Proverbs 11:30** says. When we live like this, it impacts others in ways we can't always see. Your character today can become someone's lifeline tomorrow.

Think About It

1. **Choose Peace Over Power:** When Abraham gave Lot the first choice of land, he let go of control. Where in your life can you choose peace instead of being right or in charge?

2. **Live Like a Tree of Life:** Proverbs says the righteous are like a "tree of life." Are your actions producing life-giving fruit—like love, patience, or kindness—in your school, family, or friend group?

3. **Courage to Rescue:** Abraham didn't just walk away when Lot messed up—he showed up. Are there people in your life who need someone to care enough to reach out, forgive, or help them through a tough time?

Bottom Line

Living with integrity, choosing peace, and showing up for others are powerful ways God uses us to bring life, healing, and hope into the world around us. Don't underestimate the impact of a righteous choice—it might just be someone else's rescue plan.

Prayer

Heavenly Father, thank You for showing me through Abraham's story how important it is to live with peace, wisdom, and love. Help me be someone who brings life to others through my choices. Give me the courage to step up when someone needs help, and the humility to choose peace even when it's hard. Grow in me the kind of faith that trusts You with the outcome. In Jesus' Name, Amen.

MARCH 9

Correction Course

3-Year-Bible Reading: Proverbs 12:1; Psalm 28; Genesis 15

"Whoever loves discipline loves knowledge, but he who hates reproof is stupid." — Proverbs 12:1

"The Lord is my strength and my shield; in him my heart trusts, and I am helped; my heart exults, and with my song I give thanks to him." — Psalm 28:7

"And he believed the Lord, and he counted it to him as righteousness." — Genesis 15:6

Let's be honest—no one *loves* being corrected. Whether it's your parents, a coach, or even a teacher calling you out, it can feel like a punch to your pride. But **Proverbs 12:1** reminds us that loving correction is actually a sign of wisdom. Why? Because it means we care more about growing than looking perfect. That same attitude shows up in **Psalm 28**, where David cries out to God, not with pride, but with trust—trust that even when life feels like it's falling apart, God is still strong and good.

And way back in **Genesis 15**, we see Abram believing God's promise even when it seemed impossible. He didn't argue, he didn't demand proof—he just trusted. That trust was the beginning of a legacy that would bless the entire world. When we learn to embrace correction, trust God through challenges, and believe His promises, we begin to walk the same path.

THINK ABOUT IT

1. **Love the Hard Truth:** Why do you think Proverbs says hating correction is "stupid"? How can accepting feedback actually help you become stronger and wiser?

2. **Trust in the Storm:** Psalm 28 shows David praising God *before* he even sees the answer. How do you respond when it feels like God is silent? What can you learn from David's trust?

3. **Faith that Counts:** God credited Abram's faith as righteousness. What does it look like to take God at His word in your everyday life—even when it doesn't all make sense?

BOTTOM LINE

God wants your heart more than your perfection. Embrace correction, trust Him in the struggle, and believe His promises—because that's where growth, strength, and blessing begin.

PRAYER

Heavenly Father, thank You for loving me enough to correct me. Help me not to get defensive when I'm challenged, but to learn and grow. Teach me to trust You like David did, even when I don't have all the answers. And give me faith like Abram—to believe that what You say is true, no matter how things look around me. In Jesus' Name, Amen.

March 10

Rooted, Not Shaken

3-Year-Bible Reading: Proverbs 12:2–3; Psalm 29; Genesis 16–17

"A good man obtains favor from the Lord, but a man of evil devices he condemns. No one is established by wickedness, but the root of the righteous will never be moved." — Proverbs 12:2–3

"The voice of the Lord is powerful; the voice of the Lord is full of majesty." — Psalm 29:4

"I am God Almighty; walk before me, and be blameless, that I may make my covenant between me and you, and may multiply you greatly." — Genesis 17:1–2

Life can feel like one big unknown sometimes. Whether it's trying to figure out who your real friends are, what you're good at, or what God wants from you, there's a lot that can shake your confidence. But today's readings show us something important: if you're rooted in God, you won't be moved—even when life is loud and messy.

In **Genesis 16–17**, Abram and Sarai tried to take things into their own hands instead of waiting on God's promise. Still, God didn't give up on them. Instead, He reminded Abram of His promise and called him to walk with Him. **Psalm 29** reminds us of God's power—His voice breaks the strongest trees and makes mountains shake. And **Proverbs 12** tells us that being rooted in righteousness (doing what's right in God's eyes) makes you unshakable.

Think About It

1. **What Are You Rooted In?** Are you letting your choices be guided by what feels good or by what God says is good? Proverbs says the righteous will never be moved.

2. **Listen for His Voice:** Psalm 29 shows God's voice has power—but are you listening? Sometimes He speaks in a whisper, other times like thunder. Are you tuned in or tuned out?

3. **Wait on God:** Abram and Sarai got tired of waiting and made a mess. Can you trust God's timing, even when it's slow? He always keeps His promises.

Bottom Line

When you're rooted in God's truth, nothing can shake you—not doubts, not drama, not even failure. God's promises are worth the wait, and His voice is the one worth listening to.

Prayer

Heavenly Father, Help me stay rooted in You when life feels confusing or uncertain. Teach me to trust Your promises and to walk with You even when I don't understand the path. Speak to me through Your Word, and give me the courage to wait for Your timing. Thank You for being steady when everything else feels shaky. In Jesus' Name, Amen.

MARCH 11

The Power of Character

3-Year-Bible Reading: Proverbs 12:4; Genesis 18-19

An excellent wife is the crown of her husband, but she who brings shame is like rottenness in his bones. — Proverbs 12:4

And the men said to Lot, "Have you anyone else here? Sons-in-law, sons, daughters, or anyone you have in the city, bring them out of the place." — Genesis 19:12

In life, our character speaks louder than anything else. **Proverbs 12:4** tells us that a person of good character is like a crown, something valuable and admirable, while a person who brings shame is like rottenness—something that ruins everything it touches. In **Genesis 18-19**, we see a powerful example of this when Lot, a man who lived in the wicked city of Sodom, is given a chance to escape God's judgment. While his character shines in his willingness to help strangers (the angels), we also see the consequences of living in a corrupt environment. His decision to stay and negotiate with the angels, while honorable in part, also shows the tension between the desire to protect his family and the overwhelming pull of a city full of sin.

In both Proverbs and Genesis, the lesson is clear: our choices and our character are more important than we may realize. They affect those around us, and in Lot's case, they even put his family's future in jeopardy. But, even in difficult situations, God offers grace and the opportunity to rebuild and follow Him.

THINK ABOUT IT

1. **Character Matters:** How do the choices you make reflect your character? Are you living in a way that would bring honor to God and those around you?
2. **Building on a Foundation:** Just like Lot had a choice to leave Sodom, you also have daily decisions to make. Are you choosing environments and friendships that encourage your character or lead you astray?
3. **Family Impact:** In what ways can you influence your family for good, like Lot tried to protect his loved ones? How can you stand firm in your faith even when things around you are tough?

BOTTOM LINE

Your character is a crown—wear it well. Let your choices reflect your identity in Christ, and remember: even in hard times, God's grace is shaping you into someone who honors Him.

PRAYER

Heavenly Father, thank You for teaching me the importance of my character and how it impacts those around me. Help me to make decisions that honor You and build up those I care about. Strengthen me to stand firm in my faith, especially when life gets difficult. I trust that You will guide me in building a character that reflects Your love and truth. In Jesus' Name, Amen.

MARCH 12

God's Faithfulness in Our Journeys

3-Year-Bible Reading: Proverbs 12:5-6; Psalms 30; Genesis 20-21

"The thoughts of the righteous are just; the counsels of the wicked are deceitful. The words of the wicked lie in wait for blood, but the mouth of the upright delivers them." — Proverbs 12:5-6

"I will extol you, O Lord, for you have drawn me up and have not let my foes rejoice over me. O Lord my God, I cried to you for help, and you have healed me." — Psalm 30:1

"And Abraham journeyed from there toward the territory of the Negeb and lived between Kadesh and Shur; and he sojourned in Gerar. And Abraham said of Sarah, 'She is my sister.'" — Genesis 20:1-2

Life's journey isn't always smooth. There are times when things seem to go wrong, and we wonder if anyone is on our side. You might think of the story of Abraham in **Genesis 20**, where he makes a huge mistake by lying about his wife, Sarah, to protect himself. But even in his fear and failure, God intervened and protected him. In **Psalm 30**, David cries out to God in a moment of distress, thanking Him for rescuing him. Despite the struggles, David praises God for being a faithful protector.

In **Proverbs 12:5-6**, we read that the righteous, those who seek to do what is right, will find their way. This doesn't mean life will be perfect or without struggles, but it does mean that God's guidance will always be there to help us through.

The key takeaway is that we can rely on God's faithfulness, even when we make mistakes or when the world feels uncertain. Whether we're facing our own fears, dealing with mistakes, or simply trying to understand where God is in the middle of it all, He is faithful. He doesn't abandon us. In fact, He provides protection, direction, and comfort, just as He did for Abraham and David.

THINK ABOUT IT

1. **God's Protection:** How have you seen God's protection in your life, even when things seemed scary or uncertain?
2. **Mistakes and Grace:** Like Abraham, have you ever made a mistake and wondered if God would still be with you? How can you trust His grace to cover you?
3. **Praising God in Hard Times:** Psalm 30 shows David praising God even after hard times. How can you praise God in your current situation, no matter what it looks like?

BOTTOM LINE

Even when life feels uncertain or when we mess up, God remains faithful. He will protect us, guide us, and help us to grow through every situation.

PRAYER

Heavenly Father, thank You for being faithful to me, even when I make mistakes or face difficult situations. Help me to trust in Your protection and guidance, and to praise You even in tough times. I know You are always with me, and I trust that You will never leave me. In Jesus' Name, Amen.

March 13

Stand Firm in Faith

3-Year-Bible Reading: Proverbs 12:7-8; Genesis 22

"The wicked are overthrown and are no more, but the house of the righteous will stand."— Proverbs 12:7

"By faith Abraham, when he was tested, offered up Isaac, and he who had received the promises was in the act of offering up his only son, of whom it was said, 'Through Isaac shall your offspring be named.'"— Hebrews 11:17

Sometimes life can feel like a test, right? You might face situations where you have to choose between what seems easy or what you know is right, even if it's hard. **Proverbs 12:7** reminds us that when we stand firm in what's right, even in the face of opposition, we're like a house that stands strong against the storm. But how do we stand firm when things are uncertain?

One of the best examples we can look to is the story of Abraham in **Genesis 22**. God asked Abraham to do something that sounded impossible—sacrifice his son, Isaac. But Abraham didn't hesitate. He trusted God's promise and believed that even if Isaac had to die, God would bring him back to life. That kind of faith wasn't easy, but it was what God wanted. When Abraham obeyed, God provided a ram as a substitute for Isaac, showing that God always has a plan, even when we can't see it.

Abraham's story is a reminder that faith isn't always about understanding the why or the how. It's about trusting God no matter what. **Proverbs 12:8** says, "A man is commended according to his good sense," and Abraham showed that kind of good sense when he trusted God in the hardest of circumstances.

Think About It

1. **Trust in the Unknown:** Abraham didn't know how things would work out, but he trusted God. How do you handle situations where you don't know what will happen next? Do you trust God, or do you try to figure it out on your own?

2. **Standing Firm:** The righteous stand firm like a house that won't fall. How can you build your life on God's Word so that when challenges come, you stay strong in your faith?

3. **God's Provision:** God provided a ram for Abraham. Have you seen God provide for you in ways you didn't expect? What's one thing you can thank God for today?

Bottom Line

When life gets tough, remember that God calls us to trust Him like Abraham did. Even when we don't know the outcome, we can stand firm in faith, knowing that God will provide for us in ways we can't imagine.

Prayer

Heavenly Father, Thank You for always being there for me, even when life gets tough. Help me to trust You more and stand firm in my faith, just like Abraham did. Teach me to trust Your plan, even when I can't see the full picture. Thank You for Your provision and for always being faithful. In Jesus' Name, Amen.

March 14

True Riches

3-Year-Bible Reading: Proverbs 12:9; Psalms 31; Genesis 23

"Better to be lowly and have a servant than to play the great man and lack bread." — Proverbs 12:9

"Be merciful to me, O Lord, for I am in distress; my eye is wasted from grief; my soul and my body also." — Psalm 31:9

"Abraham listened to Ephron; and Abraham weighed out for Ephron the silver that he had named in the hearing of the Hittites, four hundred shekels of silver, according to the weight current among the merchants." — Genesis 23:16

In a world that often measures success by wealth, status, or popularity, it's easy to get caught up in striving for things that don't last. **Proverbs 12:9** reminds us that true value isn't found in how the world sees us, but in how we live humbly and serve others. In **Psalm 31**, David cries out to God, recognizing his need for mercy and deliverance, showing that our true worth isn't in our achievements or comfort, but in our relationship with God. And in **Genesis 23**, we see Abraham's integrity in his dealings with others, even when it came to securing a burial place. He didn't let greed or pride control him, but rather demonstrated wisdom and fairness in all his transactions.

When we focus too much on external success, we can easily lose sight of what's truly important. Like David, we may face moments of distress, but our value is not defined by our circumstances or what we have. We also see from Abraham that our integrity matters, no matter how small the situation seems. It's a reminder that we are called to live humbly and honorably in all that we do.

Think About It

1. **True wealth:** How do you measure success in your life? Is it by the things you have or by the way you live?

2. **Humility in distress:** When you're going through a tough time, where do you turn for comfort? Do you remember that God is near to the broken-hearted?

3. **Integrity matters:** Are you always honest in your decisions, even when it's difficult? What can you learn from Abraham's example of integrity?

Bottom Line

True wealth isn't measured by what you own or how others see you. It's found in living humbly, trusting God, and acting with integrity, even in the small moments.

Prayer

Heavenly Father, thank You for reminding me that my worth is not found in what I have or in how others view me. Help me to live humbly and to trust in Your provision, especially in tough times. Guide me to always act with integrity and to seek You first above all things. In Jesus' Name, Amen.

MARCH 15

The Right Way to Lead

3-Year-Bible Reading: Proverbs 12:10-11; Genesis 24

"Whoever is righteous has regard for the life of his beast, but the mercy of the wicked is cruel." — Proverbs 12:10

"Then the man bowed his head and worshiped the Lord and said, 'Blessed be the Lord, the God of my master Abraham, who has not forsaken his steadfast love and faithfulness toward my master. As for me, the Lord has led me in the way to the house of my master's kinsmen.'" — Genesis 24:26-27

Leading others isn't about being in charge—it's about having the right heart. In **Proverbs 12:10**, we learn that true leadership is marked by kindness and responsibility, even in small things. A righteous person treats others, including animals, with care and respect. This shows us that leadership isn't about being the loudest or most powerful but about showing compassion and making wise decisions that benefit everyone around you.

In **Genesis 24**, we see an example of true leadership through Abraham's servant. He doesn't just go about his mission randomly. He prays, listens to God, and follows the path God shows him. When he finds success, he gives glory to God. This humble, prayerful, and God-centered approach teaches us that good leadership starts with listening to God's voice and acting in faith, not just relying on our own strength.

As you move through life, whether in your family, school, or with your friends, remember that leadership isn't about showing off or being the boss. It's about treating others with respect, making thoughtful decisions, and seeking guidance from God in everything you do.

THINK ABOUT IT

1. **Leadership is about care:** What are some ways you can show care for others in your daily life, like Abraham's servant did?
2. **Trust God's guidance:** When faced with a decision, do you seek God's guidance first? What does it look like to trust Him in all situations?
3. **Giving glory to God:** When you succeed at something, do you give thanks to God for His help and direction, like the servant did in Genesis 24?

BOTTOM LINE

True leadership is about humility, care for others, and trusting God's direction in your life. God wants to lead you, and when you follow His path, you'll lead others in the right way.

PRAYER

Heavenly Father, thank You for teaching me what it means to lead with kindness and humility. Help me to always seek Your guidance in my decisions and show care for others in all I do. May I trust You and give You the glory for every success. In Jesus' Name, Amen.

March 16

The Power of Choices

3-Year-Bible Reading: Proverbs 12:12-14; Psalm 32; Genesis 25

"Whoever is wicked covets the spoil of evildoers, but the root of the righteous bears fruit." — Proverbs 12:12

"Blessed is the one whose transgression is forgiven, whose sin is covered." — Psalm 32:1

"Esau said, 'Let me eat some of that red stew, for I am exhausted!' Therefore his name was called Edom." — Genesis 25:30

We all face moments where we must make choices, big or small. Some decisions are simple, but others can have lasting consequences. In **Genesis 25**, we read about Esau, who gave up his birthright for a bowl of stew. In the heat of the moment, he chose immediate satisfaction over long-term gain. He acted on impulse and ended up regretting it. Sound familiar? Maybe you've faced situations where you had to decide between what feels good right now and what will benefit you in the long run.

Psalm 32 speaks of the joy and peace that come with forgiveness. When we make poor choices, it's easy to feel burdened by guilt. But God's grace is powerful—He offers forgiveness and invites us to experience His freedom. In **Proverbs 12**, we are reminded that our actions—whether good or bad—have consequences. Our choices bear fruit, and it's up to us to decide what kind of fruit we want to grow in our lives.

Think About It

1. **Impulsive Choices:** Have you ever made a decision in the heat of the moment that you later regretted? What can you do to stop and think before acting?
2. **Consequences Matter:** How do you think the decisions you make today will impact your future? Are you living with the long-term consequences in mind?
3. **The Gift of Forgiveness:** When you make mistakes, do you turn to God for forgiveness? Psalm 32 reminds us that when we confess, God forgives and restores us.

Bottom Line

The choices you make today shape your future. Impulse may lead to regret, but God's forgiveness and guidance lead to life and peace.

Prayer

Heavenly Father, thank You for Your forgiveness and grace. Help me to make wise choices that honor You and bring lasting peace. When I stumble, remind me of Your love and forgiveness. Teach me to think before acting and trust You with my future. In Jesus' Name, Amen.

March 17

The Right Path

3-Year-Bible Reading: Proverbs 12:15; Psalms 33; Genesis 26

"The way of a fool is right in his own eyes, but a wise man listens to advice." — Proverbs 12:15

"The counsel of the Lord stands forever, the plans of his heart to all generations." — Psalm 33:11

"And Isaac dug again the wells of water that had been dug in the days of Abraham his father... and he called their names as the names that his father had called them." — Genesis 26:18

We all have decisions to make. Whether it's figuring out how to handle a tough situation with friends, making choices about school, or navigating the ups and downs of life, we're often faced with a big question: "What should I do?" The good news is that you don't have to figure it all out on your own. **God** offers wisdom and direction that can help guide you along the right path. Sometimes, it's a matter of listening and trusting that His way is better than our own.

In **Proverbs 12:15**, we are reminded that it's easy to think we know what's best for ourselves, but true wisdom comes when we listen to godly advice and guidance. In **Psalm 33**, we see that God's plans last forever—His counsel is unshakable, and His direction is always trustworthy. Just like Isaac in **Genesis 26**, who dug the wells his father had dug before him, we can find strength and guidance by going back to what God has already shown us in His Word.

When we face challenges, it's important to stop and ask, "Am I trusting God to lead me, or am I trying to figure this out on my own?" Trusting in God's wisdom will help you walk the path He's designed for you, and He'll guide you every step of the way.

Think About It

1. **What voices are you listening to?** Are you relying on your own understanding, or do you seek advice from others who are rooted in faith and God's wisdom?
2. **God's plans are eternal:** Even when things don't make sense or seem hard, remember that God's plan for you is good and will stand forever. How can you trust that He knows the best way for your life?
3. **Are you digging your own wells?** Isaac returned to the wells his father had dug. In the same way, God wants you to dig into His Word and hold onto what He has already revealed to you. Are you staying grounded in His truth?

Bottom Line

True wisdom comes from listening to God and trusting His plans. Don't go through life alone—God's guidance will lead you in the right direction if you choose to follow it.

Prayer

Heavenly Father, thank You for Your wisdom and guidance in my life. Help me to listen to Your voice and trust Your plans for me. When I face decisions, remind me to turn to You first, and to follow the path You have laid out for me. Thank You for always being faithful. In Jesus' Name, Amen.

MARCH 18

Living with Integrity

3-Year-Bible Reading: Proverbs 12:16; Genesis 27–28

"The vexation of a fool is known at once, but the prudent ignores an insult." — Proverbs 12:16

"Esau said, 'Is he not rightly named Jacob? For he has cheated me these two times. He took away my birthright, and behold, now he has taken away my blessing.'" — Genesis 27:36

"But Jacob said to him, 'I am the Lord, the God of Abraham your father and the God of Isaac. The land on which you lie I will give to you and to your offspring.'" — Genesis 28:13

In the Bible, we see examples of people struggling with dishonesty, conflict, and regret—one of the clearest being Jacob. In **Genesis 27**, Jacob tricks his father Isaac into giving him the blessing meant for his brother Esau. At first, it seems like Jacob got away with his deception, but the consequences were huge. His actions led to years of brokenness and separation in his family. Jacob's story shows us how one wrong choice can affect so much, and yet God still chose him and promised to be with him. We also see wisdom in **Proverbs 12:16** about responding to offense. It reminds us that we don't have to fight back when we're wronged. Sometimes, choosing not to react can bring peace.

Jacob's journey wasn't easy, but through it, he learned about God's grace and how much better it is to live with integrity. The journey of owning up to mistakes and seeking God's forgiveness is a hard but rewarding process. It's a reminder that even when we mess up, God is there to guide us forward.

THINK ABOUT IT

1. **What's your first reaction to being insulted or hurt?** Proverbs 12:16 tells us to ignore an insult rather than react foolishly. How can you practice responding with wisdom instead of anger?
2. **Are there times when you've tried to hide or cover up a mistake?** Jacob's deceit had big consequences, but God still used him. How can you face mistakes with honesty instead of hiding them?
3. **How does God's grace show up in your life when you make mistakes?** Even after Jacob deceived his brother, God still reached out to him. How does God's mercy give you hope after failing?

BOTTOM LINE

God calls us to live with integrity, even when it's hard. His grace meets us in our mistakes, guiding us back. Choose honesty, seek peace, and trust that He can use your story for good.

PRAYER

Heavenly Father, thank You for showing us that even when we make mistakes, You are always there to offer forgiveness and guidance. Help us to live with integrity and to respond with wisdom when we face conflict or insults. Strengthen us to make choices that honor You. In Jesus' Name, Amen.

MARCH 19

Words That Heal, Not Hurt

3-Year-Bible Reading: Proverbs 12:17-18; Genesis 29-30

"Whoever speaks the truth gives honest evidence, but a false witness utters deceit." — Proverbs 12:17

"There is one whose rash words are like sword thrusts, but the tongue of the wise brings healing." — Proverbs 12:18

"Then Jacob's anger was kindled against Rachel, and he said, 'Am I in the place of God, who has withheld from you the fruit of the womb?'" — Genesis 30:2

Have you ever said something you regret? Sometimes, our words come out without thinking, and they can hurt others deeply. Proverbs 12:18 tells us that the wise use their words to bring healing, but the rash often speak words that cut like swords. The truth matters, but how we say it matters just as much.

Take a look at how words played a huge role in the relationship between Jacob and Rachel in **Genesis 29-30**. Instead of using his words to bring comfort or encouragement, Jacob's frustration led him to respond harshly, even blaming Rachel when she was unable to have children. In that moment, his words didn't bring peace; they created tension.

We all have moments of frustration or disappointment, and it's easy to lash out or speak without thinking. But the Bible calls us to a higher standard. **Proverbs 12** reminds us that our words should be truth-filled and life-giving, not hurtful. Like Jacob, we may not always understand the struggles others are going through, but it's important to be mindful of how we speak to and about them.

THINK ABOUT IT

1. **How do you respond when you're frustrated?** When things don't go our way, it's easy to speak from anger. Think back—how could your words have built up instead of tearing down?
2. **Why do words matter so much?** In **Genesis 30**, Jacob's words had a big impact on his relationship with Rachel. The way we speak can deeply affect our relationships with friends, family, and others. Think about how your words have shaped the relationships in your life.
3. **What does it mean to use words that heal?** Healing words speak kindness, truth, and comfort—even in hard times. How can you practice that today?

BOTTOM LINE

Words are powerful. They can either hurt or heal, build up or tear down. As followers of Jesus, we're called to choose our words carefully, offering truth in love and using our speech to bring peace and healing.

PRAYER

Heavenly Father, Thank You for the gift of words and the power they hold. Help me to choose my words wisely, especially when I'm frustrated or upset. Teach me to speak truth with love, to build up those around me, and to offer healing with my words. May my speech reflect Your heart. In Jesus' Name, Amen.

March 20

Words That Heal

3-Year-Bible Reading: Proverbs 12:19-20; Psalms 34; Genesis 31

"Truthful lips endure forever, but a lying tongue is but for a moment." — Proverbs 12:19

"The righteous cry, and the Lord hears and delivers them out of all their troubles." — Psalms 34:17

"Then God said to Laban, 'Be careful not to say anything to Jacob, either good or bad.'" — Genesis 31:24

Words have power. They can either bring peace or cause harm. **Proverbs 12:19-20** reminds us that truth and kindness in our speech bring lasting results, while lies and deceit only lead to trouble. In **Psalms 34:17**, we see that when we cry out to God, He listens and delivers us, showing how even in the toughest situations, God is close and ready to help. Finally, in **Genesis 31**, God warns Laban not to speak to Jacob, either good or bad, showing how powerful our words can be. Even when tensions are high, God teaches us to be careful with what we say, knowing that words have the ability to stir up or settle conflicts.

This combination of verses speaks to the power of our words and the importance of trusting God in all circumstances. We often face situations where it's easy to say things we don't mean, or to get caught up in conflict. Yet, God's Word calls us to reflect on how we speak and to trust Him for peace and resolution. Whether it's with friends, family, or even those we don't get along with, we have the opportunity to use our words to build bridges rather than walls.

Think About It

1. **How do your words affect others?** Reflect on the times you've spoken words that were either encouraging or hurtful. What impact did they have on those around you?

2. **When you're in trouble, do you turn to God first?** Like in **Psalm 34:17**, when things get hard, do you reach out to God for help, or do you try to handle it yourself?

3. **What's the role of honesty in your relationships?** In **Proverbs 12:19**, we're reminded that truth lasts. How can you practice honesty in your friendships and family?

Bottom Line

Our words have the power to either build up or tear down. By choosing truth and kindness, and trusting God to deliver us when we face difficult situations, we honor Him and create peace in our relationships.

Prayer

Heavenly Father, thank You for reminding us of the power of our words. Help us to speak truth and kindness to others, especially when we're faced with tough situations. Teach us to trust You in every conflict and to turn to You for help when things feel out of control. May we reflect Your love and peace in all our conversations. In Jesus' Name, Amen.

March 21

Peace Over Payback

3-Year-Bible Reading: Proverbs 12:21–22; Genesis 32–33

"No ill befalls the righteous, but the wicked are filled with trouble. Lying lips are an abomination to the Lord, but those who act faithfully are his delight." — Proverbs 12:21–22

"And Jacob lifted up his eyes and looked, and behold, Esau was coming, and four hundred men with him… But Esau ran to meet him and embraced him and fell on his neck and kissed him, and they wept." — Genesis 33:1, 4

Have you ever dreaded seeing someone you hurt—or someone who hurt you? Jacob had lied, tricked, and stolen from his brother Esau years earlier. Now, in **Genesis 32–33**, he's about to face him again. And he's terrified. He thinks Esau might want revenge. But instead of fighting, Esau surprises everyone—he forgives. Their reunion is emotional and full of grace.

That moment reflects what God values most: truth, humility, and peace, just like **Proverbs 12:21–22** says. Choosing honesty and making things right may feel scary, but God blesses those who walk in integrity.

Think About It

1. **God Honors Honesty:** Are there any lies or cover-ups in your life that need to be made right? God doesn't just dislike lying—He *delights* in those who are truthful and faithful.

2. **Reconciliation Is Possible:** Jacob was scared of Esau's reaction, but Esau chose forgiveness. Are you open to giving or receiving forgiveness, even if it's been a long time?

3. **Fear Can't Stop God's Plan:** Even when we mess up, God can still bring healing. Is fear keeping you from facing a tough situation or conversation?

Bottom Line

God values truth and reconciliation. Like Jacob and Esau, you might be surprised what happens when you choose peace over payback.

Prayer

Heavenly Father, thank You for showing me that honesty and forgiveness matter more than pride or fear. Help me to walk faithfully, speak truthfully, and seek peace with others. Give me courage when I need to face the consequences of my actions, and help me to be someone who reflects Your grace and love. In Jesus' Name, Amen.

March 22

Quiet Strength and Wise Hands

3-Year-Bible Reading: Proverbs 12:23–24; Genesis 34

"A prudent man conceals knowledge, but the heart of fools proclaims folly. The hand of the diligent will rule, while the slothful will be put to forced labor." — Proverbs 12:23–24

"But Hamor spoke with them, saying, 'The soul of my son Shechem longs for your daughter. Please give her to him to be his wife.'" — Genesis 34:8

Have you ever seen someone make a situation worse just by rushing to act without thinking? In **Genesis 34**, Dinah's brothers explode in rage after she's wronged, and their response—deceptive and violent—ends in bloodshed. Instead of seeking justice with wisdom, they take it into their own hands recklessly. It's a tough chapter, but it highlights a powerful contrast with **Proverbs 12:23–24**, which reminds us that real strength lies in quiet wisdom and diligence, not in loud reaction or lazy shortcuts. In a world that often rewards noise, God honors those who are steady, wise, and faithful.

Think About It

1. **Quiet Wisdom Is Powerful:** Do you tend to speak just to be heard, or do you speak with purpose? Proverbs says a wise person knows when to speak and when to stay silent. Don't underestimate the strength in being quietly thoughtful.

2. **Anger Can Mislead You:** In Genesis 34, the brothers let anger take over, leading to choices that hurt everyone. When you feel wronged or upset, do you seek God's wisdom first—or react on impulse?

3. **Diligence Pays Off:** Proverbs 12:24 tells us that the diligent will rule. Whether it's school, relationships, or faith, choosing consistency over shortcuts builds a life of influence and trust.

Bottom Line

True strength isn't loud or reckless—it's wise, thoughtful, and rooted in doing what's right, even when it's hard or slow. Don't trade lasting impact for a quick reaction. Let your diligence and quiet wisdom speak louder than any outburst ever could.

Prayer

Heavenly Father, help me to be someone who chooses wisdom over reaction. When I'm hurt or angry, give me the strength to pause and seek You first. Teach me to be diligent in everything I do, and let my quiet faithfulness speak louder than any words I could say. In Jesus' Name, Amen.

March 23

Anxiety vs. Assurance

3-Year-Bible Reading: Proverbs 12:25; Psalm 35; Genesis 35–36

"Anxiety in a man's heart weighs him down, but a good word makes him glad." — Proverbs 12:25

"Contend, O Lord, with those who contend with me; fight against those who fight against me!" — Psalm 35:1

"And God said to him, 'Your name is Jacob; no longer shall your name be called Jacob, but Israel shall be your name.' So he called his name Israel." — Genesis 35:10

Some days feel heavy. Anxiety creeps in like a thick fog—about school, friendships, your future, or even your faith. Proverbs 12:25 reminds us how those anxious feelings can weigh us down, but also how encouragement—"a good word"—can lift us back up. David understood this in **Psalm 35** when he cried out for God to fight on his behalf.

And in **Genesis 35**, we see Jacob going through a major identity change—God reminding him that he is no longer the deceiver, but Israel, the one who wrestled with God and prevailed. In the middle of our worries and battles, God steps in to give us not only strength, but a new name and a renewed purpose.

Think About It

1. **Anxiety is real, but so is God's presence:** What weighs your heart down right now? Have you talked to God about it, or let someone speak encouragement into your situation?

2. **God fights for you:** David asked God to fight against those who fought him. What "battles" are you facing right now—internal or external—and how can you let God take the lead?

3. **You are not who you used to be:** Just like God renamed Jacob, He gives us new identity in Him. Are you living out of your past labels, or stepping into the name and future God has for you?

Bottom Line

When anxiety weighs you down, remember that God sees, God speaks, and God strengthens. Let Him fight your battles and remind you who you really are.

Prayer

Heavenly Father, You know the things that weigh on my heart even before I say a word. Thank You for caring about my worries and reminding me of who I am in You. Help me trust that You're fighting for me, even when I feel overwhelmed. Speak Your truth over my life and replace my anxiety with peace and purpose. In Jesus' Name, Amen.

March 24

Choose Your Circle Wisely

3-Year-Bible Reading: Proverbs 12; Psalm 36; Genesis 37

One who is righteous is a guide to his neighbor, but the way of the wicked leads them astray. — Proverbs 12:26

Your steadfast love, O Lord, extends to the heavens, your faithfulness to the clouds. — Psalm 36:5

So when Joseph came to his brothers, they stripped him of his robe, the robe of many colors that he wore. And they took him and threw him into a pit. — Genesis 37:23–24

Have you ever felt left out, betrayed, or hurt by someone you thought you could trust? Maybe a friend turned on you, or you were talked about behind your back. In **Genesis 37**, Joseph experienced the sting of betrayal—his own brothers threw him into a pit because they were jealous.

That story connects with **Proverbs 12:26**, which reminds us how much influence the people around us can have. Friends can either lift you up or pull you down. But in the middle of all that mess, **Psalm 36** shows us something powerful: God's love and faithfulness never give up on us, even when others do.

Think About It

1. **Friendship Matters:** Are the people closest to you pointing you toward God or pulling you away from Him? Proverbs 12:26 challenges us to surround ourselves with people who guide us in righteousness.

2. **God Sees the Hurt:** Joseph's story shows that even when people treat us unfairly, God is still at work. Are you trusting that He has a plan, even in the hard moments?

3. **Lean on God's Love:** Psalm 36 reminds us that God's love is unfailing and limitless. Do you turn to Him when you're feeling betrayed or rejected?

Bottom Line

Who you surround yourself with shapes who you become—but no matter how others treat you, God's love is constant and His plan for you is good.

Prayer

Heavenly Father, thank You for loving me even when others let me down. Help me to choose friends who push me closer to You and give me the wisdom to walk away from harmful influences. When I feel hurt or betrayed, remind me of Your faithfulness and help me trust Your plan like Joseph did. In Jesus' Name, Amen.

MARCH 25

Don't Waste the Fire

3-Year-Bible Reading: Proverbs 12:27–28; Genesis 38

Whoever is slothful will not roast his game, but the diligent man will get precious wealth. In the path of righteousness is life, and in its pathway there is no death. — Proverbs 12:27–28

She was more righteous than I, since I did not give her to my son Shelah. And he did not know her again. — Genesis 38:26

Sometimes we start something strong—like a new goal, a commitment to read the Bible, or a decision to follow God more closely—but we lose motivation halfway through. **Proverbs 12:27** paints a strange but powerful picture: a hunter catches food but never cooks it. It's like having potential but wasting it because of laziness or fear.

Then there's **Genesis 38**, one of the messiest chapters in the Bible. Judah made huge mistakes, and Tamar was deeply wronged. But even in this mess, God was at work. Tamar showed courage and persistence, and in the end, Judah recognized her righteousness. It's a reminder that even when life is messy and we feel like giving up, God can redeem the broken parts and bring life through righteousness.

THINK ABOUT IT

1. **Don't Waste What You've Been Given:** What talents, relationships, or opportunities has God placed in your hands? Are you roasting the game—or letting it spoil?

2. **Righteousness Over Reputation:** Tamar risked everything to stand up for what was right. How do you respond when doing the right thing might cost you something?

3. **God Works in the Mess:** Judah's story reminds us that God isn't only present in the "clean" parts of our lives. Where do you need to invite Him into your mess?

BOTTOM LINE

God wants you to live with purpose and courage. Don't let laziness, fear, or shame waste the fire He's put in you. Even when your story feels like a mess, He can bring redemption and life.

PRAYER

Heavenly Father, thank You for reminding me that You work even in the broken and complicated parts of my story. Help me not to waste the gifts, time, or opportunities You've given me. Give me the strength to choose what's right, even when it's hard, and the faith to trust that You are working behind the scenes. In Jesus' Name, Amen.

March 26

Lessons in the Pit and the Palace

3-Year-Bible Reading: Proverbs 13:1–2; Genesis 39–41

"A wise son hears his father's instruction, but a scoffer does not listen to rebuke. From the fruit of his mouth a man eats what is good, but the desire of the treacherous is for violence." — Proverbs 13:1–2

"But the LORD was with Joseph and showed him steadfast love and gave him favor in the sight of the keeper of the prison." — Genesis 39:21

"Then Pharaoh said to Joseph, 'Since God has shown you all this, there is none so discerning and wise as you are.'" — Genesis 41:39

Have you ever felt like doing the right thing actually made life harder? Joseph definitely could relate. He honored God, stayed out of trouble, and still got thrown into a pit, sold into slavery, lied about, and tossed in prison. Yet even in the worst places, God didn't forget him.

Through it all, Joseph chose wisdom over bitterness and faith over fear. His journey from the pit to the palace shows what happens when we stick with God—even when life feels unfair. And just like **Proverbs 13:1–2** reminds us, when we listen and live wisely, it leads to good things in the long run.

Think About It

1. **God is at work even when it's hard:** Joseph went through betrayal and prison, but Genesis 39–41 shows that God was with him the entire time. Where in your life do you need to trust that God is still working, even when you don't see the results yet?

2. **Your choices matter in every season:** Whether Joseph was a slave, a prisoner, or a leader in Egypt, he lived with integrity. How can you choose to honor God in your current situation—at school, home, or with your friends?

3. **Wisdom brings reward:** Proverbs 13 reminds us that listening to godly instruction leads to good fruit. Who are the people in your life that help you grow in wisdom? Are you open to correction when it comes?

Bottom Line

God's presence and purpose don't disappear in your hardest moments. When you live with integrity and choose wisdom like Joseph did, God can use your story in powerful ways—both in the pit and the palace.

Prayer

Heavenly Father, thank You for never leaving me, even when life feels unfair or confusing. Help me to choose wisdom, stay faithful, and trust that You're working behind the scenes. Grow in me a heart like Joseph's—one that stays close to You no matter what. In Jesus' Name, Amen.

March 27

Guard Your Mouth, Feed Your Soul

3-Year-Bible Reading: Proverbs 13:3–4; Genesis 42–45

Whoever guards his mouth preserves his life; he who opens wide his lips comes to ruin. The soul of the sluggard craves and gets nothing, while the soul of the diligent is richly supplied. — Proverbs 13:3–4

And now do not be distressed or angry with yourselves because you sold me here, for God sent me before you to preserve life. — Genesis 45:5

Then Joseph hurried out, for his compassion grew warm for his brother, and he sought a place to weep. And he entered his chamber and wept there. — Genesis 43:30

Words are powerful. They can heal or hurt, encourage or tear down. The story of Joseph and his brothers in **Genesis 42–45** is full of strong emotions and important conversations. After being betrayed by his brothers and sold into slavery, Joseph ends up saving them during a famine. He could have gotten revenge, but instead he chose grace. His words and actions showed maturity and a heart shaped by God.

In **Proverbs 13:3–4**, we're reminded that guarding our words and being diligent in our actions leads to life and blessing. Just like Joseph, we're faced with moments where we have to decide whether we'll let our mouths or our hearts lead.

Think About It

1. **Your Words Have Weight:** Are you guarding your mouth or just saying whatever pops into your head? Proverbs warns that careless words can ruin relationships and even your own life.

2. **Hard Work Pays Off:** Joseph didn't let bitterness or laziness define him. Even in prison or working for others, he stayed faithful and diligent. What kind of work ethic are you showing at school, home, or church?

3. **Grace Over Grudges:** Joseph had every reason to be angry. But he forgave his brothers, seeing God's bigger plan. Who do you need to forgive, or show grace to, even if they don't deserve it?

Bottom Line

Choose your words carefully and live with purpose. Like Joseph, God can use your faithfulness—even in hard times—to bring life to others.

Prayer

Heavenly Father, help me to be wise with my words and faithful in everything I do. Teach me to forgive like Joseph did, and to trust that You're working even when life feels unfair. I want my heart, my words, and my actions to reflect You. In Jesus' Name, Amen.

March 28

Guardrails and Guidance

3-Year-Bible Reading: Proverbs 13:5–6; Genesis 46–47

The righteous hates falsehood, but the wicked brings shame and disgrace. Righteousness guards him whose way is blameless, but sin overthrows the wicked. — Proverbs 13:5–6

So Israel took his journey with all that he had and came to Beersheba, and offered sacrifices to the God of his father Isaac. — Genesis 46:1

Then Joseph settled his father and his brothers and gave them a possession in the land of Egypt, in the best of the land… — Genesis 47:11

Have you ever felt nervous about a big change—like moving schools, starting a new job, or stepping into a situation where everything feels unfamiliar? That's exactly where Jacob (also called Israel) found himself in **Genesis 46–47**. After years of thinking his son Joseph was gone, Jacob learned Joseph was alive and ruling in Egypt. But moving his whole family there? That was a major leap. Still, Jacob paused to worship and seek God first, and God assured him it was the right move.

Meanwhile, **Proverbs 13** reminds us that doing what's right—walking in truth and righteousness—protects us, even when life takes unexpected turns.

Think About It

1. **Check the Direction:** Are you seeking God first when you face a big decision, like Jacob did in Genesis 46:1? Or are you rushing ahead without asking Him for guidance?

2. **Character Counts:** Proverbs 13:5–6 talks about how righteousness "guards" your way. What choices in your life show that you're walking in truth and integrity—even when no one's watching?

3. **God Provides:** Joseph prepared a place for his family during famine. How does this remind you that God often uses people and situations to care for you, even in unfamiliar territory?

Bottom Line

When we choose righteousness and seek God's direction, He guards our path and provides what we need—even in seasons of big change.

Prayer

Heavenly Father, thank You for always being with me, especially when life feels uncertain. Help me to choose what's right and trust that You're guiding my steps. Teach me to pause, pray, and follow Your voice just like Jacob did. Thank You for being faithful to provide, even when I can't see the whole picture. In Jesus' Name, Amen.

March 29

True Worth

3-Year-Bible Reading: Proverbs 13:7–8; Genesis 48

"One pretends to be rich, yet has nothing; another pretends to be poor, yet has great wealth. The ransom of a man's life is his wealth, but a poor man hears no threat." — Proverbs 13:7–8

"And he blessed Joseph and said, 'The God before whom my fathers Abraham and Isaac walked, the God who has been my shepherd all my life long to this day, the angel who has redeemed me from all evil, bless the boys.'" — Genesis 48:15–16

Have you ever felt like you had to "look" a certain way to fit in—wearing the right clothes, having the right phone, or being seen with the right people? In our social media world, it's easy to fall into the trap of pretending—trying to appear more impressive, more "together," or more important than we really are. But **Proverbs 13:7–8** reminds us that what we show on the outside doesn't always reflect the truth of what's inside.

Meanwhile, in **Genesis 48**, we see something radically different: Jacob (also known as Israel), at the end of his life, focuses not on what he owns but on the faithfulness of God throughout his journey—and he passes that blessing on to the next generation.

Think About It

1. **What Really Matters?** According to Proverbs, people can *look* wealthy but have nothing of real value. What does this tell you about how God views status and material things?

2. **A Life of Blessing:** Jacob's blessing over Joseph's sons is deeply spiritual, rooted in God's faithfulness. How might your words and actions bless others, especially when you focus on what God has done for you?

3. **Are You Pretending?** Do you sometimes feel pressure to hide your struggles or fake success? Remember, your true worth isn't measured by popularity or possessions but by your identity in Christ.

Bottom Line

Your value isn't in what you have or how you appear—it's in who you belong to. Live honestly, walk in God's blessings, and trust that His presence is the greatest treasure of all.

Prayer

Heavenly Father, thank You for reminding me that I don't need to pretend or perform to have value. You see me, love me, and bless me because I'm Yours. Help me live with honesty, contentment, and faith in Your promises. Teach me to see others—and myself—through Your eyes. In Jesus' Name, Amen.

March 30

Shining Light, Humble Hearts

3-Year-Bible Reading: Proverbs 13:9–10; Genesis 49–50

"The light of the righteous rejoices, but the lamp of the wicked will be put out. By insolence comes nothing but strife, but with those who take advice is wisdom." — Proverbs 13:9–10

"As for you, you meant evil against me, but God meant it for good, to bring it about that many people should be kept alive, as they are today." — Genesis 50:20

Have you ever had someone try to bring you down, only for God to turn it around and use it to grow you stronger? That's exactly what Joseph experienced. His brothers betrayed him, sold him into slavery, and thought they'd never see him again. But God had a bigger plan.

In **Genesis 50:20**, Joseph explains to his brothers that even though they meant to harm him, God used it for good. Then, in **Proverbs 13:9–10**, we're reminded that when we live righteously and walk humbly, our lives shine bright—like lights in a dark world. The proud stir up conflict, but the wise choose to listen and grow.

Think About It

1. **Let Your Light Shine:** Are your words and actions showing the joy and light of someone who follows Jesus? A righteous life doesn't mean a perfect one—but it does mean choosing to reflect God's goodness.

2. **Check Your Heart:** Are you quick to argue or slow to listen? Proverbs tells us pride leads to conflict. Humility—being willing to take advice or admit when we're wrong—is a mark of maturity and wisdom.

3. **Trust God's Bigger Picture:** Have you gone through something unfair or painful? Like Joseph, you might not understand it now, but God can bring good out of it in ways you never imagined.

Bottom Line

God calls us to be people of light and humility, trusting Him even when life feels unfair. He can turn even the darkest moments into part of a much bigger, beautiful story.

Prayer

Heavenly Father, thank You for being a God who brings light into darkness and purpose out of pain. Help me to live with a humble heart, to listen and grow in wisdom, and to trust Your plan even when it doesn't make sense. Let my life shine with Your joy. In Jesus' Name, Amen.

MARCH 31

Dreams, Delays, and Real Rewards

3-Year-Bible Reading: Proverbs 13:11–12; Psalm 37

"Wealth gained hastily will dwindle, but whoever gathers little by little will increase it. Hope deferred makes the heart sick, but a desire fulfilled is a tree of life." — Proverbs 13:11–12

"Delight yourself in the Lord, and he will give you the desires of your heart. Be still before the Lord and wait patiently for him." — Psalm 37:4, 7

Waiting is hard. Whether it's waiting for summer break, answers to prayer, or clarity about your future, it's easy to feel discouraged. You might start wondering if God's even listening. But the Bible reminds us that God cares about both the *what* and the *when*.

In **Proverbs 13:11–12**, we learn that quick wins often don't last, but steady faithfulness leads to lasting rewards. And **Psalm 37** shows us that when we find joy in God first, He aligns our hearts with His will and blesses us in His perfect timing.

THINK ABOUT IT

1. **Don't Rush the Process:** What are some things you're tempted to rush in life—relationships, success, popularity? Proverbs 13 reminds us that "little by little" growth is what truly lasts.

2. **Check Your Heart:** Are your dreams rooted in God's desires or just your own? Psalm 37:4 says if you delight in God first, He shapes your desires to match His best for you.

3. **Patience Is Powerful:** Waiting doesn't mean doing nothing. Waiting on God often involves trusting, praying, and staying faithful even when it's tough.

BOTTOM LINE

God sees your dreams and delays. He isn't ignoring you—He's shaping you. Stay close to Him, and trust that His timing is better than anything you could rush into on your own.

PRAYER

Heavenly Father, help me to trust You when things don't happen as fast as I want them to. Teach me patience, and help me to find joy in You even while I wait. Shape my dreams to match Your will, and give me the courage to keep going, step by step. In Jesus' Name, Amen.

APRIL 1

Living Water & Real Change

3-Year-Bible Reading: Proverbs 13:13-14; Mark 1

"Whoever despises the word brings destruction on himself, but he who reveres the commandment will be rewarded. The teaching of the wise is a fountain of life, that one may turn away from the snares of death." — Proverbs 13:13-14

"The beginning of the gospel of Jesus Christ, the Son of God... And a voice came from heaven, 'You are my beloved Son; with you I am well pleased.'" — Mark 1:1, 11

Have you ever been thirsty after a long run or a hot day, and that first sip of water just hits different? That's what **Proverbs 13:14** is getting at—God's wisdom is like a "fountain of life." It refreshes, it satisfies, and it keeps you from going down dangerous paths. But here's the thing: just like ignoring your thirst leads to exhaustion, ignoring God's truth leads to spiritual burnout.

In **Mark 1**, we get introduced to Jesus in a powerful way. From John the Baptist prepping the way, to Jesus being baptized, to Him healing the sick and casting out demons—everything shows that Jesus came to bring real change and new life. Notice that when Jesus was baptized, God declared, "You are my beloved Son." Before Jesus performed a single miracle, He was already fully loved and accepted by the Father. That's huge. It means our identity is rooted in God's love first, not in what we do.

Jesus invites us into a new way of living—one where we follow His Word (like Proverbs says), experience deep purpose, and overflow with living water to others. But we've got to take that first step: listen to God's voice, trust His Word, and let Him lead.

THINK ABOUT IT

1. **Respecting the Word:** Do you treat God's Word as a source of life—or something to ignore until it's convenient?
2. **Your Identity:** Are you trying to earn God's love or acceptance? Or are you living from a place of already being loved like Jesus was?
3. **Following Jesus:** Jesus called people to repent and believe the gospel (Mark 1:15). What's one step you can take today to follow Him more closely?

BOTTOM LINE

God's wisdom brings life. In Jesus, we find a new identity rooted in love—not performance. His Word refreshes and transforms us from the inside out.

PRAYER

Heavenly Father, thank You for loving me before I could do anything to earn it. Help me to take Your Word seriously and trust that it leads to life. Teach me to follow Jesus with my whole heart and to remember that my identity is secure in Your love. Let Your truth refresh me like living water today. In Jesus' Name, Amen.

APRIL 2

Wise Steps and Healing Hearts

3-Year-Bible Reading: Proverbs 13:15-16; Psalm 38; Mark 2

"Good sense wins favor, but the way of the treacherous is their ruin. Every prudent man acts with knowledge, but a fool flaunts his folly." — Proverbs 13:15–16

"I am utterly bowed down and prostrate; all the day I go about mourning. For my sides are filled with burning, and there is no soundness in my flesh." — Psalm 38:6–7

"And when Jesus saw their faith, he said to the paralytic, 'Son, your sins are forgiven.'" — Mark 2:5

Sometimes it's easy to make choices based on what feels good in the moment—snapping back at someone, going along with a crowd, or ignoring a little warning in your heart. But **Proverbs 13:15–16** reminds us that wise choices lead to favor, while foolish ones lead to trouble. In **Psalm 38**, David is overwhelmed with guilt and physical pain because of his sin. He's not just feeling bad emotionally—he feels it in his body. That's how deep regret can go when we ignore wisdom.

But here's the good news: **Mark 2** shows us Jesus doesn't just see the surface; He sees our hearts. When a group of friends brought a paralyzed man to Jesus, He didn't start by healing his legs. He started by healing his soul—by forgiving his sins. Jesus knew the man needed spiritual healing most of all.

When we've messed up or feel broken inside like David, Jesus is ready to forgive, restore, and help us start fresh. Wisdom isn't about being perfect—it's about turning to the One who is.

THINK ABOUT IT

1. **Your Choices Matter:** What small choices have you made recently that reflect wisdom—or foolishness? How can you start acting with more "knowledge," as Proverbs says?
2. **When Guilt Weighs You Down:** Have you ever felt like David in Psalm 38—overwhelmed by regret? What can you do when you feel like that?
3. **Faith That Brings Healing:** The friends in Mark 2 brought the paralyzed man to Jesus. Who can you bring to Jesus—through prayer, encouragement, or inviting them to know Him?

BOTTOM LINE

Wisdom leads to favor, but mistakes don't have to define us. Jesus sees our hearts, forgives our sins, and invites us to walk in healing and wholeness.

PRAYER

Heavenly Father, thank You for being patient with me when I mess up. Please give me a heart that desires wisdom and help me to make good choices each day. When I feel weighed down by guilt or regret, remind me of Your forgiveness and healing. Teach me to lean on You and to bring others closer to You too. In Jesus' Name, Amen.

April 3

Who's In Your Circle?

3-Year-Bible Reading: Proverbs 13:17-18; Mark 3

"A wicked messenger falls into trouble, but a faithful envoy brings healing. Poverty and disgrace come to him who ignores instruction, but whoever heeds reproof is honored." — Proverbs 13:17–18

"And he appointed twelve (whom he also named apostles) so that they might be with him and he might send them out to preach." — Mark 3:14

"And looking about at those who sat around him, he said, 'Here are my mother and my brothers! For whoever does the will of God, he is my brother and sister and mother.'" — Mark 3:34–35

Have you ever thought about the people you spend the most time with? Whether it's your closest friends, teammates, or even your family, your circle matters. In **Mark 3**, Jesus carefully chose the twelve disciples—not just to follow Him, but to be with Him, learn from Him, and be sent out for a purpose. And later, when people told Him His family was outside, He pointed to those doing God's will and called them His true family. That's a huge deal—Jesus redefined family as those who follow and obey God.

Meanwhile, **Proverbs 13:17-18** reminds us that who we listen to and what we do with correction can shape our future. A "faithful envoy" or trustworthy messenger brings healing. But ignoring advice or instruction leads to trouble. That means choosing to surround ourselves with people who tell us the truth, encourage our faith, and challenge us to grow can actually lead to honor and blessing.

So here's the question: Are the people around you helping you get closer to Jesus—or pulling you away? Are you becoming someone others can count on to bring truth, healing, and encouragement?

Think About It

1. **Your Circle Matters:** Who are the people closest to you? Are they encouraging your walk with Jesus—or making it harder?
2. **Listen and Learn:** How do you respond to correction or advice, especially when it's from someone who cares about you?
3. **Be Someone Who Builds:** Are you a faithful messenger who brings encouragement and healing, or do your words bring more drama than peace?

Bottom Line

Surround yourself with people who help you follow Jesus, and be the kind of person others can trust to speak truth and bring healing.

Prayer

Heavenly Father, thank You for the people You've placed in my life. Help me to build strong, Christ-centered relationships and be someone who brings encouragement and truth. Teach me to listen to correction and grow from it, just like You want me to. I want to be part of Your family—someone who does Your will. In Jesus' Name, Amen.

APRIL 4

Wise Vibes Only

3-Year-Bible Reading: Proverbs 13:19-20; Psalm 39; Mark 4

"A desire fulfilled is sweet to the soul, but to turn away from evil is an abomination to fools. Whoever walks with the wise becomes wise, but the companion of fools will suffer harm." — Proverbs 13:19-20

"O Lord, make me know my end and what is the measure of my days; let me know how fleeting I am!" — Psalm 39:4

"But they were filled with great fear and said to one another, 'Who then is this, that even the wind and the sea obey him?'" — Mark 4:41

Have you ever made a goal, stuck with it, and finally saw it come true? That *sweet* feeling of success hits deep—just like **Proverbs 13:19** says. But what about those times when you start drifting from your good goals because of distractions—or even worse, because you're hanging out with people who pull you the wrong way? **Proverbs 13:20** reminds us that the people around us matter. Choose your crew wisely, because their habits will rub off on you, for better or worse.

In **Psalm 39**, David is wrestling with the shortness of life. It's a big reminder: this life is fast. What we do and who we follow matters. Time is short, and we don't want to waste it chasing things that don't last.

Then there's **Mark 4**, where Jesus calms a raging storm with just a few words. The disciples are stunned. *Even the wind and waves obey Him.* Talk about ultimate power. Jesus isn't just wise—He's got authority over nature itself. He's the kind of leader worth following. When life gets stormy, you want Him in your boat.

So how do we make the most of this quick life? Walk with Jesus. Walk with people who are chasing wisdom. Say "no" to the crowd that's heading nowhere and "yes" to the One who commands even the storm.

THINK ABOUT IT

1. **Who's in your circle?** Are the people closest to you helping you grow in wisdom or dragging you into bad choices?
2. **What's your storm?** What are you facing that feels out of control? Have you invited Jesus into it—or are you trying to row through it alone?
3. **What truly lasts?** Are you spending your time and energy on things that matter for eternity, or just chasing what's temporary?

BOTTOM LINE

Life is short. Choose wisdom over hype, Jesus over the crowd, and surround yourself with people who help you stay strong when life gets wild.

PRAYER

Heavenly Father, thank You for giving me the gift of life—even though it's short, it can be filled with purpose when I follow You. Help me to choose my friends wisely, to turn away from foolish things, and to trust You when storms hit. Make me wise by walking close to You each day. In Jesus' Name, Amen.

April 5

When Jesus Steps In

3-Year-Bible Reading: Proverbs 13:21-23; Mark 5

"Disaster pursues sinners, but the righteous are rewarded with good. A good man leaves an inheritance to his children's children, but the sinner's wealth is laid up for the righteous." — Proverbs 13:21–22

"And he said to her, 'Daughter, your faith has made you well; go in peace, and be healed of your disease.'" — Mark 5:34

"But overhearing what they said, Jesus said to the ruler of the synagogue, 'Do not fear, only believe.'" — Mark 5:36

Some days feel like everything is going wrong—stress, fear, disappointment. Maybe you're trying to do what's right, but you wonder if it even matters. **Proverbs 13:21–22** reminds us that doing good and living righteously really does lead to lasting reward—even if it doesn't feel like it right away. Sometimes, we just need to be reminded that God sees and honors a life of faith.

In **Mark 5**, Jesus encounters people in desperate situations. A woman who had suffered for 12 years reached out in faith and was healed. A young girl had died, and her heartbroken dad was told there was no hope—but Jesus said, *"Do not fear, only believe."* Whether someone had been waiting for years or facing the worst day of their life, everything changed when Jesus stepped in.

Faith isn't just a church word—it's a life-changing, miracle-making, peace-giving response to Jesus. That woman was healed not because she had a perfect past, but because she believed Jesus could make her whole. The ruler's daughter was raised not because he had all the answers, but because he trusted Jesus enough to keep walking with Him.

When you're overwhelmed, scared, or unsure of what's next, remember: Jesus is still speaking peace into chaos, still healing broken hearts, and still bringing dead things back to life. Your faith in Him is never wasted.

Think About It

1. **Faith in Action:** The woman in Mark 5 reached out to Jesus even when things seemed hopeless. What would it look like for you to reach out to Jesus in faith today?
2. **Don't Fear, Only Believe:** Jesus told Jairus not to be afraid. What fears are you facing that you need to surrender to Him?
3. **Your Story Matters:** Both people in Mark 5 had powerful encounters with Jesus. How might your own struggles become part of a testimony that points others to Him?

Bottom Line

Faith in Jesus changes everything. No matter how hopeless it feels, He is always near, ready to heal, restore, and speak peace over your life.

Prayer

Heavenly Father, thank You for being the God who sees me, hears me, and loves me. When I feel afraid or overwhelmed, help me remember that You are with me. Build my faith like the woman who reached out and the man who trusted You with his daughter. Teach me to walk in confidence, knowing You are still working miracles. In Jesus' Name, Amen.

April 6

Love That Corrects

3-Year-Bible Reading: Proverbs 13:24-25; Psalm 40; Mark 6

"Whoever spares the rod hates his son, but he who loves him is diligent to discipline him." — Proverbs 13:24

"He drew me up from the pit of destruction, out of the miry bog, and set my feet upon a rock, making my steps secure." — Psalm 40:2

"And he called the twelve and began to send them out two by two, and gave them authority over the unclean spirits." — Mark 6:7

Correction isn't something any of us naturally enjoy. Whether it's getting called out by a parent, coach, or teacher—it can sting. But **Proverbs 13:24** reminds us that discipline, when done in love, is actually a form of deep care. It means someone loves you enough not to let you stay in a pattern that will hurt you. The same is true with God. He lovingly corrects us to keep us on the right path.

In **Psalm 40**, David shares how God rescued him from a pit and placed his feet on solid ground. God doesn't just point out what's wrong—He helps us out of it. His discipline is never meant to shame, but to save. When He corrects us, it's to lift us out of the muck and help us stand strong again.

And in **Mark 6**, Jesus sends out His disciples with authority and purpose. But notice—before they were sent, they were trained. Correction and guidance prepared them to step into their calling. Jesus didn't just say, "Go for it!"—He shaped them into people who could represent Him well.

In the same way, the discipline we receive—whether from God or trusted adults—is shaping us. It may be uncomfortable, but it's helping us become more like Jesus. And that's a good thing.

Think About It

1. **Correction is Care:** How does your view of discipline change when you see it as love instead of punishment?
2. **God Lifts, Not Shames:** When was a time God helped you out of a bad situation? How did He use that experience to make you stronger?
3. **Prepared with Purpose:** Are there areas in your life where God may be shaping you now for something ahead?

Bottom Line

God's correction is an act of love. He disciplines to rescue, restore, and prepare you for a life that reflects His purpose.

Prayer

Heavenly Father, thank You for loving me enough to correct me when I'm going the wrong way. Help me to receive discipline with a humble heart and trust that You're shaping me for something good. Teach me to listen, grow, and become more like You through every experience. In Jesus' Name, Amen.

April 7

Heart Check

3-Year-Bible Reading: Proverbs 14:1-2; Mark 7

"The wisest of women builds her house, but folly with her own hands tears it down. Whoever walks in uprightness fears the Lord, but he who is devious in his ways despises him." — Proverbs 14:1-2

"And he said to them, 'Well did Isaiah prophesy of you hypocrites, as it is written, "This people honors me with their lips, but their heart is far from me."'" — Mark 7:6

"There is nothing outside a person that by going into him can defile him, but the things that come out of a person are what defile him." — Mark 7:15

Have you ever said all the right things but still felt off inside? Or looked like you had it together on the outside, but deep down your heart wasn't in the right place? In **Mark 7**, Jesus confronts the religious leaders who were super focused on rituals and appearances but completely missed the heart behind it all. They honored God with their lips, but their hearts were far away. That's a big deal to Jesus—He cares more about what's going on inside us than what we try to show others.

In **Proverbs 14:1-2**, we're reminded that wisdom builds while foolishness tears down. Living wisely means walking in "uprightness," or doing what's right because we respect and love God. But when we're only pretending to follow God—doing the actions without the heart—we're not really walking with Him.

God sees beyond our filters and facades. He's not impressed by a fake version of faith. Instead, He invites us to bring Him our real selves, flaws and all, and let Him shape us from the inside out.

Think About It

1. What's Really Going On in Your Heart? Are you doing things to look good or to truly grow in your relationship with God?

2. More Than Just the Outside: How can you focus less on appearances and more on your inner life with God—your thoughts, motives, and attitude?

3. Building or Tearing Down? Are your actions and words building others up or pulling them down? What does that say about the state of your heart?

Bottom Line

God doesn't want empty words or surface-level faith—He wants your heart. Let Him shape who you are from the inside out, so you can live wisely and reflect His love in a real, powerful way.

Prayer

Heavenly Father, thank You for loving me even when I don't get it all right. Help me not to focus just on appearances but to truly give You my heart. Shape me from the inside out. Teach me to walk wisely, build others up, and live in a way that honors You. In Jesus' Name, Amen.

April 8

Messy but Worth It

3-Year-Bible Reading: Proverbs 14:3-4; Mark 8

"By the mouth of a fool comes a rod for his back, but the lips of the wise will preserve them. Where there are no oxen, the manger is clean, but abundant crops come by the strength of the ox."
— Proverbs 14:3-4

"And calling the crowd to him with his disciples, he said to them, 'If anyone would come after me, let him deny himself and take up his cross and follow me.'" — Mark 8:34

We all like things neat and easy—clean rooms, smooth friendships, minimal effort. But **Proverbs 14:4** paints a different picture. It says that while having no oxen keeps the barn spotless, it also means no harvest. In other words, real growth often comes with a little mess. Whether it's putting in the hard work for a school project, resolving a conflict with a friend, or stepping out in faith—growth can be uncomfortable, and sometimes even messy.

Jesus understood this. In **Mark 8**, He called His followers to something more than a comfy life. He told them, *"Take up your cross and follow me."* That's not easy. It means making hard choices, letting go of pride, and living for something bigger than yourself. It means accepting that following Him won't always look polished—but it will always be worth it.

If your life feels messy sometimes, don't panic. Whether you're dealing with doubts, mistakes, or learning curves, that might be where God is doing His best work in you. Don't settle for a "clean barn" life that avoids challenges but misses purpose. Let the "oxen" in—let God do something meaningful, even if it's a bit messy.

Think About It

1. **Wise Words Matter:** Are your words helping or hurting others? Are you choosing to speak wisdom or foolishness in your conversations (Proverbs 14:3)?
2. **Mess with a Mission:** Are you avoiding things that seem messy just to stay comfortable? What might God want to grow in you through that challenge?
3. **Taking Up Your Cross:** What does it look like for you to "deny yourself" and follow Jesus today?

Bottom Line

God often does His greatest work in the middle of life's messes. Don't fear discomfort—embrace the growth that comes with following Jesus wholeheartedly.

Prayer

Heavenly Father, thank You for reminding me that growth takes work and sometimes even a bit of a mess. Help me to speak with wisdom and live with purpose, even when it's hard. Give me the courage to follow Jesus, deny myself, and choose what matters most. Teach me to value what You value and to keep going when things aren't easy. In Jesus' Name, Amen.

April 9

Watch What You Believe

3-Year-Bible Reading: Proverbs 14:5–7; Mark 9

"A faithful witness does not lie, but a false witness breathes out lies. A scoffer seeks wisdom in vain, but knowledge is easy for a man of understanding. Leave the presence of a fool, for there you do not meet words of knowledge." — Proverbs 14:5–7

"Immediately the father of the child cried out and said, 'I believe; help my unbelief!'" — Mark 9:24

"And he said to them, 'This kind cannot be driven out by anything but prayer.'" — Mark 9:29

Have you ever felt unsure about what to believe? Or maybe you've heard so many voices—online, at school, even from friends—that you're not sure who's telling the truth anymore. In **Proverbs 14:5–7**, we're reminded to listen to people who are faithful and wise—not those who just talk big or stir up confusion. The Bible warns us to walk away from foolish influences because they won't lead us anywhere good.

In **Mark 9**, a father brings his suffering son to Jesus. This dad is desperate, and he says something really honest: "I believe; help my unbelief!" Isn't that how faith feels sometimes? We want to believe God can move in our lives, but we struggle with doubts. And that's okay—Jesus doesn't reject the father for his shaky faith. Instead, He meets him right where he is and heals his son.

Jesus also tells His disciples that real power—spiritual strength—comes through prayer (**Mark 9:29**). That means staying close to God is the key to understanding truth, fighting doubt, and living boldly. When we're surrounded by confusing voices, we can trust Jesus to be our source of clarity, peace, and truth.

Think About It

1. **Choose Your Influences:** Who are the "faithful witnesses" in your life? Are you spending time listening to wise voices, or are you being influenced by people who lead you away from God?
2. **Doubt Isn't Defeat:** Have you ever prayed like the father in Mark 9: "I believe; help my unbelief"? What does this verse teach you about how Jesus responds to doubt?
3. **Power Through Prayer:** Are you relying on your own strength to handle life's challenges, or are you turning to God through prayer like Jesus taught?

Bottom Line

It's okay to wrestle with doubt, but don't stay stuck there. Choose to seek wisdom, avoid foolish influences, and trust that Jesus meets you in your mess with power and truth.

Prayer

Heavenly Father, thank You for being patient with me when I doubt. Help me recognize and walk away from foolish influences. I want to be someone who speaks truth, listens well, and grows in real understanding. Teach me to pray, to trust, and to lean on You when I don't have all the answers. I believe—help my unbelief. In Jesus' Name, Amen.

April 10

Real Wisdom, Real Life

3-Year-Bible Reading: Proverbs 14:8-9; Psalm 41; Mark 10

"The wisdom of the prudent is to discern his way, but the folly of fools is deceiving. Fools mock at the guilt offering, but the upright enjoy acceptance." — Proverbs 14:8–9

"Blessed is the one who considers the poor! In the day of trouble the Lord delivers him." — Psalm 41:1

"But many who are first will be last, and the last first." — Mark 10:31

Life can often feel like a race—trying to be the smartest, the most liked, the first to succeed. But Jesus flips the script. In **Mark 10**, He teaches that greatness in God's kingdom is about serving others and putting others before yourself. That's way different from what the world teaches, right?

In **Proverbs 14**, we're reminded that real wisdom isn't just about being book-smart—it's about knowing the right way to live and actually walking in it. It's easy to pretend like we've got it all figured out, but God sees our hearts. Trying to "fake it" spiritually only leads to confusion. Wisdom comes when we slow down and ask, "Is this really honoring God?"

Psalm 41 shows that God sees and honors those who care for the weak and vulnerable. That's the heart of Jesus—lifting up those who are forgotten or hurting. When we choose compassion over competition, and wisdom over shortcuts, we reflect Jesus in a world that desperately needs Him.

Think About It

1. **Wisdom vs. Foolishness:** Are you making decisions that show God's wisdom, or are you just going with what feels good or popular in the moment?
2. **Who's First?** Jesus said the last will be first. What does it look like for you to put others first—at school, at home, or in your friend group?
3. **Compassion Counts:** How can you show God's love to someone who feels left out or is going through a hard time?

Bottom Line

True greatness comes from living wisely and serving others. When we choose God's way, even when it's hard, we gain something better than popularity—we gain purpose.

Prayer

Heavenly Father, thank You for showing me what real wisdom looks like through Jesus. Help me not to chase after what the world calls success, but to follow You with a heart that serves, loves, and lives with integrity. Teach me to notice the people around me who need encouragement and give me the courage to act with compassion. In Jesus' Name, Amen.

APRIL 11

Hope in the Wilderness

3-Year-Bible Reading: Proverbs 14:10-11; Psalms 42; Mark 11

"The heart knows its own bitterness, and no stranger shares its joy." — Proverbs 14:10

"As a deer pants for flowing streams, so pants my soul for you, O God." — Psalm 42:1

"And Jesus answered them, 'Have faith in God.'" — Mark 11:22

In **Proverbs 14:10**, we see a reminder that our deepest emotions—both joy and sorrow—are personal and often unseen by others. No one can truly understand the depth of what we feel in our hearts. In moments of joy, we may wish to share it with others, and in moments of sadness, it can feel lonely. But God knows exactly what we are going through, and He invites us to bring it all to Him.

Psalm 42 beautifully expresses the soul's longing for God. The psalmist compares his desire for God to a deer longing for water. Sometimes in life, we feel like we're in a spiritual desert, searching for peace or clarity, much like the psalmist did. But just as the deer finds the water it needs, our souls find true fulfillment and peace in God. We can trust Him to meet our deepest needs, even when everything around us feels dry.

In **Mark 11**, Jesus reminds us to have faith in God. In the context of a moment of challenge and difficulty, Jesus teaches His followers that faith can move mountains. Whether we face personal struggles, loneliness, or doubts, Jesus encourages us to keep trusting Him. Faith is not just about believing in God when things are going well; it's about clinging to Him even when it feels like we're surrounded by hardships.

When we feel alone or lost, God is always near. He invites us to trust Him fully, knowing that He understands our hearts, hears our cries, and meets our deepest needs.

THINK ABOUT IT

1. **Emotions Are Real:** What are the emotions you're dealing with right now? How can you bring those emotions to God, trusting that He understands you completely?
2. **Longing for God:** Are there times when you feel spiritually dry? How can you turn to God like the psalmist did and find refreshment in Him?
3. **Faith in the Hard Times:** Is there something you're facing that feels too big to handle? How can you step out in faith and trust that God can handle it with you?

BOTTOM LINE

No matter what we're facing, God is close and can meet our deepest needs. Our faith in Him is the key to navigating both the wilderness and the mountaintop moments of life.

PRAYER

Heavenly Father, thank You for understanding my heart and the emotions I carry. I bring my joys and struggles before You, knowing that You are with me in every moment. Help me to trust You fully, even when things are tough, and to seek You as my source of strength and peace. May my faith in You grow stronger each day. In Jesus' Name, Amen.

April 12

The Right Path

3-Year-Bible Reading: Proverbs 14:12; Psalm 118; Mark 12

"There is a way that seems right to a man, but its end is the way to death." — Proverbs 14:12

"This is the day that the Lord has made; let us rejoice and be glad in it." — Psalm 118:24

"And you shall love the Lord your God with all your heart and with all your soul and with all your mind and with all your strength." — Mark 12:30

Life is full of decisions—big ones and small ones. Every day, we choose how to spend our time, what to believe, and how to treat others. **Proverbs 14:12** warns that even when a path seems right, it may lead us away from God's best for us. Often, what seems right in the moment can lead to regret later. But just because something feels okay doesn't mean it's the right choice. That's why it's so important to seek God's wisdom and guidance in everything we do.

In **Psalm 118**, we're reminded to rejoice in the day that God has made. Life is a gift, and we can find joy in it by acknowledging God's goodness and trusting in His plans. Even when things aren't perfect, God is still working in our lives. Choosing to focus on His faithfulness and celebrate His goodness helps us find peace and purpose, even in challenging times.

When asked about the most important commandment, **Mark 12:30** tells us that loving God with all our heart, soul, mind, and strength is the best way to live. Loving God fully changes the way we see the world and the decisions we make. When we love God above all else, we are more likely to walk the path He has planned for us, avoiding the pitfalls of the wrong paths.

Think About It

1. **Choosing the Right Path:** Are there areas in your life where you might be tempted to take the easy or "right in the moment" path? How can you seek God's guidance instead?
2. **Finding Joy in Today:** What are some ways you can rejoice in the day that the Lord has made, even when things aren't going perfectly?
3. **Loving God First:** How can you love God with all your heart, soul, mind, and strength in your daily life? What would that look like for you this week?

Bottom Line

Even when a way seems right, we must trust God's wisdom to guide us. By loving God above all else and choosing His path, we find joy and purpose in each day.

Prayer

Heavenly Father, thank You for the gift of today. Help me to always seek Your wisdom and guidance in the decisions I make. I want to love You with all my heart, soul, mind, and strength. Teach me to follow Your path, not the one that seems right to me. May I find joy in Your faithfulness and trust in Your plan for my life. In Jesus' Name, Amen.

April 13

When Laughing Hurts and Watching Matters

3-Year-Bible Reading: Proverbs 14:13-14; Mark 13

"Even in laughter the heart may ache, and the end of joy may be grief. The backslider in heart will be filled with the fruit of his ways, and a good man will be filled with the fruit of his ways." — Proverbs 14:13–14

"And what I say to you I say to all: Stay awake." — Mark 13:37

Sometimes, life feels like a rollercoaster. You might laugh with friends at school or post a perfect pic online, but deep inside, you're struggling—maybe with loneliness, stress, or feeling like you're pretending to be okay. Proverbs 14:13 reminds us that not everything is as it seems. We can smile on the outside and still ache on the inside. God sees beyond our surface.

In Mark 13, Jesus talks about the end times and tells His followers to "stay awake." Not just to avoid falling asleep, but to stay spiritually alert—to be aware of what's going on in our hearts and lives. When things get tough, or the world seems dark and confusing, we're called to live with purpose and pay attention to what matters.

These verses connect in a powerful way. Whether you're feeling fake joy or real pain, or you're distracted by everything going on around you, God is calling you to check your heart and stay focused on Him.

Think About It

1. **What's really going on in your heart?** Are you laughing on the outside but hurting inside? God wants to meet you in that honest place.

2. **Are you paying attention to what matters?** Jesus tells us to "stay awake"—that means living with awareness, not drifting through life distracted or spiritually asleep.

3. **What "fruit" is your life growing?** Proverbs says both the backslider and the faithful person will be filled with the results of their choices. What direction are you heading in today?

Bottom Line

It's easy to hide behind a smile or zone out in a world full of distractions. But God sees the truth of our hearts, and He invites us to live awake—honestly, intentionally, and anchored in Him.

Prayer

Heavenly Father, thank You for seeing me completely—even when I try to hide behind a smile or get lost in distractions. Help me to stay awake to what You're doing in my life. When my heart aches, remind me You are near. When I'm tempted to drift or fall back, call me back to You. Fill me with the fruit of faithfulness and help me live with purpose each day. In Jesus' Name, Amen.

APRIL 14

Think Twice, Trust Deep

3-Year-Bible Reading: Proverbs 14:15; Psalm 43; Mark 14

"The simple believes everything, but the prudent gives thought to his steps." — Proverbs 14:15

"Send out your light and your truth; let them lead me; let them bring me to your holy hill and to your dwelling!" — Psalm 43:3

"Watch and pray that you may not enter into temptation. The spirit indeed is willing, but the flesh is weak." — Mark 14:38

Have you ever clicked on something online without thinking—and then instantly regretted it? It's easy to get caught up in the moment, especially when something feels urgent, exciting, or emotional. Whether it's a post, a rumor, or a risky decision, acting before thinking can lead us places we didn't want to go. **Proverbs 14:15** reminds us not to just go with the flow but to stop and think before we take a step.

In **Psalm 43**, the writer is overwhelmed, feeling attacked and abandoned, yet he doesn't just act out of emotion—he asks God for truth and light to guide him. That's a powerful move: choosing God's direction over our impulses. And then in **Mark 14**, we see Jesus telling His disciples to "watch and pray" in a moment of intense pressure. Why? Because even when our hearts are in the right place, we're still weak without God's help.

Think About It

1. **Are you thinking or just reacting?** Like Proverbs says, wisdom means taking a second to consider your next step instead of blindly following whatever's in front of you. Pause. Pray. Then proceed.

2. **Where do you need God's light and truth?** Psalm 43 is a reminder that when life feels confusing or dark, we can ask God to lead us with His truth—not just our feelings.

3. **How's your spiritual alertness?** Jesus' words in Mark 14 show that even the strongest intentions can fall apart without prayer. Staying spiritually awake means staying connected to God in every situation.

Bottom Line

God doesn't expect you to have it all figured out but He does call you to think wisely, seek His truth, and lean on Him when you feel weak. Don't rush your decisions. Let His light lead your steps.

Prayer

Heavenly Father, Thank You for being my source of truth and light. Sometimes I act too quickly, and I forget to think or pray first. Help me to pause, seek You, and follow Your lead—even when it's hard. Strengthen me when I'm tempted to give in or go along with the crowd. I want to live with wisdom, walk in truth, and stay spiritually awake. In Jesus' Name, Amen.

April 15

When Anger Meets Grace

3-Year-Bible Reading: Proverbs 14:16–17; Isaiah 53; Mark 15

"One who is wise is cautious and turns away from evil, but a fool is reckless and careless. A man of quick temper acts foolishly, and a man of evil devices is hated." — Proverbs 14:16–17

"He was despised and rejected by men; a man of sorrows, and acquainted with grief... But he was pierced for our transgressions; he was crushed for our iniquities." — Isaiah 53:3, 5

"And Jesus uttered a loud cry and breathed his last. And the curtain of the temple was torn in two, from top to bottom." — Mark 15:37–38

Have you ever lost your temper and done something you instantly regretted? Maybe it was yelling at someone, sending a harsh text, or walking away when someone needed you. Proverbs warns us that quick tempers lead to foolish actions (**Proverbs 14:17**).

But when we look at Jesus, especially in **Mark 15**, we see something completely different—grace under pressure, love instead of rage. Even as He was mocked, beaten, and nailed to a cross, Jesus didn't lash out. **Isaiah 53** reminds us that He carried our pain, our guilt, and even our angry outbursts—all without retaliation. He chose love. That kind of self-control and sacrificial love changes everything.

Think About It

1. What situations tend to make you "act foolishly" or lose control? What would it look like to respond with wisdom instead?

2. How does Jesus' response to suffering and rejection challenge the way you handle your emotions—especially anger?

3. The temple curtain was torn when Jesus died. That symbolized open access to God. How does knowing this help you when you feel overwhelmed or frustrated?

Bottom Line

Jesus showed us the ultimate example of strength—not in power or anger, but in grace and love. When we follow His lead, we can turn our frustration into wisdom, and our pain into purpose.

Prayer

Heavenly Father, thank You for the love and patience Jesus showed, even when He was hurt and rejected. Help me to choose wisdom over anger and grace over reaction. Teach me to reflect Your love in the way I handle my emotions. Thank You for tearing down every barrier between us so I can come to You freely. In Jesus' Name, Amen.

April 16

Wise or Whatever

3-Year-Bible Reading: Proverbs 14:18–19; Mark 16

"The simple inherit folly, but the prudent are crowned with knowledge. The evil bow down before the good, the wicked at the gates of the righteous." — Proverbs 14:18–19

"And he said to them, 'Go into all the world and proclaim the gospel to the whole creation.'" — Mark 16:15

Let's be real—nobody likes feeling clueless or like they've been played. Whether it's falling for a fake rumor or just making a dumb decision, those moments can leave us cringing. Proverbs reminds us that being "simple"—aka not thinking things through—leads to foolishness. But choosing wisdom? That leads to something way better: knowledge, respect, and ultimately, victory. In **Proverbs 14:18–19**, it's clear that wisdom puts you ahead, even when the world seems upside down.

Fast forward to **Mark 16**, and we see Jesus giving His followers the ultimate mission: *Go tell everyone about Me.* This is the call to live wisely—to live boldly and purposefully. It's not about having all the answers, but trusting the One who does. The disciples didn't always get it right, but after seeing the risen Jesus, they went all in. They weren't just "whatever" about life—they had a purpose, and it changed the world.

Think About It

1. **Your Direction Matters:** Are you living like someone who's just "going with the flow," or are you asking God for wisdom daily? Simple doesn't mean stupid—it means unwise. Start asking, "God, what's the wise choice here?"

2. **Wisdom Wins in the End:** Even if it feels like people who cheat or cut corners are winning right now, **Proverbs 14:19** promises the tables will turn. Keep walking with God. Your faithfulness will be worth it.

3. **You've Got a Mission:** Jesus didn't just rise from the dead for a cool ending—He gave us a purpose. Sharing His love and truth with others (see **Mark 16:15**) is how we live out that mission with wisdom and courage.

Bottom Line

Living wisely means trusting God, seeking truth, and walking with purpose—even when it's hard. In the end, wisdom wins, and God's mission moves forward through people like you.

Prayer

Heavenly Father, thank You for reminding me that wisdom comes from You. Help me not to live passively or foolishly but to seek Your guidance in every choice I make. Give me courage to live on mission, to share Your truth, and to trust that doing what's right will always be worth it. In Jesus' Name, Amen.

April 17

Outsiders and the Heart of God

3-Year-Bible Reading: Proverbs 14:20; Romans 1

"The poor is disliked even by his neighbor, but the rich has many friends." — Proverbs 14:20

"For although they knew God, they did not honor him as God or give thanks to him, but they became futile in their thinking, and their foolish hearts were darkened." — Romans 1:21

Ever felt invisible or overlooked? Like people only care if you're popular, talented, or have something they want? **Proverbs 14:20** nails it—sometimes people are treated better just because they seem more "successful."

And when we read **Romans 1**, it's clear that when people ignore God, their hearts and values get twisted. It's not just about breaking rules—it's about walking away from what really matters: honoring God and loving others. Our world often lifts up what's flashy and forgets the unseen, but God doesn't play favorites. He sees the heart, and He cares about how we treat people—especially those who are often ignored.

Think About It

1. **Popularity Isn't Everything:** Are you tempted to treat people differently based on what they have, how they look, or what they can offer you? God values every person—not for what they have, but because they are made in His image.

2. **Watch What You Worship:** Romans 1 shows us that when we put other things before God—whether that's popularity, stuff, or even our own opinions—we lose our way. What's taking up the most space in your heart and thoughts?

3. **Be the Difference:** While the world may ignore the "poor," God calls us to love them. Who is someone around you who might feel left out, and how can you show them God's love today?

Bottom Line

When we choose to honor God and value others like He does, we shine in a dark world. God doesn't ignore the unnoticed—He invites us to love like He does.

Prayer

Heavenly Father, Help me to see people the way You see them. Keep my heart from chasing what the world celebrates, and instead fill me with Your truth and compassion. I want to love the overlooked, honor You in my thoughts, and stay close to what truly matters. In Jesus' Name, Amen.

APRIL 18

Seen by God

3-Year-Bible Reading: Proverbs 14:21; Psalm 44; Romans 2

"Whoever despises his neighbor is a sinner, but blessed is he who is generous to the poor." — Proverbs 14:21

"Yet you have crushed us in the place of jackals and covered us with the shadow of death. If we had forgotten the name of our God or spread out our hands to a foreign god, would not God discover this? For he knows the secrets of the heart." — Psalm 44:19–21

"He will render to each one according to his works... For God shows no partiality." — Romans 2:6,11

Have you ever felt like you were doing the right thing, but no one noticed? Maybe you stood up for someone being bullied, gave up your spot so someone else could go first, or just chose kindness when no one else did. It can feel frustrating when your efforts seem invisible. But the Bible reminds us—God sees everything, even what's hidden.

Proverbs 14:21 tells us that kindness and generosity matter to God. **Psalm 44** reminds us that God knows the secrets of our hearts. And in **Romans 2**, we're told that God will reward each person according to what they've done—not based on popularity or how loud our good deeds are, but based on what's real in our lives.

Think About It

1. **Your Actions Matter:** Even small acts of kindness reflect God's heart. Are there ways you can show generosity or love today, even if no one else sees?

2. **God Knows the Heart:** Sometimes we can fool others—or even ourselves—but not God. What's something in your heart that you need to be honest with God about?

3. **God Is Fair:** Romans reminds us that God doesn't play favorites. How does knowing God is just and impartial encourage you when things seem unfair?

Bottom Line

God sees your heart, your choices, and your quiet faithfulness—even when no one else does. Keep living for Him, knowing His reward is better than any applause this world can give.

Prayer

Heavenly Father, thank You for seeing me and knowing me completely. Help me to live with integrity, to show love and generosity, and to trust that You will honor the good I do in Your name—even when no one else notices. Search my heart, and shape it to reflect You more. In Jesus' Name, Amen.

April 19

No One Seeks God?

3-Year-Bible Reading: Proverbs 14:22; Psalm 14; Psalm 53; Romans 3

"Do they not go astray who devise evil? Those who devise good meet steadfast love and faithfulness." —Proverbs 14:22

"The fool says in his heart, 'There is no God.' They are corrupt, they do abominable deeds; there is none who does good." —Psalm 14:1

"None is righteous, no, not one; no one understands; no one seeks for God." —Romans 3:10–11

Have you ever felt like you just couldn't get it right—like no matter how hard you try, you mess up again? Maybe you've looked around at the world and thought, "Why does it feel like people are drifting further from God?"

In **Romans 3**, Paul reminds us that this struggle is real—not just for some people, but for *everyone*. In fact, **Psalm 14** and **Psalm 53** say that no one naturally does good on their own. That sounds kind of heavy, but it's not the end of the story. God knows we fall short—and that's exactly why He sent Jesus.

Think About It

1. **The Truth About Us:** According to **Romans 3**, every human heart has a problem—we all fall short of God's perfect standard. This isn't to make us feel hopeless but to help us realize that we *need* God's grace. Are you aware of your need for Him?

2. **A Fool's Mistake:** Both **Psalm 14** and **Psalm 53** describe the person who says in their heart, *"There is no God,"* as a fool—not because they're unintelligent, but because they ignore the One who gives life meaning. Have you ever lived like God wasn't there, even when you believe He is?

3. **Choosing Good on Purpose:** Proverbs 14:22 points out that doing good isn't automatic—it's intentional. When you *choose* what's right, you align with God's love and faithfulness. What are some small but meaningful ways you can choose good today?

Bottom Line

We all fall short, but that doesn't mean we're without hope. God sees our brokenness and sent Jesus so that we could be made right with Him—not by trying harder, but by trusting in Him. When we admit our need for God and follow His lead, He shapes our hearts to seek good and reflect His love.

Prayer

Heavenly Father, Thank You for loving me even when I fall short. I confess that I don't always seek You or choose what's right. Help me to see my need for You and to trust in Your grace more than my own efforts. Teach me to do good on purpose, to live wisely, and to follow You daily. In Jesus' Name, Amen.

April 20

Faith That Works

3-Year-Bible Reading: Proverbs 14:23; Psalm 32; Romans 4

"In all toil there is profit, but mere talk tends only to poverty." — Proverbs 14:23

"Blessed is the one whose transgression is forgiven, whose sin is covered." — Psalm 32:1

"That is why his faith was 'counted to him as righteousness.'" — Romans 4:22

It's easy to talk about doing the right thing—studying for that test, apologizing to a friend, or spending time with God. But just talking doesn't get us anywhere. Proverbs reminds us that only when we *do* the work does it bring any real benefit (**Proverbs 14:23**).

At the same time, **Psalm 32** shows us that while we fall short and mess up, there's freedom and joy in being forgiven by God. And **Romans 4** reminds us that even before we do anything "perfect," what really counts is *faith*. Abraham was called righteous not because he earned it but because he *believed* God.

So, how do these connect? True faith isn't just belief in your head—it shows up in your choices, in the way you speak, act, and even admit when you've messed up. God sees and honors faith that's lived out, not just talked about.

Think About It

1. **Talk vs. Action:** Are there areas where you talk a lot about change, but don't follow through? What small step could you take today to turn intention into action?

2. **Owning Your Mistakes:** Psalm 32 reminds us that hiding sin only weighs us down. What might you need to bring into the light today so you can experience the joy of forgiveness?

3. **Faith That Moves:** Abraham's story in Romans 4 isn't about perfect behavior—it's about trusting God even when it's hard. Where in your life is God calling you to trust Him more deeply?

Bottom Line

Faith isn't just about what we say we believe—it's about trusting God enough to live like it's true. That means taking action, being honest when we fall short, and relying on His forgiveness to keep going.

Prayer

Heavenly Father, Thank You that my worth isn't based on being perfect but on trusting You. Help me to put my faith into action—not just in big things, but in everyday choices. When I mess up, remind me that there is forgiveness in You and joy when I'm honest. Teach me to work with purpose, trust with courage, and walk in the freedom You give. In Jesus' Name, Amen.

April 21

Wise Words & Real Love

3-Year-Bible Reading: Proverbs 14:24–25; Psalm 45; Romans 5

"The crown of the wise is their wealth, but the folly of fools brings folly. A truthful witness saves lives, but one who breathes out lies is deceitful." — Proverbs 14:24–25

"You are the most handsome of the sons of men; grace is poured upon your lips; therefore God has blessed you forever." — Psalm 45:2

"But God shows his love for us in that while we were still sinners, Christ died for us." — Romans 5:8

Life throws a lot of mixed messages at you—be smart, look good, get rich, be cool. But when you pause to look at what God values, it's something deeper. In **Proverbs 14:24–25**, we see that wisdom and truth have lasting worth.

Psalm 45 gives us a poetic image of a royal groom—ultimately pointing to Jesus—whose words overflow with grace. And in **Romans 5**, we read the most mind-blowing truth of all: God loved us at our worst. Not when we had it all together, but when we were still lost, broken, and sinful. That's when Jesus showed up to save us.

The world may try to crown you based on looks, talent, or followers—but God crowns wisdom. He sees truth, grace, and sacrificial love as real greatness. That's the kind of life Jesus modeled, and it's what He invites us into.

Think About It

1. **Real Wealth:** Are you chasing the world's version of success or growing in wisdom that lasts? What kind of "crown" are you building?

2. **Speak Life:** Proverbs says a truthful witness saves lives. Do your words reflect truth and kindness, or are they careless and reactive?

3. **Undeserved Love:** Jesus loved you when you didn't deserve it. How does that change the way you view yourself—and others?

Bottom Line

True greatness isn't about having it all together. It's about receiving God's love and living it out with wisdom, grace, and truth.

Prayer

Heavenly Father, thank You for loving me even when I fall short. Help me to grow in wisdom, speak truth, and reflect the grace of Jesus in my daily life. Show me how to love like You love—without conditions. In Jesus' Name, Amen.

April 22

Fear That Leads to Freedom

3-Year-Bible Reading: Proverbs 14:26–27; Romans 6

"In the fear of the Lord one has strong confidence, and his children will have a refuge. The fear of the Lord is a fountain of life, that one may turn away from the snares of death." — Proverbs 14:26–27

"For the wages of sin is death, but the free gift of God is eternal life in Christ Jesus our Lord." — Romans 6:23

Fear usually feels like something we should run from. Afraid of rejection, failure, or the future—those kinds of fear can trap us. But the Bible talks about a different kind of fear: *the fear of the Lord.* Not fear like being scared of a monster, but a deep awe and respect for who God is.

In **Proverbs 14:26–27**, this fear brings *confidence* and *life*. It helps us avoid the traps of sin. And **Romans 6** reminds us why that matters—because sin leads to death, but God offers a way out through Jesus. Choosing to follow Jesus is choosing freedom. But that freedom doesn't mean doing whatever we want—it means we're finally free to live the way God designed us to: full of purpose, peace, and real joy.

Think About It

1. **Real Confidence Comes from God:** Where are you trying to find your confidence—your looks, your popularity, your talents? Proverbs says that fearing God is where true confidence begins. Why do you think that is?

2. **Freedom Isn't the Same as "No Rules":** Romans 6 talks about being set free *from* sin, not just free *to* sin. How do you think following Jesus gives you more freedom—not less?

3. **Sin Has a Price, but Grace Is Free:** The Bible says sin earns death, but God *gives* eternal life. What does that say about how much God loves you?

Bottom Line

Fearing God isn't about being scared—it's about recognizing His greatness and trusting Him completely. That kind of fear leads to confidence, life, and freedom from sin through Jesus.

Prayer

Heavenly Father, Thank You for loving me enough to offer freedom through Jesus. Help me to truly understand what it means to fear You—to respect You, trust You, and follow You. I don't want to be trapped by sin or fooled by fake freedom. Teach me how to walk in the kind of freedom that leads to life. Help me find my confidence in You alone. In Jesus' Name, Amen.

April 23

Slow to Anger, Strong in Spirit

3-Year-Bible Reading: Proverbs 14:28–29; Psalm 46; Romans 7

"Whoever is slow to anger has great understanding, but he who has a hasty temper exalts folly." —Proverbs 14:29

"God is our refuge and strength, a very present help in trouble. Therefore we will not fear though the earth gives way." —Psalm 46:1–2

"For I do not do the good I want, but the evil I do not want is what I keep on doing." —Romans 7:19

Ever feel like you're fighting a battle inside yourself? One moment you're calm, and the next you're snapping at someone. Or maybe you really want to follow God, but you still mess up in ways that frustrate you. You're not alone.

In **Romans 7**, Paul talks about this exact struggle—the desire to do right but feeling pulled in the opposite direction. And in **Proverbs 14**, we're reminded that being slow to anger is a sign of real strength.

But what happens when you feel weak or overwhelmed? That's where **Psalm 46** steps in, reminding us that God is our strength when everything feels out of control—even when *we* feel out of control.

Think About It

1. **Strong Doesn't Mean Perfect:** Being "slow to anger" doesn't mean you never feel it—it means you learn to pause, reflect, and invite God into that moment instead of reacting on impulse. What helps you pause when you're mad or overwhelmed?

2. **Your Safe Place:** Psalm 46 paints a picture of God as a refuge—your safe place. Where do you go (or what do you do) when life feels like it's falling apart? Are you running *to* God or just running?

3. **The Inner Battle Is Real:** Paul's honesty in Romans 7 shows us that struggling with sin doesn't mean you've failed—it means you're aware and still fighting. How can you ask the Holy Spirit to help you choose what's right, even when it's hard?

Bottom Line

You're not alone in your struggles. God is your strength, even when you feel weak or frustrated. Slow down, breathe, and invite Him into your everyday reactions. Real strength shows up when you let Him lead your heart, especially when emotions rise.

Prayer

Heavenly Father, thank You for being my strength when I feel like a mess inside. Help me to slow down when I get angry, and to turn to You instead of reacting on my own. Teach me to trust You more in the middle of my struggles, and remind me that Your Spirit is always with me, even when I fall short. In Jesus' Name, Amen.

APRIL 24

Peace in the Chaos

3-Year-Bible Reading: Proverbs 14:30–31; Romans 8

"A tranquil heart gives life to the flesh, but envy makes the bones rot. Whoever oppresses a poor man insults his Maker, but he who is generous to the needy honors him." — Proverbs 14:30–31

"There is therefore now no condemnation for those who are in Christ Jesus." — Romans 8:1

"For you did not receive the spirit of slavery to fall back into fear, but you have received the Spirit of adoption as sons, by whom we cry, 'Abba! Father!'" — Romans 8:15

Ever felt like your heart was racing from anxiety, jealousy, or fear of not measuring up? Maybe you're scrolling through social media and comparing your life to someone else's highlight reel. Or maybe you're feeling stuck—burdened by mistakes, regrets, or stress about the future.

In moments like that, **Proverbs 14:30** reminds us that a heart at peace isn't just a nice feeling—it actually brings *life*. And the good news of **Romans 8** is that we don't have to live trapped by guilt, fear, or comparison. Because of Jesus, we are set free from condemnation and given the Spirit who reminds us that we belong to God. That changes everything.

Think About It

1. **Inner Peace Starts with Trust:** Do you believe God loves you no matter what? Romans 8:1 says there is *no condemnation* for those in Christ. Let that truth replace your self-doubt and fear.

2. **Comparison Kills Joy:** Proverbs says envy rots our bones. How has comparison affected your peace lately? What would it look like to choose gratitude over jealousy?

3. **You're Not Alone:** The Holy Spirit helps you live differently—from a place of being known, loved, and accepted. Are you listening to His voice over the noise of the world?

Bottom Line

Peace doesn't come from having it all together. It comes from knowing that, in Jesus, you already belong—and nothing can separate you from God's love.

Prayer

Heavenly Father, thank You for reminding me that peace comes from You. Help me to stop comparing myself to others and to find confidence in who I am in Christ. Thank You for Your Spirit, who comforts and leads me. Fill me with Your peace that gives life to my heart. In Jesus' Name, Amen.

April 25

Anchored in the Storm

3-Year-Bible Reading: Proverbs 14:32–33; Psalm 47; Romans 9

"The wicked is overthrown through his evildoing, but the righteous finds refuge in his death." — Proverbs 14:32

"Clap your hands, all peoples! Shout to God with loud songs of joy! For the Lord, the Most High, is to be feared, a great king over all the earth." — Psalm 47:1–2

"So then it depends not on human will or exertion, but on God, who has mercy." — Romans 9:16

Life can feel chaotic—like when everything you've planned unravels, people misunderstand you, or the pressure to be "enough" feels like too much. In those moments, you might wonder where God is or if He's even paying attention. But the truth found in **Proverbs 14:32, Psalm 47,** and **Romans 9** reminds us that God is not only in control—He is our *refuge*.

Even when it feels like everything is crashing down, He's the One we can trust with our hearts, our mistakes, and our futures. Our hope doesn't depend on being perfect—it depends on God's mercy and power.

Think About It

1. **Where's Your Refuge?** When things get hard, where do you run for comfort—friends, distractions, isolation? Proverbs says the righteous find *refuge* even in death, meaning that trusting in God gives us peace and confidence even in the worst situations.

2. **Celebrate God's Reign:** Psalm 47 invites us to *shout for joy* because God is King over *everything*. What would it look like for you to live like God is truly in charge of your life—especially when it feels like you're not?

3. **God's Mercy, Not Your Performance:** Romans 9 reminds us that our relationship with God isn't about how hard we try or how "good" we are—it's about God's *mercy*. That means you don't have to earn His love. You already have it.

Bottom Line

No matter what storms you face, you can be anchored in God's love, leadership, and mercy. He is your refuge, your King, and the one who chooses you—not because of what you do, but because of who He is.

Prayer

Heavenly Father, thank You for being my refuge when life feels overwhelming. Help me to trust Your mercy more than my own effort, and to remember that You are King even when things feel out of control. Teach me to rest in Your love and live with joy because I belong to You. In Jesus' Name, Amen.

April 26

The Heart That Honors

3-Year-Bible Reading: Proverbs 14:34-35; Romans 10-11

"Righteousness exalts a nation, but sin is a reproach to any people." — Proverbs 14:34

"For the Scripture says, 'Everyone who believes in him will not be put to shame.'" — Romans 10:11

It's easy to get caught up in the excitement of things like popularity, success, and fitting in. But the Bible reminds us that what truly matters is how we honor God with our lives. In **Proverbs 14:34**, we see that righteousness is what elevates a nation or a community—it's the core value that sets us apart and honors God. And in **Romans 10:11**, we're encouraged that when we believe in Jesus, we won't be disappointed. We're called to live in a way that reflects this righteousness, to seek God with a genuine heart.

When we honor God in our choices, we stand out in a world that often values the wrong things. Living with integrity, kindness, and love reflects God's character and draws others to Him. Our actions, words, and attitudes become a testimony of who we belong to and what we believe. So, while the world may focus on outward success, God values the heart that seeks righteousness and truth.

Think About It

1. **Righteousness vs. Sin:** What does it mean to you that "righteousness exalts a nation" and that "sin is a reproach to any people"? How do you see this play out in your life or your community?
2. **True Belief:** How can you make sure that your belief in Jesus is genuine and not just about doing the right things to "fit in"?
3. **The Role of Integrity:** What's one area in your life where you feel God is calling you to be more honest or to honor Him more clearly?

Bottom Line

Living a life that honors God and seeks righteousness is far more valuable than anything the world can offer. It's not about fitting in, but about standing out for Him.

Prayer

Heavenly Father, Thank You for calling me to live a life that honors You. Help me to seek righteousness in everything I do, from the choices I make to the way I treat others. Give me the strength to stand firm in my belief in You, and to reflect Your love and truth in all I say and do. I want to be someone who makes a difference for Your Kingdom. In Jesus' Name, Amen.

April 27

A Soft Answer

3-Year-Bible Reading: Proverbs 15:1-2; Romans 12

"A soft answer turns away wrath, but a harsh word stirs up anger." — Proverbs 15:1

"Do not be overcome by evil, but overcome evil with good." — Romans 12:21

When someone insults us or frustrates us, it's easy to react in anger. It's natural to want to defend ourselves or to strike back, especially when we feel hurt or misunderstood. But **Proverbs 15:1** reminds us that a soft answer can turn away wrath—meaning our words have the power to calm or escalate a situation. The way we speak and respond to others can either diffuse tension or make things worse.

Romans 12:21 challenges us to overcome evil with good, teaching us that responding with kindness and patience instead of fighting back shows the world the love of Christ in us. In tough moments, choosing gentle words and showing kindness can be one of the most powerful ways to reflect Christ.

How often do we let our feelings dictate our reactions? It can be so tempting to respond harshly when we feel disrespected or misunderstood. But these verses remind us that God's way is different. When we choose patience and kindness over anger, we reflect His character. It's not always easy, but God equips us to respond in a way that honors Him and brings peace to the situation.

Think About It

1. **Soft answers matter:** How do you usually respond when someone speaks harshly to you or annoys you? What would a soft answer look like in that moment?
2. **Overcoming with good:** Is there someone in your life who has hurt you, and how could you overcome their bad behavior with kindness or good actions?
3. **Reflection of Christ:** How do your words and actions reflect the love of Christ? In what ways can you be more intentional about showing His love in your interactions?

Bottom Line

God calls us to respond to conflict with kindness, patience, and love. Choosing soft answers instead of harsh words can help bring peace and show others the love of Christ.

Prayer

Heavenly Father, thank You for Your example of kindness and patience. Help me to respond with love when I am tempted to react with anger. Give me the strength to overcome evil with good and to reflect Your love in all my words and actions. In Jesus' Name, Amen.

APRIL 28

Living with Purpose and Peace

3-Year-Bible Reading: Proverbs 15:3-4; Psalm 48; Romans 13

The eyes of the Lord are in every place, keeping watch on the evil and the good. — Proverbs 15:3

Great is the Lord and greatly to be praised in the city of our God! — Psalm 48:1

Let every person be subject to the governing authorities. For there is no authority except from God, and those that exist have been instituted by God. — Romans 13:1

Life can feel like a whirlwind of distractions, decisions, and responsibilities. From school to social media, friendships to family, it's easy to feel overwhelmed. But, the Bible teaches us something crucial: God's presence is constant, and He is watching over us in every moment. In **Proverbs 15:3**, we see that God's eyes are everywhere, observing both the good and the bad. There's nothing we can do that escapes His attention, but rather than feeling intimidated by this, we should find peace in the truth that God is in control. He is with us in every situation, guiding and protecting us. **Psalm 48** takes us to a place of worship and awe, reminding us of God's greatness. The psalmist proclaims that God is greatly to be praised in the city of His people—His presence is so powerful that it fills the entire city with awe. In the midst of life's chaos, we can take time to pause and remember who God is and how worthy He is of our praise.

Then, in **Romans 13**, we are reminded to submit to the authorities that God has put over us. This doesn't mean we blindly follow, but it does mean that God has placed order in the world for a reason. We can trust that God works through the leaders and authorities, even when we don't understand everything happening around us. In all this, we see a powerful truth: God is both near and in control. No matter how loud life gets, He is with us, providing peace in the storm and purpose in the everyday moments.

THINK ABOUT IT

1. **God Sees You:** What does it mean to you personally that God sees both the good and the bad in your life? How does this truth affect the way you live each day?
2. **Praise in the Storm:** In **Psalm 48**, the psalmist praises God even in the midst of challenges. How can you practice praising God when things aren't going your way?
3. **Trusting God's Order:** How can you show respect and trust in the authorities that God has placed in your life, even when you don't agree with everything they do?

BOTTOM LINE

God sees you, He is in control, and He is worthy of your praise. No matter what life throws your way, trust that God is with you, guiding you, and giving you peace.

PRAYER

Heavenly Father, thank You for always being with me, watching over my life, and guiding me with Your wisdom. Help me to trust in Your authority and find peace in Your presence. Teach me to honor You with my actions and my words, especially when life gets difficult. May I always remember that You are great, and You are good. In Jesus' Name, Amen.

APRIL 29

The Things That Really Matter

3-Year-Bible Reading: Proverbs 15:5-6; Psalm 49; Romans 14

"A fool despises his father's instruction, but whoever heeds reproof is prudent." — Proverbs 15:5

"For the ransom of their life is costly and can never suffice, that he should live on forever and never see the pit." — Psalm 49:8

"So then each of us will give an account of himself to God." — Romans 14:12

We all care about what others think of us, whether it's how we look, how much we know, or how successful we seem. But when we focus too much on appearances and worldly things, we can lose sight of what truly matters in God's eyes.

The Bible reminds us in **Proverbs 15:5** that wisdom comes from being open to correction and learning from those who care about us. In **Psalm 49**, we are warned that material wealth and earthly accomplishments can't save us from death or give us eternal life. And in **Romans 14**, we're reminded that our actions are ultimately accountable to God, not to anyone else.

As young people, it's easy to get caught up in the pressure to succeed or impress. Social media, school, and even family expectations can make us feel like we need to be perfect. But the truth is, what matters most isn't what people see on the outside—it's how we live before God. It's about humility, wisdom, and the understanding that our value isn't tied to our achievements or how much we have. We are made in God's image, and He calls us to live for Him and care about what He thinks, not just for others.

Think About It

1. **True Wisdom:** Are you open to correction or advice from others, especially when it might be hard to hear?

2. **Eternal Value:** What things in your life do you focus on that may not have eternal value? How can you shift your focus to what truly matters in God's eyes?

3. **Living for God:** In what areas of your life do you need to remember that you're ultimately accountable to God, not to the opinions of others?

Bottom Line

God cares about our hearts and our relationship with Him. Success, popularity, and material wealth won't last, but how we live for God and serve others will have eternal value.

Prayer

Heavenly Father, thank You for reminding me that my worth isn't tied to what the world values. Help me to focus on what truly matters—following You, learning from others, and living in a way that pleases You. Give me the wisdom to make choices that reflect Your heart, and help me remember that I am ultimately accountable to You. In Jesus' Name, Amen.

April 30

The Power of Words

3-Year-Bible Reading: Proverbs 15:7-9; Romans 15-16

"The lips of the wise spread knowledge; not so the hearts of fools." — Proverbs 15:7 (ESV)

"For whatever was written in former days was written for our instruction, that through the endurance and the encouragement of the Scriptures we might have hope." — Romans 15:4 (ESV)

"Let the word of Christ dwell in you richly, teaching and admonishing one another in all wisdom, singing psalms and hymns and spiritual songs, with thankfulness in your hearts to God." — Colossians 3:16 (ESV)

We've all heard the saying, "Sticks and stones may break my bones, but words will never hurt me." But let's be real—words can hurt. In fact, they can have a deeper impact than any physical wound.

That's why **Proverbs 15** reminds us of the power our words carry: *"The lips of the wise spread knowledge..."* When we speak, we can either bring life and understanding or chaos and confusion.

Romans 15 encourages us to remember why the scriptures exist—to give us hope through the endurance and encouragement they offer. The Bible itself is full of words that can change lives. And just like the scriptures, we, as followers of Christ, are called to use our words in a way that encourages, uplifts, and gives hope to others. Our words are powerful tools, and we are stewards of them.

Think About It

1. **Your Words Matter:** How do the things you say impact the people around you? Do you use your words to build up or tear down?
2. **Encouraging Others:** How can you use your words today to encourage someone? Think about a verse or a kind word you could share that would make someone's day better.
3. **Reflecting Christ:** In what ways can you make sure your words reflect Christ's love and hope? Are there areas where you could improve in being more intentional with your speech?

Bottom Line

Your words have the power to shape hearts and minds, whether for good or bad. Let's use our words to spread knowledge, offer encouragement, and reflect the love of Christ.

Prayer

Heavenly Father, thank You for the power of words and the wisdom in Your Scriptures. Help me to be mindful of what I say and how I say it. May my words always reflect Your love and bring encouragement to those around me. Teach me to use my speech to build up, not tear down. Thank You for the hope You give through Your Word. In Jesus' Name, Amen.

May 1

No Shortcuts to Wisdom

3-Year-Bible Reading: Proverbs 15:10–11; 1 Corinthians 1–2

"There is severe discipline for him who forsakes the way; whoever hates reproof will die. Sheol and Abaddon lie open before the Lord; how much more the hearts of the children of man!" — Proverbs 15:10–11

"For the word of the cross is folly to those who are perishing, but to us who are being saved it is the power of God." — 1 Corinthians 1:18

"Now we have received not the spirit of the world, but the Spirit who is from God, that we might understand the things freely given us by God." — 1 Corinthians 2:12

Ever feel like following God is *harder* than just going with the flow? Like when you know the right thing to do but everything inside you wants to take the shortcut? **Proverbs 15** reminds us that turning away from God's path leads to serious consequences, and avoiding correction is dangerous. But here's the good news—God knows us deeply and offers us a better way.

In **1 Corinthians 1–2**, Paul reminds us that the world might see God's ways as foolish, but to those who believe, it's actually the key to real strength and wisdom. God doesn't just give us a rulebook—He gives us His Spirit to help us understand and live out His truth.

Think About It

1. **Correction is Love:** When someone points out something you need to work on, do you push back or listen? God uses correction not to shame you but to *shape* you.

2. **God's Wisdom Looks Different:** The cross didn't make sense to the world—but it changed everything. Are you okay with following God even when it feels countercultural or misunderstood?

3. **You're Not Alone:** You've been given the Holy Spirit to understand God's truth. What would change if you started asking Him to help you every day?

Bottom Line

God's wisdom may seem upside-down to the world, but it leads to real life. Don't run from correction—lean into it, trust the Spirit, and walk in God's power.

Prayer

Heavenly Father, thank You for loving me enough to correct me and for giving me the Holy Spirit to guide me. Help me not to be stubborn or chase what the world calls "wise," but instead to follow You with humility and courage. Teach me to listen when You speak and to trust that Your way leads to life. In Jesus' Name, Amen.

May 2

Joy Starts with Listening

3-Year-Bible Reading: Proverbs 15:12-13; Psalm 50; 1 Corinthians 3

"A scoffer does not like to be reproved; he will not go to the wise. A glad heart makes a cheerful face, but by sorrow of heart the spirit is crushed." — Proverbs 15:12-13

"Offer to God a sacrifice of thanksgiving, and perform your vows to the Most High, and call upon me in the day of trouble; I will deliver you, and you shall glorify me." — Psalm 50:14-15

"So neither he who plants nor he who waters is anything, but only God who gives the growth." — 1 Corinthians 3:7

Have you ever had a hard time taking advice? Sometimes it feels easier to just do things our way instead of listening to others, especially when it means admitting we need to grow. But **Proverbs 15** shows us that when we're open to wise advice, it actually leads to a happier heart. **Psalm 50** reminds us that God isn't asking for perfection—He's looking for our thankful hearts and our trust when things get tough. And in **1 Corinthians 3**, Paul reminds us that real growth comes from God, not from trying to be impressive or doing it all alone. When we listen, trust, and stay connected to God, He changes us from the inside out.

Think About It

1. **Are you willing to listen?** When someone gives you advice or correction, do you take it seriously or get defensive?

2. **God loves thankful hearts:** How can you make gratitude a regular part of your relationship with God this week?

3. **Remember who grows you:** It's not about being the best—it's about letting God work in you. How can you depend on Him more today?

Bottom Line

Joy and real growth come when we listen to wisdom, stay thankful, and trust God to lead our journey.

Prayer

Heavenly Father, Thank You for loving me even when I don't have it all figured out. Help me to listen to wise advice and not be stubborn. Teach me to have a heart full of gratitude and trust that You are growing me, even when I can't see it right away. I want my life to show Your love and joy to others. In Jesus' Name, Amen.

MAY 3

A Healthy Heart and Humble Service

3-Year-Bible Reading: Proverbs 15:14-15; 1 Corinthians 4

"The heart of him who has understanding seeks knowledge, but the mouths of fools feed on folly. All the days of the afflicted are evil, but the cheerful of heart has a continual feast." — Proverbs 15:14-15

"This is how one should regard us, as servants of Christ and stewards of the mysteries of God. Moreover, it is required of stewards that they be found faithful. But with me it is a very small thing that I should be judged by you or by any human court. In fact, I do not even judge myself. For I am not aware of anything against myself, but I am not thereby acquitted. It is the Lord who judges me." —1 Corinthians 4:1-4

Have you ever noticed that when your heart is in a good place, it's so much easier to stay positive and find joy in the day? But when you're feeling down or your thoughts are stuck on negative things, it can feel like everything is going wrong. **Proverbs 15:14-15** points out that a cheerful heart can experience joy in the midst of struggles, while those who are focused on negativity or foolishness will always feel weighed down.

In **1 Corinthians 4**, Paul teaches us that our lives are not about proving ourselves to others or seeking praise. Instead, we are called to serve humbly as stewards of God's grace, faithfully living out His purposes. Paul reminds us that judgment doesn't come from the opinions of others, but from God alone. This connects with the idea in Proverbs that the heart of the wise seeks knowledge, while the heart of the foolish is distracted by the wrong things. A heart that focuses on God's wisdom will find peace, even when circumstances are tough.

THINK ABOUT IT

1. **Heart of Understanding:** Proverbs says that those with understanding seek knowledge. Are you seeking knowledge that helps you grow in wisdom, or are you distracted by things that don't lead to peace or growth?
2. **The Power of a Cheerful Heart:** Proverbs says that a cheerful heart has a continual feast. How can you shift your focus from negative thoughts to gratitude, even when things are difficult?
3. **Serving Humbly:** In **1 Corinthians 4**, Paul talks about how he doesn't care to be judged by others but seeks to be faithful to God. How do you handle the opinions of others? Do you focus on seeking approval from people, or are you more concerned with pleasing God in your actions?

BOTTOM LINE

A heart focused on God's truth finds joy even in hard times, serving humbly and trusting Him as the ultimate judge. When we live to honor God and love others, His peace and joy fill our lives.

PRAYER

Heavenly Father, Thank You for the wisdom You offer through Your Word. Help me to seek knowledge and understanding that brings me closer to You. I want to be faithful in serving You, not seeking approval from others, but trusting in Your judgment. Please help me to cultivate a cheerful heart, even when life is hard, and to find joy in the midst of struggles. I want to be a faithful steward of the gifts

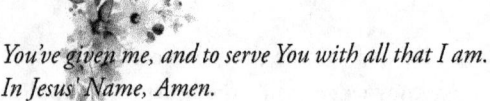
*You've given me, and to serve You with all that I am.
In Jesus' Name, Amen.*

May 4

More Than Stuff

3-Year-Bible Reading: Proverbs 15:16-17; 1 Corinthians 5–6

"Better is a little with the fear of the Lord than great treasure and trouble with it. Better is a dinner of herbs where love is than a fattened ox and hatred with it."— Proverbs 15:16-17

"Your boasting is not good. Do you not know that a little leaven leavens the whole lump?" — 1 Corinthians 5:6

"Or do you not know that your body is a temple of the Holy Spirit within you, whom you have from God? You are not your own." — 1 Corinthians 6:19

Have you ever thought that having more stuff would make life better? Like, if you just had a better phone, more friends, cooler clothes—then you'd really be happy? Proverbs reminds us that real happiness isn't about *what* we have, but *Who* we fear and love: God. In **1 Corinthians 5-6**, Paul talks to a church that got distracted by pride and selfishness, letting sin spread like mold in bread. He reminds them (and us) that our bodies and lives actually belong to God. Real life isn't found in chasing things—it's found in loving God, living purely, and letting His love fill every part of who we are.

Think About It

1. **What really matters:** Would you rather have a lot of "stuff" but feel alone—or a simple life full of real love, friendships, and God's peace?

2. **Be careful of what spreads:** Paul warns that sin doesn't just stay small—it spreads. How can you protect your heart from influences that pull you away from God?

3. **You're God's temple:** How would your choices change if you really believed that God's Spirit lives inside you?

Bottom Line

True peace and joy come from loving God and living for Him, not from chasing after stuff or trying to fit in with the world.

Prayer

Heavenly Father, Thank You for reminding me that my worth isn't found in what I have or what the world says about me. Help me to love You more than anything else. Teach me to live in a way that honors You and shows Your love to others. Protect my heart from anything that would pull me away from You. Thank You for making me Your temple. In Jesus' Name, Amen.

MAY 5

Peace and Purpose in Relationships

3-Year-Bible Reading: Proverbs 15:18-19; 1 Corinthians 7

"A hot-tempered man stirs up strife, but he who is slow to anger quiets contention. The way of a sluggard is like a hedge of thorns, but the path of the upright is a level highway." —Proverbs 15:18-19

"To the unmarried and the widows I say that it is good for them to remain single, as I am. But if they cannot exercise self-control, they should marry. For it is better to marry than to burn with passion." —1 Corinthians 7:8-9 (ESV)

Have you ever been in a situation where someone's anger made everything more complicated? Maybe it was a heated argument with a friend or a family member, or even a time when you reacted in anger, and things escalated quickly. **Proverbs 15:18** reminds us that a hot-tempered person stirs up strife, while someone who is slow to anger helps to bring peace. It's easy to let our emotions take over, but taking a step back and choosing calmness can be a game-changer in any relationship.

In **1 Corinthians 7**, Paul talks about relationships, specifically marriage. He says that being single has its own advantages, as it allows for more focus on serving God without distractions. However, he also acknowledges that not everyone is called to singleness, and for those who struggle with self-control, marriage is a good option. Paul encourages us to make choices based on what will allow us to live in a way that honors God.

THINK ABOUT IT

1. **Anger and Strife:** Proverbs says a hot temper stirs trouble, but calm brings peace. How do your reactions shape your relationships? What might change if you responded with calm instead of anger?

2. **The Gift of Singleness and Marriage:** Paul talks about the advantages of being single and serving God fully, but also acknowledges the reality of desire and passion. How does this balance of perspectives affect the way you view relationships and your own choices in relationships right now?

3. **Choosing Peace and Purpose:** Proverbs and Paul remind us to live with purpose—in our emotions and relationships. How can you choose peace and wisdom with others today?

BOTTOM LINE

Living in peace starts with controlling our anger and making choices that honor God, bringing His peace, joy, and purpose into every part of our lives.

PRAYER

Heavenly Father, Thank You for Your guidance in relationships and in how to handle conflict. Help me to be slow to anger and quick to bring peace into my relationships. Give me wisdom in my choices, whether I am single or in a relationship, and help me to honor You in all I do. Help me to

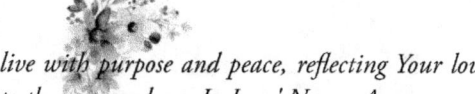
live with purpose and peace, reflecting Your love to those around me. In Jesus' Name, Amen.

May 6

Wisdom in Relationships

3-Year-Bible Reading: Proverbs 15:20-21; 1 Corinthians 8-9

"A wise son makes a glad father, but a foolish man despises his mother. Folly is a joy to him who lacks sense, but a man of understanding walks straight ahead." —Proverbs 15:20-21

"For though I am free from all, I have made myself a servant to all, that I might win more of them. To the Jews I became as a Jew, in order to win Jews. To those under the law I became as one under the law (though not being myself under the law) that I might win those under the law." —1 Corinthians 9:19

In **Proverbs 15:20-21**, we see the difference between someone who seeks wisdom and someone who chooses foolishness. A wise son brings joy to his parents, and a person of understanding walks with purpose. But those who reject wisdom and live recklessly end up stuck in foolishness. In our lives, the choices we make, especially how we treat those around us, impact not only our relationships but also our own personal growth and understanding.

In **1 Corinthians 8-9**, Paul talks about the importance of being willing to adjust our actions and behaviors for the benefit of others, especially when it comes to issues of faith and freedom. Paul explains how he is willing to give up certain rights and freedoms to avoid causing others to stumble in their walk with God. He makes it clear that true freedom in Christ doesn't mean we live for ourselves; instead, it means living in a way that helps others come closer to Christ.

Think About It

1. **Living Wisely in Relationships:** Proverbs says that a wise son makes his father glad and walks in understanding. Think about your relationships with your family, friends, or mentors. How do your actions reflect wisdom or foolishness?

2. **Serving Others for God's Glory:** True freedom in Christ means choosing what helps others grow. How can you put others' needs first in your relationships, school, or community?

3. **Adjusting for the Sake of Others:** In **1 Corinthians 9**, Paul became all things to all people to reach them for Christ. What could that look like in your life? How might your words or actions help others be more open to Jesus?

Bottom Line

Wisdom comes from living for the good of others, helping them grow in faith and bringing glory to God, not just seeking our own enjoyment.

Prayer

Heavenly Father, Thank You for the wisdom You give through Your Word. Help me to live with understanding in all my relationships and to make choices that honor You and build up those around me. Teach me to serve others with love and humility, just as Paul did, and to adjust my behavior for their benefit. Help me to reflect Your heart in everything I do. In Jesus' Name, Amen.

MAY 7

The Power of Wise Counsel and Intentional Living

3-Year-Bible Reading: Proverbs 15:22-23; 1 Corinthians 10

"Without counsel plans fail, but with many advisers they succeed. To make an apt answer is a joy to a man, and a word in season, how good it is!" —Proverbs 15:22-23 (ESV)

"So, whether you eat or drink, or whatever you do, do all to the glory of God." — 1 Corinthians 10:31 (ESV)

Have you ever had an important decision to make and wished you could get a bit of advice? Whether it's choosing a career, deciding on friendships, or handling a tough situation, seeking counsel can make all the difference.

Proverbs 15:22-23 highlights that making decisions without seeking advice is risky, but wise counsel can bring success and joy. It's not just about asking for advice, but knowing that those words can help guide you in the right direction.

In **1 Corinthians 10**, Paul challenges us to live intentionally in everything we do—whether it's as simple as eating or drinking. He says that we should do all things for God's glory. That means every action, even the small ones, can be an opportunity to reflect God's wisdom and love. When we choose to act wisely and with purpose, we honor God and move toward success in our lives.

THINK ABOUT IT

1. **The Power of Counsel:** Proverbs says that plans succeed with good advice. Have you ever made a big decision on your own? What would have been different if you had asked for advice from a trusted friend, mentor, or leader?

2. **Living for God's Glory:** Paul reminds us that everything we do should bring glory to God. How can you change your attitude or actions today to reflect that you're living with God's purposes in mind, even in the small choices you make?

3. **Wisdom in Words:** Proverbs says a timely word brings joy. When has someone's words lifted you? How can you speak wisdom and encouragement to others today?

BOTTOM LINE

Life is full of decisions, big and small, and having the right advice can make all the difference. God invites us to live intentionally and to seek counsel from those who can guide us toward His will. As we live for His glory, we begin to see that our decisions align with His purpose for our lives.

PRAYER

Heavenly Father, Thank You for the people in my life who offer wise counsel. Help me to seek guidance from others and to make decisions that honor You. Teach me to live intentionally and to do all things for Your glory. May my actions, words, and choices reflect Your wisdom and love. In Jesus' Name, Amen.

May 8

Humble Hearts and True Worship

3-Year-Bible Reading: Proverbs 15:24-25; Psalm 51; 1 Corinthians 11

"The path of life leads upward for the prudent, that he may turn away from Sheol beneath. The Lord tears down the house of the proud but maintains the widow's boundaries."—Proverbs 15:24-25

"Create in me a clean heart, O God, and renew a right spirit within me."—Psalm 51:10

"For I received from the Lord what I also delivered to you, that the Lord Jesus on the night when He was betrayed took bread, and when He had given thanks, He broke it and said, 'This is My body, which is for you. Do this in remembrance of Me.'"—1 Corinthians 11:23-24

Have you ever found yourself caught in a moment where you felt like you couldn't quite approach God with a full heart? Maybe you've messed up, and it feels like the weight of your mistakes is pulling you down. **Proverbs 15:24** reminds us that the path of life leads upward for those who choose humility, but the proud are brought down. God values humility over pride, and a humble heart allows us to turn away from destruction and move toward the fullness of life that He offers. In **Psalm 51**, David pours out his heart to God after realizing the weight of his sin. He doesn't try to justify himself or cover up what he did. Instead, he asks God to create a clean heart and renew a right spirit within him. David knows that true restoration comes from God alone. It's not about looking good on the outside; it's about having a heart that is genuinely seeking God's forgiveness and guidance.

In **1 Corinthians 11**, Paul speaks about the importance of the Lord's Supper, which is a moment for believers to remember Jesus' sacrifice. When we come to the table, it's a time for us to reflect, repent, and renew our commitment to Christ. Just like David, we are called to approach God with a humble heart, recognizing our need for His grace. The Lord's Supper isn't just a ritual; it's an opportunity to reconnect with God and let Him transform us.

THINK ABOUT IT

1. **The Pride Trap:** Proverbs says God opposes the proud but honors the humble. Are there areas where pride is leading you? How can you choose humility and follow God's path instead?
2. **A Clean Heart:** David's prayer in Psalm 51 asks God to create a clean heart within him. Is there something you need to ask God to clean up in your heart today?
3. **True Worship:** In 1 Corinthians 11, Paul says the Lord's Supper is about remembering Jesus' sacrifice. Are you coming to God with a heart seeking His forgiveness and peace? What does true worship look like for you?

BOTTOM LINE

True worship begins with a humble heart open to God's forgiveness and transformation, not just outward actions or appearances.

PRAYER

Heavenly Father, Thank You for Your constant grace and forgiveness. I know that I fall short, and sometimes I let pride get in the way of my relationship with You. Please create in me a clean heart, O God, and renew a right spirit within me. Help me to approach You with humility, to seek Your forgiveness, and to worship You with a sincere heart. I want to live in the fullness of life that You offer. In Jesus' Name, Amen.

MAY 9

Building with the Right Foundation

3-Year-Bible Reading: Proverbs 15:26-27; 1 Corinthians 12

"The thoughts of the wicked are an abomination to the Lord, but gracious words are pure. The greedy bring ruin to their households, but the one who hates bribes will live."—Proverbs 15:26-27

"Now there are varieties of gifts, but the same Spirit; and there are varieties of service, but the same Lord; and there are varieties of activities, but it is the same God who empowers them all in everyone."—1 Corinthians 12:4-6

Ever wonder how you can make a difference? Or how you can use your unique talents and abilities in a way that makes a positive impact? **Proverbs 15:26-27** shows us how our words and actions can either build or destroy. Gracious words are pure and pleasing to God, while greed and selfishness bring ruin. If we're seeking to build something meaningful in our lives, we need to start with the right foundation—using words that are kind and actions that are selfless.

In **1 Corinthians 12**, Paul reminds us that we all have different gifts and abilities, but they all come from the same Spirit—God. He's given each of us something unique to contribute to His work. Whether it's serving others, encouraging, teaching, or something else, each of us has a role to play. We're all part of God's big picture, and when we use our gifts to build others up, we reflect His love and grace.

THINK ABOUT IT

1. **Your Words Matter:** Proverbs 15:26-27 tells us that **gracious words** are pure. How do your words impact others? Do you use them to encourage, build up, or tear down?

2. **Unique Gifts for a Greater Purpose:** Just as each part of the body has a unique role in **1 Corinthians 12**, you have a unique gift to use. Have you thought about how you can use your talents, skills, or passions to serve God and others?

3. **Building a Strong Foundation:** Both your words and actions lay the foundation for the life you're building. Are you focusing on things that honor God? How can you shift your mindset or actions today to reflect His love and purpose?

BOTTOM LINE

To build a life that honors God, it's important to start with the right foundation—gracious words and selfless actions. As Paul reminds us in **1 Corinthians 12**, we each have a unique gift to offer, and when we use it to serve others, we reflect God's love and make a positive impact. Let's build wisely with the gifts God has given us!

PRAYER

Heavenly Father, Thank You for the unique gifts You've given me. Help me to use my words and actions in a way that reflects Your love and builds up those around me. I want to honor You with how I serve others, knowing that each gift I have is a blessing from You. Please guide me today in using my talents to make a difference in the world for Your glory. In Jesus' Name, Amen.

May 10

The Power of Thoughtful Words

3-Year-Bible Reading: Proverbs 15:28-29; 1 Corinthians 13

"The heart of the righteous ponders how to answer, but the mouth of the wicked pours out evil things. The Lord is far from the wicked, but he hears the prayer of the righteous." —Proverbs 15:28-29 (ESV)

"If I speak in the tongues of men and of angels, but have not love, I am a noisy gong or a clanging cymbal. And if I have prophetic powers, and understand all mysteries and all knowledge, and if I have all faith, so as to remove mountains, but have not love, I am nothing." —1 Corinthians 13:1-2 (ESV)

Words are powerful. They can build someone up or tear them down. Have you ever said something without thinking and immediately regretted it? Maybe it was a comment you thought was funny but hurt someone, or you spoke in anger without considering how it would affect the other person.

Proverbs 15:28-29 shows us that the righteous person thinks carefully before speaking, while the wicked just let harmful words fly. What's inside of us—our hearts—determines what comes out of our mouths.

In **1 Corinthians 13**, Paul challenges us to understand that love is the true power behind our words and actions. Without love, even the most impressive speech or talents are meaningless. No matter how great your skills, knowledge, or faith might be, without love, it's like being a noisy distraction—like a clanging cymbal that just annoys everyone around you.

Paul reminds us that the heart matters. Just as Proverbs teaches us to think carefully before speaking, Paul teaches that love is the driving force behind everything we do. We can be the most gifted person, but without love, those gifts will not make a lasting impact.

THINK ABOUT IT

1. **Words with Impact:** Proverbs tells us that the righteous think before speaking, and God listens to their prayers. How can you be more thoughtful with your words today?

2. **Love Over Everything:** In **1 Corinthians 13**, Paul says love is the most important thing. Think about a time you acted in love, even when it was hard. How did that affect others around you?

3. **What's Inside Comes Out:** Our words reflect what's going on inside. Do you ever find yourself saying things you regret? How can you start to fill your heart with love and wisdom so that your words reflect that?

BOTTOM LINE

Our words can build up or break down—so let love be the foundation. When we speak with love, our words can heal and lift others. Today, pause and make sure your words reflect God's love.

PRAYER

Heavenly Father, Thank You for the gift of speech and for the power of words. Help me to be thoughtful in what I say and to let love guide my conversations. Please fill my heart with love so that I can speak words that bring encouragement and peace. Help me to reflect Your love in everything I do. In Jesus' Name, Amen.

MAY 11

The Power of Words and Wisdom

3-Year-Bible Reading: Proverbs 15:30-31; Psalm 52; 1 Corinthians 14

"The light of the eyes rejoices the heart, and good news refreshes the bones. The ear that listens to life-giving reproof will dwell among the wise." —Proverbs 15:30-31

"Why do you boast of evil, O mighty man? The steadfast love of God endures all the day. Your tongue plots destruction, like a sharp razor, you worker of deceit." —Psalm 52:1

"For God is not a God of confusion but of peace. As in all the churches of the saints, the women should keep silent in the churches. For they are not permitted to speak, but should be in submission, as the Law also says." —1 Corinthians 14:33-34

Have you ever said something that you instantly regretted? Maybe it was a hurtful comment or a harsh word spoken in anger. **Proverbs 15:30** says that "good news refreshes the bones," reminding us that the right words can bring life and joy, while the wrong ones can cause pain. Words have the power to build others up or tear them down, and in the moment, it can feel like it's just a quick reaction. But the truth is, what we say matters more than we think.

In **Psalm 52**, David speaks about the evil of those who use their words to plot destruction, boasting in their deceit. He paints a picture of someone using their words as a weapon, a sharp razor, cutting down others for personal gain. It's a reminder that our words can either reflect God's love or be used for destruction. We must choose to speak in ways that honor God and build others up, not tear them down.

In **1 Corinthians 14**, Paul gives instructions about orderly worship, emphasizing that **peace** and **order** are essential when believers gather. God doesn't want confusion—He desires unity. In the same way, our words should promote peace and clarity. When we speak in love and with wisdom, we reflect God's character. When we're quick to speak or act in anger, we risk causing division and confusion.

THINK ABOUT IT

1. **Words as Life or Death:** Proverbs says the wise receive life-giving correction. Have you ever grown from being challenged? How can you respond more wisely next time?

2. **Power to Harm:** Psalm 52 shows how words can destroy. Have you hurt someone with your words? How can you speak with more kindness, even when upset?

3. **Promoting Peace:** 1 Corinthians 14 reminds us God values peace. How can your words bring peace today? Is there someone you need to make things right with?

BOTTOM LINE

Our words have the power to heal or hurt, and when we speak with wisdom, kindness, and love, we reflect God's character and build others up.

PRAYER

Heavenly Father, Thank You for the gift of words and for the opportunity to speak life into others. Help me to be mindful of the things I say and to choose my words carefully. May I use my words to encourage, heal, and bring peace, not to hurt or destroy. When

I need correction, give me a heart that is willing to listen and learn. Help me to reflect Your love in everything I say. In Jesus' Name, Amen.

MAY 12

The Wisdom of Humility and the Victory of Resurrection

3-Year-Bible Reading: Proverbs 15:32-33; 1 Corinthians 15

"Whoever ignores instruction despises himself, but whoever listens to reproof gains intelligence. The fear of the Lord is instruction in wisdom, and humility comes before honor."—Proverbs 15:32-33

"But in fact Christ has been raised from the dead, the firstfruits of those who have fallen asleep. For as by a man came death, by a man has come also the resurrection of the dead." — 1 Corinthians 15:20-21 (ESV)

We all want to be successful, and we often look for shortcuts to get ahead. It's tempting to ignore advice or feel like we don't need to listen to anyone. But **Proverbs 15:32-33** reminds us that humility and a willingness to learn lead to wisdom and honor. If we reject correction, we're only hurting ourselves, but if we humble ourselves and listen, we grow in understanding.

Humility isn't just about accepting correction—it's also about recognizing that we don't have all the answers and being open to the wisdom of others. The fear of the Lord—a deep respect for God—leads us to wisdom, and humility is the path that leads to honor.

In **1 Corinthians 15**, Paul reminds us of the ultimate victory that comes through Jesus' resurrection. Death entered the world because of sin, but through Jesus' death and resurrection, we have hope beyond the grave. Jesus is the "firstfruits" of the resurrection, showing us that death doesn't have the final word. Just as humility comes before honor, death was followed by resurrection—proof that God's plan brings victory from what seems like defeat.

THINK ABOUT IT

1. **Learning from Correction:** Proverbs warns that ignoring correction hurts us. When have you resisted advice? How can you grow by staying open to correction?
2. **Fear of the Lord:** Wisdom starts with reverence for God. How does that shape your decisions? Where do you need more humility and trust in His wisdom?
3. **Victory in Christ:** 1 Corinthians 15 celebrates Jesus' victory over death. How does that truth impact your daily life and choices?

BOTTOM LINE

Humility and wisdom go hand in hand. When we listen to correction and live in the fear of the Lord, we grow in understanding and honor. And just as Jesus' resurrection brought victory over death, we can experience the victory He offers in our lives. Humble yourself, learn from God, and walk in the victory He has already won for you.

PRAYER

Heavenly Father, Thank You for Your wisdom and for teaching me that humility leads to honor. Help me to listen to correction and grow in wisdom, always seeking Your guidance. Thank You for the victory that Jesus' resurrection brings, and help me to live today with the hope and confidence that I am victorious in Him. In Jesus' Name, Amen.

May 13

True Wisdom, Genuine Faith, and Steadfast Service

3-Year-Bible Reading: Proverbs 15:33; Psalm 53; 1 Corinthians 16

"The fear of the Lord is instruction in wisdom, and humility comes before honor." —Proverbs 15:33

"The fool says in his heart, 'There is no God.' They are corrupt, doing abominable iniquity; there is none who does good." —Psalm 53:1

"Be watchful, stand firm in the faith, act like men, be strong. Let all that you do be done in love." —1 Corinthians 16:13-14

Have you ever met someone who seems to have everything figured out, but they just can't seem to make wise choices? Or someone who rejects God and insists on going their own way? **Proverbs 15:33** reminds us that true wisdom comes from the fear of the Lord—a deep respect and reverence for God. This wisdom leads us to humility and honor, but without that foundation, we're left wandering aimlessly, just like the person described in **Psalm 53**.

Psalm 53 warns us about the foolishness of denying God's existence. The world may say there is no God, but for those who know Him, we recognize that denying Him leads to emptiness and moral failure. The psalmist points out that those who turn away from God fall into sin and corruption. It's a reminder that without God, we have no true guide for our lives.

Then, in **1 Corinthians 16**, Paul gives instructions to the church to be steadfast in faith, to be strong, and to act with love in all things. It's a call to stand firm, to not be swayed by the distractions or pressures of the world. This ties in perfectly with the wisdom we gain from Proverbs: when we fear the Lord, we build our lives on a solid foundation that helps us remain strong, act honorably, and be courageous in following God's ways.

Think About It

1. **The Foundation of Wisdom:** Proverbs tells us that wisdom begins with the fear of the Lord. What does it look like in your life to "fear the Lord"? How can you make God the foundation of your decisions, actions, and relationships?

2. **Foolishness of Denying God:** Psalm 53 warns about the foolishness of those who say there is no God. How does this challenge you in a world that often denies God's existence? How can you stand firm in your faith and point others toward God's truth?

3. **Steadfast Faith in Action:** In **1 Corinthians 16**, Paul encourages believers to be strong and act with love. How can you apply this to your life as a teen? Are there areas where you need to stand firm in your faith, even when it's difficult or unpopular? How can you show God's love in the way you act and speak?

Bottom Line

True wisdom starts with honoring God and trusting Him, giving us the strength, courage, and love to boldly live out our faith.

Prayer

Heavenly Father, Thank You for the wisdom You offer through Your Word. Help me to grow in my fear and respect for You, so that I can make wise choices in my life. Strengthen my faith and help me stand firm in You, even when the world around me tries to pull me away. May all that I do be done in love, and may my life reflect Your honor and truth. In Jesus' Name, Amen.

May 14

Planned, But Not Perfect

3-Year-Bible Reading: Proverbs 16:1; 2 Corinthians 1–2

"The plans of the heart belong to man, but the answer of the tongue is from the Lord." — Proverbs 16:1

"For all the promises of God find their Yes in him. That is why it is through him that we utter our Amen to God for his glory." — 2 Corinthians 1:20

"Now if anyone has caused pain… you should rather turn to forgive and comfort him, or he may be overwhelmed by excessive sorrow." — 2 Corinthians 2:5,7

Have you ever made a plan that totally fell apart? Maybe you studied hard for a test and still didn't get the grade you hoped for. Or you planned a big moment—like saying something important to a friend—and it didn't come out right. That can be so frustrating.

But **Proverbs 16:1** reminds us that even when we make plans, it's God who ultimately directs what happens. And in **2 Corinthians 1**, Paul teaches that all of God's promises are trustworthy—even when things go sideways. In **chapter 2**, he also reminds us that when others mess up, forgiveness matters just as much as planning ahead.

Think About It

1. **God's Direction Over Our Plans:** What's something you've planned recently? Did it go as expected? How might trusting God more with your plans give you peace, even when things change?

2. **God's Promises Are Steady:** When Paul says that all of God's promises are "Yes" in Christ, what promise from God do you need to cling to today?

3. **Grace for Others:** Paul encourages forgiveness instead of piling on guilt. Is there someone you might need to show compassion to, even if they've hurt you?

Bottom Line

You can make plans—and you should—but trust that God sees the whole picture. His promises never fail, and His grace isn't just for you; it's for you to share with others too.

Prayer

Heavenly Father, thank You for reminding me that while I can make plans, You are the one who guides the outcome. Help me trust in Your promises, even when life doesn't go the way I expect. Teach me to be gracious and forgiving, just like You are with me. Let my plans be surrendered to You and my heart always open to Your direction. In Jesus' Name, Amen.

May 15

Heart Check

3-Year-Bible Reading: Proverbs 16:2; Psalm 54; 2 Corinthians 3

"All the ways of a man are pure in his own eyes, but the Lord weighs the spirit." — Proverbs 16:2

"Behold, God is my helper; the Lord is the upholder of my life." — Psalm 54:4

"Not that we are sufficient in ourselves to claim anything as coming from us, but our sufficiency is from God." — 2 Corinthians 3:5

We all want to believe we're doing okay—maybe even great. We like to think our motives are right, our choices are good, and our hearts are in the right place. But **Proverbs 16:2** reminds us that just because something seems right to *us* doesn't mean it's actually right in God's eyes. He sees what's under the surface—our thoughts, intentions, and the stuff we don't post online. That can feel intense, but it's not meant to shame us. It's meant to *free* us.

When we feel overwhelmed by the pressure to be enough or do everything perfectly, **Psalm 54** brings comfort: God is our helper. He doesn't leave us to figure things out alone. And in **2 Corinthians 3**, Paul reminds us that we don't have to be "sufficient" on our own—our strength, value, and ability come *from God*. That's where real confidence and freedom begin.

Think About It

1. **Check Your Motives:** Why do you do what you do—especially when no one is watching? Ask God to reveal what's really going on in your heart.

2. **Admit the Pressure:** Do you ever feel like you're not enough or like you have to keep proving yourself? Remember, your *sufficiency is from God*—not your grades, your popularity, or your performance.

3. **Let God Be Your Helper:** What would change if you actually believed that God was the "upholder of your life"? Would you stress less? Would you pray more?

Bottom Line

God sees your heart, helps you when you feel weak, and reminds you that your worth doesn't come from your own strength—but from Him.

Prayer

Heavenly Father, thank You for seeing my heart, even when I'm confused about what's going on inside. Help me not to rely on my own understanding or chase approval, but to trust that You are my helper and that You are enough for me. Search my heart and lead me in Your truth. In Jesus' Name, Amen.

MAY 16

Fully Committed

3-Year-Bible Reading: Proverbs 16:3; 2 Corinthians 4

"Commit your work to the Lord, and your plans will be established." — Proverbs 16:3

"So we do not lose heart. Though our outer self is wasting away, our inner self is being renewed day by day. For this light momentary affliction is preparing for us an eternal weight of glory beyond all comparison." — 2 Corinthians 4:16-17

Have you ever felt like you're working really hard at something—school, friendships, sports—but still not seeing the results you hoped for? It's frustrating when your plans fall apart, especially when you're giving it your all.

Proverbs 16:3 gives us a huge piece of wisdom: God doesn't just want our effort—He wants our commitment. And 2 Corinthians 4 reminds us that even when things are tough or slow to change, God is working *in* us, renewing us and building something that lasts forever.

When we give our work and our hearts fully to Him, He transforms it into something way more meaningful than we could on our own.

THINK ABOUT IT

1. **What does it mean to "commit"?** It's more than just asking God to "bless" what you're doing. Committing means trusting Him with the outcome, even when things don't go how you planned.

2. **God's perspective is bigger than ours:** Paul calls our troubles "light and momentary"—not because they're easy, but because God is doing something eternal through them. What's something you're going through right now that might feel different if you saw it from God's view?

3. **God renews us daily:** Life wears us down, but God promises renewal from the inside out. Are you letting Him strengthen your inner self, or are you trying to power through on your own?

BOTTOM LINE

When you commit your work, dreams, and struggles to God, He doesn't just fix your plans—He forms your heart. What feels heavy or hard now is preparing something amazing in you that will last forever.

PRAYER

Heavenly Father, Thank You for seeing the big picture when I can't. Help me to commit all I do to You—not just the big stuff, but everything. When I feel like quitting or when things don't go my way, remind me that You're still at work in me. Teach me to trust You with both the process and the outcome. Renew my heart every day so I can walk with purpose and peace. In Jesus' Name, Amen.

MAY 17

God's Purpose in the Pain

3-Year-Bible Reading: Proverbs 16:4; Psalm 55; 2 Corinthians 5

"The Lord has made everything for its purpose, even the wicked for the day of trouble." — Proverbs 16:4

"Cast your burden on the Lord, and he will sustain you; he will never permit the righteous to be moved." — Psalm 55:22

"Therefore, if anyone is in Christ, he is a new creation. The old has passed away; behold, the new has come." — 2 Corinthians 5:17

Let's be real—life can feel like a mess sometimes. Maybe you've dealt with betrayal from a friend like David describes in **Psalm 55**, or you've wondered why things seem so unfair. You might even question if there's a purpose behind the pain you're feeling.

But here's the truth: **Proverbs 16:4** reminds us that God has a purpose for *everything*—even the hard stuff. When life feels overwhelming, **2 Corinthians 5:17** is a game-changer. In Christ, we're not stuck in the past or defined by what's been done to us. We are made new, with a fresh start and a purpose. No matter what you're going through, you're never without hope—and never alone.

THINK ABOUT IT

1. **God Has a Plan:** How does knowing that *everything* has a purpose help you trust God even when life doesn't make sense?
2. **You Can Trust Him with Your Pain:** What burdens are you carrying right now? Have you truly "cast" them onto God, or are you still holding on?
3. **You Are Not Who You Were:** When you feel stuck in guilt, shame, or regret, how can remembering that you are a "new creation" in Christ help you walk in freedom?

BOTTOM LINE

Even when life feels confusing or unfair, God is still working out His perfect purpose. You can trust Him with your pain because He's making something new in you through it all.

PRAYER

Heavenly Father, sometimes I don't understand why things happen the way they do. But I believe You have a purpose, even when I can't see it. Help me to cast my burdens on You and trust that You will carry me through. Remind me that I am a new creation in Christ, made for Your glory. Give me strength, peace, and hope as I walk through every season. In Jesus' Name, Amen.

May 18

Pride, Grace, and a Changed Heart

3-Year-Bible Reading: Proverbs 16:5–6; 2 Corinthians 6–7

"Everyone who is arrogant in heart is an abomination to the Lord; be assured, he will not go unpunished. By steadfast love and faithfulness iniquity is atoned for, and by the fear of the Lord one turns away from evil." — Proverbs 16:5–6

"We put no obstacle in anyone's way, so that no fault may be found with our ministry… as sorrowful, yet always rejoicing; as poor, yet making many rich; as having nothing, yet possessing everything." — 2 Corinthians 6:3, 10

"For godly grief produces a repentance that leads to salvation without regret, whereas worldly grief produces death." — 2 Corinthians 7:10

Sometimes we wear a mask—trying to seem like we've got it all together, that we're strong, confident, maybe even a little better than others. But **Proverbs 16:5** reminds us that pride isn't something God overlooks. It's not just a bad attitude—it's a heart condition that separates us from Him. The good news? God doesn't leave us stuck there.

Proverbs 16:6 shows us the way back: love, faithfulness, and reverent respect for God. In **2 Corinthians 6–7**, Paul shares how real change happens—not through shame, but through godly sorrow that leads to repentance. God isn't after fake perfection. He's after a real, humble, surrendered heart that's willing to be changed.

Think About It

1. **Pride vs. Humility:** What are some ways pride can quietly sneak into your thoughts or actions? How can choosing humility open the door for God's grace?

2. **Godly Grief = Real Change:** Have you ever felt genuinely sorry for something because you knew it hurt your relationship with God—not just because you got caught? That's godly sorrow. It leads to freedom and transformation.

3. **What Are You Clinging To?** Paul said he had "nothing, yet possessed everything" (**2 Corinthians 6:10**). What things are you holding tightly to that may be getting in the way of truly depending on God?

Bottom Line

God isn't looking for perfect people—He's looking for hearts willing to be honest, humbled, and transformed by His love. Real strength comes when we let go of pride and let God reshape us.

Prayer

Heavenly Father, I confess that sometimes pride creeps into my heart. I try to handle things on my own or pretend I'm fine when I'm not. Help me to turn to You with a humble heart, to be real about where I've messed up, and to trust Your love to guide me. Thank You for grace that changes me from the inside out. Make me more like You. In Jesus' Name, Amen.

May 19

When Peace and Purpose Collide

3-Year-Bible Reading: Proverbs 16:7; Psalm 56; 2 Corinthians 8–9

"When a man's ways please the Lord, he makes even his enemies to be at peace with him." — Proverbs 16:7

"When I am afraid, I put my trust in you. In God, whose word I praise, in God I trust; I shall not be afraid. What can flesh do to me?" — Psalm 56:3–4

"Each one must give as he has decided in his heart, not reluctantly or under compulsion, for God loves a cheerful giver." — 2 Corinthians 9:7

Life is full of moments where we feel unsure, afraid, or even misunderstood. Maybe you've had a fight with a friend, been left out of a group, or struggled with doing the right thing when it wasn't popular.

In **Psalm 56**, David pours out his fears but keeps choosing to trust God. **Proverbs 16:7** reminds us that when we live to please God, He can even calm tensions with people who don't like us. And in **2 Corinthians 8–9**, Paul talks about generosity—how giving with joy reflects a heart that trusts in God's goodness. These passages together show how trusting God leads to peace, courage, and a heart that wants to give.

Think About It

1. **Pleasing God Over People:** Are you more focused on what people think of you or what God thinks? Pleasing God can bring unexpected peace in difficult relationships.

2. **Faith Over Fear:** What's something you're afraid of right now? Like David, you can bring your fear to God and still choose to trust Him.

3. **Giving With Joy:** Do you see giving as a chore or a joy? God doesn't just look at what we give—but how we give. A generous heart reflects a heart full of trust.

Bottom Line

When you trust God with your fears, relationships, and resources, He can turn anxiety into courage, conflict into peace, and giving into joy.

Prayer

Heavenly Father, thank You for being trustworthy and good. Help me to live in a way that pleases You—even when it's hard. Teach me to trust You when I'm afraid, and give generously with joy, knowing You are my provider and peace. In Jesus' Name, Amen.

MAY 20

Better With Less

3-Year-Bible Reading: Proverbs 16:8; 2 Corinthians 10–11

"Better is a little with righteousness than great revenues with injustice." — Proverbs 16:8

"Let the one who boasts, boast in the Lord." — 2 Corinthians 10:17

"And no wonder, for even Satan disguises himself as an angel of light." — 2 Corinthians 11:14

Have you ever felt pressured to prove yourself—maybe by getting more likes, impressing certain people, or standing out in a crowd? Our world shouts that "more" means "better." But the Bible challenges that idea.

Proverbs 16:8 reminds us that having a little with integrity is actually better than having a lot through shady means. **2 Corinthians 10–11** shows Paul defending his ministry, not by bragging about his success, but by pointing to God's strength in his weakness. He even warns that things aren't always what they seem—Satan himself can show up looking like something good. That's why it's so important to stay anchored in truth and live with godly character, not just outward success.

THINK ABOUT IT

1. **What Really Matters?** Are you chasing what looks impressive or what is truly right in God's eyes? Remember, *a little with righteousness* is worth more to God than a lot gained the wrong way.

2. **Who Gets the Credit?** When people compliment you, do you give credit to God or try to boost your image? Paul said, *"Let the one who boasts, boast in the Lord."* That's a mindset shift we all need.

3. **Don't Be Fooled by Appearances:** Not everything that *looks* good is *actually* good. Satan disguises himself as an angel of light. Are you paying attention to what's truly from God?

BOTTOM LINE

God cares more about *how* you live than *how much* you have. When you live with honesty, humility, and a heart that points back to Him, you're already winning.

PRAYER

Heavenly Father, Help me to choose what is right, even when it's not popular or flashy. Teach me to value integrity over attention and faithfulness over fame. I want to live a life that brings You honor and not just one that impresses others. Help me recognize what's truly from You and not be fooled by what only looks good. In Jesus' Name, Amen.

MAY 21

Direction in the Detour

3-Year-Bible Reading: Proverbs 16:9; Psalm 57; 2 Corinthians 12–13

"The heart of man plans his way, but the Lord establishes his steps." — Proverbs 16:9

"God will send out his steadfast love and his faithfulness!" — Psalm 57:3b

"For the sake of Christ, then, I am content with weaknesses, insults, hardships, persecutions, and calamities. For when I am weak, then I am strong." — 2 Corinthians 12:10

Ever make a plan that totally fell apart? You studied hard but didn't make the grade. You trained for months but didn't make the team. You thought things were finally looking up, and then… they weren't. That can be frustrating—especially when you feel like you're doing everything right.

But **Proverbs 16:9** reminds us that while we can make plans, it's God who ultimately guides our steps. Even when it looks like everything's going sideways, God isn't lost or confused. He's faithful—**Psalm 57** says He sends out His steadfast love to meet us where we are. And Paul reminds us in **2 Corinthians 12** that sometimes our weakness is exactly where God's power shows up best.

Think About It

1. **Whose Plan Wins?** Are you willing to trust God's plan even when it doesn't match your own? Proverbs 16:9 reminds us that He sees the bigger picture we can't.

2. **Pain with Purpose:** Paul's "thorn" in 2 Corinthians wasn't removed, but God used it to show His strength. What hardship might God be using in your life to grow your faith?

3. **Praise in the Waiting:** In Psalm 57, David praises God *before* he's rescued. What would it look like for you to worship even while you're still in the middle of the mess?

Bottom Line

God isn't thrown off by detours. His love, power, and purpose remain steady—even when life doesn't go the way you planned. Trust that His steps are better than your schedule.

Prayer

Heavenly Father, help me trust You when my plans don't work out. Teach me to lean on You in weakness, to praise You in uncertainty, and to follow You even when the path isn't clear. Show me how You're working in the middle of my mess, and give me strength to walk with You. In Jesus' Name, Amen.

May 22

Following the Right Voice

3-Year-Bible Reading: Proverbs 16:10–15; Galatians 1–2

"An oracle is on the lips of a king; his mouth does not sin in judgment." — Proverbs 16:10

"For am I now seeking the approval of man, or of God? Or am I trying to please man? If I were still trying to please man, I would not be a servant of Christ." — Galatians 1:10

"I have been crucified with Christ. It is no longer I who live, but Christ who lives in me." — Galatians 2:20

It's not always easy to know who to listen to. Your friends say one thing, social media says another, and sometimes, even adults can contradict each other. In **Proverbs 16:10–15**, we're reminded that true leadership comes from wisdom rooted in righteousness.

Meanwhile, in **Galatians 1–2**, Paul shares how he stopped living to impress others and started living to honor Christ. He knew that if he wanted to serve God faithfully, he couldn't let popular opinion control him. That's something we all face—choosing whose voice we follow.

Think About It

1. **Approval vs. Truth:** Who are you trying to impress—God or people? Take a moment to reflect on **Galatians 1:10**. What does it look like for you to live to please God today?

2. **Living with Purpose:** Paul says, *"It is no longer I who live, but Christ who lives in me"* (Galatians 2:20). What are some ways you can let Jesus lead your thoughts, words, and decisions this week?

3. **Wise Influence:** Proverbs 16 reminds us that leaders are meant to speak and act with justice. Whether you're leading in school, youth group, or at home, how can your words reflect God's wisdom?

Bottom Line

Don't let pressure from others steer your life. Like Paul, choose to live for the One who gave everything for you. When Jesus lives in you, you don't have to prove yourself—you just have to follow Him.

Prayer

Heavenly Father, Help me to stop chasing approval from others and start listening to Your voice above all. I want to be someone who lives with wisdom, courage, and truth. Teach me to follow Jesus more closely and let His life be seen in me. In Jesus' Name, Amen.

May 23

More Valuable Than Gold

3-Year-Bible Reading: Proverbs 16:16–17; Galatians 3–4

"How much better to get wisdom than gold! To get understanding is to be chosen rather than silver. The highway of the upright turns aside from evil; whoever guards his way preserves his life." — Proverbs 16:16–17

"So then, the law was our guardian until Christ came, in order that we might be justified by faith." — Galatians 3:24

"So you are no longer a slave, but a son, and if a son, then an heir through God." — Galatians 4:7

Ever feel like you have to earn your worth—whether it's getting perfect grades, being noticed on social media, or proving yourself to your friends or family? It's easy to chase things that the world tells us matter—like popularity, money, or success—but **Proverbs 16:16–17** reminds us that wisdom and understanding are *way* more valuable than all that.

In **Galatians 3–4**, Paul explains that we are no longer trying to earn our place with God through rules. Instead, we are welcomed into His family by faith. You're not just someone trying to measure up—you're God's child, deeply loved and accepted. That truth can change everything about how you live and what you chase after.

Think About It

1. **What Are You Chasing?** Are you more focused on gaining popularity, money, or stuff—or growing in wisdom and understanding? What would it look like to make God's wisdom your top priority?

2. **Faith Over Rules:** Galatians teaches that we're justified by faith, not by following a bunch of religious rules. Do you ever feel like you need to "do more" to be right with God? How does knowing you're accepted by faith change that?

3. **Know Your Identity:** If you truly believed you were God's child and heir (Galatians 4:7), how would that affect your self-worth and the choices you make every day?

Bottom Line

You don't have to earn God's love or your place in His family. In Christ, you are already a beloved child and heir. Choose wisdom over worldly success, and live like someone who knows they belong.

Prayer

Heavenly Father, thank You that I don't have to earn Your love. Help me to value wisdom more than anything the world offers. Teach me to trust in faith, not in trying to be perfect. Remind me daily that I am Your child and heir, and help me to live like it—with confidence, love, and purpose. In Jesus' Name, Amen.

May 24

Stumbling Blocks & Stepping Stones

3-Year-Bible Reading: Proverbs 16:18; Psalms 58; Galatians 5

"Pride goes before destruction, and a haughty spirit before a fall." — Proverbs 16:18

"The wicked are estranged from the womb; they go astray from birth, speaking lies." — Psalm 58:3

"But the fruit of the Spirit is love, joy, peace, forbearance, kindness, goodness, faithfulness, gentleness, and self-control. Against such things there is no law." — Galatians 5:22-23

Have you ever had a moment when you felt unstoppable, maybe because of your talents or accomplishments? It's easy to let that feeling of confidence turn into pride. **Proverbs 16:18** warns us about the danger of pride, which can cause us to stumble. When we think we're above others or better than we truly are, we can set ourselves up for a fall.

In **Psalm 58**, we're reminded that sin is a part of human nature, starting from birth. It's not just about big acts of rebellion—it's also in the smaller, subtle ways we hurt others or make decisions apart from God. But here's the good news: we don't have to stay stuck in sin.

Galatians 5:22-23 tells us about the fruit of the Spirit—qualities like love, peace, and kindness—that can transform our hearts. When we allow the Holy Spirit to guide us, He helps us rise above the stumbles of pride and selfishness.

Think About It

1. **Pride Check:** Are there areas in your life where pride might be influencing your thoughts or actions? How can you humble yourself and seek God's guidance?
2. **True Transformation:** The fruit of the Spirit is a result of God's work in us. Which of these traits do you want to grow more in your life? How can you invite the Holy Spirit to help you with that?
3. **Lies We Believe: Psalm 58** talks about how lying is a natural part of our human nature. Are there lies or half-truths you've believed about yourself or others that need to be replaced with God's truth?

Bottom Line

Pride can cause us to stumble, but God offers us a better way through the Holy Spirit, who helps us grow in love, joy, and self-control.

Prayer

Heavenly Father, thank You for reminding me that pride leads to destruction, but with Your help, I can live differently. I ask You to help me grow the fruit of Your Spirit in my life, so that I can love others and honor You in everything I do. Keep me humble and open to Your guidance, and help me replace any lies with Your truth. In Jesus' Name, Amen.

May 25

Humble Paths & Heavy Burdens

3-Year-Bible Reading: Proverbs 16:19-20; Psalms 59; Galatians 6

"It is better to be of a lowly spirit with the poor than to divide the spoil with the proud." — Proverbs 16:19

"Deliver me from my enemies, O my God; protect me from those who rise up against me." — Psalm 59:1

"Bear one another's burdens, and so fulfill the law of Christ." — Galatians 6:2

There's something powerful about humility. In **Proverbs 16:19**, we're reminded that it's better to have a humble heart and walk alongside those who are struggling than to live with pride and selfish ambition. But why is that? Humility opens the door to serving others and connecting with them on a deeper level. On the flip side, pride often leads us to want recognition or rewards that are empty and fleeting.

In **Psalm 59**, David calls out to God for deliverance from those who are against him, showing us that when life gets tough and people turn against us, it's okay to ask God for help. Finally, in **Galatians 6:2**, Paul encourages us to carry each other's burdens—whether that's emotional, physical, or spiritual struggles. This is what it means to love others as Christ loved us.

Think About It

1. **Humility vs. Pride:** Are you more likely to lift others up or try to get ahead of them? How can you embrace humility and avoid the trap of pride in your daily life?
2. **Dealing with Opposition:** When you face opposition or feel like people are against you, how do you usually respond? How can you turn to God for strength and guidance in those moments?
3. **Helping Others:** What burdens do the people around you carry? How can you practically help lighten their load and show Christ's love to them?

Bottom Line

Humility leads to peace and connection with others, while pride can isolate us. We are called to help bear one another's burdens and seek God's strength when facing struggles.

Prayer

Heavenly Father, thank You for reminding me of the importance of humility and the need to help others. Help me to be mindful of others' struggles and show love by bearing their burdens with them. When I feel weighed down, help me to turn to You for strength. May my life reflect Your love, and may I live humbly, just as You have called me to. In Jesus' Name, Amen.

May 26

Wisdom, Worth, and Worship

3-Year-Bible Reading: Proverbs 16:21-22; Ephesians 1

"The wise of heart is called discerning, and sweetness of speech increases persuasiveness." — Proverbs 16:21

"Having the eyes of your hearts enlightened, that you may know what is the hope to which he has called you, what are the riches of his glorious inheritance in the saints." — Ephesians 1:18

Have you ever wondered why wisdom is so important? **Proverbs 16:21** shows us that being wise in heart leads to being persuasive and trustworthy. It's not about being the loudest or most impressive—it's about being discerning, knowing when to speak, and how to listen. We all have moments when we can speak wisely and bring peace into situations, and in doing so, we point others to Christ.

Then, in **Ephesians 1:18**, Paul prays that our hearts would be enlightened so that we can truly understand the hope of our calling in Christ. This is more than just head knowledge—it's about knowing the riches of what it means to belong to God, and that knowledge should shape how we live and how we treat others. Wisdom comes from understanding our value in Christ, and it encourages us to use our words and actions to reflect His love.

Think About It

1. **Wisdom in Action:** How can you be more discerning in your speech and actions this week? What's one situation where you could practice speaking wisely instead of reacting impulsively?
2. **Understanding Your Worth:** What do you think it means to have an "inheritance in the saints"? How does understanding your worth in Christ change how you view your life and purpose?
3. **Enlightened Hearts:** How can you actively invite God to enlighten your heart and mind so that you can know His calling and purpose for you?

Bottom Line

Wisdom isn't just about knowing the right things—it's about understanding your worth in Christ and using that knowledge to live out His calling in your life, especially in how you speak and act.

Prayer

Heavenly Father, thank You for the wisdom You offer and for the incredible inheritance I have in You. Help me to speak wisely and live with a heart that is discerning. Open the eyes of my heart to fully understand the hope of Your calling and the purpose You've given me. May my life reflect Your love and wisdom in everything I do. In Jesus' Name, Amen.

MAY 27

Words That Heal

3-Year-Bible Reading: Proverbs 16:23-24; Psalms 60; Ephesians 2

"The heart of the wise makes his speech judicious and adds persuasiveness to his lips." — Proverbs 16:23

"Oh, grant us help against the foe, for vain is the salvation of man! With God we shall do valiantly; it is he who will tread down our foes." — Psalm 60:11-12

"But God, being rich in mercy, because of the great love with which he loved us, even when we were dead in our trespasses, made us alive together with Christ—by grace you have been saved." — Ephesians 2:4-5

Have you ever noticed how the words we speak can change the atmosphere in a room? **Proverbs 16:23** tells us that wise hearts speak in ways that are persuasive and full of wisdom. Words have power to heal, encourage, or tear down, and when we choose our words carefully, we bring life to those around us.

But sometimes, life can feel like a battle, like **Psalm 60** describes. We face challenges, and we may feel weak or helpless, but we are reminded that true victory comes from God. Just like the psalmist calls out to God for help against their enemies, we too can trust in God's power and His ability to help us in our struggles.

Finally, **Ephesians 2** reminds us of God's incredible mercy. Even when we were lost in sin, He reached out and saved us by grace, making us alive in Christ. This new life in Christ should shape the way we speak and act, reflecting His love and grace in all that we do.

THINK ABOUT IT

1. **The Power of Words:** How do you use your words with those around you? Do you speak in ways that build others up? What can you do today to speak more wisely and kindly?
2. **God's Strength in Struggles:** Are there battles you're facing right now, whether big or small? How can you trust God to help you, as the psalmist did?
3. **Grace in Action:** How does understanding God's grace to save you change the way you interact with others? How can you show grace to those around you?

BOTTOM LINE

Our words are powerful, and God's grace transforms how we speak and live. With His help, we can use our words to encourage others, trust Him in our battles, and reflect His love and mercy.

PRAYER

Heavenly Father, thank You for the gift of wisdom and the power of words. Help me to speak in ways that honor You and bring life to others. When I face challenges, remind me that You are my strength, and I can trust in Your power to overcome. Thank You for Your amazing grace that saved me. Help me to extend that grace to others, reflecting Your love in all I do. In Jesus' Name, Amen.

May 28

The Right Way Isn't Always the Easy Way

3-Year-Bible Reading: Proverbs 16:25-26; Ephesians 3

"There is a way that seems right to a man, but its end is the way to death. A worker's appetite works for him; his mouth urges him on." — Proverbs 16:25-26

"That according to the riches of his glory he may grant you to be strengthened with power through his Spirit in your inner being." — Ephesians 3:16

Have you ever followed your gut or trusted your feelings, only to realize later it wasn't the best move? **Proverbs 16:25** warns that sometimes the way that *feels* right can actually lead us the wrong direction. That's a big deal—especially when you're trying to make choices about friends, dating, school, or even what to post online.

It's easy to get pulled into what's popular or what feels good in the moment, but God invites us to walk His way—even when it's harder. Thankfully, we're not expected to figure it all out on our own.

In **Ephesians 3**, Paul reminds us that God *strengthens us from the inside out* through His Spirit. That means when life gets confusing or exhausting, we can ask God for real power to keep going and keep growing. He wants us to be rooted in His love, guided by His truth, and strong enough to follow the path that leads to life.

Think About It

1. **Looks Can Be Deceiving:** Have you ever made a decision that *seemed right* but ended badly? How can you seek God's direction instead of just trusting your own instincts?
2. **Real Strength:** Where do you feel weak right now—in your faith, your choices, or your relationships? What would it look like to ask God for strength in your "inner being" like Paul prayed?
3. **Hunger That Motivates:** Proverbs 16:26 talks about how hunger drives a worker. What "hunger" or goal is pushing you forward in life—and is it leading you toward God or away from Him?

Bottom Line

Not everything that seems right is truly right. We need God's wisdom and strength to follow His path, even when it's hard. His way leads to life, peace, and purpose.

Prayer

Heavenly Father, help me not to lean on my own understanding or follow what just feels right. Give me Your wisdom to see clearly and Your strength to follow You when it's hard. Fill my heart with the hunger to know You more and to live out Your truth each day. Strengthen me in my inner being so I can live the life You've called me to. In Jesus' Name, Amen.

May 29

Watch Your Words

3-Year-Bible Reading: Proverbs 16:27-30; Psalms 61; Ephesians 4

"A worthless man plots evil, and his speech is like a scorching fire. A dishonest man spreads strife, and a whisperer separates close friends." — Proverbs 16:27-28

"Lead me to the rock that is higher than I, for you have been my refuge, a strong tower against the enemy." — Psalm 61:2b-3

"Let no corrupting talk come out of your mouths, but only such as is good for building up, as fits the occasion, that it may give grace to those who hear." — Ephesians 4:29

Words can be powerful. You've probably felt it—whether someone made you feel amazing with a compliment or crushed your spirit with a mean comment. **Proverbs 16** warns about people who stir up drama, lie, or tear others down with their words. It's a reminder that how we talk matters.

Ephesians 4:29 says we should use our words to *build others up* and give *grace* to those listening. That doesn't mean being fake or overly sweet—it means being intentional, kind, and truthful. And when we're overwhelmed or tempted to snap, **Psalm 61** shows us where to run: straight to God, our refuge and strong tower. He's the one who helps us keep our words (and hearts) in check when everything around us feels loud and messy.

Think About It

1. **Check Your Words:** Are your words helping or hurting others? Think about your recent texts, posts, or conversations—are they building people up or tearing them down?
2. **Guard Your Heart:** What kind of things are you letting into your mind and heart (music, shows, friends)? Could any of those be influencing the way you speak?
3. **Run to the Rock:** When you're stressed, angry, or tempted to say something you shouldn't, how can you turn to God like David did in Psalm 61?

Bottom Line

Your words hold power. Use them to encourage, not destroy. God is your safe place, and He can help you speak with grace—even when it's tough.

Prayer

Heavenly Father, help me to be careful with my words. I want what I say to reflect Your love, not cause hurt or division. When I'm tempted to speak out of anger or frustration, remind me to run to You first. Be my strength and guide. Teach me how to build others up and bring grace into every conversation. In Jesus' Name, Amen.

May 30

Strong on the Inside

3-Year-Bible Reading: Proverbs 16:31-32; Ephesians 5

"Gray hair is a crown of glory; it is gained in a righteous life. Whoever is slow to anger is better than the mighty, and he who rules his spirit than he who takes a city." — Proverbs 16:31-32

"Therefore be imitators of God, as beloved children. And walk in love, as Christ loved us and gave himself up for us. Look carefully then how you walk, not as unwise but as wise, making the best use of the time, because the days are evil." — Ephesians 5: 1-2, 15-16

In a world that celebrates flashy moments, loud personalities, and instant reactions, God's Word points us in a different direction. **Proverbs 16:32** says real strength isn't about being the toughest or loudest—it's about *self-control*. Controlling your reactions, holding your anger, and being wise in how you live takes true inner strength.

That's not easy, especially in high-stress moments like group chats blowing up, drama at school, or family tension. But **Ephesians 5** reminds us that we're called to *imitate God*—to walk in love and live wisely, using our time well. When you choose patience over lashing out, or love over bitterness, you're showing the world what God's strength really looks like in everyday life.

Think About It

1. **Real Power:** What does it look like to "rule your spirit" in real-life situations—like when someone makes you mad or pushes your buttons?
2. **Time Check:** How are you spending your time? Are you using it in ways that reflect God's wisdom and love—or are there areas that could shift?
3. **Walking Like Jesus:** Think about how Jesus showed love through self-control and sacrifice. What's one way you can "walk in love" today?

Bottom Line

Real strength isn't about being the loudest or most powerful—it's about living with love, patience, and wisdom, just like Jesus.

Prayer

Heavenly Father, help me grow strong on the inside. Teach me to be slow to anger and quick to love. Show me how to make wise choices with my time and how to reflect Your heart in the way I treat others. I want to live like Jesus, even when it's hard. Thank You for Your Spirit that gives me strength. In Jesus' Name, Amen.

May 31

Strength in Stillness

3-Year-Bible Reading: Proverbs 16:33; Psalm 62; Ephesians 6

"The lot is cast into the lap, but its every decision is from the Lord." — Proverbs 16:33

"For God alone my soul waits in silence; from him comes my salvation. He only is my rock and my salvation, my fortress; I shall not be greatly shaken." — Psalm 62:1-2

"Put on the whole armor of God, that you may be able to stand against the schemes of the devil." — Ephesians 6:11

Life can feel super unpredictable. You study hard and still bomb a test. You try to be kind but still get misunderstood. It's like rolling dice—you're never sure what you'll get. But **Proverbs 16:33** reminds us that even when things feel random or out of our control, God is still in charge.

When the world around us is noisy and chaotic, **Psalm 62** calls us to *wait in silence*—to trust that God is our unshakable foundation. And while we wait, **Ephesians 6** tells us not to just sit back, but to *gear up* spiritually. We're in a battle every day—against doubts, distractions, and the temptation to quit.

That's why we need God's armor: truth, righteousness, faith, and the Word. When we trust in His strength and stand firm, we're not just surviving—we're living with purpose.

Think About It

1. **Trust God's Control:** Are there areas of your life that feel out of control? How can you remind yourself that God is still guiding your steps?
2. **Stand in Stillness:** What does it look like to "wait in silence" for God? How can slowing down help you grow stronger in faith?
3. **Armor Up Daily:** Which piece of God's armor (see Ephesians 6:10–18) do you need most right now—truth, peace, faith, God's Word, etc.?

Bottom Line

Even when life feels uncertain, God is in control. Wait on Him, stand firm, and suit up with His armor every day.

Prayer

Heavenly Father, thank You that even when life feels unpredictable, You are always in control. Teach me to wait on You and trust that You're working things out for my good. Help me put on Your armor daily and stand strong in Your truth. Be my strength and my peace. In Jesus' Name, Amen.

June 1

God's Faithfulness in Unexpected Places

3-Year-Bible Reading: Proverbs 17:1–2; Exodus 1–2

"Better is a dry morsel with quiet than a house full of feasting with strife." —Proverbs 17:1

"Now a man from the house of Levi went and took as his wife a daughter of Levi. The woman conceived and bore a son… When she saw that he was a fine child, she hid him three months." —Exodus 2:1–2

Life doesn't always go the way we expect, right? Sometimes we face struggles that seem unfair or overwhelming. But even when things seem uncertain, we can trust that God is working behind the scenes.

In **Exodus 1–2**, we read about a time when God's people, the Israelites, were enslaved in Egypt. They were oppressed, mistreated, and their lives were anything but peaceful. In the middle of this hardship, **Moses** was born. His mother, seeing that he was a special child, decided to hide him from the Pharaoh's orders to kill all the Hebrew baby boys. She trusted God and took a huge step of faith to protect him.

But here's the thing: Moses' story didn't start with a grand miracle or a powerful leader—it started in the middle of fear and uncertainty. Moses' family didn't have everything they wanted. They had to live in difficult circumstances, yet they chose faith. And that faith led to God using Moses to lead His people to freedom.

Now, **Proverbs 17:1** tells us, **"Better is a dry morsel with quiet than a house full of feasting with strife."** This verse reminds us that peace, even in small things, is better than having everything we think we want but being surrounded by chaos. A quiet, humble life with peace is far more valuable than a loud, over-the-top life filled with drama and conflict.

Think About It

1. **Struggle vs. Faith** – Life might feel like it's going wrong sometimes, but can you think of a time when God showed up in a surprising way during a difficult situation? What did that teach you about trusting Him even when things feel hard?
2. **Quiet Peace** – Proverbs says peace is better than "feasting with strife." Are there areas in your life where you might be trading peace for drama? Maybe in friendships, school, or your thoughts? How can you choose peace over chaos?
3. **God's Plan** – Moses' journey didn't look easy, but God was working in the background. Where in your life can you trust that God is doing something even if you can't see it yet?

Bottom Line

When everything around you feels uncertain, remember that God is at work even when things seem chaotic. Trusting Him, even in the smallest things, can lead to peace and a bigger story than you could imagine. The beginning of Moses' life didn't look perfect, but God had a plan all along—and He has one for you too.

Prayer

God, sometimes life feels out of control, and I don't always see how You're working. Help me trust that even in the mess, You have a plan for me. Teach me to choose peace over chaos and trust You, even when I don't have all the answers. Thank You for Your faithfulness, even in the hardest moments. Amen.

JUNE 2

God Refines Us for His Purpose

3-Year-Bible Reading: Proverbs 17:3-4; Psalm 63; Exodus 3-4

"The crucible is for silver, and the furnace is for gold, and the Lord tests hearts. An evildoer listens to wicked lips, and a liar gives ear to a mischievous tongue."—Proverbs 17:3-4

"O God, you are my God; earnestly I seek you; my soul thirsts for you; my flesh faints for you, as in a dry and weary land where there is no water."—Psalm 63:1

Have you ever felt like you're being tested? Like you're going through tough moments that make you wonder if you'll ever get through them? Maybe it's dealing with school stress, a friendship that's falling apart, or even moments of doubt about who you really are. Proverbs tells us that just like silver and gold are refined in fire, God allows us to be tested to shape our hearts.

Psalm 63 shows us what it looks like when we *thirst* for God, when we're desperate for Him in our hearts. David, the psalmist, was in a dry and weary place, but he recognized that only God could satisfy him. The same way we feel thirsty when we're dehydrated, our souls are thirsty for God when we face challenges. But the good news is, He's there to fill us.

In **Exodus 3-4**, we see how God uses testing to refine Moses. God calls Moses to a big task—to free the Israelites from slavery in Egypt. But Moses doubts himself, he's unsure, and he feels unqualified. God's response? He tells Moses, *"I will be with you."* Even though Moses doesn't feel ready, God knows exactly what he's capable of because He's the one who made him. And He's refining Moses for a purpose far greater than he could imagine.

THINK ABOUT IT

1. **Testing and Refining:** Think about the struggles you're going through. How do they feel like fire or pressure in your life? What do you think God might be teaching you through these moments?
2. **Thirsting for God:** Like David in **Psalm 63**, do you ever feel like your soul is thirsty for God? What are some ways you can actively seek Him in your life, even when things feel dry or difficult?
3. **God's Calling:** Moses didn't think he was the right person for the job, but God saw something in him. Do you ever feel unqualified for something God might be calling you to do? How can you trust God to use you, even when you don't feel ready?

BOTTOM LINE

God allows us to go through testing, just like silver and gold are refined in fire. It's in these moments that we get to see what we're really made of and who we're becoming. Like David, we're called to thirst for God, to seek Him in the dry moments, and trust that He will fill us. And like Moses, we can trust that when God calls us to something, He will be with us every step of the way.

PRAYER

God, I know I'm going through tests and struggles in my life right now. It's hard, and I sometimes feel unqualified or unsure. But I trust that You are refining me and shaping me into who You want me to be. Help me to seek You like David did, to thirst for You even in the hard moments. And when You call me to something big, help me to trust that You'll be with me every step of the way. Amen.

June 3

No Laughing Matter

3-Year-Bible Reading: Proverbs 17:5; Exodus 5-7

"Whoever mocks the poor insults his Maker; he who is glad at calamity will not go unpunished." — Proverbs 17:5

"Afterward Moses and Aaron went and said to Pharaoh, 'Thus says the Lord, the God of Israel, "Let my people go, that they may hold a feast to me in the wilderness."' But Pharaoh said, 'Who is the Lord, that I should obey his voice and let Israel go? I do not know the Lord, and moreover, I will not let Israel go.'" — Exodus 5:1–2

"But I will harden Pharaoh's heart, and though I multiply my signs and wonders in the land of Egypt, Pharaoh will not listen to you." — Exodus 7:3–4

It's easy to laugh at someone else's struggle when we're not the ones going through it. But **Proverbs 17:5** reminds us that mocking the poor or taking joy in someone's misfortune is actually insulting to God—the very One who made them. In **Exodus 5–7**, we see this attitude in Pharaoh. He not only mocked Moses and Aaron, but also ignored God completely. His pride caused him to harden his heart even when God showed him powerful signs. It can be tempting to act like Pharaoh—dismissing God's voice, thinking we're too important to be corrected, or joking at someone else's expense. But God sees the heart, and He calls us to humility, compassion, and obedience instead.

Think About It

1. **How do you treat others who are struggling?** Do you speak with kindness, or do you ever laugh at others to look cool or feel better about yourself?

2. **God sees the heart:** Just like Pharaoh's heart was hardened, we can also resist God's voice. Are you open to what He might be teaching you through others or through His Word?

3. **Compassion reflects God's character:** When we treat people with dignity—especially the vulnerable—we reflect God's love. How can you show kindness to someone who's hurting today?

Bottom Line

God takes how we treat others seriously—especially those who are hurting. Choose compassion over mockery and humility over pride.

Prayer

Heavenly Father, thank You for reminding me that every person matters to You. Help me not to laugh at others or ignore people who are struggling. Instead, give me a heart that shows kindness, stands up for what's right, and listens to Your voice—even when it's hard. Soften my heart and lead me to walk in Your ways. In Jesus' Name, Amen.

June 4

Legacy and Lips

3-Year-Bible Reading: Proverbs 17:6–7; Psalm 64; Exodus 8

"Grandchildren are the crown of the aged, and the glory of children is their fathers. Fine speech is not becoming to a fool; still less is false speech to a prince." — Proverbs 17:6–7

"They hold fast to their evil purpose; they talk of laying snares secretly, thinking, 'Who can see them?'" — Psalm 64:5

"Then the magicians said to Pharaoh, 'This is the finger of God.' But Pharaoh's heart was hardened, and he would not listen to them, as the Lord had said." — Exodus 8:19

Have you ever been caught saying something you regret—or not saying something you should have? Whether it's gossip, sarcasm, or silence when truth is needed, our words carry a lot of weight. In **Proverbs 17:6–7**, we see the value of legacy and how speech reflects character. A fool can't fake wisdom with fancy words, and someone in a position of influence shouldn't lie—it just doesn't fit. In **Psalm 64**, David describes people who use their words to trap others. They think no one notices, but God does. And in **Exodus 8**, Pharaoh's refusal to listen—even when truth stared him in the face—shows how a hardened heart resists what God is clearly doing.

The Bible connects words, hearts, and legacy. What you say (and how you listen) matters more than you think.

Think About It

1. **Your Words Reflect Your Heart:** Are your words encouraging, truthful, and life-giving—or sarcastic, dishonest, or hurtful? What would someone learn about your heart by listening to you?

2. **Listening to God Matters:** Pharaoh had every chance to listen, but he didn't. Are there areas in your life where you know what God is saying but keep ignoring it?

3. **What Kind of Legacy Are You Building?** Proverbs reminds us that kids look up to their parents and grandparents. Whether you realize it or not, you're already shaping a legacy. What do you want to be remembered for?

Bottom Line

God cares about your words and your heart. When you speak truth, listen well, and live wisely, you leave behind a legacy that honors Him and blesses others.

Prayer

Heavenly Father, Help me to speak words that bring life, truth, and hope. Guard my heart so I won't be like Pharaoh—prideful and closed off. Teach me to listen to You and to build a legacy that reflects Your love. Let my life point others to You through what I say and how I live. In Jesus' Name, Amen.

June 5

The Power of Forgiveness and Grace

3-Year-Bible Reading: Proverbs 17:8-9; Exodus 9

"A bribe is like a magic stone in the eyes of the one who gives it; wherever he turns he prospers. Whoever covers an offense seeks love, but he who repeats a matter separates close friends."—Proverbs 17:8-9

"Then the Lord said to Moses, 'Stretch out your hand toward the heavens, so that there may be hail in all the land of Egypt, on man and beast and every plant of the field in the land of Egypt.' Then Moses stretched out his staff toward heaven, and the Lord sent thunder and hail, and fire ran down to the earth. And the Lord rained hail upon the land of Egypt."—Exodus 9:22-23

Have you ever been hurt by someone, maybe even betrayed by a friend, and found it difficult to let go of the offense? Or maybe you've been the one who hurt someone and felt the tension of broken trust? Proverbs 17:9 tells us that covering an offense is a way of showing love, but repeating the matter only creates division. It's like trying to repair a broken bond between friends by constantly bringing up the past hurt. True peace comes when we choose to forgive and not hold onto grudges.

In **Exodus 9**, God unleashes one of the ten plagues on Egypt—hail. Pharaoh had repeatedly refused to listen to God, and despite multiple chances to repent, he remained stubborn. The hail was a warning, a consequence of Pharaoh's refusal to acknowledge God's power. Yet, God still offered Pharaoh a chance to let go of his stubbornness and choose obedience.

Just like Pharaoh, sometimes we are stubborn in our own lives. We may hold onto anger or bitterness, refusing to forgive others. But Proverbs challenges us to cover offenses with love. The way forward is through forgiveness, not through repeating the hurt or letting bitterness fester.

Think About It

1. **Forgiveness vs. Repeating the Offense:** Proverbs says that covering an offense seeks love, but repeating it causes separation. Is there someone in your life that you've been holding a grudge against? How can you begin to let go of that offense and seek healing in the relationship?

2. **God's Grace to Pharaoh:** In Exodus 9, Pharaoh receives multiple chances to repent, but he keeps refusing. God still gives him a chance. How can you open your heart to God's grace and forgiveness, both for yourself and others?

3. **The Power of Letting Go:** What would happen in your life if you stopped holding onto offenses, but instead chose to forgive? How would that change your relationships with friends, family, and even God?

Bottom Line

Forgiveness can be tough, especially when the hurt feels justified—but God calls us to let go, just as He offers us grace. Like Pharaoh, we have a choice: to stay hardened or to walk in the freedom that forgiveness brings.

Prayer

God, I know it's hard to forgive sometimes, especially when I've been hurt or betrayed. But I thank You for showing me grace and patience. Help me to follow Your example and cover offenses with love instead of repeating the hurt. Heal my heart and help me to forgive, just as You forgive me. Amen.

June 6

The Power of Correction and Trusting in God's Timing

3-Year-Bible Reading: Proverbs 17:10-11; Psalm 65; Exodus 10-11

"A rebuke goes deeper into a man of understanding than a hundred blows into a fool. An evil man seeks only rebellion, and a cruel messenger will be sent against him." —Proverbs 17:10-11

"You visit the earth and water it; you greatly enrich it; the river of God is full of water; you provide their grain, for so you have prepared it. You water its furrows abundantly, settling its ridges, softening it with showers, and blessing its growth." —Psalm 65:9-10

Have you ever been corrected or rebuked by someone? Maybe a parent, teacher, or even a friend? It doesn't always feel good, right? Proverbs tells us that for someone who is wise, a rebuke has the power to go deep and change them for the better. But for a fool, it's like hitting a brick wall—nothing changes. Correction is a tool that helps us grow, but only if we're willing to listen and learn.

In **Exodus 10-11**, we see God continuing to show His power through Moses as He brings more plagues on Egypt. Pharaoh, the ruler of Egypt, is repeatedly warned, but he refuses to listen to God's instructions. Each time God sends a plague, Pharaoh's heart grows harder. Despite the repeated warnings, Pharaoh stubbornly rebels against God, and eventually, the consequences of his rebellion become more severe.

God was giving Pharaoh time and opportunities to repent, but Pharaoh chose to harden his heart. In contrast, the psalmist in **Psalm 65** reminds us that God is a God of abundance, who waters and nourishes the earth. He is patient with us, and He gives us everything we need, even in the waiting. When we trust in God's timing, we recognize that He is working behind the scenes, preparing something good for us, just like He prepared the earth with rain to make it flourish.

Think About It

1. **Listening to Correction:** Proverbs says that a wise person accepts correction, but a fool ignores it. How do you usually respond when someone tries to correct you?

2. **God's Patience and Timing:** In Exodus, Pharaoh repeatedly rejects God's commands, and the consequences get worse. How can you learn to trust God's plans for your life, knowing that He's always working in His perfect timing?

3. **Nourishment in God:** Psalm 65 speaks of how God nourishes and enriches the earth. Are there areas in your life where you need God's spiritual nourishment and growth? How can you seek God to help you grow in your relationship with Him?

Bottom Line

God patiently corrects us to help us grow, but like Pharaoh, we can resist if our hearts aren't willing to listen. When we trust His timing and grace, we can rest knowing He's always working for our good.

Prayer

Heavenly Father, Thank You for Your patience and for the times You've corrected me with love. Help me to have a heart that listens to Your guidance, that I may grow in wisdom and understanding. I know You are working in my life, even when I can't see it, and I trust Your perfect timing. Please nourish my heart with Your Word, and help me to grow in my relationship with You every day. In Jesus' Name, Amen.

June 7

The Danger of Rebellion and the Power of Obedience

3-Year-Bible Reading: Proverbs 17:12-13; Exodus 12

"Let a man meet a she-bear robbed of her cubs rather than a fool in his folly." —Proverbs 17:12

"The blood shall be a sign for you on the houses where you are. And when I see the blood, I will pass over you, and no plague will befall you to destroy you when I strike the land of Egypt." —Exodus 12:13

Have you ever had one of those moments where you've done something that you immediately knew was a huge mistake? Maybe you didn't listen to a parent or teacher, or you ignored your gut feeling and made a bad decision. **Proverbs 17:12** says that it would be safer to meet a wild bear than to encounter someone who is stuck in their foolishness. It paints a vivid picture—foolishness leads to danger and destruction.

In **Exodus 12**, we see God preparing the Israelites to leave Egypt, but not before the most significant judgment would take place: the death of the firstborns of Egypt. However, God provides a way of escape for the Israelites—through the Passover lamb. The Israelites were commanded to kill a lamb, take its blood, and mark their doorposts. When God saw the blood, He would "pass over" their homes, sparing their lives.

This moment is a powerful reminder that obedience brings protection, while rebellion leads to destruction. Pharaoh's rebellion to God's command cost him the lives of his people, but the Israelites were saved through their obedience to God's instructions. The same applies to us: when we follow God's commands, even when they seem difficult, we're protected and blessed. But when we choose to ignore God's guidance, we end up facing consequences.

Think About It

1. **Folly and Consequences:** Proverbs warns us that foolishness leads to harm. Think about a time when you made a decision without thinking through the consequences. How did that decision affect you or those around you?

2. **Obedience to God:** The Israelites' obedience to God during the Passover saved their lives. What are some areas of your life where God is calling you to obey? Are there situations where you find it difficult to trust God's instructions?

3. **The Passover Lamb:** The lamb's blood on the doorposts was a sign of God's protection. Just like that, Jesus is the Lamb whose blood saves us from the consequences of sin. How does remembering Jesus' sacrifice help you respond to God's calls for obedience?

Bottom Line

Foolishness leads to destruction, but obedience brings blessing—just as the Israelites were saved through the Passover, we are saved through Jesus, who calls us to trust and follow Him.

Prayer

Heavenly Father, Thank You for the gift of Your protection and for sending Jesus as the ultimate sacrifice to save us. Help me to recognize the danger of foolish choices and the importance of obeying Your guidance. Give me the strength to trust You in all areas of my life, knowing that You protect and care for me. Help me to live in a way that honors You, walking in Your wisdom and love. In Jesus' Name, Amen.

June 8

Don't Open the Floodgates

3-Year-Bible Reading: Proverbs 17:14; Psalm 66; Exodus 13

"The beginning of strife is like letting out water, so quit before the quarrel breaks out." — Proverbs 17:14

"Come and hear, all you who fear God, and I will tell what he has done for my soul." — Psalm 66:16

"By a strong hand the Lord brought us out of Egypt, from the house of slavery." — Exodus 13:14

Ever turned on a water hose just a little and then suddenly—*WHOOSH*—water blasts out everywhere? That's what **Proverbs 17:14** is saying about arguments. A little strife may seem harmless at first, but once it starts, things can escalate fast—like a flood of words and emotions you can't control. Instead of letting conflict spill out, God calls us to *walk away before it explodes.*

But conflict isn't all there is. **Psalm 66** reminds us to zoom out and remember the bigger picture—how God has worked in our lives. Sharing what He's done can give us peace in tense moments. And **Exodus 13** shows that when God brings freedom, He leads us forward with purpose. Just like He freed the Israelites from Egypt, He frees us from reacting with anger, holding grudges, or staying stuck in drama.

Think About It

1. **Stop the Flood Early:** What small conflict in your life could turn into something bigger if left unchecked? How can you "quit before the quarrel breaks out"?
2. **Share What God's Done:** What has God done in your life that you can share to encourage others or even calm a situation down?
3. **Let God Lead:** The Israelites followed God after being freed. Are you letting God lead your actions, especially in how you handle tough moments?

Bottom Line

It's better to stop conflict before it floods your heart. Remember what God has done and let Him lead you into peace.

Prayer

Heavenly Father, help me recognize when conflict is starting and give me the strength to walk away before things go too far. Remind me of all You've done in my life, and help me speak peace, not strife. Lead me like You led the Israelites—out of the mess and into freedom. In Jesus' Name, Amen.

June 9

Who's Really in Charge?

3-Year-Bible Reading: Proverbs 17:15–16; Exodus 14–15

"He who justifies the wicked and he who condemns the righteous are both alike an abomination to the Lord. Why should a fool have money in his hand to buy wisdom when he has no sense?" — Proverbs 17:15-16

"And Moses said to the people, 'Fear not, stand firm, and see the salvation of the Lord, which he will work for you today. The Lord will fight for you, and you have only to be silent." — Exodus 14:13-14

"The Lord is my strength and my song, and he has become my salvation." — Exodus 15:2

Have you ever been in a situation where something seemed totally unfair, and you wondered why the wrong person was being praised—or why someone who did the right thing got punished? That's what **Proverbs 17:15** talks about. God cares deeply about justice. But when the world seems upside down, how do we respond?

In **Exodus 14**, the Israelites faced what looked like a hopeless situation: trapped between the Red Sea and the Egyptian army. But Moses told them to "stand firm." Why? Because God was about to show them He was still in control. He split the sea, led them through it, and crushed their enemies. Their response in **Exodus 15**? A full-on worship session, praising God for being their strength and salvation.

It's easy to want to fix injustice ourselves, to speak out in frustration, or to question if God even notices. But these passages remind us that even when we can't see how things will work out, God is still fighting for us. Sometimes, we just need to be still—and trust.

Think About It

1. **God Sees Injustice:** What's a situation in your life or in the world that feels unfair? Do you believe God sees it and cares?
2. **Trust Before You Understand:** The Israelites didn't know God would part the sea—they just had to trust. Is there something you need to trust God with right now before you know the outcome?
3. **Don't Waste Wisdom:** Proverbs 17:16 warns against chasing wisdom without actually wanting to learn. Are you seeking God's truth with a teachable heart?

Bottom Line

Even when life feels unfair or scary, God is in control—and He fights for those who trust Him.

Prayer

Heavenly Father, sometimes things feel so unfair, and I don't understand what You're doing. Help me to stand firm and trust You, even when I can't see the way forward. Teach me to seek true wisdom and to be still, knowing that You're working behind the scenes. You are my strength and my salvation. In Jesus' Name, Amen.

June 10

Faithful Friendships and Fresh Manna

3-Year-Bible Reading: Proverbs 17:17–18; Psalm 67; Exodus 16

"A friend loves at all times, and a brother is born for adversity. One who lacks sense gives a pledge and puts up security in the presence of his neighbor." — Proverbs 17:17–18

"May God be gracious to us and bless us and make his face to shine upon us, that your way may be known on earth, your saving power among all nations." — Psalm 67:1–2

"Then the Lord said to Moses, 'Behold, I am about to rain bread from heaven for you...'" — Exodus 16:4

Have you ever been hangry—so hungry that your mood completely flips? That was the Israelites in **Exodus 16.** Just days after being rescued by God through the Red Sea, they started complaining about being hungry. Instead of snapping at them, God provided bread from heaven (called manna), teaching them to trust Him for daily needs.

In **Proverbs 17**, we see another kind of faithfulness—through friendship. A true friend isn't just there for the fun stuff. They stick with you in tough times. Real friends reflect God's faithful love, showing up when you're struggling, not just when life's easy.

And **Psalm 67** reminds us why all this matters: when God provides for us and we show His love to others, the world sees what God is like. God blesses us so His goodness can be known everywhere—at your school, on your team, in your friend group.

Whether it's God providing food in the desert, a friend standing by you, or you being that kind of friend for someone else—God is showing us what faithfulness looks like. It's daily. It's generous. And it points people to Him.

THINK ABOUT IT

1. **Daily Dependence:** What's one area of your life where you need to trust God to provide—emotionally, physically, or spiritually?
2. **Faithful Friendships:** Are you the kind of friend who shows up when others are struggling? Who's someone that might need your encouragement today?
3. **Living as a Blessing:** How can your life reflect God's blessing to others this week? Think about how your words, attitude, or actions can make His love visible.

BOTTOM LINE

God is faithful to meet our daily needs and calls us to reflect that same love and faithfulness in our friendships and everyday lives.

PRAYER

Heavenly Father, thank You for being faithful even when I forget to trust You. Help me to depend on You every day, like the Israelites learned to do in the wilderness. Make me a faithful friend to others and use my life to show the world Your love and goodness. In Jesus' Name, Amen.

June 11

Hands Up, Hearts Strong

3-Year-Bible Reading: Proverbs 17:19–20; Psalm 68; Exodus 17

"Whoever loves transgression loves strife; he who makes his door high seeks destruction. A man of crooked heart does not discover good, and one with a dishonest tongue falls into calamity." — Proverbs 17:19–20

"Blessed be the Lord, who daily bears us up; God is our salvation." — Psalm 68:19

"Whenever Moses held up his hand, Israel prevailed, and whenever he lowered his hand, Amalek prevailed." — Exodus 17:11

Have you ever tried to hold your hands in the air for a long time—like, really long? In **Exodus 17**, Moses had to do just that. While Israel was in battle, whenever he raised his hands, they were winning. When he lowered them, they started losing. So his friends came and helped hold his hands up. The victory wasn't just about strength—it was about trusting God, staying steady, and supporting each other.

In **Proverbs 17**, we see a warning: if you chase drama or stir up conflict, it only leads to destruction. A "crooked heart" leads you away from peace, while honesty and humility bring you closer to God's way.

Then **Psalm 68** reminds us of the good news: God carries us daily. Every burden, every worry, every struggle—He's strong enough to handle it all. But sometimes, like Moses, we need friends to help us lift our arms and keep going when we're tired.

Whether you're facing school stress, friendship drama, or just feeling overwhelmed, remember you're not in it alone. God is your strength, and He often sends people—friends, mentors, parents—to help you stand firm and steady in faith.

THINK ABOUT IT

1. **Avoid the Drama:** Are you someone who brings peace or starts problems? How can you guard your heart and words today?
2. **Daily Strength:** What's weighing you down right now? Have you talked to God about it—and who might help you carry the load?
3. **Lift Each Other Up:** Who in your life needs encouragement? How can you be the one holding up someone else's hands today?

BOTTOM LINE

God gives us strength every day—and sometimes that strength shows up through people who help us stay faithful and focused when life is hard.

PRAYER

Heavenly Father, thank You for being my daily strength. I don't always feel like I can keep going, but You are faithful to lift me up. Help me avoid conflict, speak with honesty, and support the people around me. Use me to be a source of peace and encouragement. In Jesus' Name, Amen.

June 12

Joy That Lifts, Wisdom That Lasts

3-Year-Bible Reading: Proverbs 17:21–22; Exodus 18

"He who sires a fool gets himself sorrow, and the father of a fool has no joy. A joyful heart is good medicine, but a crushed spirit dries up the bones."
— Proverbs 17:21–22

"Moses' father-in-law said to him, 'What you are doing is not good… You and the people with you will certainly wear yourselves out, for the thing is too heavy for you. You are not able to do it alone.'"
— Exodus 18:17–18

Have you ever tried to do everything yourself—homework, chores, even helping friends—until you totally burned out? In **Exodus 18**, Moses was in that exact spot. He was working nonstop, trying to lead the entire nation of Israel by himself, until his father-in-law Jethro stepped in and basically said, "This is not working—you can't do it all." Jethro's wisdom helped Moses make changes that brought life and peace not just for himself but for everyone around him.

Proverbs 17 reminds us that joy is powerful—like medicine for your heart. But trying to carry the world on your shoulders, or ignoring good advice, can dry out your spirit fast. Sometimes we think being strong means doing it all, but real strength comes from knowing when to ask for help and how to guard your heart with joy.

God never meant for you to walk through life alone or overloaded. He places people in your life—friends, family, leaders—to speak truth, offer support, and share the load. Whether you're stressed, sad, or just trying to figure life out, God's wisdom offers a way forward. And it often starts with listening, letting go of pride, and choosing joy even in the middle of chaos.

Think About It

1. **Joy Check:** Are you letting God fill your heart with joy, or are you holding on to stress and pressure?
2. **Don't Go Alone:** Who in your life gives wise advice like Jethro? Are you listening to them—or trying to do everything on your own?
3. **Lighten the Load:** Is there something you need to let go of, share, or ask for help with this week?

Bottom Line

A joyful heart refreshes your soul, and wise choices—especially ones that involve letting others help—lead to strength that lasts.

Prayer

Heavenly Father, thank You for reminding me that I don't have to do life alone. Help me to recognize the people You've placed in my life to encourage and guide me. Give me wisdom to listen, courage to ask for help, and joy that fills my heart even on hard days. In Jesus' Name, Amen.

June 13

Clear Eyes, Clean Heart

3-Year-Bible Reading: Proverbs 17:23–24; Exodus 19–20

"The wicked accepts a bribe in secret to pervert the ways of justice. The discerning sets his face toward wisdom, but the eyes of a fool are on the ends of the earth." — Proverbs 17:23–24

"Now therefore, if you will indeed obey my voice and keep my covenant, you shall be my treasured possession among all peoples... And God spoke all these words, saying, 'I am the Lord your God... You shall have no other gods before me.'" — Exodus 19:5; 20:1–3

Have you ever zoned out while trying to do something important—like studying or praying—because your mind was all over the place? In **Proverbs 17:24**, it says that wisdom comes from focusing, but a fool's eyes are everywhere. And in **Exodus 20**, God gives His people the Ten Commandments, not to weigh them down, but to give them a solid path to walk on—a way to stay focused on Him.

God had just rescued the Israelites from slavery, and He didn't want them wandering aimlessly anymore. Instead, He invited them into a relationship with Him, giving clear boundaries and instructions for living differently from the world. Sadly, people often try to bend the rules for their own gain or chase every distraction possible—just like that warning in **Proverbs 17:23** about accepting bribes and perverting justice.

God's Word is like a compass that helps us see through the noise and live with integrity. Whether it's choosing honesty over cheating, truth over gossip, or God over distractions, wisdom starts with looking straight ahead—keeping your eyes on what matters most.

Think About It

1. **Keep Your Focus:** Are you chasing distractions or setting your heart toward God's wisdom each day?
2. **What Guides You?** Do you follow what feels good in the moment, or are you allowing God's Word to shape your decisions?
3. **Obedience Is Worship:** When you hear God's commands, do you see them as rules—or as a way to stay close to the One who calls you His treasured possession?

Bottom Line

God gives us clear direction, not to limit us, but to lead us into freedom and purpose. Wisdom starts when we fix our eyes on Him.

Prayer

Heavenly Father, thank You for giving me Your Word to guide my life. Help me to focus on wisdom instead of chasing distractions. Teach me to love Your commands and live in a way that honors You. I want to walk in Your truth and keep You at the center of everything I do. In Jesus' Name, Amen.

JUNE 14

When It's Hard to Do What's Right

3-Year-Bible Reading: Proverbs 17:25–26; Psalm 69; Exodus 21

"A foolish son is a grief to his father and bitterness to her who bore him. To impose a fine on a righteous man is not good, nor to strike the noble for their uprightness." — Proverbs 17:25–26

"I am weary with my crying out; my throat is parched. My eyes grow dim with waiting for my God… But as for me, my prayer is to you, O Lord. At an acceptable time, O God, in the abundance of your steadfast love answer me in your saving faithfulness." — Psalm 69:3, 13

"You shall not wrong a sojourner or oppress him, for you were sojourners in the land of Egypt." — Exodus 22:21

Have you ever felt like doing the right thing cost you something—maybe a friendship, a good grade, or even just your peace of mind? In **Proverbs 17:26**, it talks about how unfair it is to punish someone for doing what's right. And in **Psalm 69**, David pours out his heart to God because doing right has made him feel worn out and alone. But even when things got tough, David didn't stop talking to God—he trusted that God would respond at just the right time.

The truth is, sometimes choosing to do the right thing can feel lonely or painful. Standing up for someone who's being mistreated, refusing to lie when others do, or not going along with gossip—it can make you feel left out or even attacked. But just like God told His people in **Exodus 22**, He sees those who are overlooked or mistreated, and He wants His people to treat others with compassion because He's done the same for them.

When you feel discouraged for doing what's right, remember that God sees it all. He honors integrity, and even when others don't understand your choices, God does.

THINK ABOUT IT

1. **Righteous but Rejected:** Have you ever been hurt or criticized for doing what was right? What helped you stay strong—or what would help next time?
2. **God Hears the Honest Heart:** When life feels unfair or heavy, do you bring those feelings to God like David did, or try to carry them alone?
3. **Justice Is God's Heart:** Are you living in a way that reflects God's justice and kindness—especially to those who are often overlooked?

BOTTOM LINE

Doing what's right won't always be easy—but God sees, God cares, and He promises to be faithful in every battle you face.

PRAYER

Heavenly Father, sometimes doing what's right feels hard, especially when others don't understand or when it costs me something. Help me to stay strong in those moments and keep trusting You. Remind me that You care about justice, and that You're always with me when I stand for what's right. Give me courage and a heart like Yours. In Jesus' Name, Amen.

June 15

The Power of Quiet Strength

3-Year-Bible Reading: Proverbs 17:27–28; Exodus 22

"Whoever restrains his words has knowledge, and he who has a cool spirit is a man of understanding. Even a fool who keeps silent is considered wise; when he closes his lips, he is deemed intelligent." — Proverbs 17:27–28

If ever you take your neighbor's cloak in pledge, you shall return it to him before the sun goes down, for that is his only covering... If he cries to me, I will hear, for I am compassionate." — Exodus 22:26–27

Have you ever said something in the heat of the moment and immediately regretted it? Maybe you snapped at a friend or posted something online you wish you could take back. It's easy to think that having the last word or speaking loudly makes us strong—but **Proverbs 17:27–28** shows us that true wisdom often shows up in the form of self-control and quiet strength.

In **Exodus 22**, God gives laws to protect the vulnerable, showing His heart for people who can't defend themselves. He reminds His people to act with compassion and responsibility. In the same way, we're called to use our influence—not to hurt or stir up drama—but to bring peace and care to others.

In a world that celebrates loud opinions and viral arguments, God invites us to something better: to speak with wisdom, to stay calm when things get tense, and to be compassionate, especially toward those who have less power or voice. Being quick to listen and slow to speak isn't weakness—it's strength that reflects the heart of God.

Think About It

1. **When to Speak, When to Stay Silent:** Do you pause and think before you speak—or respond in the moment? How might holding back your words actually show maturity?
2. **Reflecting God's Heart:** How can your actions reflect God's compassion toward others, especially those who are hurting or vulnerable?
3. **Influence with Purpose:** Are you using your words to build others up, or tear them down? What's one way you can show wisdom and kindness with your speech this week?

Bottom Line

Wisdom isn't about being loud—it's about knowing when to speak, when to stay silent, and always reflecting God's heart in the way you treat others.

Prayer

Heavenly Father, thank You for reminding me that real strength often looks like self-control. Help me to use my words wisely and with love. When I'm tempted to speak too quickly or harshly, give me the wisdom to pause. Teach me to reflect Your compassion in the way I treat others—especially those who need kindness most. In Jesus' Name, Amen.

June 16

Don't Go Solo

3-Year-Bible Reading: Proverbs 18:1–2; Psalm 70; Exodus 23

"Whoever isolates himself seeks his own desire; he breaks out against all sound judgment. A fool takes no pleasure in understanding, but only in expressing his opinion." — Proverbs 18:1–2

"Make haste, O God, to deliver me! O Lord, make haste to help me!... Let those who love your salvation say evermore, 'God is great!'" — Psalm 70:1, 4

"You shall not spread a false report. You shall not join hands with a wicked man to be a malicious witness." — Exodus 23:1

Have you ever felt like shutting everyone out—pulling away from your family, friends, or even God—just to do your own thing? It might feel like a way to protect yourself, but **Proverbs 18:1** warns that isolating ourselves leads us away from wisdom. When we stop listening to others and only care about saying what we think, we're more likely to make poor choices.

Psalm 70 is a cry for help—a reminder that we need God, and we need His people. And **Exodus 23** reminds us how important it is to act with integrity, especially in how we speak and treat others. God calls us to live in community with truth and justice, not selfishness or isolation.

We weren't made to go solo. Whether it's struggling through something hard, fighting off temptation, or just trying to figure out life, God designed us to need Him and need each other. Wise friends, parents, mentors, and Scripture help guide us. When we cut off those voices, we're missing out on help we were never meant to live without.

THINK ABOUT IT

1. **Don't Isolate—Connect:** Are there times when you pull away from others just to do things your own way? How could that be keeping you from wise input or God's help?
2. **Cry Out Like David:** Do you ask God for help when you're in trouble or confused, like David did in Psalm 70? What would change if you made that your first instinct?
3. **Live with Integrity:** Are you being honest and fair in your relationships, especially when it's easier to go along with gossip or unfair treatment like Exodus 23 warns against?

BOTTOM LINE

Wisdom grows in community, not isolation. God designed you to walk with Him and with others in truth and love.

PRAYER

Heavenly Father, help me not to shut people out or think I have to figure life out alone. Give me wisdom to stay connected to the right voices, and courage to cry out to You when I'm overwhelmed. Help me live honestly and with integrity, reflecting Your heart in every decision. In Jesus' Name, Amen.

June 17

True Power

3-Year-Bible Reading: Proverbs 18:3–5; Exodus 24

"When the wicked comes, contempt also comes, and with dishonor comes disgrace. The words of a man's mouth are deep waters; the fountain of wisdom is a bubbling brook. It is not good to be partial to the wicked or to deprive the righteous of justice." — Proverbs 18:3–5

"Then Moses went up on the mountain, and the cloud covered the mountain. The glory of the Lord dwelt on Mount Sinai, and the cloud covered it six days. And on the seventh day he called to Moses out of the midst of the cloud." — Exodus 24:15–16

Have you ever noticed how powerful words can be? **Proverbs 18:3–5** talks about how words can either lift us up or drag us down, especially when used with dishonor or injustice. The verses remind us that true wisdom, like a refreshing fountain, brings life and understanding, while wickedness brings only destruction. In this life, you'll face a choice every day: Will you choose to speak life and truth, or will you let selfishness and dishonor take the lead?

In **Exodus 24**, Moses experiences the awe-inspiring presence of God on Mount Sinai. For six days, he waits in the presence of God's glory, and then on the seventh day, God calls to him. It's a reminder of the power and majesty of God—He is the source of true wisdom and honor. And just like Moses, we are invited into His presence.

When we align ourselves with God, our words and actions become a reflection of His wisdom and glory, just as Moses' encounter with God on the mountain shaped his entire leadership. Choosing to speak with integrity and wisdom, to not indulge in partiality, or to bring dishonor to others, reflects God's glory in us. We are not meant to live by our own wisdom or selfish desires, but by His truth and righteousness.

Think About It

1. **The Power of Words:** How do the words you speak reflect who you are? Are they a source of life and wisdom, or do they bring dishonor and disgrace to others?
2. **True Honor:** What does it look like for you to honor God with your words and actions? How can you stand firm in speaking truth in a world that often prefers shortcuts?
3. **God's Presence:** Just as Moses waited in God's presence for six days, are you taking time to listen for God's voice and allow His glory to shape you?

Bottom Line

Our words hold power—let's use them wisely to reflect God's glory and wisdom.

Prayer

Heavenly Father, thank You for inviting me into Your presence and giving me the gift of Your wisdom. Help me to choose my words carefully, that they might bring life and honor, not dishonor or destruction. May I reflect Your glory in everything I say and do. In Jesus' Name, Amen.

June 18

Words Matter

3-Year-Bible Reading: Proverbs 18:6–7; Psalm 71; Exodus 25

"A fool's lips walk into a fight, and his mouth invites a beating. A fool's mouth is his ruin, and his lips are a snare to his soul." — Proverbs 18:6–7

"In you, O Lord, do I take refuge; let me never be put to shame. In your righteousness deliver me and rescue me; incline your ear to me, and save me!" — Psalm 71:1–2

"And you shall make a mercy seat of pure gold. Two cubits and a half shall be its length, and a cubit and a half its breadth." — Exodus 25:17

Have you ever said something that you instantly regretted? **Proverbs 18:6–7** warns us about the power of our words—how they can cause destruction and even ruin our lives. A fool's words can lead to conflict, division, and harm. Just as a careless person can talk themselves into trouble, their mouth can also become a trap that causes pain for themselves and others. Sometimes, it's hard to stop and think before we speak, but the Bible gives us a clear reminder: our words matter.

In **Psalm 71**, the psalmist cries out for God's protection and rescue. It's a beautiful example of trusting God, especially when feeling vulnerable or in trouble. When we face moments where our words could bring damage, it's important to remember to lean on God for strength and wisdom. When we can't seem to control our mouths, we can always turn to God to help us speak wisely and find refuge in Him.

In **Exodus 25**, God gives specific instructions for building the Ark of the Covenant, with a mercy seat that will rest on top. This is where God will meet His people. It's a reminder that God's presence is a place of refuge, where we can find peace and healing. Just as the mercy seat symbolizes God's presence among His people, we can seek His presence when our words are causing conflict or hurt. God is a place of safety, and we can run to Him for help.

Think About It

1. Think Before You Speak: Have you ever noticed the way your words impact your relationships? Are they building others up or tearing them down?

2. Running to God: When you face situations where your words could hurt others, how can you ask God for help? Do you trust Him to guide your speech?

3. Presence of God: Just like the mercy seat in Exodus represented God's presence, how can you invite His presence into your life and words today?

Bottom Line

Our words hold power, and with God's help, we can use them wisely to build others up and reflect His presence.

Prayer

Heavenly Father, thank You for the reminder that my words have the power to bring either life or destruction. Help me to speak with wisdom, kindness, and love. When I feel tempted to speak in anger or foolishness, remind me to seek Your presence and to trust You to guide my words. In Jesus' Name, Amen.

June 19

The Power of Words and the Strength of Unity

3-Year-Bible Reading: Proverbs 18:8–9; Exodus 26

"The words of a whisperer are like delicious morsels; they go down into the inner parts of the body. Whoever is slack in his work is a brother to him who destroys." — Proverbs 18:8-9

"You shall make the tabernacle with ten curtains of fine linen, and blue and purple and scarlet yarns. You shall make them with cherubim skillfully worked into them." — Exodus 26:1

Words can be powerful. **Proverbs 18:8** describes how gossip or slander can feel like "delicious morsels"—easy to take in, yet harmful to the soul. We might find ourselves drawn to hearing juicy details or spreading rumors, but the reality is that words can damage relationships, just like the fabric of a garment can tear apart when it's mishandled. Similarly, **Proverbs 18:9** shows that laziness or not putting in our best effort can lead to destruction. When we slack off, whether in our responsibilities or our relationships, we damage the strength of our community and our bond with others.

In **Exodus 26**, God gives detailed instructions on how to build the tabernacle. This tabernacle is meant to be a holy and unified space, where God's presence can dwell among His people. Each part of the tabernacle, from the fine linens to the cherubim woven into the curtains, is crafted with care, as it is a symbol of unity and beauty in God's kingdom. Just like the intricate details of the tabernacle, our words and actions should be intentional and done with care to build up, rather than tear down, the unity of the body of Christ.

The connection here is clear: Just as the tabernacle needed to be carefully built to represent God's glory and unity, our words and efforts must be intentional and aligned with God's purpose for our lives. When we speak wisely and work diligently, we contribute to building a strong and unified community.

Think About It

1. **Gossip's Damage:** Have you ever witnessed the harm that gossip or careless words can do? How can you choose to speak in a way that builds others up instead of tearing them down?
2. **Slackness in Action:** Do you ever find yourself slacking off in your responsibilities? What would it look like if you gave your best effort in everything you do, especially in your relationships and tasks?
3. **Building Unity:** Just as the tabernacle was made with intentionality to bring God's presence among His people, how can you contribute to the unity and strength of your community through your words and actions?

Bottom Line

Our words and actions, when used wisely and with care, can build strong relationships and communities, reflecting God's unity and glory.

Prayer

Heavenly Father, help me to be mindful of my words and actions. May I speak with kindness and purpose, building up those around me rather than tearing them down. Help me to put in my best effort in all that I do, so that I can bring unity and strength to my relationships and to Your kingdom. In Jesus' Name, Amen.

JUNE 20

The Strength of God's Name

3-Year-Bible Reading: Proverbs 18:10–11; Exodus 27

"The name of the Lord is a strong tower; the righteous man runs into it and is safe. A rich man's wealth is his strong city, and like a high wall in his imagination."— Proverbs 18:10-11

"You shall make the altar of acacia wood, five cubits long and five cubits broad. The altar shall be square, and its height shall be three cubits."— Exodus 27:1

Have you ever felt the need to seek safety or refuge when life gets overwhelming? **Proverbs 18:10** reminds us that the name of the Lord is like a strong tower, a place where we can run for safety and security. It's easy to rely on things like money, fame, or popularity for protection, but **Proverbs 18:11** warns that these can be deceptive. Wealth or status may seem like a "strong city," but they are temporary and unreliable. True security only comes from the name of the Lord, who is unchanging and always present to protect and guide us.

In **Exodus 27**, God instructs the Israelites to build an altar of acacia wood, symbolizing a place of sacrifice and worship. The altar was a central part of their relationship with God, where they sought His presence and forgiveness. The structure of the altar, like the strong tower in **Proverbs 18**, provided a tangible space for the people to encounter God's strength and protection.

Just like the Israelites had a physical altar to approach God, we have access to the ultimate refuge in God's name. When life feels chaotic or uncertain, we can always turn to Him, knowing that He is the true source of security and peace.

THINK ABOUT IT

1. **Source of Strength:** Where do you usually turn when you feel unsafe or uncertain? How can you make God your first refuge in times of trouble?
2. **The Illusion of Wealth:** Have you ever put too much trust in things like money or status? What are some ways you can remember that these things won't give you the true security that God offers?
3. **The Power of God's Name:** How can you make God's name central to your life, just as the altar was central to the Israelites' worship?

BOTTOM LINE

When life feels unstable, we can always find safety in God's name, our true strong tower, where we find security and peace.

PRAYER

Heavenly Father, thank You for being my strong tower and the source of my security. Help me to remember that true strength comes from You alone, not from the things of this world. I choose to turn to You when I feel overwhelmed, trusting in Your name for refuge and peace. In Jesus' Name, Amen.

June 21

Humility Before Honor

3-Year-Bible Reading: Proverbs 18:12; Exodus 28

"Before destruction a man's heart is haughty, but humility comes before honor." — Proverbs 18:12

"And you shall make holy garments for Aaron your brother, for glory and for beauty." — Exodus 28:2

In **Proverbs 18:12**, we are reminded of the danger of pride. The verse tells us that before a person's downfall, they often become prideful. But the opposite, humility, leads to honor. It's a powerful reminder that putting others first and being humble before God opens the door to true greatness.

In **Exodus 28**, we see the story of God's instructions for the garments of the priests, specifically Aaron. The garments are to be made for glory and beauty, symbolizing honor and respect in God's eyes. However, these garments, while beautiful, were not to be a reflection of Aaron's own pride or status—they were meant to symbolize his humble service before God and the people. The priest's true honor came not from the clothes themselves, but from his heart and willingness to serve with humility.

Just like Aaron's garments were intended for glory and beauty, our actions and hearts are called to reflect God's honor. True honor comes when we serve others with humility, just as Jesus did. When we allow pride to creep in, it can lead to destruction, but when we humble ourselves before God, He lifts us up in His time.

Think About It

1. **The Danger of Pride:** How have you seen pride lead to negative outcomes in your life or the lives of others? What are some ways to guard against becoming prideful?
2. **Humility Brings Honor:** What does humility look like in your day-to-day life? How can you practice humility, even in situations where it might be hard?
3. **Serving with Purpose:** Aaron's garments were meant for glory and beauty in service to God. How can your actions reflect God's glory and honor in your own life?

Bottom Line

True honor comes from humility, not pride. When we humble ourselves before God and serve others, we reflect His glory and receive His honor.

Prayer

Heavenly Father, thank You for reminding me that humility comes before honor. Help me to stay humble in all that I do, and to serve You and others with a heart that seeks Your glory. I pray that You would guard me against pride and help me to always reflect Your love and grace. In Jesus' Name, Amen.

June 22

Words Matter, Hearts Matter More

3-Year-Bible Reading: Proverbs 18:13-14; Exodus 29

"If one gives an answer before he hears, it is his folly and shame." — Proverbs 18:13

"And you shall consecrate them, that they may be most holy. Whatever touches them will become holy." — Exodus 29:37

In **Proverbs 18:13**, we're warned about jumping to conclusions. Have you ever given an answer before truly listening to someone? It's easy to speak without fully understanding, but this often leads to mistakes and misunderstandings. The verse reminds us that true wisdom comes from listening carefully before responding.

In **Exodus 29**, God is giving detailed instructions to Moses about the consecration of the priests. These priests were to be made holy, set apart for God's work. This process involved offering sacrifices and following specific rituals. The priests were not just to look holy; they were to be holy, with their hearts dedicated to serving God. The consecration wasn't just about appearances—it was about a true transformation, inside and out.

Just like the priests, we are called to be set apart for God. Our actions, but more importantly, our hearts, need to reflect His holiness. We don't want to just look good on the outside—we want our words and actions to flow from a heart that listens to God and seeks to honor Him.

Think About It

1. **Listen First:** Have you ever given a quick response without fully understanding what was said? How can taking a moment to truly listen change the way you communicate?
2. **Holiness from the Inside Out:** The priests were set apart for God, not just in their actions but in their hearts. How can you make sure that your heart is set apart for God, not just your behavior?
3. **God Sees the Heart:** God cares more about the condition of our hearts than our outward appearances. How can you focus on honoring God from the inside out today?

Bottom Line

Listening carefully and focusing on the condition of our hearts are key to truly honoring God. It's not just about what we say or do, but about who we are on the inside.

Prayer

Heavenly Father, thank You for reminding me that words matter, but the state of my heart matters even more. Help me to listen carefully and respond wisely. Make me holy, inside and out, so that I can truly honor You in everything I do. In Jesus' Name, Amen.

June 23

A Heart That Listens, A Life That Serves

3-Year-Bible Reading: Proverbs 18:15-16; Psalm 72; Exodus 30

"An intelligent heart acquires knowledge, and the ear of the wise seeks knowledge." — Proverbs 18:15

"Give the king your justice, O God, and your righteousness to the royal son! May he judge your people with righteousness, and your poor with justice." — Psalm 72:1-2

"You shall consecrate the altar with it, and make it most holy. Whatever touches the altar shall become holy." — Exodus 30:29

In **Proverbs 18:15**, we see that true wisdom begins with a heart that seeks knowledge and ears that are eager to learn. It's not just about knowing facts but being open to God's wisdom and listening to others. In a world that often values quick answers, it's important to remember that true understanding takes time and intention. As you grow, you'll realize that listening carefully can often be more important than speaking quickly.

Psalm 72 is a prayer for the king, asking God to bless him with justice and righteousness. It's a powerful reminder that leaders, whether they are in the public eye or close to home, are called to serve with wisdom and fairness. Just like the king, we are called to lead with justice in the small, everyday decisions we make. God's call to righteousness and justice is for everyone, not just the powerful.

In **Exodus 30**, we read about the consecration of the altar. The altar, a place of sacrifice and worship, was to be set apart as holy. Everything that touched it would become holy too. This is a picture of how God's holiness transforms the things it touches, and it reminds us that, as we draw near to Him, He makes us holy as well.

Think About It

1. **Seek Knowledge:** Are you actively seeking to grow in wisdom and understanding, especially in your walk with God? How can you cultivate a heart that listens and learns?
2. **Serve with Justice:** Whether in school, sports, or friendships, you have opportunities to serve others. How can you show justice and fairness in your actions today?
3. **God's Transforming Power:** Just like the altar in Exodus was consecrated, God wants to make your life holy. How can you invite God's transforming power into your everyday choices?

Bottom Line

True wisdom comes from a heart that listens and seeks knowledge, and God calls us to serve with justice and holiness, just as He makes us holy through His presence.

Prayer

Heavenly Father, thank You for giving me a heart that can seek wisdom and knowledge. Help me to listen well and serve others with justice and fairness. May Your holiness transform me and make me more like You every day. In Jesus' Name, Amen.

JUNE 24

The Power of Listening and Building

3-Year-Bible Reading: Proverbs 18:17-19; Exodus 31

"The one who states his case first seems right, until the other comes and examines him." — Proverbs 18:17

"And I have filled him with the Spirit of God, with ability and intelligence, with knowledge and all craftsmanship, to devise artistic designs, to work in gold, silver, and bronze..." — Exodus 31:3-4

In **Proverbs 18:17**, we learn that first impressions or the initial arguments might seem convincing, but it's important to hear both sides before making a judgment. Whether it's a disagreement with a friend or a situation where you feel conflicted, it's wise to listen carefully to both perspectives before forming an opinion. It reminds us that fairness and patience lead to wiser decisions.

In **Exodus 31**, we read about Bezalel, whom God filled with His Spirit to give him the skills necessary to craft the tabernacle and all its elements. God gave him wisdom, knowledge, and the ability to create beautiful things. This passage shows us that our talents, whether in art, sports, music, or other areas, are gifts from God. He equips us to build and create, not just for our own benefit but for His glory and the good of others.

Both of these scriptures challenge us to think beyond ourselves. Proverbs 18:17 teaches the value of hearing others out, and Exodus 31 encourages us to use the talents God has given us to make something meaningful.

Think About It

1. **Listen Fairly:** Do you tend to jump to conclusions before hearing both sides of a story? How can you practice being more patient and fair in situations where you're forming an opinion or resolving a conflict?
2. **Use Your Gifts:** God has given you talents for a reason. How can you use your skills and abilities, whether big or small, to serve others and bring glory to Him?
3. **Building for a Purpose:** Just as Bezalel built the tabernacle for God's purposes, how can you build your life, relationships, and passions in a way that honors God and serves those around you?

Bottom Line

Take time to listen carefully to others and use the gifts God has given you to build something meaningful. Both of these things bring honor to God and help create a stronger, more compassionate world.

Prayer

Heavenly Father, thank You for the wisdom You give us to listen carefully and consider both sides of a situation. I pray that You help me use the talents and skills You've blessed me with to build things that honor You and help others. Help me build my life on Your truth and use my abilities for Your glory. In Jesus' Name, Amen.

June 25

The Power of Words and Trusting God's Plan

3-Year-Bible Reading: Proverbs 18:20-21; Psalm 73; Exodus 32

"From the fruit of a man's mouth his stomach is satisfied; he is satisfied by the yield of his lips. Death and life are in the power of the tongue, and those who love it will eat its fruits." — Proverbs 18:20-21

"But as for me, my feet had almost stumbled, my steps had nearly slipped. For I was envious of the arrogant when I saw the prosperity of the wicked." — Psalm 73:2-3

"When the people saw that Moses delayed to come down from the mountain, the people gathered themselves together to Aaron and said to him, 'Up, make us gods who shall go before us.'" — Exodus 32:1

Words are powerful. Proverbs 18:20-21 reminds us that our words can bring life or death, satisfaction or harm. How we speak can shape not just our relationships but our own experiences. Think about the way you speak to others, and also how you speak to yourself. Are you using your words to build others up, or tear them down? Are your words full of faith and encouragement, or doubt and negativity?

Psalm 73 shows the struggle of the psalmist as he looks at the prosperity of the wicked and feels discouraged. He nearly loses his footing, envious of those who seem to have it all. It's easy to get caught up in comparing ourselves to others, especially when it seems like they're succeeding without facing the same struggles. But the psalmist realizes that the prosperity of the wicked is only temporary, and the ultimate peace comes from trusting in God's plan.

In **Exodus 32**, the people of Israel grew impatient waiting for Moses. Instead of trusting that God had a plan, they turned to Aaron to make them idols. In their impatience, they forgot how God had already shown His faithfulness. When things aren't going as we expect, it's easy to lose faith and try to take control in unhealthy ways, just like the Israelites did. But true peace comes from trusting God, even when we don't see the full picture.

THINK ABOUT IT

1. **The Power of Words:** How do your words impact others and your own life? Do you use words to bring life, encouragement, and positivity, or do you sometimes use words to hurt or criticize?
2. **Trusting God's Timing:** When was the last time you felt like things weren't going your way? How can you remind yourself to trust God's timing, even when it feels like He's taking too long?
3. **Patience and Faith:** Like the Israelites, have you ever grown impatient with God's plan? How can you wait with faith instead of rushing ahead and making decisions that might not be part of His plan?

BOTTOM LINE

Our words are powerful—use them wisely. Trust in God's plan and timing, even when things don't make sense, because He is faithful and His plan is always better than anything we can imagine.

PRAYER

Heavenly Father, thank You for the reminder that my words have the power to build up or tear down. Help me use my words to encourage and bring life to others. When I feel impatient or discouraged, help me trust Your plan and Your timing. Thank You for Your faithfulness, even when I don't see the full picture. In Jesus' Name, Amen.

June 26

The Blessing of Finding a Good Partner

3-Year-Bible Reading: Proverbs 18:22; Exodus 33-34

"He who finds a wife finds a good thing and obtains favor from the Lord." — Proverbs 18:22

"And Moses said to the Lord, 'See, You say to me, "Bring up this people," but You have not let me know whom You will send with me. Yet You have said, "I know you by name, and you have also found favor in My sight."'" — Exodus 33:12

"The Lord descended in the cloud and stood with him there, and proclaimed the name of the Lord. The Lord passed before him and proclaimed, 'The Lord, the Lord, a God merciful and gracious, slow to anger, and abounding in steadfast love and faithfulness.'" — Exodus 34:5-6

In **Proverbs 18:22**, we read that finding a good partner is a blessing, one that comes with favor from the Lord. It's not just about having someone by your side; it's about finding someone who brings out the best in you and who encourages you to grow closer to God. This is a key reminder that relationships—whether friendships, family, or romantic—should be centered around mutual respect and God's love. A good partner isn't just about personality or looks; it's about God's favor shining through them and making your life better.

In **Exodus 33**, Moses is having a conversation with God, feeling unsure about the mission ahead of him. He needs help, but God assures him that He knows Moses by name and has shown him favor. Moses is seeking reassurance that God's presence will be with him as he leads Israel, and God responds with a promise of His companionship and guidance. Moses learns that God's presence is the true source of power and success, and this truth applies to us as well. No matter what we face in life, God's presence is our ultimate blessing and the key to overcoming obstacles.

In **Exodus 34**, God reveals His nature to Moses, describing Himself as merciful, gracious, slow to anger, and abounding in love. These characteristics are what we should reflect in our relationships with others, especially in close partnerships. Whether we're leading a group, working with teammates, or in a romantic relationship, embracing God's character in how we treat others will deepen our connections and help us navigate challenges with grace and humility.

Think About It

1. **Value of Relationships:** What qualities do you value most in your friendships and relationships? How do you think God's favor shapes your connections with others?
2. **God's Presence:** When was the last time you felt unsure about something you had to do? How can you remember that God is with you, just like He was with Moses?
3. **Reflecting God's Character:** How can you be more merciful, gracious, and slow to anger in your relationships? What would it look like to show God's love in your daily interactions?

Bottom Line

The best relationships are those centered around God's love and favor. As we seek His presence in our lives, we'll be better equipped to reflect His character and navigate challenges, building stronger connections with others along the way.

Prayer

Heavenly Father, thank You for the gift of relationships and for the reminder that You bless us with good partners who help us grow. Please help me to reflect Your love and mercy in my interactions with others. I want to be a person who mirrors Your character, bringing grace and love into every relationship. Thank You for always being with me, guiding me through life's challenges. In Jesus' Name, Amen.

June 27

Choosing Your Friends Wisely

3-Year-Bible Reading: Proverbs 18:23-24; Exodus 35-36

"The poor use entreaties, but the rich answer roughly. A man of many companions may come to ruin, but there is a friend who sticks closer than a brother." — Proverbs 18:23-24

"Then Moses said to the people of Israel, 'See, the Lord has called by name Bezalel the son of Uri, son of Hur, of the tribe of Judah; and He has filled him with the Spirit of God, with skill, with intelligence, with knowledge, and with all craftsmanship.'" — Exodus 35:30-31

"And they received from Moses all the contribution that the people of Israel had brought for doing the work of the sanctuary. They still kept bringing him freewill offerings every morning." — Exodus 36:3

Proverbs 18:23-24 speaks to the impact of our relationships. It warns that while some people may be quick to speak and may have many companions, true friendship is found in those who stick with you, especially during tough times. The Bible shows us that there are friends who are like family, loyal and steady. As young people, we can often be tempted to gather as many friends as possible, but the Bible teaches us that the quality of our friendships is far more important than the quantity.

In **Exodus 35-36**, we see a beautiful example of people coming together with the right heart to do God's work. The Israelites willingly gave their talents and resources to build the Tabernacle, and the work was done with dedication and unity. Just as Bezalel was filled with the Spirit of God to carry out a special task, we, too, are called to use our gifts in community. The teamwork shown here teaches us that great things happen when we work with the right people, doing the work God has called us to do. Our closest relationships should be with those who encourage us in our faith, who challenge us to be better, and who bring us closer to God.

When we surround ourselves with friends who share our values and support our growth, it strengthens us for the tasks God has for us. It's important to build relationships that help us to walk faithfully and help others do the same.

Think About It

1. **Friendships and Influence:** Who are the people you spend the most time with? Do they bring you closer to God, or do they pull you away?
2. **Quality vs. Quantity:** Do you have a lot of friends, or just a few close ones? How do you think the friendships you choose affect your life and your faith journey?
3. **Using Your Gifts:** Just as Bezalel used his talents for God's work, what gifts or abilities has God given you that you can use to help others or serve in your community?

Bottom Line

True friends are those who help you grow in your faith and reflect God's love. Choose relationships carefully, and always prioritize quality over quantity in your friendships.

Prayer

Heavenly Father, thank You for the gift of friendship. Help me to choose my friends wisely, so I am surrounded by people who encourage me to grow closer to You. Teach me to use the gifts You've given me to serve others and work together for Your purposes. May my friendships reflect Your love and faithfulness. In Jesus' Name, Amen.

June 28

Living with Integrity

3-Year-Bible Reading: Proverbs 19:1-2; Exodus 37-38

"Better is a poor person who walks in his integrity than one who is crooked in speech and is a fool. Desire without knowledge is not good, and whoever makes haste with his feet misses his way." — Proverbs 19:1-2

"And he made the mercy seat of pure gold. Two cubits and a half was its length, and a cubit and a half its breadth." — Exodus 37:6

"And he made the bronze basin and its stand of bronze, for washing, with a mirror of bronze from the women of the service, who served at the entrance of the tent of meeting." — Exodus 38:8

In **Proverbs 19:1-2**, Solomon highlights the value of integrity. It's easy to think that wealth and success are the most important things in life, but the Bible tells us that living a life of honesty and integrity is far better than chasing after riches in dishonest ways. A person with integrity values truth, even when it's hard or unpopular. Integrity doesn't just mean doing the right thing when others are watching, it's about having a character that aligns with your beliefs in every situation, whether anyone notices or not.

In **Exodus 37-38**, we see the Israelites putting their resources into building the Tabernacle. The detailed work shows how each person's contribution was essential to God's work, and the craftsmanship was done with excellence and care. Bezalel and Oholiab, for example, were skilled artisans who used their talents for the glory of God. In the same way, we are called to use our gifts and resources with integrity and excellence to honor God, whether we're serving in the church or at school.

In life, it's easy to fall into the trap of wanting shortcuts or trying to impress others. However, when we act with integrity—when we choose to do what's right even when it's difficult—we show the world that we belong to God. And just like the Israelites building the Tabernacle, when we put in the effort to do things with excellence, we reflect God's goodness and bring glory to Him.

THINK ABOUT IT

1. **Integrity in Action:** How do you show integrity in your daily life? Are there areas where you could be more honest or consistent with your values?
2. **Using Your Gifts for God:** What talents or skills do you have? How can you use them to honor God, both at church and in your everyday life?
3. **Avoiding Shortcuts:** Have you ever been tempted to take a shortcut or be dishonest to get ahead? How can you stay focused on doing things the right way?

BOTTOM LINE

Living with integrity and using your gifts to serve God brings true fulfillment and honor. Don't let the pressure of success or shortcuts cloud your desire to walk in honesty and excellence.

PRAYER

Heavenly Father, thank You for the gift of integrity and for showing me how to live with honesty and truth. Help me to honor You in everything I do, whether it's in my relationships, my work, or the way I use my talents. Give me the strength to do what's right, even when it's hard. May my life reflect Your goodness and love to others. In Jesus' Name, Amen.

June 29

The Power of Choices

3-Year-Bible Reading: Proverbs 19:3-4; Exodus 39

"When a man's folly brings his way to ruin, his heart rages against the Lord. Wealth brings many new friends, but a poor man is deserted by his friend." — Proverbs 19:3-4

"And they made the holy garments for Aaron, as the Lord had commanded Moses." — Exodus 39:1

"And they did all the work of the tabernacle of the tent of meeting; and Moses saw all the work, and behold, they had done it; as the Lord had commanded, so had they done it. Then Moses blessed them." — Exodus 39:32

Proverbs 19:3-4 warns us about the consequences of foolish decisions and how they affect our lives. It's easy to blame others or God when things go wrong, but the Bible teaches that our own choices can lead to our downfall. We may be tempted to blame bad circumstances on God or others, but ultimately, our own decisions have a lot to do with where we end up. Choosing to follow our impulses and desires can often lead to disappointment and heartache. On the other hand, choosing wisdom leads to better outcomes.

In **Exodus 39**, we see the Israelites carefully crafting the holy garments for Aaron, following God's instructions down to the last detail. They did all the work as God had commanded, and their obedience resulted in the Tabernacle being built exactly as God wanted it. This attention to detail and obedience shows how every choice we make, no matter how small, matters. Our choices can either bring us closer to God's perfect plan or lead us further away.

The Israelites didn't just stumble into creating the Tabernacle; they made intentional choices to follow God's guidance. Similarly, we must choose wisely in our daily lives, especially in the decisions we make that may seem insignificant. Each choice matters in shaping our future and bringing us closer to God's will.

Think About It

1. **The Power of Choices:** What choices in your life have led to positive outcomes? What about negative ones? How can you make wiser decisions moving forward?
2. **Wisdom in Action:** How can you better align your choices with God's Word and His will? Are there specific areas in your life where you feel you need more wisdom?
3. **Following God's Plan:** Just like the Israelites, you have a part to play in God's plan. How can you take intentional steps to follow God's will in your everyday life?

Bottom Line

The choices we make—big or small—have a direct impact on our lives and our relationship with God. Choosing wisdom, following God's guidance, and being intentional in our actions lead us toward His perfect plan.

Prayer

Heavenly Father, thank You for the gift of wisdom and the opportunity to make choices that align with Your will. Help me to make decisions that honor You and lead to a life that reflects Your love and truth. Guide me in every step I take, and remind me of the importance of my choices in shaping my future. In Jesus' Name, Amen.

June 30

God's Presence, Our Purpose

3-Year-Bible Reading: Proverbs 19:5-6; Psalm 74; Exodus 40

"A false witness will not go unpunished, and he who breathes out lies will not escape." — Proverbs 19:5

"For God is my King from of old, working salvation in the midst of the earth." — Psalm 74:12

"Then the cloud covered the tent of meeting, and the glory of the Lord filled the tabernacle." — Exodus 40:34

In **Proverbs 19:5-6**, we are reminded of the consequences of dishonesty. A false witness may think they are getting away with lying, but ultimately, truth will prevail. The world may offer rewards for deceitful actions, but God's justice is certain. Trust in God's truth, and He will always expose what is false in the end. The pursuit of truth and integrity is far more rewarding than any temporary gain from dishonesty. In **Psalm 74**, the psalmist acknowledges that God is the King from of old, working salvation. Even when things seem hopeless, God is still on His throne, actively working to bring about salvation and restoration. It's easy to feel overwhelmed or lost in the world, but knowing that God is always working, even in difficult times, can bring peace. His purpose is always moving forward, even when we don't fully see it.

Finally, in **Exodus 40**, we see the culmination of God's detailed instructions to the Israelites.

The Tabernacle is complete, and the glory of the Lord fills the temple. The cloud that covered the tent of meeting is a visible sign of God's presence among His people. The Tabernacle was the place where the Israelites would experience God's presence and guidance. This moment reminds us that God's presence is not distant or abstract—it's here with us. When we align ourselves with His purpose, we experience His presence in real and tangible ways.

THINK ABOUT IT

1. **Integrity Matters:** How does living with integrity impact your relationship with God and others? Have you ever faced a situation where you had to choose between honesty and deceit?
2. **God's Sovereignty:** Even when life feels out of control, how does knowing that God is working salvation help you remain hopeful? In what areas of your life do you need to trust God more deeply?
3. **Experiencing God's Presence:** Like the Israelites with the Tabernacle, how can you create space for God's presence in your life? What steps can you take to align yourself more closely with God's purpose for you?

BOTTOM LINE

God's presence is with us, and His truth is unshakable. When we live with integrity and trust in His plan, we can experience His peace and purpose in our lives, no matter what challenges come our way.

PRAYER

Heavenly Father, thank You for being a God of truth and justice. Help me to live with integrity and to trust in Your sovereignty, especially when life feels uncertain. May Your presence fill my life, just like You filled the Tabernacle, and lead me in Your purpose. In Jesus' Name, Amen.

July 1

Friends, Forgotten, and Favored

3-Year-Bible Reading: Proverbs 19:7; Luke 1

"All a poor man's brothers hate him; how much more do his friends go far from him! He pursues them with words, but does not have them." — Proverbs 19:7

"For he has looked on the humble estate of his servant. For behold, from now on all generations will call me blessed; for he who is mighty has done great things for me, and holy is his name." — Luke 1:48–49

Have you ever felt invisible—like people only notice you when they need something, but forget you the rest of the time? Maybe you've experienced what **Proverbs 19:7** talks about: people pulling away when you're struggling, or feeling abandoned by the very ones you trusted. That hurts. But the amazing thing is, God sees those who are overlooked.

In **Luke 1**, Mary wasn't rich or famous. She was a young, humble girl in a small town. But God saw her, chose her, and lifted her up. Her response wasn't pride—it was praise. God didn't choose Mary because she was perfect, but because she was willing. That same God sees *you*, too—right where you are, whether you feel forgotten or favored.

Think About It

1. **When Friends Disappear:** Have you ever felt like people avoided you when you were going through something hard? What did that feel like, and how did you respond?

2. **God Notices the Overlooked:** Mary wasn't the most "important" person by the world's standards, but God noticed her. What might it look like for you to trust God even when others don't see your value?

3. **Your Praise Is Powerful:** Mary responded to God's favor with worship, not worry. How can you develop a heart like Mary's—a heart that praises even when things don't make sense?

Bottom Line

Even when people walk away or overlook you, God never does. He sees you, chooses you, and wants to use you for His purpose—just like He did with Mary.

Prayer

Heavenly Father, thank You for seeing me even when others don't. Help me to trust that Your plan for me is good, even when I feel forgotten. Teach me to respond like Mary—with faith, obedience, and praise. Remind me that my worth comes from You, not from the approval of others. In Jesus' Name, Amen.

July 2

Choose What Lasts

3-Year-Bible Reading: Proverbs 19:8; Psalm 75; Luke 2

"Whoever gets sense loves his own soul; he who keeps understanding will discover good." — Proverbs 19:8

"At the set time that I appoint I will judge with equity." — Psalm 75:2

"And Jesus increased in wisdom and in stature and in favor with God and man." — Luke 2:52

Have you ever scrolled through your feed and felt like you're supposed to have your life completely figured out already? There's pressure to know who you are, what your purpose is, and how to succeed—before you've even finished high school. But here's the thing: God's Word doesn't expect you to have it all together right now. Instead, it invites you to grow in wisdom step by step, like Jesus did in **Luke 2:52**.

Life isn't about chasing likes or temporary success—it's about becoming the person God created you to be. And that starts with choosing wisdom.

THINK ABOUT IT

1. **Wisdom is self-care:** According to Proverbs 19:8, when you pursue wisdom and understanding, you're actually showing love to yourself. Are you taking time to seek truth, or are you filling your mind with empty stuff?

2. **God's timing is perfect:** Psalm 75:2 reminds us that God judges at *His* appointed time. You don't have to stress about controlling everything. Can you trust God's timing, even when things feel slow or uncertain?

3. **Jesus grew slowly, and so can you:** In Luke 2, even Jesus didn't skip the growing-up part. He matured in wisdom and found favor step by step. What's one way you can grow in wisdom this week?

BOTTOM LINE

True growth takes time, and it starts by choosing what matters most—wisdom, trust in God, and becoming more like Jesus.

PRAYER

Heavenly Father, thank You for showing me that it's okay not to have it all figured out. Help me to grow in wisdom like Jesus did, to love myself enough to pursue understanding, and to trust in Your perfect timing. Teach me to value what truly lasts. In Jesus' Name, Amen.

July 3

Truth Matters

3-Year-Bible Reading: Proverbs 19:9–10; Luke 3

"A false witness will not go unpunished, and he who breathes out lies will perish. It is not fitting for a fool to live in luxury, much less for a slave to rule over princes." — Proverbs 19:9–10

"Bear fruits in keeping with repentance. And do not begin to say to yourselves, 'We have Abraham as our father.' For I tell you, God is able from these stones to raise up children for Abraham." — Luke 3:8

Have you ever been in a situation where telling the truth felt risky or uncomfortable? Or maybe you've seen someone pretend to be something they're not just to impress others. The Bible is super clear—God cares deeply about truth and integrity. In **Proverbs 19**, we're warned that lies always catch up with us, and in **Luke 3**, John the Baptist challenges people to show real change in their lives, not just talk the talk. Following Jesus isn't about putting on a good show or pretending to be perfect. It's about a real heart change that shows up in how we live.

Think About It

1. **Why Truth Matters:** Proverbs reminds us that lies have consequences. Even if no one else sees it, God does. Are there any areas in your life where you need to choose truth, even when it's hard?

2. **Real Repentance Shows:** John the Baptist wasn't impressed by people's family history or religious background—he wanted to see *fruit*. What actions in your life show that your heart is genuinely following Jesus?

3. **Don't Just Look the Part:** It's easy to fake it—say the right things at youth group or post Bible verses online. But is your daily life reflecting a growing relationship with God? What's one change you could make today to live more authentically?

Bottom Line

God isn't looking for perfect people—He's looking for real ones. Living truthfully and with integrity shows that our hearts are truly turning toward Him.

Prayer

Heavenly Father, Thank You for caring about the condition of my heart more than just how I appear on the outside. Help me to live honestly, speak truthfully, and show real change in my actions. When I mess up, give me the courage to repent and grow. Make me someone who lives out my faith in a way that honors You. In Jesus' Name, Amen.

July 4

Slow to Snap, Quick to Shine

3-Year-Bible Reading: Proverbs 19:11; Psalm 76; Luke 4

"Good sense makes one slow to anger, and it is his glory to overlook an offense." — Proverbs 19:11

"But you, you are to be feared! Who can stand before you when once your anger is roused?" — Psalm 76:7

"And Jesus answered him, 'It is written, "You shall worship the Lord your God, and him only shall you serve."'" — Luke 4:8

Have you ever had someone say something rude or unfair to you, and your first reaction was to fire back? It's tempting to respond out of anger, especially when we feel disrespected or hurt. But **Proverbs 19:11** reminds us that there's strength in patience. Being slow to anger isn't weakness—it's wisdom. In **Psalm 76**, we're reminded that even God's power is measured and purposeful. And in **Luke 4**, Jesus models self-control when He's tempted in the wilderness. Instead of reacting emotionally, He responds with truth and focus. That kind of calm strength is something we can grow in too.

Think About It

1. **Patience is Power:** What happens when you choose to stay calm instead of clapping back? Think of a time when you held your tongue. How did it impact the situation or the way others saw you?

2. **God's Strength, God's Way:** Psalm 76 reminds us that God's anger isn't random—it's just and holy. How can we reflect that kind of measured response in our own lives?

3. **Fighting Back with Truth:** In Luke 4, Jesus didn't argue or get defensive. He simply stood on God's Word. What are some truths you can keep in your heart to help you stay steady when you feel attacked or tempted?

Bottom Line

Being slow to anger and grounded in truth doesn't make you weak—it shows that you're growing in wisdom, just like Jesus. Real strength is shown in how you choose to respond, not how loud you can react.

Prayer

Heavenly Father, thank You for showing us what true strength looks like through Your Word and through the example of Jesus. Help me to be patient, to overlook offenses, and to respond with wisdom and grace. Teach me to fight my battles with truth and to trust You when things get tough. Fill me with Your peace and self-control today. In Jesus' Name, Amen.

July 5

Kingdom Over Clout

3-Year-Bible Reading: Proverbs 19:12–13; Luke 5

"A king's wrath is like the growling of a lion, but his favor is like dew on the grass. A foolish son is ruin to his father, and a wife's quarreling is a continual dripping of rain." — Proverbs 19:12–13

"And when they had brought their boats to land, they left everything and followed him." — Luke 5:11

Have you ever been in a situation where you had to choose between doing what was popular and doing what was right? It's not always easy, especially when others are watching. In **Luke 5**, we see Jesus calling His first disciples. These were ordinary guys—fishermen—who had just experienced a massive catch after a long night of failure. But when Jesus called them, they didn't cling to success. They *left everything* to follow Him. That kind of decision only makes sense when you know who Jesus really is. It's a decision to value the favor of the King of kings over any other reward, popularity, or comfort this world can offer.

Think About It

1. **Whose approval matters most?** Proverbs talks about the power of a king's wrath and favor. If you're living to impress people, you'll always feel pressure to perform. But what if the King you're aiming to please is Jesus—the one who loves you completely and unconditionally?

2. **Letting go to follow Jesus:** The disciples didn't just believe in Jesus—they took action. They left their jobs, their routines, and their plans to follow Him. What might Jesus be asking you to let go of so you can follow Him more fully?

3. **Foolish or faithful?** Proverbs warns about foolishness bringing destruction, especially in close relationships. Following Jesus often includes becoming more like Him in how we treat others. Are your actions bringing peace or drama into your world?

Bottom Line

When Jesus calls, He's inviting you to something greater than popularity, comfort, or control. Choosing to follow Him may cost you something—but you'll gain so much more.

Prayer

Heavenly Father, Thank You for calling me into something bigger than myself. Help me to hear Your voice above all the noise, and to have the courage to follow You even when it's hard. I want to live for Your approval, not the world's. Teach me to let go of anything that holds me back from fully following You. In Jesus' Name, Amen.

JULY 6

Waiting with Purpose

3-Year-Bible Reading: Proverbs 19:14–15; Psalm 77; Luke 6

"House and wealth are inherited from fathers, but a prudent wife is from the Lord. Slothfulness casts into a deep sleep, and an idle person will suffer hunger." — Proverbs 19:14–15

"I will remember the deeds of the Lord; yes, I will remember your wonders of old." — Psalm 77:11

"But I say to you who hear, Love your enemies, do good to those who hate you, bless those who curse you, pray for those who abuse you." — Luke 6:27–28

Some days feel like everything is on pause—like life is stuck buffering. You might be waiting for answers about your future, for friendships to heal, or just for God to show up in a way that feels real. In **Psalm 77**, the writer is deep in sorrow, but he doesn't stay stuck in his feelings. Instead, he *remembers* God's past faithfulness. That shift in focus gives him hope.

Proverbs 19 warns us not to waste the waiting with laziness or distraction—idleness can starve your soul. And in **Luke 6**, Jesus challenges us to live with purpose even in the hard moments: love radically, forgive freely, and keep doing good—especially when it's tough. What if this season of waiting is actually where God is shaping you the most?

THINK ABOUT IT

1. **Stay Awake, Stay Ready:** Are you letting boredom or discouragement lull you into spiritual sleep? God may be preparing something amazing for you—don't miss it by zoning out.

2. **Shift Your Focus:** Like the psalmist, take time to remember what God has already done in your life. Gratitude can turn your doubt into faith.

3. **Live Like Jesus—Even Now:** How can you show love and forgiveness this week, even if someone doesn't deserve it? That's exactly what Jesus teaches in **Luke 6**—and it's what sets you apart.

BOTTOM LINE

Waiting isn't wasted when you live with purpose. Stay active in faith, remember God's goodness, and love like Jesus—right where you are.

PRAYER

Heavenly Father, help me to stay awake in my faith and not drift into spiritual laziness. Teach me to remember all the ways You've been faithful in the past, and give me the strength to love and serve others like Jesus, even when it's hard. Thank You that waiting seasons still have purpose. In Jesus' Name, Amen.

July 7

Living with Heart

3-Year-Bible Reading: Proverbs 19:16–17; Luke 7

"Whoever keeps the commandment keeps his life; he who despises his ways will die. Whoever is generous to the poor lends to the Lord, and he will repay him for his deed." — Proverbs 19:16–17

"And he said to the woman, 'Your faith has saved you; go in peace.'" — Luke 7:50

Have you ever felt invisible—like no one sees your effort, your kindness, or even your pain? In **Luke 7**, we meet a woman like that. She had a reputation, and not the good kind. But when she approached Jesus, pouring out her heart and tears, Jesus didn't turn her away. He saw her. He valued her. And He forgave her. That moment changed her life.

Meanwhile, **Proverbs 19** reminds us that when we care for others, especially those in need, we're not just being "nice"—we're lending to the Lord Himself. That means every act of kindness, every time we choose compassion over judgment, God sees it and values it deeply.

Think About It

1. **God Notices the Small Stuff:** You don't have to be famous or perfect to be seen by God. Like the woman in Luke 7, it's your heart and faith that matter most to Him. Are you offering Him your whole heart?

2. **Kindness is Kingdom Work:** When you help someone in need, you're not just doing a good deed—you're honoring God. Who around you might need encouragement or help today?

3. **Obedience Protects:** Proverbs reminds us that keeping God's commands leads to life. That's not just about avoiding trouble—it's about living with purpose and peace. Are you paying attention to the way you're walking through life?

Bottom Line

God values a heart that is humble, kind, and full of faith. He sees your love, your efforts, and your obedience—even when no one else does.

Prayer

Heavenly Father, Thank You for seeing me and loving me just as I am. Help me to walk in Your ways, to care for others with a generous heart, and to trust that You are always near. Teach me to live with a faith that honors You, even when no one else notices. In Jesus' Name, Amen.

JULY 8

Tough Love and Unshakable Hope

3-Year-Bible Reading: Proverbs 19:18–19; Psalm 78; Luke 8

Discipline your son, for there is hope; do not set your heart on putting him to death. — Proverbs 19:18

They should set their hope in God and not forget the works of God, but keep his commandments. — Psalm 78:7

As for that in the good soil, they are those who, hearing the word, hold it fast in an honest and good heart, and bear fruit with patience. — Luke 8:15

No one *loves* being corrected—especially when it feels like your freedom is being challenged. Whether it's your parents, a teacher, or even God through His Word, discipline can sting. But **Proverbs 19:18** reminds us that discipline isn't about punishment—it's about hope. God's correction is a sign that He believes in your future. Psalm 78 tells the story of a generation that forgot God's faithfulness, even after seeing His miracles. When we forget what He's done, we lose our direction.

Then in **Luke 8**, Jesus talks about the different kinds of soil, or hearts, that receive God's Word. Only one kind produces lasting fruit—the one that holds on to God's truth, even when life gets hard. These three passages together show us that God is working to shape us into something better. It won't always be easy, but it will always be worth it.

THINK ABOUT IT

1. **Correction is love:** When have you experienced discipline that actually helped you grow? What might God be teaching you in hard moments?

2. **Remember God's work:** Psalm 78 shows that forgetting God's past faithfulness can lead to poor choices. How can you remind yourself of God's goodness daily?

3. **Rooted in truth:** Are you the kind of "soil" that holds onto God's Word with patience? What helps you stay grounded when life feels chaotic?

BOTTOM LINE

God disciplines us because He loves us, and when we remember His faithfulness and cling to His Word, our lives can produce real, lasting fruit.

PRAYER

Heavenly Father, thank You for loving me enough to correct me. Help me not to push away the lessons You're teaching me, but to see them as signs of Your care. Remind me of all the times You've come through for me, and give me a heart that holds tightly to Your Word, even when it's tough. Make my life good soil that grows something beautiful for You. In Jesus' Name, Amen.

July 9

God's Plan > My Plan

3-Year-Bible Reading: Proverbs 19:20–21; Luke 9

"Listen to advice and accept instruction, that you may gain wisdom in the future. Many are the plans in the mind of a man, but it is the purpose of the Lord that will stand." — Proverbs 19:20–21

"And he said to all, 'If anyone would come after me, let him deny himself and take up his cross daily and follow me.'" — Luke 9:23

You probably have some plans for your future—college, sports, a dream career, or maybe even what you're doing this weekend. It's great to have goals and ambition, but **Proverbs 19:21** reminds us that no matter how many plans we make, it's *God's* purpose that will ultimately stand. That doesn't mean your dreams don't matter—it means they're safest and strongest when they align with God's plan.

In **Luke 9:23**, Jesus invites us to follow Him, which means sometimes letting go of our own way and trusting His. That's hard, especially when our plans feel exciting or important. But following Jesus means trusting that His way is always better—even when it requires sacrifice.

Think About It

1. **Whose voice are you listening to?** Are you seeking advice and wisdom from godly people in your life—parents, leaders, friends who follow Jesus? Or are you only listening to your own plans and feelings?

2. **Purpose > Plans:** God's purpose is bigger than our plans. That can feel scary when we're not sure what His purpose is. But it's also comforting, because it means we don't have to have it all figured out.

3. **Following Jesus daily:** Taking up your cross *daily* means following Jesus isn't a one-time decision—it's an everyday choice. What's one way you can put His plan before your own today?

Bottom Line

God's plan is better and lasting. Trusting Him means letting go of control, listening to wise advice, and choosing to follow Jesus every day.

Prayer

Heavenly Father, thank You that Your purpose for my life is greater than anything I could plan. Help me to listen to wise advice and to trust You when things don't go the way I imagined. Give me courage to follow Jesus daily, even when it's hard. In Jesus' Name, Amen.

July 10

What's Better Than Gold?

3-Year-Bible Reading: Proverbs 19:22–23; Psalm 79; Luke 10

What is desired in a man is steadfast love, and a poor man is better than a liar. The fear of the Lord leads to life, and whoever has it rests satisfied; he will not be visited by harm — Proverbs 19:22–23

Help us, O God of our salvation, for the glory of your name; deliver us, and atone for our sins, for your name's sake! — Psalm 79:9

But a Samaritan, as he journeyed, came to where he was, and when he saw him, he had compassion — Luke 10:33

We live in a world that often values popularity over kindness, image over integrity, and comfort over compassion. But in **Proverbs 19**, we're reminded that what really matters is *steadfast love*—being someone who loves deeply, honestly, and consistently. Even being poor with integrity is better than living a lie. That's big. **Psalm 79** shows us what it's like to be in deep trouble and still turn to God, trusting His mercy and asking Him to save not just for our sake—but because His name is worth it.

Then in **Luke 10**, Jesus flips the script with a story that challenges everything we think we know about love: the Good Samaritan. The hero wasn't the religious guy or the rule-follower—it was the one who stopped, saw the hurting, and *did something* about it. That kind of love is rare. And it's what God wants from us.

Think About It

1. **Love That Costs Something:** The Samaritan didn't just feel bad for the hurt man—he acted. Real love looks like getting involved, even when it's messy or inconvenient. Who might need your help or kindness today?

2. **Integrity Over Image:** Proverbs says being honest is better than having money but living a lie. How are you choosing integrity in your daily life—online, in friendships, or at school?

3. **God's Mercy is Personal:** Psalm 79 shows us it's okay to cry out to God when things are hard. Are you turning to Him when you're overwhelmed, or trying to handle it all on your own?

Bottom Line

God values love that is real, bold, and compassionate. It's not about how perfect you look on the outside—it's about living with integrity, choosing kindness, and trusting God to be your strength and help, even when life is hard.

Prayer

Heavenly Father, Thank You for showing us what real love looks like through Jesus. Help us be people who don't just talk about love but actually live it out—especially when it's uncomfortable or hard. Teach us to choose honesty over appearances and to trust You when things feel overwhelming. Give us eyes to see others the way You do. In Jesus' Name, Amen.

July 11

Wake Up and Wise Up

3-Year-Bible Reading: Proverbs 19:24–25; Luke 11

"The sluggard buries his hand in the dish and will not even bring it back to his mouth. Strike a scoffer, and the simple will learn prudence; reprove a man of understanding, and he will gain knowledge." — Proverbs 19:24–25

"Blessed rather are those who hear the word of God and keep it!" — Luke 11:28

Ever feel like doing nothing? Like zoning out on your phone instead of doing homework—or ignoring advice because you just don't feel like hearing it? You're not alone. In **Proverbs 19**, we meet a lazy person who won't even lift his hand to feed himself. That's extreme, but it makes a point: laziness and ignoring wisdom don't just waste time—they lead us nowhere.

And in **Luke 11**, Jesus calls out people who hear God's Word but don't actually live it out. It's one thing to hear truth; it's another to let it change you. Being wise and growing in faith means being alert, teachable, and willing to act.

Think About It

1. **Are You Just Listening?** Jesus says the blessing isn't just in *hearing* God's Word but in *keeping* it. Do you read the Bible or hear sermons but then forget them by lunch? What's one way you can live out something you've recently learned?

2. **How Do You Handle Correction?** Proverbs says that wise people *gain knowledge* when corrected. It's not fun being called out, but do you take advice seriously—or get defensive and tune out?

3. **Laziness or Action:** The image of the sluggard with his hand in the dish is a funny but powerful warning. What area of your life needs a little more effort or discipline—school, friendships, your relationship with God?

Bottom Line

God's Word is meant to change us, not just fill our heads. Wisdom means being awake to what God is saying and brave enough to follow through.

Prayer

Heavenly Father, thank You for speaking through Your Word. Help me not to be lazy with my time, my choices, or my faith. Give me a heart that listens to You—and actually lives out what You say. Teach me to receive correction with humility and to grow wiser every day. In Jesus' Name, Amen.

July 12

Walk in the Light

3-Year-Bible Reading: Proverbs 19:26–27; Psalm 80; Luke 12

"He who does violence to his father and chases away his mother is a son who brings shame and reproach. Cease to hear instruction, my son, and you will stray from the words of knowledge." —Proverbs 19:26–27

"Restore us, O God of hosts; let your face shine, that we may be saved!" —Psalm 80:7

"You also must be ready, for the Son of Man is coming at an hour you do not expect." —Luke 12:40

Ever get annoyed when someone tries to tell you what to do? Maybe it's a parent, teacher, or even a friend. In the moment, it feels easier to tune them out and just do your own thing. But **Proverbs 19** warns us that shutting out wisdom can lead us down a path we really don't want to walk. **Psalm 80** reminds us that when we drift, we can always ask God to restore us.

And in **Luke 12**, Jesus calls us to be ready—to live each day with our hearts aligned to Him. The truth is, how we respond to instruction and how we live each day shows what we really believe.

Think About It

1. **Check Your Attitude:** Are you open to correction and guidance, or do you automatically resist it? Learning to receive instruction is a sign of maturity and wisdom.

2. **Be Ready, Always:** Jesus could return at any time. What would it look like for you to live today like He's coming back tomorrow?

3. **Seek Restoration:** If you've been walking your own way, Psalm 80 is a prayer you can make your own: *"Restore me, God. Let Your face shine on me."*

Bottom Line

Choosing to listen, stay alert, and seek God's presence leads to a life of purpose, peace, and readiness. Don't tune out wisdom—lean in and walk in the light.

Prayer

Heavenly Father, help me to have a heart that listens and a life that's ready for You. Forgive me for the times I've pushed away truth or ignored Your voice. Shine Your face on me and lead me in the way I should go. I want to walk in Your light every day. In Jesus' Name, Amen.

July 13

Consequences Are Coming

3-Year-Bible Reading: Proverbs 19:28–29; Luke 13

"A worthless witness mocks at justice, and the mouth of the wicked devours iniquity. Condemnation is ready for scoffers, and beating for the backs of fools." — Proverbs 19:28–29

"Unless you repent, you will all likewise perish." — Luke 13:5

We've all heard the phrase, "Play stupid games, win stupid prizes." It's a harsh way of saying that our choices have consequences. Whether it's lying to get out of trouble or making fun of people who try to do the right thing, we often act like our actions are no big deal. But **Proverbs 19** reminds us that mocking justice and doing wrong will eventually catch up to us.

In **Luke 13**, Jesus says something even more direct: if we don't repent—meaning turn away from sin—we'll face serious consequences. Jesus isn't being mean. He's giving us a heads-up. He loves us too much to let us walk blindly into danger.

Think About It

1. **Truth Has Weight:** Have you ever lied or bent the truth and thought, "It's not a big deal"? God sees lying as serious, especially when it covers up injustice. Our words have power. Are you using them to build truth or tear it down?

2. **Mocking What's Right:** It's easy to joke about things we don't understand or to go along with others who make fun of good choices. But Proverbs says scoffing leads to consequences. Are you standing up for what's right—or laughing it off?

3. **A Wake-Up Call:** Jesus wasn't trying to scare people in **Luke 13**—He was giving a loving warning. Repentance is about changing direction, not just feeling bad. Are there things in your life you need to turn away from before they lead to more pain?

Bottom Line

God is patient and loving, but He's also just. He wants us to take our actions seriously—not to scare us, but to save us. Turning away from sin and choosing His way brings life, not regret.

Prayer

Heavenly Father, thank You for loving me enough to tell me the truth, even when it's hard to hear. Help me recognize when I'm going the wrong way, and give me the courage to turn back to You. Teach me to value truth and justice and to walk in a way that honors You. In Jesus' Name, Amen.

July 14

Wise Warnings and Open Doors

3-Year-Bible Reading: Proverbs 20:1–2; Psalm 81; Luke 14

"Wine is a mocker, strong drink a brawler, and whoever is led astray by it is not wise. The terror of a king is like the growling of a lion; whoever provokes him to anger forfeits his life." — Proverbs 20:1–2

"Oh, that my people would listen to me, that Israel would walk in my ways!" — Psalm 81:13

"For I tell you, none of those men who were invited shall taste my banquet." — Luke 14:24

Imagine being invited to the most epic party of the year—amazing food, the coolest people, and music that hits just right. But instead of going, you say you're too busy. Sounds crazy, right? That's the kind of story Jesus tells in **Luke 14**—a parable about people missing out on God's feast because they chose other things over Him. Pair that with **Psalm 81**, where God is literally longing for His people to just *listen* and follow Him.

Then you've got **Proverbs 20**, reminding us how easy it is to get distracted or even wrecked by things like alcohol or reckless choices. All three passages speak to a simple but deep truth: God offers us His best, but we've got to be wise enough to say "yes."

Think About It

1. **God Wants You In:** Jesus paints a picture of God as a host, throwing open the doors of His Kingdom. Are you showing up to the party—or are other things keeping you away?

2. **Listening Is Loving:** Psalm 81 shows how much God longs for us to simply hear His voice and trust Him. How often do you take time to really listen to what God might be saying?

3. **Choices Have Consequences:** Proverbs warns us about the dangers of letting anything—substances, pride, peer pressure—take the lead in our lives. What influences are shaping your decisions right now?

Bottom Line

God is offering you something amazing—His presence, His wisdom, and a place at His table. Don't miss it because you're chasing something less. Stay focused, stay wise, and say yes to Him.

Prayer

Heavenly Father, thank You for inviting me into something greater than anything this world can offer. Help me to listen to Your voice, to walk in wisdom, and to say "yes" when You call. Keep my heart steady when distractions come, and remind me of the joy that comes from following You. In Jesus' Name, Amen.

July 15

Choose Peace Over Proving a Point

3-Year-Bible Reading: Proverbs 20:3; Luke 15

"It is an honor for a man to keep aloof from strife, but every fool will be quarreling." — Proverbs 20:3

"But when he came to himself, he said, 'How many of my father's hired servants have more than enough bread, but I perish here with hunger! I will arise and go to my father...'" — Luke 15:17–18

Ever had an argument that started over something small, but suddenly you're in a full-blown battle with someone—maybe a sibling, a friend, or even your parents? It's easy to feel like you *have* to prove you're right, especially when emotions are running high. But **Proverbs 20:3** reminds us that real strength and honor come from walking away from fights, not diving into them.

And in **Luke 15**, Jesus tells a story about a younger son who made a huge mess of his life but chose to go back home with humility instead of pride. That choice—swallowing his pride and returning to his father—changed everything.

Think About It

1. **Peace Over Pride:** Why do we sometimes feel like we *have* to win an argument? How can choosing peace actually make you stronger and more respected?

2. **Coming to Your Senses:** The younger son had a turning point—he "came to himself." What does that look like in your life when you realize you're wrong or heading down a bad path?

3. **God Welcomes You Back:** No matter how far we've messed up or how heated things get, God is ready to welcome us with open arms. How does that change the way you respond when you've blown it?

Bottom Line

You don't have to win every fight. Choosing peace and humility reflects strength and opens the door for healing, restoration, and a better path forward with God and others.

Prayer

Heavenly Father, help me to choose peace over pride. Teach me to walk away from arguments that don't honor You and give me the humility to admit when I'm wrong. Thank You for always being ready to forgive and welcome me back when I mess up. Help me show that same grace to others. In Jesus' Name, Amen.

July 16

Dig Deep, Live Wise

3-Year-Bible Reading: Proverbs 20:4–5; Luke 16

"The sluggard does not plow in the autumn; he will seek at harvest and have nothing. The purpose in a man's heart is like deep water, but a man of understanding will draw it out." — Proverbs 20:4–5

"One who is faithful in a very little is also faithful in much... You cannot serve God and money." — Luke 16:10, 13

Have you ever crammed for a test the night before and wished you had prepared earlier? Or maybe you've felt torn between doing what's right and doing what's easiest. The Bible speaks to both those moments in **Proverbs 20** and **Luke 16**.

Whether it's avoiding laziness or choosing who (or what) you'll serve, God wants us to live with purpose and wisdom. It's not always flashy or fun, but being faithful in small things today leads to real reward later. And the good stuff—our God-given purpose—isn't always obvious. Sometimes we have to dig deep to discover it.

Think About It

1. **What are you planting?** Proverbs talks about a person who doesn't plow and then wonders why there's no harvest. If you're not making time for God, friendships, goals, or growth now, what do you hope to reap later? Your future harvest depends on today's choices.

2. **Faithfulness in the small stuff:** Jesus says that if you're trustworthy in little things, you'll be trusted with more. Are you showing up with effort, honesty, and heart—even when no one is watching?

3. **What's driving you?** Luke reminds us that we can't serve both God and money. It's bigger than money—it's about what rules your heart. Is it popularity, success, comfort? Or is it Jesus?

Bottom Line

Faithfulness today shapes your tomorrow. God has placed deep purpose in your heart, but you've got to dig it out—and that starts with small, consistent steps in the right direction.

Prayer

Heavenly Father, help me not to be lazy with the life You've given me. Teach me to be faithful in the little things and to make choices that honor You. Give me the courage to dig deep and follow Your purpose for my life, even when it's not easy. I want to serve You, not the things that pull me away from You. In Jesus' Name, Amen.

July 17

Walk the Walk

3-Year-Bible Reading: Proverbs 20:6–7; Luke 17

Many a man proclaims his own steadfast love, but a faithful man who can find? The righteous who walks in his integrity—blessed are his children after him! — Proverbs 20:6–7

And Jesus said to his disciples, "Temptations to sin are sure to come, but woe to the one through whom they come! … Pay attention to yourselves! If your brother sins, rebuke him, and if he repents, forgive him." — Luke 17:1, 3

Everyone wants to be seen as loyal, kind, and trustworthy—especially in the eyes of friends, family, and even God. But **Proverbs 20:6–7** points out something important: while lots of people *say* they're loyal, it's rare to find someone who truly *lives* that way. Real faith shows up in our actions, not just our words.

Then in **Luke 17**, Jesus gets real with His disciples: life is going to bring challenges, including the temptation to mess up—and people will. That's why He teaches us to keep an eye on our own hearts and also to practice forgiveness when others fall short. It's not always easy, but it's the kind of faith that makes a difference in the world and in us.

Think About It

1. **Integrity is rare:** What does it mean to "walk in integrity"? How would your actions change if you thought about your example influencing others—like younger siblings, friends, or even classmates?

2. **Real faith forgives:** Jesus tells us to forgive those who repent—even if they mess up more than once (see the rest of **Luke 17**). Is there someone you're struggling to forgive? What would it look like to offer them grace like Jesus does?

3. **Watch yourself:** Jesus says, "Pay attention to yourselves!" That means we have to stay alert, not just to others' faults, but our own. What temptations or habits do you need to guard against right now?

Bottom Line

Living out your faith means walking with integrity, forgiving like Jesus, and keeping your heart in check. Words are easy—real faith shows up in how you live.

Prayer

Heavenly Father, Thank You for showing me what real faith looks like through Jesus. Help me to walk in integrity, even when no one's watching. Give me a heart that forgives like You do, and eyes to see where I need to grow. Teach me to live in a way that reflects You to the people around me. In Jesus' Name, Amen.

July 18

Clear Vision, Clean Heart

3-Year-Bible Reading: Proverbs 20:8–9; Psalm 82; Luke 18

"A king who sits on the throne of judgment winnows all evil with his eyes. Who can say, 'I have made my heart pure; I am clean from my sin?'" — Proverbs 20:8–9

"Give justice to the weak and the fatherless; maintain the right of the afflicted and the destitute." — Psalm 82:3

"For everyone who exalts himself will be humbled, but the one who humbles himself will be exalted." — Luke 18:14b

---

We live in a world that often judges by outward appearances—how we look, how many likes we get, or how confident we seem. But the Bible reminds us that God sees past the surface. In **Proverbs 20**, we're told that even the best leaders can't claim a perfectly clean heart. **Psalm 82** calls out for justice, especially for those who are overlooked or treated unfairly.

And in **Luke 18**, Jesus tells a story about two people praying—one proud, the other humble—and how only one walks away right with God. Spoiler alert: it's not the proud guy.

Think About It

1. **Check Your Heart:** Do you ever catch yourself trying to look like you have it all together on the outside while struggling on the inside? God isn't looking for a perfect image—He wants a heart that's honest and open to Him.

2. **Justice Isn't Just a Trend:** Psalm 82 reminds us to care for those who are often ignored—people who are struggling, hurting, or feeling left out. What's one way you can stand up for someone in need this week?

3. **Humility Wins:** In Jesus' parable, the humble man was the one God lifted up. What does humility look like in your everyday life—in your friendships, social media, or when you mess up?

Bottom Line

God sees our hearts, not just our highlight reels. He calls us to live with humility, care for others, and be real with Him. When we stop pretending and start trusting, He meets us with grace.

Prayer

Heavenly Father, Thank You for seeing me completely and loving me anyway. Help me to be honest with You about where I struggle. Teach me to care for others the way You care for me, especially those who are hurting or forgotten. Fill my heart with humility and give me the courage to live with compassion and truth. In Jesus' Name, Amen.

July 19

Check Your Heart

3-Year-Bible Reading: Proverbs 20:10–11; Psalm 83; Luke 19

Unequal weights and unequal measures are both alike an abomination to the Lord. Even a child makes himself known by his acts, by whether his conduct is pure and upright. —Proverbs 20:10–11

O my God, make them like whirling dust, like chaff before the wind. As fire consumes the forest, as the flame sets the mountains ablaze, so may you pursue them with your tempest and terrify them with your hurricane! —Psalm 83:13–15

When he drew near and saw the city, he wept over it, saying, "Would that you, even you, had known on this day the things that make for peace! But now they are hidden from your eyes." —Luke 19:41–42

Have you ever been called out for something you thought no one noticed—like saying something rude under your breath, or pretending not to hear your parents ask for help? **Proverbs 20:11** reminds us that even when we're young, our actions say a lot about who we really are. The way we treat people, how we act when no one's watching, and the choices we make all show what's going on in our hearts.

In **Luke 19**, Jesus weeps over Jerusalem because they didn't recognize what would bring them peace. It broke His heart to see people missing the chance to truly know Him. And in **Psalm 83**, there's a cry for justice—God sees every unfair and evil act, and He doesn't ignore it. Put together, these verses challenge us to check ourselves: Are we living with honesty, kindness, and awareness of God's presence?

Think About It

1. **Your Actions Matter:** What do your choices say about your character? You may be young, but your actions still have meaning and impact.

2. **Jesus Sees the Heart:** Jesus isn't looking for perfection—He's looking for honesty, humility, and a heart that wants peace with Him.

3. **Be Real About Right and Wrong:** It's easy to overlook "small" wrongs—like cheating a little or being fake to friends—but God cares about fairness and truth in all things.

Bottom Line

God sees our hearts and our actions. Even when we're young, how we live matters. Choose honesty, pursue peace, and live in a way that reflects the love of Jesus.

Prayer

Heavenly Father, thank You for seeing me and caring about what's in my heart. Help me to live in a way that honors You, even in the little things. Show me where I need to grow and help me choose peace, honesty, and love every day. In Jesus' Name, Amen.

July 20

Eyes Open, Heart Ready

3-Year-Bible Reading: Proverbs 20:12–13; Psalm 118; Luke 20

"The hearing ear and the seeing eye, the Lord has made them both. Love not sleep, lest you come to poverty; open your eyes, and you will have plenty of bread." —Proverbs 20:12–13

"This is the day that the Lord has made; let us rejoice and be glad in it." —Psalm 118:24

"But he looked directly at them and said, 'What then is this that is written: "The stone that the builders rejected has become the cornerstone"?'" —Luke 20:17

Have you ever slept through your alarm and woke up feeling totally behind? It's the worst. You scramble to catch up, and all day feels off. Proverbs warns us about more than just physical sleep—it's about not *sleepwalking* through life spiritually. God gave us eyes and ears for a reason (see **Proverbs 20:12**). We're meant to be alert—to see what He's doing and listen for His direction. And when we do, we begin to notice that every single day is a gift (**Psalm 118:24**).

In **Luke 20**, Jesus talks about being rejected, even though He was the cornerstone—the most important part of God's plan. It's a wake-up call: don't miss what God is building in and around you. Open your eyes. He's already moving.

Think About It

1. **Spiritual Alarm Clock:** Are you "awake" to what God is doing in your life? Or are you coasting through your days without noticing His hand in the little things?

2. **Today Matters:** Psalm 118 says this day was made by God. How can you live with more purpose and joy *today*, even if it's not a perfect day?

3. **Cornerstone Check:** Jesus was rejected, but He's the foundation of everything. Is He at the center of your life, or have you unintentionally left Him out of your plans?

Bottom Line

God created you to see, hear, and live fully alert to His presence. Don't miss what He's building—He has something powerful planned for today.

Prayer

Heavenly Father, thank You for creating me with eyes to see and ears to hear. Help me not to sleepwalk through life, but to be fully awake to what You're doing. Show me how to live with purpose and joy each day. Remind me that Jesus is my cornerstone, and help me build my life on Him. In Jesus' Name, Amen.

July 21

Wise Eyes and True Treasure

3-Year-Bible Reading: Proverbs 20:14–15; Luke 21

"'Bad, bad,' says the buyer, but when he goes away, then he boasts. There is gold and abundance of costly stones, but the lips of knowledge are a precious jewel." — Proverbs 20:14–15

"He looked up and saw the rich putting their gifts into the offering box, and he saw a poor widow put in two small copper coins. And he said, 'Truly, I tell you, this poor widow has put in more than all of them.'" — Luke 21:1–3

Have you ever bought something cheap and bragged about how you got a great deal—even if it meant someone else got the short end of the stick? Or maybe you've seen people show off their wealth and thought, *"They must be doing everything right."*

But **Proverbs 20:14–15** reminds us that wisdom and honesty are more valuable than gold, and **Luke 21** shows us that God sees the heart, not just the numbers. A poor widow gave only two small coins, but Jesus said her gift was greater than all the rich offerings. Why? Because she gave with trust, not for attention.

Think About It

1. **Value Check:** Are you chasing the kind of wealth the world values—or the kind God treasures? The world sees money and stuff; God sees faith, wisdom, and generosity.

2. **Heart Over Hype:** Why do you give, serve, or speak? Is it to be noticed, or because it's right? Jesus saw the widow's humble heart and praised her, not the rich and flashy givers.

3. **Honest Gains:** Proverbs warns against being sneaky or boastful in deals. Are you honest in how you treat others, even when no one's watching?

Bottom Line

True treasure isn't in what you own or how much you give—it's in the heart behind it. God values faith, honesty, and wisdom more than wealth or reputation.

Prayer

Heavenly Father, help me to see the world the way You see it. Teach me to value what truly matters and to give with a sincere heart. Help me to be honest in my actions and wise in my words. May I seek to please You, not just impress people. In Jesus' Name, Amen.

July 22

Sweet or Bitter?

3-Year-Bible Reading: Proverbs 20:16–17; Psalm 84; Luke 22

"Bread gained by deceit is sweet to a man, but afterward his mouth will be full of gravel." —Proverbs 20:17

"For a day in your courts is better than a thousand elsewhere." —Psalm 84:10

"Father, if you are willing, remove this cup from me. Nevertheless, not my will, but yours, be done." —Luke 22:42

You know that moment when you get away with something? Maybe it's sneaking extra time on your phone, copying homework, or telling a white lie to stay out of trouble. At first, it can feel like a win—a quick fix that tastes sweet. But then comes the guilt, the stress, or the fallout—and suddenly, that "sweet" victory turns to gravel in your mouth (**Proverbs 20:17**).

God offers a better way: not the easy path, but the right one. The psalmist says just one day close to God is better than a thousand lived chasing our own way (**Psalm 84:10**). And in **Luke 22:42**, Jesus gives us the ultimate example of surrender—choosing God's will, even when it's hard. He didn't take the easy way out. He chose obedience out of love.

Think About It

1. **Quick Fix or Lasting Reward?** When you're tempted to take the easy way out, ask yourself—what will this cost later? Is it worth the "gravel" in your mouth?

2. **Where's Your Sweet Spot?** The psalmist says just being with God is better than anywhere else. What's one way you can spend time in God's presence this week?

3. **Jesus Chose the Hard Way:** In the garden, Jesus didn't want to suffer—but He chose to trust God. Is there something hard you're facing where you need to say, "Not my will, but Yours"?

Bottom Line

God's way isn't always easy, but it's always best. What seems sweet in the moment can turn bitter—choose the lasting joy of walking with Him.

Prayer

Heavenly Father, sometimes I want what's easy more than what's right. Help me to see beyond the moment and trust You, even when it's hard. I want to live in a way that brings You honor and keeps me close to You. Give me the courage to say, "Not my will, but Yours." In Jesus' Name, Amen.

July 23

Plans, Pain, and Purpose

3-Year-Bible Reading: Proverbs 20:18; Psalm 69; Luke 23

"Plans are established by counsel; by wise guidance wage war."—Proverbs 20:18

"But as for me, my prayer is to you, O Lord. At an acceptable time, O God, in the abundance of your steadfast love answer me in your saving faithfulness."—Psalm 69:13

"And Jesus said, 'Father, forgive them, for they know not what they do.'"—Luke 23:34

Have you ever been totally misunderstood or unfairly blamed for something you didn't do? That gut-punch feeling can be the worst. In **Luke 23**, Jesus faced the ultimate injustice—He was innocent but still nailed to a cross. And yet, He forgave. In **Psalm 69**, David cries out to God from a place of deep pain, feeling mocked and overwhelmed.

And in **Proverbs 20:18**, we're reminded that wise decisions and good plans come through seeking godly advice. Life can be confusing and painful, but these verses show us that God is with us in every part of the journey—from planning, to suffering, to forgiving.

Think About It

1. **Plan with God's Wisdom:** Are you trying to make big decisions on your own? Proverbs tells us to seek wise advice. God often speaks through trusted mentors, parents, youth leaders, and His Word. Who are you letting speak into your choices?

2. **Pain Has a Purpose:** Like David in Psalm 69, it's okay to be honest with God about your struggles. He can handle your feelings. What tough thing are you facing right now that you need to give to Him?

3. **Forgiveness Over Revenge:** Jesus forgave people who were literally killing Him. That's next-level love. Is there someone in your life you're struggling to forgive? How can Jesus' example help you take a step toward letting go?

Bottom Line

Even when life feels unfair or painful, God calls us to trust His plan, cry out to Him honestly, and follow Jesus' example of forgiveness.

Prayer

Heavenly Father, sometimes life doesn't make sense, and it really hurts. Help me to trust You when things feel confusing. Teach me to seek wisdom, to be real with You in my struggles, and to choose forgiveness even when it's hard. Thank You for showing me what love and strength really look like through Jesus. In Jesus' Name, Amen.

July 24

Watch Your Words, Follow His Voice

3-Year-Bible Reading: Proverbs 20:19; Luke 24

"Whoever goes about slandering reveals secrets; therefore do not associate with a simple babbler." — Proverbs 20:19

"And beginning with Moses and all the Prophets, he interpreted to them in all the Scriptures the things concerning himself… They said to each other, 'Did not our hearts burn within us while he talked to us on the road, while he opened to us the Scriptures?'" — Luke 24:27, 32

Have you ever shared something with a friend only to find out later it's been passed around like a trending meme? Gossip spreads fast—and it hurts. **Proverbs 20:19** reminds us to be careful about who we trust with our words and how we speak about others. But there's another side to this: whose words are we *listening* to?

In **Luke 24**, Jesus meets two disciples who are confused and heartbroken. But when He walks with them and explains the Scriptures, something powerful happens—they feel their hearts come alive. Gossip may stir drama, but God's Word stirs truth, clarity, and passion. So the real question is: are we tuning in to the voice of the world or the voice of Jesus?

Think About It

1. **Words Can Wound:** Who are you listening to, and how are their words shaping your heart or mindset?
2. **Jesus Speaks Life:** The disciples didn't recognize Jesus right away, but they felt the impact of His words. When you read Scripture, do you pay attention to how God might be speaking to you through it?
3. **Walk With the Right People:** Proverbs warns us not to stick close to "babblers"—those who stir drama. What kind of people are you surrounding yourself with? Are they helping you grow closer to Jesus?

Bottom Line

Words have power. Avoid those who use them to tear others down, and lean into the words of Jesus that give life, truth, and purpose.

Prayer

Heavenly Father, help me to be wise with my words and cautious with the voices I let influence me. Teach me to recognize Your voice in Scripture and in the quiet moments of life. Surround me with people who point me to You, and make me someone who speaks life into others. In Jesus' Name, Amen.

July 25

Respect, Roots, and Real Growth

3-Year-Bible Reading: Proverbs 20:20–21; Philippians 1

"If one curses his father or his mother, his lamp will be put out in utter darkness. An inheritance gained hastily in the beginning will not be blessed in the end." — Proverbs 20:20–21

"And I am sure of this, that he who began a good work in you will bring it to completion at the day of Jesus Christ." — Philippians 1:6

Have you ever wanted to grow up *fast*? Maybe you've thought, "I just want to be done with school," or "I wish I had all the freedom and money right now." It's tempting to want the rewards without the journey.

But **Proverbs 20:20–21** warns against rushing ahead without respect or wisdom, especially when it comes to relationships with parents and chasing blessings too quickly. In **Philippians 1**, Paul reminds us that God is working in us slowly, surely, and on purpose. The process matters—and so does our attitude during it.

Think About It

1. **Respect Is the Root:** Proverbs warns about dishonoring parents—not just because it's wrong, but because it leads to darkness. Why do you think respect for authority is so connected to spiritual growth?

2. **Quick Gains Can Miss the Point:** What are some things you've wanted *right now* that might be better with time? How can waiting and learning prepare you for those blessings?

3. **God Is Still Working:** According to Philippians 1:6, God has already started something amazing in you. Are you trusting His timing, or trying to rush ahead? How can you lean into the process today?

Bottom Line

Real growth takes time, respect, and trust in God's process. Don't trade long-term blessing for a shortcut that leaves you empty. Let God do His work—He's not done with you yet.

Prayer

Heavenly Father, thank You for starting a good work in me and for promising to finish it. Help me to honor the people You've placed in my life, even when it's tough. Give me patience to trust Your timing and to grow the right way. In Jesus' Name, Amen.

July 26

Trusting God's Timing

3-Year-Bible Reading: Proverbs 20:22; Psalm 85; Philippians 2

"Do not say, 'I will repay evil'; wait for the Lord, and he will deliver you." — Proverbs 20:22

"Restore us again, O God of our salvation, and put away your indignation toward us." — Psalm 85:4

"Do nothing from selfish ambition or conceit, but in humility count others more significant than yourselves." — Philippians 2:3

We all want things to happen right now. Whether it's getting that new phone, passing an important test, or seeing a situation change for the better, we often feel the pressure to fix everything on our own terms. But what happens when the timing isn't right, or when the outcome isn't exactly what we expected? **Proverbs 20:22** reminds us that instead of rushing to fix things or take matters into our own hands, we are called to wait for God's perfect timing.

In **Psalm 85**, we see the psalmist crying out to God for restoration, trusting that only God can bring the peace and change they need. It's a reminder that God is in control, and His timing is always better than ours. And in **Philippians 2**, we are called to adopt a heart of humility, looking out for others and serving them rather than always seeking our own way. It's a message that teaches us to trust God, to wait on His plan, and to live with a servant's heart, even when it's tough.

Think About It

1. **Trust God's Timing:** What situations in your life are you tempted to rush? How can you practice waiting on God's perfect timing instead of forcing your own solutions?
2. **Humble Yourself:** Philippians 2 challenges us to consider others more important than ourselves. What does it look like to put someone else's needs before your own?
3. **God Brings Restoration:** In Psalm 85, the psalmist asks for restoration. Are there areas in your life where you need God's healing or restoration? What does it look like to trust Him for that change?

Bottom Line

God's timing is always better than our own. Instead of rushing through life, we can trust Him to make things right in His time, knowing that He is always working for our good. Humility, patience, and trust in God's plan will lead to the peace and restoration we long for.

Prayer

Heavenly Father, thank You for Your perfect timing and for always working things out for our good. Help me to trust You when I want to rush ahead. Teach me to be patient, humble, and to put others before myself. I know that You are always with me, guiding me. Please restore and strengthen me in the areas where I need Your help. In Jesus' Name, Amen.

July 27

True Treasure

3-Year-Bible Reading: Proverbs 20:23; Philippians 3

"Unequal weights are an abomination to the Lord, and false scales are not good." — Proverbs 20:23

Indeed, I count everything as loss because of the surpassing worth of knowing Christ Jesus my Lord." — Philippians 3:8

Have you ever found yourself weighing things differently depending on what you value? It's easy to let the world's standards influence the way we measure success, happiness, or even friendships. But in **Proverbs 20:23**, we're reminded that using "false scales" — whether in how we view ourselves or others — doesn't honor God. Instead of focusing on what the world says is valuable, **Philippians 3** teaches us to prioritize knowing Christ above everything else. When we value Him above all things, everything else finds its proper place.

It's easy for young people to get caught up in comparing themselves to others. Whether it's the latest trends, social media likes, or the pressure to be perfect, it can feel like we have to "weigh" ourselves against a set of standards that don't truly reflect who we are in Christ. But remember, God sees you for who you are, not what you appear to be on the outside. The treasure you should pursue is not earthly fame or achievements, but the "surpassing worth of knowing Christ" (Philippians 3:8).

Think about it: if you spent less time measuring your worth by others' standards, and more time focusing on growing in your relationship with Jesus, how would your life change? This doesn't mean you can't have goals or aspirations, but it does mean that your identity and value should never depend on what's on the outside. When you weigh everything against the truth of Christ's love and purpose for you, you'll find that the scales tip in a different direction — one that leads to lasting joy and peace.

Think About It

1. **True Value:** What are some things you tend to value most in life? Are they things that align with God's perspective?
2. **Measuring by God's Standards:** How can you shift your focus to value your relationship with Jesus above everything else?
3. **True Treasure:** How does knowing that Christ's love is more valuable than anything this world offers change your perspective?

Bottom Line

The world's standards may seem appealing, but true treasure is found in knowing Christ. Let Him be the one who sets the value in your life.

Prayer

Heavenly Father, thank You for showing us that true worth is found in You alone. Help me to focus less on what the world says is valuable and more on growing in my relationship with You. Teach me to measure my life by Your standards, so that I may treasure what truly matters. In Jesus' Name, Amen.

July 28

God's Got This

3-Year-Bible Reading: Proverbs 20:24; Psalms 86; Philippians 4

"A man's steps are from the Lord; how then can man understand his way?" — Proverbs 20:24 (ESV)

"Teach me your way, O Lord, that I may walk in your truth; unite my heart to fear your name." — Psalm 86:11 (ESV)

"Do not be anxious about anything, but in everything by prayer and supplication with thanksgiving let your requests be made known to God." — Philippians 4:6 (ESV)

Have you ever been unsure about the direction your life is heading? Maybe you're making big decisions about your future, or maybe it feels like things are just moving too fast. It's easy to feel confused or overwhelmed. But did you know that God is not only with you but also guiding your steps? **Proverbs 20:24** reminds us that our steps come from the Lord, meaning even when we don't fully understand the path ahead, He's in control. And when we seek Him like David does in **Psalm 86**, asking God to teach us His ways, He will guide us through everything, even the tough stuff. Plus, **Philippians 4** tells us that we don't need to be anxious. Instead, we can pray and trust that God will give us peace. Isn't that comforting?

You might be feeling uncertain about your plans or the future. You might have some big questions or moments of doubt. But this is where faith comes in. Trusting that God knows the best way forward is something we can rely on every day. And when you bring those questions to God in prayer, He listens. No matter how big or small your concerns might seem, God cares about every detail.

Think About It

1. **God's Plan for You:** How does knowing that your steps are from the Lord change the way you approach decisions?

2. **Seeking God's Guidance:** What are some ways you can actively ask God to teach you His ways in your daily life?

3. **Peace in Prayer:** What's one thing you can start praying about today instead of worrying over?

Bottom Line

You don't have to figure everything out on your own. God is with you, guiding your steps, and giving you peace when you trust in Him.

Prayer

Heavenly Father, thank You for always being with me and guiding my steps. When I feel uncertain or worried, help me to remember that You are in control. Teach me Your ways and help me to trust You more. Please give me peace as I bring my concerns to You in prayer. In Jesus' Name, Amen.

July 29

Wisdom for Living Well

3-Year-Bible Reading: Proverbs 20:25-26; Colossians 1

"It is a snare to say rashly, 'It is holy,' and to reflect only after making vows. A wise king winnows the wicked and drives the wheel over them." — Proverbs 20:25-26

"And he is the head of the body, the church. He is the beginning, the firstborn from the dead, that in everything he might be preeminent." — Colossians 1:18

Sometimes, life can feel like a whirlwind. Decisions, big and small, are coming at you all the time. You might feel pressure to act quickly or make promises without really thinking about them. In **Proverbs 20:25**, the Bible reminds us that we shouldn't rush into making commitments or decisions. It's a trap to say something is "holy" or make promises on the fly without considering the consequences. Even when it comes to something good or noble, like being involved in church or serving others, it's important to think carefully first. God wants us to live wisely, not impulsively.

In **Colossians 1**, we see that Jesus is the head of the church—He is the ultimate authority in all things, and He should be the one guiding our choices. When we keep Him at the center of our lives, our decisions will reflect His wisdom and peace. He is the beginning, the firstborn, and in everything, He deserves to be preeminent, or first place, in our lives. If we truly want to live wisely, we need to put Jesus first, allowing His wisdom to shape how we live, serve, and make decisions.

Think About It

1. **Rash Decisions:** Have you ever made a snap decision or promise and later regretted it? What could you do next time to avoid rushing into things?

2. **Jesus First:** In what areas of your life might you need to let Jesus take the lead? How can you make Him the "head" of those areas?

3. **Wisdom in Choices:** When making decisions, are you taking the time to reflect and pray for God's guidance, or do you tend to act first and think later?

Bottom Line

Living wisely means making thoughtful decisions, especially when it comes to commitments. Don't rush into things; let Jesus guide you. He deserves to be first in everything, and when you put Him there, your choices will reflect His wisdom.

Prayer

Heavenly Father, thank You for being the ultimate source of wisdom. Help me to slow down and think carefully before making decisions, especially the big ones. I want to put You first in my life, trusting You to lead me with Your wisdom. In Jesus' Name, Amen.

July 30

The Light Inside You

3-Year-Bible Reading: Proverbs 20:27-28; Colossians 2

"The spirit of man is the lamp of the Lord, searching all his innermost parts. Steadfast love and faithfulness preserve the king, and by steadfast love his throne is upheld." — Proverbs 20:27-28

"Therefore, as you received Christ Jesus the Lord, so walk in him, rooted and built up in him and established in the faith, just as you were taught, abounding in thanksgiving." — Colossians 2:6-7

Your heart is like a lamp. No, really. Proverbs talks about how the spirit of a person is like a lamp, shining light into the deepest parts of who you are. That light, your soul, is something the Lord uses to lead you. But it doesn't always feel like a glowing beacon, does it? Sometimes, it feels like the light is flickering or going out. Maybe you feel like you're in a dark spot in life, trying to figure out your purpose or feeling uncertain about the future. This is where **Colossians 2** offers something powerful: it encourages you to be "rooted and built up in Him" — in Jesus. When you stay connected to Jesus, your inner light stays strong, no matter how tough things get.

Think about how much you trust your phone to charge when it's plugged in. If you stop plugging it in, the battery dies, right? The same is true for your spiritual life. Jesus is the source of your strength, your purpose, your everything. Without Him, you'll lose your way. But with Him, you'll be anchored in faith, and that light will shine brighter.

Think About It

1. **The Lamp Inside You:** How can your spirit be a light for others? Do you let your faith show in how you treat people and make decisions?
2. **Rooted in Jesus:** What are some ways you can make sure you're staying connected to Jesus daily? Are there habits, like prayer or reading your Bible, that can help you grow?
3. **Steadfast Love:** How can you show God's love and faithfulness to others? What difference does it make in your life when you remember how much God loves you?

Bottom Line

Your light is strongest when you stay rooted in Jesus. Let His love and faithfulness fuel your life and guide you through all the ups and downs.

Prayer

Heavenly Father, Thank You for being the light in our lives, guiding us through every challenge. Help us to stay rooted in You and to shine Your love to those around us. Give us the strength to live faithfully, even when things feel dark. We trust in Your faithfulness to uphold us. In Jesus' Name, Amen.

July 31

Strong in the Lord

3-Year-Bible Reading: Proverbs 20:29-30; Psalms 87; Colossians 3-4

"The glory of young men is their strength, but the splendor of old men is their gray hair. Blows that wound cleanse away evil; strokes make clean the innermost parts." — Proverbs 20:29-30

"Glorious things of you are spoken, O city of God." — Psalms 87:3

"Put on then, as God's chosen ones, holy and beloved, compassionate hearts, kindness, humility, meekness, and patience, bearing with one another and, if one has a complaint against another, forgiving each other; as the Lord has forgiven you, so you also must forgive." — Colossians 3:12-13

When you're young, there's a lot of attention placed on strength, energy, and what you're capable of doing. **Proverbs 20:29** talks about how the strength of youth is something to be proud of, but it also reminds us that strength can come with responsibility. You're not just strong to show off, but to help others and grow into the person God has made you to be. But this strength doesn't just come from muscles or energy—it's also found in your character and your ability to love and forgive, which **Colossians 3:12-13** emphasizes. God calls you to be strong in the ways that matter most: kindness, patience, humility, and compassion.

In **Psalms 87**, we are reminded of the importance of belonging to God's family, His kingdom. Just like the city of God is glorious, so are those who belong to Him. Your strength is not just for your own glory, but to serve God's bigger purpose. God's glory shines through in your life when you act with love, humility, and grace, reflecting His goodness and bringing glory to Him.

Think About It

1. **What does it mean to be strong in the Lord?** Think about how your strength isn't just physical. How can you show strength through kindness and patience?

2. **How does forgiveness fit into your strength?** In **Colossians 3:13**, we are called to forgive others just like God forgives us. Why is forgiveness a sign of strength rather than weakness?

3. **Belonging to God's kingdom: Psalms 87** reminds us that being part of God's family is a glorious thing. How does knowing that change the way you see yourself and your purpose in life?

Bottom Line

True strength comes from being rooted in Christ. It's about more than what you can do on your own; it's about showing the love, patience, and forgiveness that reflects who God is. You are called to be a part of something greater—God's kingdom—and in that, you can stand strong, not just in body, but in spirit.

Prayer

Heavenly Father, thank You for making me strong, not only in my body but in my heart and spirit. Help me to be strong in kindness, humility, and forgiveness, reflecting Your love to others. Guide me in using my strength for Your glory, and help me to remember that I belong to You, part of Your kingdom. In Jesus' Name, Amen.

August 1

Hearts in His Hands

3-Year-Bible Reading: Proverbs 21:1; 1 Thessalonians 1–3

"The king's heart is a stream of water in the hand of the Lord; he turns it wherever he will." — Proverbs 21:1

"For we know, brothers loved by God, that he has chosen you." — 1 Thessalonians 1:4

"Now may our God and Father himself, and our Lord Jesus, direct our way to you." — 1 Thessalonians 3:11

Sometimes, life can feel like it's completely out of our control—because, honestly, a lot of it is. Whether it's school, relationships, family stuff, or decisions about the future, it's easy to get overwhelmed or wonder if things will ever fall into place. But **Proverbs 21:1** reminds us that even the hearts of kings—people with major power and influence—are like streams of water in God's hands. That means God's not just involved in the big picture; He's personally shaping and guiding the details, even when we can't see it yet. And in **1 Thessalonians**, we see how God doesn't just guide us, He *chooses* us, loves us, and desires to be close to us. Paul's prayer in chapter 3 shows that God is always working behind the scenes, directing our steps and drawing us toward what's good and true.

Think About It

1. **God's in control:** Where in your life do you feel like things are uncertain or out of your hands? How can remembering that God turns hearts like streams give you peace?

2. **You are chosen:** Paul reminded the Thessalonians that they were *loved by God and chosen*. How might your confidence change if you remembered every day that God has handpicked *you*?

3. **God guides relationships:** Paul longed to reconnect with people he loved, and he trusted God to "direct his way." Are there friendships or family situations where you need to trust God's timing and direction?

Bottom Line

God lovingly guides every heart and situation—including yours. You are chosen, cared for, and never alone in what you're facing.

Prayer

Heavenly Father, thank You for holding every heart and every plan in Your hands. Help me trust that You're in control even when I feel overwhelmed or uncertain. Remind me daily that I am loved and chosen by You, and help me follow Your direction with faith. In Jesus' Name, Amen.

August 2

Heart Check

3-Year-Bible Reading: Proverbs 21:2–3; Psalm 88; 1 Thessalonians 4–5

"Every way of a man is right in his own eyes, but the Lord weighs the heart. To do righteousness and justice is more acceptable to the Lord than sacrifice." — Proverbs 21:2–3

"But I, O Lord, cry to you; in the morning my prayer comes before you." — Psalm 88:13

"For God has not destined us for wrath, but to obtain salvation through our Lord Jesus Christ, who died for us so that whether we are awake or asleep we might live with him." — 1 Thessalonians 5:9–10

It's easy to think we're doing okay—especially when we're checking the boxes: going to church, helping out, being (mostly) nice. But Proverbs **21:2–3** reminds us that God isn't just looking at what we do on the outside. He sees our *hearts*. That can feel intimidating, especially on the days when we're wrestling with hard emotions, doubts, or just feel distant from Him—kind of like the raw honesty in **Psalm 88**, where the writer is crying out in deep pain. But the good news? God isn't put off by our mess.

In **1 Thessalonians 5**, we're reminded that Jesus *died for us*—not because we had it all together, but so that we could *live with Him*, whether we're on fire with faith or struggling just to show up.

Think About It

1. **Heart Over Hype:** Are you doing things to look good on the outside, or is your heart truly seeking to do what's right in God's eyes?

2. **God Can Handle It:** Psalm 88 shows someone being brutally honest with God. Do you believe God is safe to run to, even with your darkest thoughts and deepest hurts?

3. **Your Hope Is Secure:** In 1 Thessalonians 5, we're reminded that salvation is *God's plan for you*. How can this truth give you peace when you're feeling overwhelmed or unsure?

Bottom Line

God cares more about your heart than your performance. He welcomes your honesty, even in your pain, and He's already made a way for you to live with Him—now and forever.

Prayer

Heavenly Father, Thank You for seeing my heart and still loving me completely. Help me to live in a way that pleases You, not just on the outside, but deep inside too. Teach me to come to You with honesty, like the psalmist, and to trust that my hope is secure in Jesus. Even when life is hard or I feel distant, remind me that You are near and that I belong to You. In Jesus' Name, Amen.

August 3

When Pride Gets in the Way

3-Year-Bible Reading: Proverbs 21:4; II Thessalonians 1–3

"Haughty eyes and a proud heart, the lamp of the wicked, are sin." — Proverbs 21:4

"To this end we always pray for you, that our God may make you worthy of his calling and may fulfill every resolve for good and every work of faith by his power." — 2 Thessalonians 1:11

"But the Lord is faithful. He will establish you and guard you against the evil one." — 2 Thessalonians 3:3

Have you ever felt like you had to prove something to the world? Maybe it's getting the most likes, crushing your goals, or just being seen as the best. Our culture celebrates pride and self-promotion, but **Proverbs 21:4** reminds us that pride isn't just an attitude—it's sin. It blocks our hearts from fully depending on God.

Paul's letters in **2 Thessalonians** show us a better way: relying on God's strength, being faithful, and living lives that reflect His calling. Instead of being led by ego, we're invited to be led by the Spirit and shaped by God's purposes.

Think About It

1. **Pride Check:** Where in your life are you tempted to rely on yourself more than on God?

2. **Living Worthy:** What does it mean to live "worthy of His calling" (2 Thessalonians 1:11)? How can you pursue that this week?

3. **God's Got You:** When things get hard or scary, how does knowing "the Lord is faithful" (2 Thessalonians 3:3) give you peace?

Bottom Line

Pride blinds us to God's best. But when we live by faith and rely on God's power, He shapes us into people who reflect His goodness, not our own greatness.

Prayer

Heavenly Father, help me to recognize when pride tries to take over. I don't want to live for my own glory—I want to live for Yours. Teach me to depend on Your strength and stay faithful, even when it's hard. Thank You for being with me and guarding me every step of the way. In Jesus' Name, Amen.

August 4

Smart Steps, Not Shortcuts

3-Year-Bible Reading: Proverbs 21:5–6; 1 Timothy 1–2

"The plans of the diligent lead surely to abundance, but everyone who is hasty comes only to poverty. The getting of treasures by a lying tongue is a fleeting vapor and a snare of death." — Proverbs 21:5–6

"The aim of our charge is love that issues from a pure heart and a good conscience and a sincere faith." — 1 Timothy 1:5

"For there is one God, and there is one mediator between God and men, the man Christ Jesus." — 1 Timothy 2:5

Let's be honest—shortcuts can be tempting. Whether it's cheating on homework, exaggerating on social media, or rushing into something without thinking, it's easy to want quick results. But **Proverbs 21:5–6** warns that chasing fast success through dishonesty or laziness can actually mess us up.

In contrast, **1 Timothy 1–2** calls us to live with a clear heart, real love, and sincere faith. That means slowing down and walking with purpose, not racing ahead without God. And the best part? We don't have to do it alone. **1 Timothy 2:5** reminds us that Jesus is our bridge to God—He's not only cheering us on, He's walking with us step by step.

Think About It

1. **Patience Pays Off:** Are there areas in your life where you're tempted to take shortcuts? What might it look like to choose diligence and honesty instead?

2. **Real Love Requires Real Faith:** Paul says love comes from a pure heart, good conscience, and sincere faith. Are you letting God shape those things in your life?

3. **Who Are You Following?** Jesus is your mediator, your go-between, your guide. Are you letting Him lead your decisions—or are you trying to run the show?

Bottom Line

Lasting success and real peace come from slow, steady steps with God—not quick fixes. Walk in love, hold onto your faith, and trust that God's path is worth the wait.

Prayer

Heavenly Father, help me not to chase after shortcuts or things that don't last. Teach me to be patient, honest, and faithful in everything I do. Shape my heart to love others sincerely and to trust You fully. Thank You for Jesus, who walks with me every step of the way. In Jesus' Name, Amen.

August 5

The Real Deal

3-Year-Bible Reading: Proverbs 21:7–8; Psalm 89; 1 Timothy 3–4

"The violence of the wicked will sweep them away, because they refuse to do what is just. The way of the guilty is crooked, but the conduct of the pure is upright." — Proverbs 21:7–8

"Righteousness and justice are the foundation of your throne; steadfast love and faithfulness go before you." — Psalm 89:14

"Let no one despise you for your youth, but set the believers an example in speech, in conduct, in love, in faith, in purity." — 1 Timothy 4:12

Do you ever feel like the world is rewarding the wrong people? Maybe the ones who lie, cheat, or play dirty seem to get ahead. It's easy to wonder, "Does doing the right thing even matter?" But God's Word gives us a strong reminder today: God *sees* the difference between the fake and the faithful. In **Proverbs 21**, we're told the wicked will fall because they refuse justice. **Psalm 89** tells us God's throne is built on righteousness and love.

And in **1 Timothy 4**, Paul encourages a young Timothy—and you—to rise above low expectations and live in a way that reflects God's truth. God isn't impressed by empty actions or appearances. He's looking for real hearts, faithful steps, and lives shaped by His Spirit.

Think About It

1. **What Does "Real" Faith Look Like?** It's not about being perfect. It's about being consistent—loving well, choosing truth, and letting your life speak louder than your words.

2. **Your Life is an Example:** Even as a teen, you're a leader. What you say, how you treat people, and the choices you make show others what you believe. Don't underestimate your influence.

3. **God's Standard is Steady:** While the world may celebrate the wrong things, God stays the same. Righteousness, love, and faithfulness are still what He values.

Bottom Line

God isn't calling you to be popular—He's calling you to be faithful. You don't have to wait to be older to live for Him. Start now. Be the real deal.

Prayer

Heavenly Father, Thank You for reminding me that faithfulness matters, even when it feels unnoticed. Help me live with integrity—in what I say, how I act, and how I treat others. I want to set an example that points people to You. Keep me grounded in Your love and truth, no matter what others are doing. In Jesus' Name, Amen.

August 6

Peace in the Chaos

3-Year-Bible Reading: Proverbs 21:9–10; Psalm 90; 1 Timothy 5–6

"It is better to live in a corner of the housetop than in a house shared with a quarrelsome wife. The soul of the wicked desires evil; his neighbor finds no mercy in his eyes." — Proverbs 21:9–10

"So teach us to number our days that we may get a heart of wisdom." — Psalm 90:12

"But godliness with contentment is great gain, for we brought nothing into the world, and we cannot take anything out of the world." — 1 Timothy 6:6–7

Have you ever been around someone who argues just to argue, constantly stirring up drama or making life feel like a battle zone? Whether it's at school, at home, or even in group chats, conflict can wear us down. **Proverbs 21** reminds us that peace—even if it means having less or being alone for a while—is better than constant conflict. **Psalm 90** zooms out and shows us how short life really is. It encourages us to live wisely, to value our time, and not get caught up in things that don't really matter.

And then **1 Timothy 6** drops this truth bomb: real gain comes not from having more stuff, popularity, or winning arguments, but from godliness and being content with what God has already given us.

Think About It

1. **Do you bring peace or drama?** When things get tense, do your words and actions calm things down or add fuel to the fire?

2. **How are you using your time?** Life is short—what are you spending most of your time thinking about, doing, or chasing after? Does it reflect wisdom?

3. **What does contentment look like for you?** Are you constantly comparing your life to others? Or are you learning to be thankful and joyful in what God's already given you?

Bottom Line

Living a wise, peaceful, and content life is better than chasing approval, winning arguments, or having it all. Focus on growing in godliness, using your time well, and being a source of peace wherever you go.

Prayer

Heavenly Father, Help me to be someone who brings peace, not chaos. Teach me to number my days and live with wisdom. Keep my heart content and focused on You instead of what the world says I need. Help me to grow in godliness and to value what truly matters. In Jesus' Name, Amen.

August 7

Learn It, Live It, Pass It On

3-Year-Bible Reading: Proverbs 21:11–12; 2 Timothy 1–2

"When a scoffer is punished, the simple becomes wise; when a wise man is instructed, he gains knowledge." — Proverbs 21:11

"The Lord knows those who are his, and, 'Let everyone who names the name of the Lord depart from iniquity.'" — 2 Timothy 2:19

"For God gave us a spirit not of fear but of power and love and self-control." — 2 Timothy 1:7

Have you ever watched someone make a big mistake and thought, "I definitely don't want to do that"? Life is full of chances to learn—from others' failures and from our own experiences. **Proverbs 21:11** shows that a wise person takes instruction seriously and grows because of it.

And when Paul wrote to Timothy, he reminded him (and us) that God didn't give us a spirit of fear, but one of *power, love,* and *self-control* (**2 Timothy 1:7**). As young people navigating challenges at school, with friends, and online, these truths can help us grow in wisdom and courage, so we can live faithfully and influence others for good.

Think About It

1. **Be Teachable:** Are you open to correction? Wise people learn from instruction—even from the mistakes of others. Don't let pride keep you from growing.

2. **You've Got Power:** Fear may whisper that you're not enough, but God says otherwise. He's given you the Holy Spirit to live with strength, love, and self-control. What's one area you can step out in bold faith this week?

3. **Pass It On:** Paul mentored Timothy, and Timothy was expected to teach others (see **2 Timothy 2:2**). Who can you encourage or guide in your own life—maybe a younger sibling, friend, or teammate?

Bottom Line

God calls you to grow in wisdom, walk in courage, and help others do the same. You don't have to be perfect—you just have to be willing.

Prayer

Heavenly Father, thank You for giving me a spirit of power, love, and self-control. Help me to be teachable, courageous, and faithful in following You. Show me how to learn from life, live boldly for You, and share what I've learned with others. In Jesus' Name, Amen.

AUGUST 8

When No One's Watching

3-Year-Bible Reading: Proverbs 21:13; Psalm 91; 2 Timothy 3–4

"Whoever closes his ear to the cry of the poor will himself call out and not be answered." — Proverbs 21:13

"He who dwells in the shelter of the Most High will abide in the shadow of the Almighty." — Psalm 91:1

"Indeed, all who desire to live a godly life in Christ Jesus will be persecuted... But as for you, continue in what you have learned and have firmly believed..." — 2 Timothy 3:12, 14

Some days, it's tough to live out your faith—especially when it feels like no one else cares or notices. You might see others doing wrong and getting rewarded, or people ignoring the needs around them. It can feel tempting to blend in or give up.

But **Proverbs 21:13** reminds us that how we treat others, especially the hurting, matters deeply to God. **Psalm 91** reassures us that when we stick close to God—even when no one sees—He is our refuge. And **2 Timothy 3–4** tells us to stay grounded in the truth, no matter how hard life gets, because we're not living to impress people but to be faithful to God.

THINK ABOUT IT

1. **How do you respond to people in need?** Do you notice the cries of others—friends who are struggling, classmates who are lonely, or people who are hurting? God calls us to listen and act with compassion.

2. **Where's your shelter?** When life feels overwhelming or you're facing pressure to compromise your faith, are you turning to God for strength and peace, or trying to handle it alone?

3. **Stay rooted in truth:** Paul tells Timothy that living for Jesus won't always be easy. But when you stick with what you've learned from God's Word, He gives you the strength to stand firm—even when it's hard.

BOTTOM LINE

Even when no one is watching, God sees your faithfulness. Stay close to Him, care for others, and hold on to His truth—because living for Him is always worth it.

PRAYER

Heavenly Father, Help me to care deeply for others, even when it's inconvenient or unnoticed. Teach me to listen when someone's hurting and to be a source of Your love in their life. When life gets tough or I feel alone in my faith, remind me that I'm never alone with You. Help me stay rooted in Your Word and stand strong for what's right. In Jesus' Name, Amen.

AUGUST 9

Surprise Generosity

3-Year-Bible Reading: Proverbs 21:14; Titus 1–3

"A gift in secret averts anger, and a concealed bribe, strong wrath." —Proverbs 21:14

"To the pure, all things are pure, but to the defiled and unbelieving, nothing is pure; but both their minds and their consciences are defiled." —Titus 1:15

"But when the goodness and loving kindness of God our Savior appeared, he saved us, not because of works done by us in righteousness, but according to his own mercy…" —Titus 3:4–5

Let's be real—when someone wrongs you, your first instinct usually isn't to hand them a surprise gift. But *Proverbs 21:14* drops a truth bomb: quietly giving can dissolve tension and even stop anger in its tracks. Pair that with *Titus 1–3*, where Paul reminds us that we're saved not because we've got it all together, but because of God's mercy.

These verses together paint a picture of grace in action—unexpected kindness that changes hearts. Just like God gave us mercy we didn't earn, we can reflect that by offering kindness even when it's hard. And sometimes, that kind of love shocks people—in the best way possible.

THINK ABOUT IT

1. **Kindness as a Strategy:** Have you ever tried being kind to someone who annoyed or hurt you? What happened? How might a "gift in secret" change the tone of your relationships?

2. **God's Mercy Over Our Resume:** *Titus 3:5* makes it clear—God didn't save us because of our good deeds. How does that challenge the way we treat people who "don't deserve" kindness?

3. **What's in Your Heart?** *Titus 1:15* reminds us that purity starts on the inside. Are your actions a reflection of a heart that's been shaped by God's love and mercy?

BOTTOM LINE

God's grace is undeserved and unexpected—and we're called to reflect that same mercy in how we treat others, even when it's hard. Sometimes, the most powerful move is a quiet act of kindness that shows people a glimpse of God's love.

PRAYER

Heavenly Father, thank You for showing me what real love and mercy look like. Help me to reflect Your grace in the way I treat others, especially when it's tough. Teach me to love not just with words but with actions, and to live from a heart changed by You. In Jesus' Name, Amen.

AUGUST 10

The Right Kind of Rebel

3-Year-Bible Reading: Proverbs 21:15–16; Psalm 92; Philemon 1

"When justice is done, it is a joy to the righteous but terror to evildoers. One who wanders from the way of good sense will rest in the assembly of the dead." — Proverbs 21:15–16

"The righteous flourish like the palm tree and grow like a cedar in Lebanon. They are planted in the house of the Lord; they flourish in the courts of our God." — Psalm 92:12–13

"I appeal to you for my child, Onesimus, whose father I became in my imprisonment." — Philemon 1:10

Sometimes doing the right thing feels like you're swimming upstream—like you're the only one who cares about truth, kindness, or what God says is right. But the Bible shows us that standing for what's right—even when it's hard—leads to real growth and impact.

In **Proverbs 21**, God says justice brings joy to those who follow Him. **Psalm 92** reminds us that when we stay rooted in God, we'll flourish. And in **Philemon**, we see a powerful story of grace as Paul fights for the redemption of a runaway slave, Onesimus. In all these passages, one message rings clear: following God's way might make you different, but it's always worth it.

THINK ABOUT IT

1. **Doing Right Feels Right (Eventually):** Why do you think doing the right thing sometimes feels so hard in the moment but brings peace later? Think about a time when choosing God's way made a difference.

2. **Stay Planted:** Psalm 92 talks about flourishing when we are planted in God's presence. What are some practical ways you can "plant" yourself in God's house—at school, with friends, or even online?

3. **Fight for Others:** Paul didn't have to speak up for Onesimus, but he did. Who in your life might need someone to stand up for them, even if it costs you something?

BOTTOM LINE

Being different because you follow Jesus might feel like rebellion in this world—but it's the right kind of rebellion. Choosing what's right, staying rooted in God, and standing up for others brings life, joy, and real growth.

PRAYER

Heavenly Father, thank You for showing me that living for You is worth it. Help me to choose justice, stay rooted in You, and speak up for others, even when it's hard. Make me bold in doing what's right and faithful in loving people like You do. In Jesus' Name, Amen.

August 11

Chasing What Matters Most

3-Year-Bible Reading: Proverbs 21:17–18; Hebrews 1–2

Whoever loves pleasure will be a poor man; he who loves wine and oil will not be rich. — Proverbs 21:17

He is the radiance of the glory of God and the exact imprint of his nature, and he upholds the universe by the word of his power. — Hebrews 1:3

Therefore we must pay much closer attention to what we have heard, lest we drift away from it. — Hebrews 2:1

Let's be honest—most of us love a good time. Whether it's video games, shopping sprees, binge-watching our favorite shows, or just chasing the next fun thing, we're wired to enjoy life. But **Proverbs 21:17** throws a curveball: chasing pleasure too hard can actually leave us empty. Then, in **Hebrews 1**, we're reminded of who Jesus really is—the powerful, glorious Son of God.

And **Hebrews 2** warns us not to drift away from the truth we've heard. That "drifting" doesn't usually happen in big leaps; it happens when we get so distracted by things that don't really matter that we lose sight of the One who does.

Think About It

1. **What are you chasing?** Are you putting your energy into things that will last or just chasing short-term fun? It's not that fun is bad—but if it becomes your main goal, it can lead to spiritual poverty.

2. **Who really holds your world together?** Jesus "upholds the universe" (Hebrews 1:3). That means your life, your future, your purpose—it's all in His hands. Are you living like that's true?

3. **Pay attention:** Hebrews 2:1 is a wake-up call. If you don't stay focused on Jesus, you'll slowly drift. What distractions might be pulling your attention away from Him right now?

Bottom Line

Fun fades, but Jesus remains. Keep your eyes on Him, and you'll find more joy and purpose than any temporary pleasure could offer.

Prayer

Heavenly Father, thank You for giving me good things to enjoy, but help me not to live for them. Remind me every day that Jesus is better, stronger, and worth more than anything else. Help me stay focused on Him and not drift away. In Jesus' Name, Amen.

AUGUST 12

Peace Over Pressure

3-Year-Bible Reading: Proverbs 21:19–20; Psalm 93; Hebrews 3–4

"It is better to live in a desert land than with a quarrelsome and fretful woman. Precious treasure and oil are in a wise man's dwelling, but a foolish man devours it." —Proverbs 21:19–20

"Mightier than the thunders of many waters, mightier than the waves of the sea, the Lord on high is mighty!" —Psalm 93:4

"For we who have believed enter that rest… So then, there remains a Sabbath rest for the people of God." —Hebrews 4:3, 9

Sometimes life feels like a constant storm—school pressure, friend drama, family stress, and everything in between. It's easy to get swept up in the noise and react with stress, impatience, or even anger. Proverbs reminds us that drama-filled relationships aren't just annoying—they drain peace. But God offers us something different: rest, stillness, and strength in the middle of chaos.

Psalm **93** describes God's power as mightier than the ocean's biggest waves. And in **Hebrews 4**, we're reminded that faith in Jesus brings real rest—not just physical sleep, but deep, soul-level peace.

THINK ABOUT IT

1. **Choose Peace Over Drama:** Proverbs paints a vivid picture—it's better to be alone in the desert than stuck in constant conflict. Are your actions adding fuel to the fire, or helping create a peaceful space for yourself and others?

2. **God Is Bigger Than the Waves:** Psalm 93 reminds us that God isn't overwhelmed by the storms we face. He is unshaken. Do you turn to Him when things get rough, or do you try to handle it all on your own?

3. **Rest Isn't Laziness:** Hebrews shows us that rest isn't about doing nothing—it's about trusting that Jesus has done enough. Are you finding time to pause and recharge in His presence, or are you caught up in proving yourself?

BOTTOM LINE

God offers a peace that no chaos can steal and a rest that refreshes your soul. You don't have to live in constant stress—choose His rest, trust His strength, and walk in His peace.

PRAYER

Heavenly Father, thank You for being stronger than any storm I face. Help me choose peace when things around me feel overwhelming. Teach me to rest in You—not just on the outside, but deep in my heart. Show me how to be someone who brings calm instead of conflict. In Jesus' Name, Amen.

AUGUST 13

Chasing What Lasts

3-Year-Bible Reading: Proverbs 21:21; Hebrews 5–6

Whoever pursues righteousness and kindness will find life, righteousness, and honor. — Proverbs 21:21

But solid food is for the mature, for those who have their powers of discernment trained by constant practice to distinguish good from evil. — Hebrews 5:14

We desire each one of you to show the same earnestness to have the full assurance of hope until the end, so that you may not be sluggish, but imitators of those who through faith and patience inherit the promises. — Hebrews 6:11–12

Ever feel like life is a race with a finish line you can't see? School, friendships, goals, and expectations pile up, and it's easy to get stuck chasing the wrong things—like popularity, perfection, or approval. But **Proverbs 21:21** flips the script. It says if you chase *righteousness and kindness*, you'll actually *find* what your heart really wants: life, purpose, and honor.

The book of **Hebrews**, especially chapters 5 and 6, challenges us to grow up in our faith, not just snack on surface-level stuff, but dive deeper—learning to make wise choices and sticking with it even when things get hard. Following Jesus isn't always easy, but it's always worth it.

THINK ABOUT IT

1. **What Are You Pursuing?** Everyone is chasing *something*. Are your goals leading you closer to God or just making you tired? Proverbs 21:21 reminds us that chasing what *matters*—righteousness and kindness—leads to true reward.

2. **Time to Grow Up:** Hebrews 5 talks about moving from spiritual "milk" to "solid food." Are you still in the baby stage of faith, or are you training yourself to know right from wrong through God's Word?

3. **Stay Steady:** Hebrews 6 tells us not to be lazy in our faith. Faith and patience are key. What does steady, patient trust in God look like in your life right now?

BOTTOM LINE

A life that chases Jesus—filled with righteousness, kindness, and growing faith—is a life that finds real purpose and lasting joy. Don't settle for less.

PRAYER

Heavenly Father, help me to chase what really matters—righteousness, kindness, and a deeper walk with You. Grow my faith so I can move beyond just knowing about You to truly trusting and following You, even when it's hard. Give me patience and strength to keep going when I feel stuck. I want to live a life that honors You. In Jesus' Name, Amen.

AUGUST 14

Watch Your Words

3-Year-Bible Reading: Proverbs 21:23; Psalm 94; Hebrews 7–8

"Whoever keeps his mouth and his tongue keeps himself out of trouble."—Proverbs 21:23

"When the cares of my heart are many, your consolations cheer my soul."—Psalm 94:19

"But as it is, Christ has obtained a ministry that is as much more excellent than the old as the covenant he mediates is better, since it is enacted on better promises."—Hebrews 8:6

Have you ever said something in the heat of the moment and immediately regretted it? We all have. Words are powerful, and once they're out there, we can't take them back. **Proverbs 21:23** reminds us that guarding what we say can save us from a lot of drama. But let's be real—life gets overwhelming, and in the middle of the stress, we often lash out, complain, or just say things that don't reflect who we want to be.

That's where **Psalm 94** meets us. It reminds us that even when our hearts are heavy, God offers comfort. And the best part? **Hebrews 7–8** shows us that Jesus is our perfect High Priest. His promise isn't based on how well we behave but on a better covenant—one where He helps us live a life that reflects His grace, even in how we speak.

THINK ABOUT IT

1. **Words Matter:** How do your words affect the people around you? Are they encouraging or hurtful? What can you do to be more intentional with your speech?

2. **God's Comfort Is Real:** When you're feeling overwhelmed or anxious, where do you turn? How can you let God's comfort in, like Psalm 94 describes?

3. **A Better Promise:** Jesus' new covenant is based on grace. Are you living like you have to earn God's approval, or are you trusting in His better promise?

BOTTOM LINE

The way we speak reflects what's going on in our hearts. Guarding our words, trusting God in hard times, and living in the freedom of Jesus' better promise can change how we handle life—and help us grow into who God created us to be.

PRAYER

Heavenly Father, thank You for Your wisdom, comfort, and grace. Help me to guard my words and speak life to those around me. When I'm stressed or anxious, remind me of Your peace. Thank You for the better promise I have in Jesus. Teach me to walk in that truth every day. In Jesus' Name, Amen.

August 15

Strength from the Inside Out

3-Year-Bible Reading: Proverbs 21:22, 24; Hebrews 9–10

"A wise man scales the city of the mighty and brings down the stronghold in which they trust. Scoffer is the name of the arrogant, haughty man who acts with arrogant pride." — Proverbs 21:22, 24

"But when Christ had offered for all time a single sacrifice for sins, he sat down at the right hand of God." — Hebrews 10:12

We all face battles that seem way too big for us. Whether it's pressure at school, drama with friends, or just the struggle to stay strong in our faith, it's easy to feel outnumbered or outpowered. But God doesn't call us to win by being the loudest or the strongest in a worldly sense—He shows us another way. In **Proverbs 21:22**, we see that wisdom—not brute strength—can bring down mighty strongholds.

And in **Hebrews 10**, we learn that Jesus' sacrifice has already won the ultimate battle for us. We don't need to act prideful or put others down to feel powerful (see **Proverbs 21:24**); instead, we're invited to live with confidence, knowing Christ has already done the heavy lifting.

Think About It

1. **True Strength:** What does it mean to "scale the city of the mighty" with wisdom? Think of a time when a calm, wise decision had more impact than getting angry or showing off.

2. **Check Your Pride:** Are you trying to prove something by acting tough or sarcastic? Proverbs warns us about arrogance. Ask God to help you be confident without being prideful.

3. **Rest in the Finished Work:** Hebrews 10 reminds us that Jesus' sacrifice was "once for all." You don't have to keep earning God's love—it's already yours. How can you live in that freedom today?

Bottom Line

You don't need to be loud, proud, or powerful by the world's standards—God gives strength through wisdom and confidence through Christ.

Prayer

Heavenly Father, thank You for showing me that true strength comes from You, not from trying to impress others or prove myself. Help me to choose wisdom over pride and to remember that Jesus' sacrifice has already made me right with You. Teach me to trust in Your power instead of my own. In Jesus' Name, Amen.

AUGUST 16

Chasing More Than Dreams

3-Year-Bible Reading: Proverbs 21:25-26; Hebrews 11

"The desire of the sluggard kills him, for his hands refuse to labor. All day long he craves and craves, but the righteous gives and does not hold back." — Proverbs 21:25–26

"Now faith is the assurance of things hoped for, the conviction of things not seen." — Hebrews 11:1

"And without faith it is impossible to please him, for whoever would draw near to God must believe that he exists and that he rewards those who seek him." — Hebrews 11:6

Ever feel like you're stuck wanting things to change—your grades, your habits, your future—but not really doing anything about it? Or maybe you've dreamed big but stopped short because it felt too hard or too far away. In **Proverbs 21:25–26**, we're warned about letting desire replace action.

And in **Hebrews 11**, we're reminded of what really moves us forward: faith. Not just believing in something, but *acting* like it's true. The people listed in Hebrews 11 didn't just wish—they *walked* in obedience. They moved when God said "go," even when they couldn't see the outcome. This chapter reminds us: faith isn't about sitting still. It's about stepping forward, even when it's scary or unclear.

THINK ABOUT IT

1. **Desire vs. Doing:** What's something you've been wanting to see change in your life? Are you just craving, or are you willing to put in effort and trust God with the results?

2. **Faith in Motion:** Look at the people in Hebrews 11—Noah built a boat before rain existed, Abraham left everything without a map. What does real faith look like in your life today?

3. **Give It Away:** Proverbs talks about the righteous giving freely. Are you living generously with your time, your encouragement, your gifts—or holding back because you don't feel "ready" yet?

BOTTOM LINE

Faith isn't just about believing—it's about moving. God honors those who trust Him enough to act, even when the future is fuzzy. Don't just crave change—walk in faith toward it.

PRAYER

Heavenly Father, thank You for showing us that faith is more than a feeling—it's a way of living. Help me to trust You with both my dreams and my daily steps. Teach me to work hard, give freely, and walk boldly even when I can't see what's ahead. I don't want to just wish for more—I want to follow You into it. In Jesus' Name, Amen.

August 17

Worship That Means Something

3-Year-Bible Reading: Proverbs 21:27; Hebrews 12

"The sacrifice of the wicked is an abomination; how much more when he brings it with evil intent." — Proverbs 21:27

"Let us offer to God acceptable worship, with reverence and awe, for our God is a consuming fire." — Hebrews 12:28b–29

Have you ever gone through the motions just to check something off your list? Maybe you've sung a worship song without really thinking about the words or prayed a quick prayer just to say you did. **Proverbs 21:27** warns us that it's not just about what we do for God—it's about *why* we do it.

And in **Hebrews 12**, we're reminded that true worship comes from a place of awe and deep respect for who God really is. Worship isn't just about showing up at church or youth group. It's about a heart that's surrendered and real.

Think About It

1. **Check Your Motives:** Why do you do what you do for God? Are you doing it to look good, to fit in, or because you truly want to honor Him? God sees past the action straight to the heart.

2. **Worship with Awe:** What does "reverence and awe" look like in your life? It's not about being perfect; it's about recognizing God's holiness and responding with sincere respect and love.

3. **God Isn't Fooled:** God can tell when your heart isn't in it. Instead of offering half-hearted worship, take a moment to refocus your mind and spirit before jumping into prayer or praise.

Bottom Line

God wants real worship—worship that flows from a heart that truly knows and loves Him. He's not impressed by performance but moved by sincerity.

Prayer

Heavenly Father, thank You for seeing my heart even when I get distracted or go through the motions. Help me to worship You with sincerity, reverence, and awe. Show me when my motives need correcting and teach me to love You more deeply. May my life reflect true worship that pleases You. In Jesus' Name, Amen.

AUGUST 18

Real vs. Fake Faith

3-Year-Bible Reading: Proverbs 21:28–29; Psalm 95; Hebrews 13

"A false witness will perish, but the word of a man who hears will endure. A wicked man puts on a bold face, but the upright gives thought to his ways." — Proverbs 21:28–29

"Today, if you hear his voice, do not harden your hearts, as at Meribah..." — Psalm 95:7b–8

"Do not neglect to do good and to share what you have, for such sacrifices are pleasing to God." — Hebrews 13:16

Let's be real—there's a big difference between looking faithful and actually living it out. In **Proverbs 21**, we see that people can fake it with a bold front, but only those who truly listen and reflect will last.

Psalm 95 warns us not to harden our hearts when God is speaking, and **Hebrews 13** reminds us that our actions—doing good, sharing, living sacrificially—are what please God. Together, these verses paint a picture of what real faith looks like. It's not about pretending to be "perfect" or religious—it's about listening to God, staying humble, and loving others in real, visible ways.

THINK ABOUT IT

1. **Real Faith Listens:** Are you someone who actually hears God's voice and lets it change you, or do you just go through the motions?
2. **Hearts Matter:** Psalm 95 reminds us that hard hearts block God's voice. What things might be hardening your heart—pride, distraction, fear?
3. **Faith in Action:** Hebrews 13:16 is super clear—doing good and sharing is part of worship. What's one way you can live out your faith today?

BOTTOM LINE

God wants faith that's real—not just words, but hearts that listen and lives that love. When we stay soft to His voice and step out to care for others, we reflect who He really is.

PRAYER

Heavenly Father, help me to be someone who really listens to You—not just someone who acts like I've got it all together. Keep my heart soft, even when it's easier to shut You out. Show me where I can do good and love others like You've loved me. I want a faith that's real, not fake. In Jesus' Name, Amen.

August 19

Unstoppable God

3-Year-Bible Reading: Proverbs 21:30–31; James 1

"No wisdom, no understanding, no counsel can avail against the Lord. The horse is made ready for the day of battle, but the victory belongs to the Lord." — Proverbs 21:30–31

"Count it all joy, my brothers, when you meet trials of various kinds, for you know that the testing of your faith produces steadfastness." — James 1:2–3

"But be doers of the word, and not hearers only, deceiving yourselves." — James 1:22

Ever feel like life throws you into a battlefield you didn't sign up for? School stress, drama with friends, pressure to fit in—it can feel like you're constantly preparing for a fight. You plan, you worry, and you try to take control. But **Proverbs 21:30–31** reminds us that even our best plans can't override what God is doing. It's not about being the strongest or the smartest—it's about trusting the One who holds the victory.

And when things get tough, like **James 1** says, God isn't absent. He's using the hard stuff to make us stronger, more faithful, and more like Him. But we also have a part to play—we can't just hear God's Word and forget it. We're called to live it.

Think About It

1. **Whose strength are you trusting?** Are you relying on your own abilities, or are you bringing your plans and struggles to God?

2. **Trials are training:** What challenges are you facing right now, and how might God be using them to grow your faith and character?

3. **Live it out:** Are there areas in your life where you know what God says but haven't put it into action yet?

Bottom Line

You can prepare all you want, but real victory comes from trusting and obeying God—especially when life gets tough.

Prayer

Heavenly Father, thank You that no plan can succeed against You. Help me to trust You more than I trust myself. When things get hard, remind me that You are using every trial to grow my faith. Give me the courage not just to hear Your Word, but to live it every day. In Jesus' Name, Amen.

August 20

More Than Gold

3-Year-Bible Reading: Proverbs 22:1–2; Psalm 96; James 2

"A good name is to be chosen rather than great riches, and favor is better than silver or gold. The rich and the poor meet together; the Lord is the Maker of them all." — Proverbs 22:1–2

"Ascribe to the Lord the glory due his name; bring an offering, and come into his courts! Worship the Lord in the splendor of holiness; tremble before him, all the earth!" — Psalm 96:8–9

"If you really fulfill the royal law according to the Scripture, 'You shall love your neighbor as yourself,' you are doing well." — James 2:8

Ever feel like life's just one big popularity contest? Whether it's likes on your latest post, who you sit with at lunch, or the brand of shoes you're wearing—so much can seem to revolve around status. But God flips all of that on its head. In **Proverbs 22**, we're reminded that who you are—your character and reputation—matters way more than how much money you have or how many people know your name. In **Psalm 96**, we're called to give God the glory, not chase our own.

And in **James 2**, God challenges us to treat everyone with the same love and respect, no matter their status or background. These passages together are a wake-up call: you are valuable not because of what you own or how popular you are, but because of who God is and who you are in Him.

Think About It

1. **What Are You Known For?** If people had to describe you in one word, what would they say? Is your reputation something that reflects Christ? A good name—built on kindness, honesty, and love—is worth more than any material thing.

2. **Everyone's Equal at the Cross:** Proverbs reminds us that God made both the rich and the poor. That means no one is more valuable than someone else. Are you showing that same kind of equality and respect in how you treat others?

3. **Worship with Your Life:** Psalm 96 isn't just about singing songs—it's about giving God the honor He deserves with your whole life. Are you living in a way that shows your life is more about Him than yourself?

Bottom Line

God cares more about your heart than your status. Live with integrity, worship Him with your life, and treat others with the same love He shows you.

Prayer

Heavenly Father, thank You for loving me not because of what I have, but because of who I am in You. Help me to value character over popularity, to treat everyone with love, and to live in a way that gives You glory. Help me build a good name—not for myself, but to honor You. In Jesus' Name, Amen.

August 21

Watch Where You're Going

3-Year-Bible Reading: Proverbs 22:3; Psalm 97; James 3

"The prudent sees danger and hides himself, but the simple go on and suffer for it." —Proverbs 22:3

"O you who love the Lord, hate evil! He preserves the lives of his saints; he delivers them from the hand of the wicked." —Psalm 97:10

"But the wisdom from above is first pure, then peaceable, gentle, open to reason, full of mercy and good fruits, impartial and sincere." —James 3:17

You've probably seen one of those videos where someone walks into a pole while looking at their phone. Funny, sure—but it's also a reminder: when you're not paying attention, you can end up somewhere you never meant to be. Life is like that, too. **Proverbs 22:3** tells us that wise people watch out for danger and steer clear of it. God doesn't want us just stumbling along, getting hurt because we didn't think ahead.

And in **James 3**, we learn what real wisdom looks like—not just being smart, but being peace-loving, sincere, and kind. When we truly love God, as **Psalm 97** encourages, we learn to hate the things that hurt us and others—especially evil. God gives us the tools to stay on track, but we have to choose to use them.

Think About It

1. **Look Before You Leap:** Are there areas in your life where you've ignored warning signs and suffered because of it? How can you practice wisdom by paying closer attention?

2. **Real Wisdom Check:** According to James 3, godly wisdom isn't just about knowing stuff—it's about how we treat people. Which of the qualities in James 3:17 do you want to grow in?

3. **Hating Evil, Loving God:** Psalm 97:10 says if you love God, you should hate evil. What does that look like in your daily life—at school, online, with your friends?

Bottom Line

Living wisely means being alert to the world around you, choosing God's way over your own, and letting His wisdom shape your thoughts, actions, and words.

Prayer

Heavenly Father, help me to see the danger in paths that lead me away from You. Give me the courage to turn around when I need to and the wisdom to walk with integrity, peace, and love. Teach me to hate what is evil and hold on to what is good. Thank You for guiding and protecting me. In Jesus' Name, Amen.

August 22

The Riches You Really Want

3-Year-Bible Reading: Proverbs 22:4–5; James 4–5

"The reward for humility and fear of the Lord is riches and honor and life." — Proverbs 22:4

"You desire and do not have, so you murder. You covet and cannot obtain, so you fight and quarrel. You do not have, because you do not ask. You ask and do not receive, because you ask wrongly, to spend it on your passions." — James 4:2–3

"Come now, you rich, weep and howl for the miseries that are coming upon you." — James 5:1

Let's be real: we live in a world where "success" is usually measured by likes, followers, fame, or what you own. It's easy to believe that if you just had a little more—money, popularity, influence—you'd finally be satisfied. But the Bible gives us a different picture. In **Proverbs 22:4**, it says that *true* riches come from humility and honoring God, not from chasing everything the world says is valuable.

And in **James 4–5**, we're reminded that selfish ambition and greed don't end well. Instead of filling us up, they leave us empty and hurting others in the process.

Think About It

1. **What Are You Really Chasing?** Are your goals about honoring God or just getting ahead? James reminds us that when our hearts are in the wrong place, even our prayers can miss the mark.

2. **Heart Check:** Proverbs connects humility and the fear of the Lord with *true* rewards—life, honor, and real riches. What does it look like in your life to choose humility over pride?

3. **Success Redefined:** James 5 warns the rich not because wealth is bad, but because trusting in wealth instead of God leads to destruction. Where are you placing your trust?

Bottom Line

God doesn't define success the way the world does. When we walk in humility and keep God at the center, we gain something better than money—we gain a life filled with His peace, purpose, and presence.

Prayer

Heavenly Father, Help me to stop chasing what the world says will make me happy and start chasing after You. Teach me to be humble, to honor You in all I do, and to trust You with my future. Show me how to live for things that last. In Jesus' Name, Amen.

August 23

Stay on Track

3-Year-Bible Reading: Proverbs 22:6; 1 Peter 1–2

Train up a child in the way he should go; even when he is old he will not depart from it. —Proverbs 22:6

As obedient children, do not be conformed to the passions of your former ignorance... but as he who called you is holy, you also be holy in all your conduct. —1 Peter 1:14–15

But you are a chosen race, a royal priesthood, a holy nation, a people for his own possession, that you may proclaim the excellencies of him who called you out of darkness into his marvelous light. —1 Peter 2:9

We all have dreams of becoming something amazing—maybe it's a doctor, an artist, a YouTuber, or a star athlete. But when it comes to who we *really* are becoming, God's Word points us in a much deeper direction. **Proverbs 22:6** is often quoted to parents, but it's also a challenge to *us*—to stay on the right path once we've been shown it.

Then **1 Peter 1–2** picks up that thought and tells us exactly what that path looks like: it's a holy, set-apart life, full of purpose and light. That may sound intense, but it's actually incredibly freeing. Instead of blending in or getting lost trying to find yourself, God gives you an identity that's solid and full of meaning.

Think About It

1. **Set on the Path:** What are some ways you've been trained or taught to follow Jesus? Are there habits or truths from your childhood that still shape you today?

2. **Be Different on Purpose:** Peter challenges us not to copy the world but to live holy lives. What's one way you can choose holiness instead of going along with what everyone else is doing?

3. **You Belong:** Do you see yourself the way God sees you—a chosen, royal, and holy part of His family? How might this identity affect the way you live, speak, or make decisions this week?

Bottom Line

God has set you on a path for a reason. When you remember who you are in Him, you can live with confidence, purpose, and holiness—no matter what distractions come your way.

Prayer

Heavenly Father, thank You for calling me into Your light and giving me a purpose that lasts. Help me to walk in the way You've trained me, to choose holiness even when it's hard, and to always remember that I belong to You. Strengthen me to stay on track and shine for You in everything I do. In Jesus' Name, Amen.

August 24

More Than Money

3-Year-Bible Reading: Proverbs 22:7–8; 1 Peter 3–5

"The rich rules over the poor, and the borrower is the slave of the lender. Whoever sows injustice will reap calamity, and the rod of his fury will fail." — Proverbs 22:7–8

"But even if you should suffer for righteousness' sake, you will be blessed. Have no fear of them, nor be troubled..." — 1 Peter 3:14

"Casting all your anxieties on him, because he cares for you." — 1 Peter 5:7

Money. Power. Status. These things seem to rule the world. Whether it's the pressure to look a certain way, wear the latest styles, or have the newest phone, it's easy to feel like we're stuck in a cycle of comparison and control. **Proverbs 22** warns us how debt can make us feel trapped, and how living unjustly comes back around. Then in **1 Peter 3–5**, we're reminded that standing for what's right might cost us something—but we're never alone in it. God cares. And that changes everything.

Think About It

1. **Who (or what) is in control?** Are you letting money, popularity, or fear control your decisions? Proverbs reminds us that being in debt—financially or emotionally—can make us feel like slaves to those things. What are you borrowing from the world that might be holding you back?

2. **Do the right thing, even when it's hard:** 1 Peter 3 talks about suffering for righteousness. That's not fun, but it's real. Maybe you've stood up for someone or refused to go along with something wrong—and it cost you. But Peter says you're *blessed* for it. God sees your courage.

3. **Worry is heavy—God's got it:** Life gets stressful, and anxiety creeps in. But **1 Peter 5:7** says we can hand those burdens over to God, not because He *has to* take them, but because He *wants to*. He cares for you personally.

Bottom Line

What controls you reveals what you trust. Let go of fear, pressure, and control, and give it all to the God who cares deeply for you.

Prayer

Heavenly Father, thank You for reminding me that I don't have to be ruled by fear, money, or pressure. Help me to stand strong for what's right, even when it's tough, and to trust You with every part of my life. I know You care about me. Help me to cast all my worries on You and walk in Your peace. In Jesus' Name, Amen.

August 25

Overflow Generosity

3-Year-Bible Reading: Proverbs 22:9; 2 Peter 1–3

Whoever has a bountiful eye will be blessed, for he shares his bread with the poor. — Proverbs 22:9

His divine power has granted to us all things that pertain to life and godliness… — 2 Peter 1:3

But according to his promise we are waiting for new heavens and a new earth in which righteousness dwells. — 2 Peter 3:13

You know that feeling when someone shares their favorite snack with you? It's simple, but it matters—especially when they didn't have to. In **Proverbs 22:9**, the Bible calls this kind of person "bountiful" or generous, someone who looks for chances to bless others.

Now, skip forward to **2 Peter 1–3**, where we see how God has already poured out everything we need to live for Him. Not only that, but He's given us a future hope—something solid to live for beyond this life. So here's the connection: when we realize how much we've been given by God, it becomes easier (and more exciting!) to live generously and with purpose, right now.

Think About It

1. **Check Your Vision:** Do you have a "bountiful eye"? That means looking for ways to give—your time, your attention, your stuff—to others who need it. Sometimes the biggest blessings come from the smallest acts.

2. **Power Source:** According to **2 Peter 1:3**, God has already given you *everything* you need to live for Him. Are you trying to handle life on your own, or are you tapping into what He's already made available?

3. **Future-Focused Living:** In **2 Peter 3:13**, Peter talks about the "new heavens and new earth." How does knowing that something better is coming shape how you live today? Are you living with eternity in mind?

Bottom Line

God has blessed you with more than enough—His power, His promises, and a future full of hope. Let His generosity inspire you to live with open hands and a full heart.

Prayer

Heavenly Father, thank You for being so generous with me. You've given me everything I need to follow You and live a godly life. Help me to see others with a generous heart and to give freely, just like You do. Keep my eyes focused on the hope You've promised and help me live like it really matters. In Jesus' Name, Amen.

AUGUST 26

True Freedom: Living in His Light

3-Year-Bible Reading: Proverbs 22:10; Psalms 98; 1 John 1-2

"Drive out a scoffer, and strife will go out, and quarreling and abuse will cease." — Proverbs 22:10

"Oh sing to the Lord a new song, for he has done marvelous things; his right hand and his holy arm have worked salvation for him." — Psalm 98:1

"If we say we have fellowship with him while we walk in darkness, we lie and do not practice the truth. But if we walk in the light, as he is in the light, we have fellowship with one another, and the blood of Jesus his Son cleanses us from all sin." — 1 John 1:6-7

Have you ever noticed how much better things feel when you walk in the light? Not just physically, but spiritually too. **1 John 1:6-7** tells us that when we choose to walk in the light with God, things change for the better—our relationships improve, and we experience true fellowship with others. In contrast, when we walk in darkness, our hearts get clouded, and conflict becomes harder to avoid.

Proverbs 22:10 shows us that when we push away negativity and people who stir up strife, peace has room to grow. In **Psalm 98**, we see a beautiful picture of how God has done marvelous things through His salvation. He calls us to sing a new song because of the marvelous work He's done in our lives. When we recognize how much God has already done for us, it makes it easier to walk in His light and share His love with others.

Living in God's light doesn't just mean knowing what's right. It means choosing to live it out every day, especially when it's hard. That's what walking in fellowship with Jesus looks like—choosing His way over our own.

THINK ABOUT IT

1. **What's in your heart?** Are there any areas in your life where you're walking in darkness or keeping things hidden from God?
2. **How can you bring light to others?** How can you use God's love to bring peace and healing to a situation where there's strife or conflict?
3. **New songs, new life:** What are some ways you can respond to God's marvelous works in your life with a "new song"? How can you celebrate His goodness daily?

BOTTOM LINE

Walking in the light with God brings peace, fellowship, and freedom. It's a choice we make every day to live out His love and truth.

PRAYER

Heavenly Father, thank You for sending Your Son to cleanse us from all sin and for the light that You offer us. Help us to walk in that light, bringing peace to our hearts and to those around us. Teach us to reflect Your love in all we do, and guide us when we face conflict or struggle. May we live in Your freedom, sharing Your marvelous works with the world. In Jesus' Name, Amen.

August 27

Pure Heart, Pure Actions

3-Year-Bible Reading: Proverbs 22:11-12; 1 John 3

"He who loves purity of heart, and whose speech is gracious, will have the king as his friend." — Proverbs 22:11

"But if anyone has the world's goods and sees his brother in need, yet closes his heart against him, how does God's love abide in him?" — 1 John 3:17

"Beloved, if our heart does not condemn us, we have confidence before God." — 1 John 3:21

God cares deeply about what's in our hearts—what we think, what we feel, and how we act toward others. In **Proverbs 22:11**, we're told that someone who loves purity in their heart and speaks with grace will earn the respect of others. Think about that: having a pure heart isn't just about keeping our actions in check, it's about the inside being clean, too. And in **1 John 3**, we see how what's in our hearts plays a crucial role in our relationship with God. If our heart is pure, we can approach God with confidence, knowing that we're living in alignment with His will.

But sometimes, our hearts get clouded. We get selfish, we act out of pride, or we simply forget to love those around us. Yet, God's love for us remains, and He invites us to live with a heart that reflects His love toward others. It's a reminder that living for God isn't just about avoiding the bad things—it's about actively choosing to love as He loves us.

Think About It

1. **Heart Check:** How can you ensure your heart is aligned with God's will today? Are there areas where you've been closing your heart to others?
2. **Loving with Action:** How does the way you treat others reflect what's in your heart? When was the last time you showed love to someone in need?
3. **Confidence in God:** When you reflect on your heart, do you feel confident that it aligns with God's love? If not, what's one step you can take to change that?

Bottom Line

A pure heart leads to gracious speech and actions that reflect God's love to the world. When our hearts are aligned with God, we can walk confidently in His love, showing kindness to others and reflecting His heart to those around us.

Prayer

Heavenly Father, thank You for Your love that never leaves us, no matter what's in our hearts. Help me to love others the way You love me, with purity and grace. Show me areas where I need to let go of selfishness and make room for Your heart to shine through me. Help me to live with confidence before You, knowing that my actions and words reflect Your love. In Jesus' Name, Amen.

AUGUST 28

The Path of Wisdom

3-Year-Bible Reading: Proverbs 22:13-14; Psalms 99; 1 John 4

"The sluggard says, 'There is a lion outside! I shall be killed in the streets! The words of the wicked are like a deep pit; the one who is abhorred by the Lord will fall into it." — Proverbs 22:13-14

"The Lord reigns; let the peoples tremble! He sits enthroned upon the cherubim; let the earth quake!" — Psalm 99:1

"Anyone who does not love does not know God, because God is love." — 1 John 4:8

Sometimes, life can feel like a maze of challenges and fears. Maybe you've thought, "What if I mess up? What if I fail?" These worries can make us freeze or run in the wrong direction, just like the lazy person in **Proverbs 22:13** who is afraid of a lion that doesn't even exist. Fear can cloud our judgment and cause us to miss opportunities. But what if we let the truth of **Psalm 99:1**, where God reigns and is in control, take away our fear and lead us to action?

In **1 John 4:8**, we're reminded that God is love. His perfect love casts out fear (1 John 4:18). This love is the key to living boldly, without being paralyzed by fear or worry. When we remember that God's love is always with us, we can face each challenge with courage, knowing He's guiding us. Instead of worrying about the "lions" in our lives, we can trust that God's wisdom will help us navigate through tough situations.

THINK ABOUT IT

1. **Fear vs. Wisdom:** What are some things that make you anxious or fearful? How can God's wisdom and love help you face those fears instead of avoiding them?

2. **God's Authority:** How does recognizing that "The Lord reigns" (Psalm 99:1) change the way you approach life's problems?

3. **Love as the Foundation:** How does knowing that God is love encourage you to show love to others, especially in tough situations?

BOTTOM LINE

When fear tries to hold you back, remember that God's love and wisdom give you the strength to face anything with courage. Trust Him to guide you through the challenges, and let His love help you step forward without fear.

PRAYER

Heavenly Father, thank You for Your love and wisdom that guide me through life. Help me to trust in Your authority and not be ruled by fear. Teach me to lean on You when challenges come my way, knowing that Your love will give me the courage I need. In Jesus' Name, Amen.

AUGUST 29

A Heart for Wisdom

3-Year-Bible Reading: Proverbs 22:15-16; 1 John 5

"Folly is bound up in the heart of a child, but the rod of discipline drives it far from him. Whoever oppresses the poor to increase his own wealth, or gives to the rich, will only come to poverty." — Proverbs 22:15-16 (ESV)

"For everyone who has been born of God overcomes the world. And this is the victory that has overcome the world—our faith." — 1 John 5:4 (ESV)

Sometimes, life feels like a series of tough choices. Whether it's making the right decision in a friendship, sticking to your values when everyone else is compromising, or facing challenges that seem bigger than you—every day brings its own set of tests. But the Bible gives us wisdom for these times, showing us how to choose well, walk in faith, and overcome.

In **Proverbs 22:15**, we see that folly (bad choices) is a natural part of growing up. It's not about if we make mistakes—it's how we respond. Discipline helps shape us into wise people. And when we choose to live wisely, it not only benefits us, but also helps those around us. In **1 John 5:4**, we're reminded that our faith is what helps us overcome the world and its struggles. Through God, we have the power to rise above the challenges we face, even when it feels impossible.

But it's easy to forget that we have access to that strength. We sometimes forget that wisdom is not just about being smart—it's about trusting God's guidance and allowing Him to direct our paths. The world might say, "Do what feels good," but God invites us to live according to His wisdom and grace, which leads to lasting success.

THINK ABOUT IT

1. **Wisdom vs. Folly:** What areas of your life do you struggle with foolish decisions? What is one thing you can do today to make a wiser choice?
2. **Faith's Power:** When you face difficulties, how often do you lean on your faith? How can trusting in God's victory change your perspective on challenges?
3. **Discipline and Growth:** What role does discipline play in your life? How can discipline help you grow into a person who reflects God's wisdom?

BOTTOM LINE

God gives us the strength to overcome the world's pressures, but it starts with wisdom and faith. Don't let folly take root—choose wisdom, and trust God's guidance.

PRAYER

Heavenly Father, thank You for the wisdom You offer through Your Word. Help me to make wise choices and to trust in Your power when life gets hard. Strengthen my faith and guide me in every decision. May I live in a way that honors You and reflects Your love. In Jesus' Name, Amen.

AUGUST 30

Walking in Truth and Joy

3-Year-Bible Reading: Proverbs 22:17-21; Psalm 100; 2 John 1; 3 John 1

"Incline your ear, and hear the words of the wise, and apply your heart to my knowledge, for it will be pleasant if you keep them within you, if all of them are ready on your lips." — Proverbs 22:17-18

"Make a joyful noise to the Lord, all the earth. Serve the Lord with gladness! Come into his presence with singing!" — Psalm 100:1-2

"I have no greater joy than to hear that my children are walking in the truth." — 3 John 1:4

There's something powerful about receiving wisdom and living it out. Proverbs reminds us to listen to the wise, apply what we learn, and keep it close to our hearts. When we do this, we find joy and peace. Psalm 100 calls us to bring our praise to God, not out of obligation, but out of the joy of knowing Him. 2 and 3 John are letters written to believers, encouraging them to walk in truth and show love to others. John even says that his greatest joy is seeing others walk in the truth, which is something that God loves as well.

The common theme here is joy—joy in truth, in wisdom, and in our relationship with God. But living this way requires some action: listening, choosing to live out what we know, and encouraging others to do the same.

THINK ABOUT IT

1. **Wisdom:** How can you apply wisdom from the Bible to your daily life, especially in how you treat others and make decisions?
2. **Joyful Praise:** What are some ways you can serve God with gladness and express your joy in Him, even on tough days?
3. **Walking in Truth:** Is there an area in your life where you need to step up and walk more closely with the truth of God's Word?

BOTTOM LINE

When we embrace wisdom, walk in truth, and praise God with joy, we reflect His love and light to the world.

PRAYER

Heavenly Father, thank You for Your wisdom and truth. Help me to listen to Your Word, apply it to my life, and serve You with gladness. Fill my heart with joy as I walk in Your truth and encourage others to do the same. In Jesus' Name, Amen.

August 31

Guard Your Heart, Stand Firm in Truth

3-Year-Bible Reading: Proverbs 22:22-23; Jude 1

"Do not rob the poor, because he is poor, or crush the afflicted at the gate, for the Lord will plead their cause and rob of life those who rob them." — Proverbs 22:22-23

"But you, beloved, building yourselves up in your most holy faith and praying in the Holy Spirit, keep yourselves in the love of God, waiting for the mercy of our Lord Jesus Christ that leads to eternal life." — Jude 1:20-21

In a world where opinions and voices seem to constantly compete for attention, it can be tough to know where to stand. People push their ideas on us all the time—at school, on social media, and even among our friends. In **Proverbs 22:22-23**, God reminds us of a powerful truth: He sees and defends those who are oppressed and vulnerable. If we are to follow Him, we must care for the poor and not take advantage of others, especially when it's easier to do so. It's a call to stand up for what's right and just, even when it might not be popular.

In **Jude 1**, we see a different kind of call: to keep ourselves firm in God's truth and love. Jude encourages believers to build their faith, stay rooted in prayer, and guard their hearts against false teachings. He reminds us that, while there are challenges and trials, God's mercy will lead us to eternal life. This is a call to stay firm in our faith, no matter how difficult the world around us might get.

As you face daily pressures—whether from friends, school, or your own internal struggles—remember that God is calling you to live with integrity. When you choose to protect the vulnerable and remain grounded in His truth, you are actively reflecting His character. It's not easy, but it's worth it. By standing firm in His love, you'll be empowered to face whatever challenges come your way, knowing that God is always on your side.

Think About It

1. **What does it mean to stand up for those who are vulnerable?** How can you take action to help those in need, whether at school or in your community?

2. **How can you build your faith today?** Are you making time for prayer or reflecting on God's word? What's one way you can stay strong in His love?

Bottom Line

God calls us to care for others, stand up for what's right, and stay grounded in His truth. We can live out these truths by protecting the vulnerable and staying strong in faith, trusting that His mercy will lead us to eternal life.

Prayer

Heavenly Father, thank You for Your love and guidance. Help me to stand firm in my faith and to protect those who are vulnerable. Give me strength to choose what is right, even when it's hard. I pray that I would remain grounded in Your truth, trusting in Your mercy and love. In Jesus' Name, Amen.

SEPTEMBER 1

Guard Your Circle

3-Year-Bible Reading: Proverbs 22:24–25; Leviticus 1–2

"Make no friendship with a man given to anger, nor go with a wrathful man, lest you learn his ways and entangle yourself in a snare." — Proverbs 22:24–25

"He shall bring it to Aaron's sons the priests. And he shall take from it a handful of the fine flour and oil with all of its frankincense, and the priest shall burn this as its memorial portion on the altar, a food offering with a pleasing aroma to the Lord." — Leviticus 2:2

"If his offering is a burnt offering from the herd, he shall offer a male without blemish." — Leviticus 1:3

Who you spend time with can shape who you become. Have you ever noticed how someone else's mood—especially if it's angry or negative—can change the vibe of a whole group? **Proverbs 22:24–25** reminds us that constantly hanging out with people who are always angry or reckless can lead us into trouble ourselves. On the flip side, **Leviticus 1–2** talks about offerings given to God—gifts that are chosen carefully and given from the heart. It's about giving God our best, not just following rules but showing devotion through actions.

Just like those offerings had to be "without blemish" and done in the right way, the people we allow close to us shape how we live out our devotion to God. Your life, your time, your relationships—they're like an offering. Are you offering God something pure and pleasing, or are you letting yourself be influenced in a way that draws you away from Him?

THINK ABOUT IT

1. **Choose Your People Wisely:** Who are you surrounding yourself with? Are your friends encouraging you to grow closer to God, or pulling you away?

2. **Guard Your Influence:** Are you more influenced by others, or are you influencing them in a way that honors God?

3. **Living Your Offering:** What kind of "offering" is your life to God? Are there areas where you need to be more intentional in honoring Him—like your attitude, habits, or friendships?

BOTTOM LINE

The people we spend time with shape the way we live—and our lives are like offerings to God. Let's make sure we're surrounding ourselves with people who help us grow in faith and offer our best to Him.

PRAYER

Heavenly Father, thank You for reminding me how important it is to guard my friendships and live a life that honors You. Help me choose the right people to walk with and give You my best in everything I do. Teach me to be a positive influence and to live in a way that's pleasing to You. In Jesus' Name, Amen.

SEPTEMBER 2

Avoid the Trap

3-Year-Bible Reading: Proverbs 22:26–27; Psalm 101; Leviticus 3–4

"Be not one of those who give pledges, who put up security for debts. If you have nothing with which to pay, why should your bed be taken from under you?" — Proverbs 22:26–27

"I will not set before my eyes anything that is worthless. I hate the work of those who fall away; it shall not cling to me." — Psalm 101:3

"If anyone of the common people sins unintentionally in doing any one of the things that by the Lord's commandments ought not to be done…he shall bring for his offering a goat…so the priest shall make atonement for him, and he shall be forgiven." — Leviticus 4:27–28, 31

You've probably heard the phrase, "Don't sign up for something you can't handle." **Proverbs** warns against making promises—especially financial ones—that could leave you broke or trapped. **Psalm 101** shows King David's commitment to living with integrity, refusing to let evil influence his heart.

Leviticus reminds us that sin, even unintentional, has consequences—but God makes a way to be made right with Him. Together, these verses call us to live wisely, guard our hearts, and remember God's mercy when we fall short. Whether it's debt, bad habits, or wrong choices, God doesn't want us stuck—He wants us free.

THINK ABOUT IT

1. **Guard Your Commitments:** Are you quick to say "yes" without thinking? Proverbs 22:26–27 challenges us to be wise about what we agree to. It's not just about money—it's about any choice that could end up controlling you.

2. **What Are You Watching?** Psalm 101:3 is a solid check for our screens and minds. What we let in influences who we become. Would you be proud of what you're feeding your soul with?

3. **Grace for Mistakes:** Leviticus 4 shows that even accidental sins matter to God—but so does His forgiveness. We're not perfect, but God provides a way to be clean again through Jesus.

BOTTOM LINE

Be careful what you commit to, stay focused on what honors God, and remember—His forgiveness is always available when you mess up.

PRAYER

Heavenly Father, thank You for caring about every part of my life—from the choices I make to the things I watch and listen to. Help me be wise, stay focused on what's right, and turn to You when I mess up. Thank You for always offering forgiveness and a fresh start. In Jesus' Name, Amen.

September 3

Keep the Landmarks

3-Year-Bible Reading: Proverbs 22:28–29; Leviticus 5–6

"Do not move the ancient landmark that your fathers have set. Do you see a man skillful in his work? He will stand before kings; he will not stand before obscure men." — Proverbs 22:28–29

"If anyone sins in that he hears a public adjuration to testify, and though he is a witness...he shall bear his iniquity." — Leviticus 5:1

"The Lord spoke to Moses, saying, 'If anyone sins and commits a breach of faith against the Lord by deceiving his neighbor...he shall restore it in full and shall add a fifth to it.'" — Leviticus 6:1,5

Ever walk by a "Do Not Touch" sign and feel *extra* tempted to touch it? Sometimes boundaries make us curious—but they also protect what matters. Proverbs 22:28 talks about not moving the "ancient landmark," which back then meant the physical property lines set by older generations. But it's also a reminder to respect the moral and spiritual boundaries God's given us.

Leviticus 5–6 shows how serious God is about honesty, responsibility, and making things right when we mess up. Together, these passages teach us that God's boundaries aren't there to limit us—they're there to help us live with purpose, integrity, and honor.

Think About It

1. **Respect the Boundaries:** What "landmarks" or boundaries has God placed in your life—like truth, purity, or respect? Are you honoring them or trying to push past them?

2. **Skill Brings Honor:** Proverbs 22:29 says those who are skillful in what they do will stand before kings. Are you giving your best to what God's called you to—school, friendships, talents?

3. **Make It Right:** In **Leviticus 6**, when someone wrongs another person, they have to not only admit it but also *make it right*—plus extra. Is there someone you need to apologize to or repay?

Bottom Line

God's boundaries are meant to protect us and guide us toward lives of excellence and integrity. Don't ignore them—learn to respect them, live skillfully, and make things right when you fall short.

Prayer

Heavenly Father, thank You for the boundaries You've placed in my life and the wisdom that comes from Your Word. Help me to live with integrity, to give my best in everything I do, and to make things right when I mess up. Teach me to respect what You've set in place and to trust that Your way is the best way. In Jesus' Name, Amen.

September 4

Feasting with Focus

3-Year-Bible Reading: Proverbs 23:1–3; Leviticus 7–8

"When you sit down to eat with a ruler, observe carefully what is before you, and put a knife to your throat if you are given to appetite. Do not desire his delicacies, for they are deceptive food."
— Proverbs 23:1–3

"This is the law of the burnt offering, of the grain offering, of the sin offering, of the guilt offering, of the ordination offering, and of the peace offering."
— Leviticus 7:37

"And Moses did as the Lord commanded him, and the congregation was assembled at the entrance of the tent of meeting." — Leviticus 8:4

Have you ever been super hungry and then found yourself eating way too fast—or way too much—only to regret it afterward? In **Proverbs 23:1–3**, the writer warns us to be cautious, even when good things are in front of us. Food isn't the enemy—it's about learning self-control and remembering who we're living for.

The offerings in **Leviticus 7–8** may seem a bit technical or outdated at first glance, but they show us something powerful: God is a God of order, worship, and purpose. Every offering had a meaning, and the people couldn't just approach Him however they wanted. They had to come with reverence. Whether it's a meal or a moment of worship, the Bible is calling us to be intentional—focused on God more than what's on the table or happening around us.

Think About It

1. **What's really feeding you?** In a world full of "delicacies"—from social media to popularity to achievements—what are you really craving? Are you being filled by things that satisfy for a moment but leave you empty?

2. **Worship is more than music:** The detailed offerings in Leviticus show that God cares how we come to Him. How can you bring more intention and respect into your daily relationship with God?

3. **Discipline protects purpose:** Proverbs talks about controlling your appetite. That applies to food, but also your desires, habits, and even emotions. What area of your life could use more self-control to help you stay focused on God?

Bottom Line

Whether you're sitting at a feast or standing in worship, your focus should be on honoring God with discipline, reverence, and purpose.

Prayer

Heavenly Father, thank You for being a God of purpose and order. Help me not to chase after things that only look good on the outside but don't lead me closer to You. Teach me to live with self-control, to worship You with intention, and to keep my focus on what truly matters. In Jesus' Name, Amen.

SEPTEMBER 5

Chasing What Lasts

3-Year-Bible Reading: Proverbs 23:4–5; Psalm 102; Leviticus 9–10

"Do not toil to acquire wealth; be discerning enough to desist. When your eyes light on it, it is gone, for suddenly it sprouts wings, flying like an eagle toward heaven." — Proverbs 23:4–5

"My days are like an evening shadow; I wither away like grass... But you, O Lord, are enthroned forever; you are remembered throughout all generations." — Psalm 102:11–12

"Then fire came out from before the Lord and consumed them, and they died before the Lord." — Leviticus 10:2

Life moves fast—especially when you're a teen trying to balance school, friends, sports, family, and maybe even a part-time job. It's easy to get caught up chasing things that seem so important now: good grades, popularity, or even money. But **Proverbs 23:4–5** reminds us that when we make those things our top priority, they vanish just like a dream when you wake up. **Psalm 102** brings the focus back to what really lasts—God's unchanging presence, even when everything else feels temporary or falling apart.

And in **Leviticus 10**, we see a harsh reminder that treating God's holiness lightly has real consequences. Nadab and Abihu thought they could worship God their own way, but it cost them their lives.

These passages challenge us to ask: What am I really living for?

THINK ABOUT IT

1. **What Are You Chasing?** Are you spending most of your time trying to impress others, get more stuff, or be the best? Take a step back and ask yourself—will any of that still matter in 10 years? How about in eternity?

2. **God Is Constant:** When everything else changes—your friend group, your emotions, even your goals—God remains the same. How can you anchor your life in Him instead of what's temporary?

3. **Respect God's Holiness:** Nadab and Abihu's story might seem extreme, but it shows that God takes our worship seriously. Are you treating Him with reverence, or casually like a side hobby?

BOTTOM LINE

Everything in this world fades, but God is forever. Don't waste your life chasing what won't last. Choose what matters: honoring God, knowing Him, and living for His glory.

PRAYER

Heavenly Father, thank You for reminding me that not everything I chase after is worth it. Help me to see what truly matters and to put You first in my life. Teach me to honor You with my time, my choices, and my heart. Help me walk closely with You and not get distracted by things that fade. In Jesus' Name, Amen.

SEPTEMBER 6

Watch What You Take In

3-Year-Bible Reading: Proverbs 23:6–8; Psalm 103; Leviticus 11–12

"Do not eat the bread of a man who is stingy; do not desire his delicacies, for he is like one who is inwardly calculating. 'Eat and drink!' he says to you, but his heart is not with you. You will vomit up the morsels that you have eaten, and waste your pleasant words." — Proverbs 23:6–8

"Bless the Lord, O my soul, and forget not all his benefits, who forgives all your iniquity, who heals all your diseases." — Psalm 103:2–3

"For I am the Lord your God. Consecrate yourselves therefore, and be holy, for I am holy." — Leviticus 11:44

Let's be honest: not everything that looks good on the outside is actually good for us. Whether it's food, music, social media, or even certain people—there's a lot out there that can seem harmless or even appealing but actually messes with our hearts and minds. **Proverbs 23** warns us about being influenced by people who might seem generous or cool but don't have good intentions. **Leviticus 11–12** reminds us that God called His people to be set apart—to live differently. And in **Psalm 103**, we're reminded of what really satisfies: the goodness, forgiveness, and healing of God.

THINK ABOUT IT

1. **Guard Your Influences:** Who are you "eating with"? Are there people or situations in your life that seem fun or exciting but are pulling you away from what's right?

2. **Feed on What Heals:** Psalm 103 says God forgives and heals. What are you feeding your soul with—God's truth or the world's distractions?

3. **Set Apart for a Reason:** God's call to be holy isn't about being perfect—it's about being different for Him. What's one area of your life where you could make a cleaner, healthier, more God-honoring choice?

BOTTOM LINE

Not everything that looks good is good for you. God calls you to be wise about what you let into your life—so you can live healed, whole, and holy in Him.

PRAYER

Heavenly Father, help me be wise about what I take in—whether it's people, influences, or habits. Thank You for Your forgiveness and healing, and for calling me to something better. Teach me to live set apart for You. In Jesus' Name, Amen.

SEPTEMBER 7

Watch What You Take In

3-Year-Bible Reading: Proverbs 23:9; Leviticus 13–15

"Do not speak in the hearing of a fool, for he will despise the good sense of your words." — Proverbs 23:9

"He shall remain unclean as long as he has the disease. He is unclean. He shall live alone. His dwelling shall be outside the camp." — Leviticus 13:46

"Thus you shall keep the people of Israel separate from their uncleanness, lest they die in their uncleanness by defiling my tabernacle that is in their midst." — Leviticus 15:31

Have you ever felt like you were doing your best to do what's right, but everything around you seemed to pull you down? Whether it's the toxic friend group, the music you listen to, or even just what you scroll through online—it all affects your spiritual health. In **Proverbs 23:9**, we're reminded that some conversations just aren't worth having.

And in **Leviticus 13–15**, God gives very specific rules about cleanliness—not just about health, but as a symbol of keeping His people pure and separate from sin. It wasn't about judging people with diseases but about protecting the entire community from harm. Spiritually, it's the same with sin—it spreads fast, and it separates us from God. That's why we have to be intentional about what we allow into our hearts and minds.

THINK ABOUT IT

1. **Guard Your Words:** Are you trying to speak truth into someone's life who has no interest in listening? Sometimes the wisest move is to step back and let your actions speak instead.

2. **Be Aware of Contamination:** Just like in Leviticus, where uncleanness could isolate someone, sin and spiritual compromise can slowly isolate us from God and others. What "unclean" influences might be sneaking into your daily life?

3. **Spiritual Hygiene Matters:** We take showers and brush our teeth daily—but what about spiritual cleansing? Confession, prayer, and spending time with God's Word helps keep us clean inside.

BOTTOM LINE

What you allow into your life shapes your heart. Choose carefully what voices you listen to, what you dwell on, and how you respond. God calls us to stay spiritually clean not to limit us, but to protect us and help us live in His presence fully.

PRAYER

Heavenly Father, thank You for caring about every part of my life—inside and out. Help me to be wise with my words and cautious about the influences I allow into my heart. Give me discernment to walk away from foolishness and courage to pursue what is pure and honoring to You. Keep me spiritually clean so I can live in closeness with You. In Jesus' Name, Amen.

SEPTEMBER 8

Guardrails and Grace

3-Year-Bible Reading: Proverbs 23:10–11; Leviticus 16–18

"Do not move an ancient landmark or enter the fields of the fatherless, for their Redeemer is strong; he will plead their cause against you." — Proverbs 23:10–11

"For on this day shall atonement be made for you to cleanse you. You shall be clean before the Lord from all your sins." — Leviticus 16:30

"You shall therefore keep my statutes and my rules; if a person does them, he shall live by them: I am the Lord." — Leviticus 18:5

We live in a world that's constantly shifting the lines—what used to be considered wrong is now "up for debate," and sometimes it feels like there are no solid answers. But **Proverbs 23:10–11** reminds us not to mess with the "landmarks," or the boundaries God has set. Why? Because they protect people—especially the vulnerable—and God Himself defends those boundaries.

In **Leviticus 16**, we see how God made a way for people to be forgiven through the Day of Atonement. Then in **Leviticus 18**, He gives clear guidelines on how to live differently from the world. It's not about rules for rules' sake—it's about living a life that honors the God who gave everything for us.

THINK ABOUT IT

1. **God's Boundaries Are for Our Good:** God's commands aren't about limiting your fun; they're about protecting your heart and your future. Where in your life might you be tempted to "move a landmark" and step outside God's design?

2. **Grace Covers Our Gaps:** The Day of Atonement in Leviticus was a huge deal—it was God's way of saying, "I know you'll mess up, but I've made a way back." Today, Jesus is our perfect atonement. Do you believe God's forgiveness is enough for your mistakes?

3. **Live Set Apart:** Leviticus 18 lays out some serious instructions for God's people. Why? Because He called them to live differently. As a follower of Jesus, what are some areas where your life should look different from the world around you?

BOTTOM LINE

God sets up boundaries not to restrict us, but to protect us—and when we fail, His grace makes a way to bring us back. Live in His love, trust His ways, and remember that you are set apart for something greater.

PRAYER

Heavenly Father, Thank You for being a God of both boundaries and grace. Help me to see Your commands as a gift, not a burden. When I mess up, remind me that Jesus has already made a way back for me. Teach me to live in a way that honors You, even when it's hard or unpopular. I want my life to reflect Your love and truth. In Jesus' Name, Amen.

SEPTEMBER 9

Tune Your Heart

3-Year-Bible Reading: Proverbs 23; Psalm 104; Leviticus 19

"Apply your heart to instruction and your ear to words of knowledge." — Proverbs 23:12

"I will sing to the Lord as long as I live; I will sing praise to my God while I have being." — Psalm 104:33

"You shall be holy, for I the Lord your God am holy." — Leviticus 19:2

Some days it feels like your brain is full—homework, social media, friend drama, future plans. It's easy to tune out when God is trying to speak through His Word. But in **Proverbs 23:12**, we're reminded to lean in with our hearts and ears—to intentionally choose wisdom. **Psalm 104** shows us a God who's powerful and creative, worthy of praise.

And **Leviticus 19** might seem like a bunch of old rules, but it's really God calling His people (that includes us!) to live differently—to live holy. When you put these together, they paint a picture: a heart tuned to God is a heart ready to live for Him.

THINK ABOUT IT

1. **Heart and Ears Check:** Are you taking time to listen to God—not just with your ears but with your heart? What might help you stay more focused on His voice each day?

2. **Praise Is Powerful:** Psalm 104 is full of awe for who God is. How can singing, journaling, or just noticing nature help you praise Him more during your everyday routines?

3. **Holy Living Today:** Being holy doesn't mean being perfect—it means being set apart. What's one small way you can reflect God's character in how you treat others or make decisions?

BOTTOM LINE

God invites us to live with hearts that are open to His wisdom, filled with praise, and shaped by His holiness.

PRAYER

Heavenly Father, thank You for being a God who speaks, creates, and calls us to something higher. Help me tune my heart to Your instruction and choose to praise You, even when life is noisy or hard. Teach me what it means to live set apart and to reflect who You are. In Jesus' Name, Amen.

SEPTEMBER 10

Straight Talk and Sacred Living

3-Year-Bible Reading: Proverbs 23:13–14; Leviticus 20–22

"Do not withhold discipline from a child; if you strike him with a rod, he will not die. If you strike him with the rod, you will save his soul from Sheol." — Proverbs 23:13–14

"Consecrate yourselves, therefore, and be holy, for I am the Lord your God." — Leviticus 20:7

"You shall not profane my holy name, that I may be sanctified among the people of Israel. I am the Lord who sanctifies you." — Leviticus 22:32

Let's be honest—discipline and holiness aren't exactly the most exciting topics. In fact, they can feel a little... intense. When someone talks about rules or correction, it's easy to zone out or push back. But God doesn't call us to a boring or restrictive life—He calls us to something greater. In **Proverbs 23:13–14**, discipline is seen not as punishment, but as protection.

And in **Leviticus 20–22**, God lays out what it means to be set apart—holy—because He is holy. That's not about being perfect, but about belonging to Him and living differently in a way that reflects His character.

THINK ABOUT IT

1. **Discipline is love:** When has a hard truth or correction actually helped you? God uses correction not to shame us, but to shape us—because He cares too much to leave us stuck in harmful habits.

2. **Holy means set apart:** God isn't calling you to fit in—He's calling you to stand out. What's one way your choices, words, or actions can reflect God's holiness today?

3. **God does the sanctifying:** Leviticus reminds us that it's *God* who makes us holy. You don't have to "earn" your way to being enough. Trust that He's working in you, even when you feel like you fall short.

BOTTOM LINE

God's correction and His call to holiness are acts of love. He disciplines to protect us and sets us apart for a greater purpose—so we can live in a way that honors Him and draws others to His goodness.

PRAYER

Heavenly Father, thank You for loving me enough to correct me when I need it and for calling me to a life that's set apart. Help me to see discipline as Your care, not condemnation, and to trust that You are making me holy through Your Spirit. Teach me to live in a way that reflects who You are. In Jesus' Name, Amen.

September 11

Let It Make You Smile

3-Year-Bible Reading: Proverbs 23:15–16; Leviticus 23–24

"My son, if your heart is wise, my heart too will be glad. My inmost being will exult when your lips speak what is right."—Proverbs 23:15–16

"These are the appointed feasts of the Lord that you shall proclaim as holy convocations; they are my appointed feasts."—Leviticus 23:2

"Command the people of Israel to bring you pure oil from beaten olives for the lamp, that a light may be kept burning regularly."—Leviticus 24:2

Ever had that moment when someone you care about—like a parent, mentor, or coach—sees you make a wise choice and beams with pride? That's what's happening in **Proverbs 23:15–16**. A parent is saying, "When you make good choices and speak the truth, it brings me deep joy." And God feels the same way about us.

In **Leviticus 23**, God sets up rhythms—like feasts and special days—for His people to rest, celebrate, and remember Him. He wanted their lives to be filled with regular reminders of who He is and how much He cares. Then in **Leviticus 24**, there's a reminder to keep the lamps burning in the tabernacle—a picture of staying close to God's presence consistently.

So what's the connection? When we live wisely, honor God, and walk in truth, it lights up His heart—and our own lives too.

Think About It

1. **Wise Choices Shine Bright:** What does it look like to live wisely in your world—at school, at home, online? Who sees your choices, and how might they be impacted?

2. **God's Rhythm, Your Life:** God gave His people regular times to stop and remember Him. What kind of "holy habits" do you have in your life that help you stay connected to God?

3. **Keep the Light On:** The lamps in the tabernacle had to stay lit. What's one small thing you can do daily to keep your relationship with God burning bright?

Bottom Line

When you live wisely and stay connected to God, it brings joy to others—and lights the way for your own journey.

Prayer

Heavenly Father, thank You for the joy that comes from living wisely and walking in Your truth. Help me create rhythms in my life that keep me close to You. May my choices bring You joy and shine Your light to those around me. In Jesus' Name, Amen.

SEPTEMBER 12

Hope That Holds

3-Year-Bible Reading: Proverbs 23:17–18; Psalm 105; Leviticus 25

"Let not your heart envy sinners, but continue in the fear of the Lord all the day. Surely there is a future, and your hope will not be cut off." — Proverbs 23:17–18

"Seek the Lord and his strength; seek his presence continually! Remember the wondrous works that he has done…" — Psalm 105:4–5

"And you shall consecrate the fiftieth year, and proclaim liberty throughout the land to all its inhabitants. It shall be a jubilee for you…" — Leviticus 25:10

It's hard not to feel like you're missing out sometimes. You scroll through social media and see people who don't care about God living their best lives. They seem free, confident, and like everything is working out for them. Meanwhile, trying to follow Jesus can feel hard and, honestly, kind of invisible. But **Proverbs 23** reminds us that there's a deeper story playing out — one where those who trust God have a future full of hope. **Psalm 105** urges us to look back and remember all the times God came through for His people.

And **Leviticus 25** shows us that God is serious about freedom, restoration, and second chances — the Jubilee year was like a divine reset button! When we're tempted to envy others or feel like God's way is slower or harder, these verses remind us: God's path leads to a lasting kind of freedom and hope that nothing in this world can match.

THINK ABOUT IT

1. **What's Real Freedom?** The Jubilee year in Leviticus was all about releasing people from debt and giving them a fresh start. What areas of your life do you wish you could reset? God offers you spiritual freedom and a new beginning through Jesus every day.

2. **Don't Envy, Stay Focused:** Proverbs tells us not to envy those who ignore God. Why do you think it's easy to feel jealous of people who seem to have it all without living for God? What helps you stay focused on your hope in Christ?

3. **God's Track Record:** Psalm 105 encourages us to remember what God has done. Take time today to list 2–3 ways God has come through for you or someone you know. How can that reminder give you strength right now?

BOTTOM LINE

Even when following God feels tough or invisible, His promises lead to real freedom, lasting hope, and a future you can count on.

PRAYER

Heavenly Father, Thank You for giving me a hope that will never be cut off. Help me not to get distracted by what the world calls success or freedom. Remind me of Your faithfulness, and give me the strength to keep trusting You, even when it's hard. Help me walk in the freedom You've given me through Jesus. In Jesus' Name, Amen.

September 13

Feast or Famine?

3-Year-Bible Reading: Proverbs 23:19–21; Psalm 106; Leviticus 26

"Hear, my son, and be wise, and direct your heart in the way. Be not among drunkards or among gluttonous eaters of meat, for the drunkard and the glutton will come to poverty, and slumber will clothe them with rags." — Proverbs 23:19–21

"Yet he saved them for his name's sake, that he might make known his mighty power." — Psalm 106:8

"If you walk in my statutes and observe my commandments and do them…I will give peace in the land…I will turn to you and make you fruitful and multiply you and will confirm my covenant with you." — Leviticus 26:3, 6, 9

Life offers us a buffet of choices—some are good for us, and others… not so much. Whether it's junk food, binge-watching, or jumping into stuff we know isn't right, it's easy to lose direction. **Proverbs 23** warns us not to let indulgence and laziness take over. **Psalm 106** reminds us of how God's people messed up repeatedly—but still, God showed up for them because of who He is.

And in **Leviticus 26**, God lays out a pretty clear "if-then" plan: if you follow Him, there's peace and blessing; if not, life gets a lot harder. These chapters show us something huge—God gives us choices, but our direction determines our destination.

Think About It

1. **Who's Driving Your Life?** Are you letting emotions, desires, or the crowd guide your choices? Proverbs encourages us to *"direct your heart in the way."* That means living intentionally, not aimlessly.

2. **God's Patience is Powerful:** Even when Israel rebelled, Psalm 106 says God saved them "for His name's sake." Have you seen God's mercy in your own life—even when you didn't deserve it?

3. **Blessing Comes with Obedience:** Leviticus 26 isn't about earning God's love—it's about living in a way that aligns with His heart. Do you believe that following God brings real peace and joy?

Bottom Line

God wants the best for you, but that means choosing His way over your own. Stay awake, stay wise, and remember: the path you take shapes the life you live.

Prayer

Heavenly Father, thank You for giving me choices and for loving me even when I mess up. Help me to be wise with my decisions and to follow the path You've set for me. Teach me to seek Your peace and not just chase what feels good in the moment. Thank You for Your patience, grace, and promises. In Jesus' Name, Amen.

September 14

Bought With a Price

3-Year-Bible Reading: Proverbs 23:22–23; Leviticus 27

"Listen to your father who gave you life, and do not despise your mother when she is old. Buy truth, and do not sell it; buy wisdom, instruction, and understanding." — Proverbs 23:22–23

"But nothing that a person devotes to the Lord, whether man or beast, or of his inherited field, shall be sold or redeemed; every devoted thing is most holy to the Lord." — Leviticus 27:28

Have you ever saved up for something big—maybe a concert, a new game, or your first pair of shoes you really wanted? You thought about it, counted the cost, and made it yours. That's the kind of commitment today's passages are talking about. **Proverbs 23:23** tells us to "buy" truth, wisdom, and understanding—things that don't go on sale and can't be returned.

Meanwhile, **Leviticus 27** talks about what it means to dedicate something completely to God. Once it's given, it's His—no refunds, no take-backs. When we choose to follow Jesus, we're making a lifelong commitment to value what God values and to live like we belong to Him—because we do.

Think About It

1. **What's Worth Your Investment?** What are you spending your time, energy, and attention on? Are you "buying" truth and wisdom daily by spending time in God's Word or chasing after temporary things?

2. **No Take-Backs:** In Leviticus, once something was devoted to God, it became most holy. What would it look like for you to devote parts of your life—like your talents, your time, or your goals—fully to Him?

3. **Wisdom Over Hype:** Proverbs reminds us that wisdom, understanding, and truth are worth the cost. How can you remind yourself to value God's truth more than popularity, trends, or peer approval?

Bottom Line

God calls us to live like people who have been purchased with something priceless—His love and grace. When we choose to give our lives to Him, it's not about giving Him part of who we are; it's about handing over everything in trust and worship, knowing He is worth it all.

Prayer

Heavenly Father, thank You for valuing us so much that You gave everything to make us Yours. Help me to see the true worth of Your truth and wisdom and to choose those things over what the world offers. Teach me to devote my life fully to You, knowing You're faithful and good. Give me courage to live like someone who belongs to You. In Jesus' Name, Amen.

SEPTEMBER 15

The Joy of Being Known

3-Year-Bible Reading: Proverbs 23:24–25; Numbers 1–2

"The father of the righteous will greatly rejoice; he who fathers a wise son will be glad in him. Let your father and mother be glad; let her who bore you rejoice."— Proverbs 23:24–25

"Take a census of all the congregation of the people of Israel, by clans, by fathers' houses, according to the number of names, every male, head by head." — Numbers 1:2

"The people of Israel shall camp each by his own standard, with the banners of their fathers' houses." — Numbers 2:2

Have you ever felt like just another face in the crowd? Like you're one of many, and your voice doesn't really stand out? In **Numbers 1**, God tells Moses to take a census—not because He needed the numbers, but because every person mattered. Each name was known. Each tribe had a place.

And in **Proverbs 23**, we see the heart of a parent beaming with joy over a child who walks in wisdom. God is like that too. He delights in seeing you choose what's right, and He celebrates you as uniquely His. You're not just a name on a list—you're deeply known and deeply loved.

THINK ABOUT IT

1. **You Matter to God**: In a world of billions, God sees *you*. Like the Israelites counted one by one, God never loses track of you. How does it change the way you see yourself, knowing that God knows your name?

2. **Your Choices Impact Others**: Proverbs reminds us that wise living brings joy, not just to us, but to those who care about us. Have you ever made a choice that made someone proud? How can you walk in wisdom today?

3. **You Belong**: Each tribe had a banner and a place to camp. God gave His people both identity and community. Who are the people God has placed around you to support you—and how can you be that for others?

BOTTOM LINE

God knows you by name, delights in your growth, and has a unique place for you in His family.

PRAYER

Heavenly Father, thank You for seeing me and knowing me completely. Help me to make wise choices that honor You and bring joy to those around me. Remind me that I belong to something bigger than myself and that You have a special purpose for me. In Jesus' Name, Amen.

September 16

A Joy Worth Living For

3-Year-Bible Reading: Proverbs 23:24–25; Numbers 3–4

"The father of the righteous will greatly rejoice; he who fathers a wise son will be glad in him. Let your father and mother be glad; let her who bore you rejoice."— Proverbs 23:24–25

"But the Levites were not listed along with them by their ancestral tribe. For the Lord spoke to Moses, saying, 'Only the tribe of Levi you shall not list, and you shall not take a census of them among the people of Israel.'"— Numbers 3:47–49

"They shall guard all the furnishings of the tent of meeting, and keep guard over the people of Israel as they minister at the tabernacle."— Numbers 3:8

Everyone wants to make someone proud—whether it's your parents, a mentor, or even just your younger sibling. In **Proverbs 23:24–25**, we see the deep joy that a parent feels when their child chooses wisdom and righteousness. It's the kind of joy that isn't just a momentary smile, but a lasting satisfaction.

In **Numbers 3–4**, we see God giving specific responsibilities to the Levites—not just busywork, but meaningful roles that helped preserve the holiness of the tabernacle. They were set apart for something special, and their faithfulness made a difference. Just like the Levites, you have a calling. It may not be guarding a sacred tent, but it *is* about living your life in a way that honors God and brings joy to those who love you.

Think About It

1. **Living for Joy:** What does it look like in your life to bring joy to those who care about you—not by trying to impress them, but by choosing what's right even when it's hard?

2. **You Have a Role:** Just like the Levites had a special role in serving God, you have a role too. What are some ways you can serve God with your unique gifts, whether it's at church, school, or with your friends?

3. **Making It Count:** The Levites didn't have flashy jobs—they set up tents and carried furniture—but their faithfulness mattered. How can you be faithful in the small things today?

Bottom Line

Living wisely and faithfully brings joy—not just to the people around you, but to the heart of God. Every choice you make matters, even the small ones.

Prayer

Heavenly Father, thank You for giving me a purpose and for placing people in my life who care about me. Help me live in a way that brings joy to them and honors You. Show me how to be faithful in the little things and give me courage to live wisely, even when it's hard. In Jesus' Name, Amen.

September 17

Blurred Vision

3-Year-Bible Reading: Proverbs 23:29–35; Numbers 5–6

"Who has woe? Who has sorrow? Who has strife? Who has complaining? Who has wounds without cause? Who has redness of eyes? Those who tarry long over wine; those who go to try mixed wine."
— Proverbs 23:29–30

"Then the man shall bring his wife to the priest and bring the offering required of her... The priest shall make her take an oath..." — Numbers 5:15, 19

"And the Lord spoke to Moses, saying, 'Speak to the people of Israel and say to them, When either a man or a woman makes a special vow, the vow of a Nazirite, to separate himself to the Lord...'"
— Numbers 6:1–2

Life is full of choices. Some of them are easy, like choosing your favorite ice cream flavor. Others, like who you hang out with, what you watch, or how you handle temptation, have deeper consequences. In **Proverbs 23**, we're warned about the trap of things like alcohol—not because God wants to kill our fun, but because He knows how easily it can blur our vision, literally and spiritually.

In **Numbers 5**, God gives specific instructions to handle situations that test truth and faithfulness. And in **Numbers 6**, He introduces a way for people to live wholly dedicated to Him through the Nazirite vow. All these scriptures point to one big theme: our choices shape our direction—and our devotion.

Think About It

1. **What's Blurring Your Vision?** The Proverbs passage warns about how things that seem fun or harmless can lead to regret and confusion. Is there something in your life right now that's causing you to lose focus on God?

2. **God Cares About Integrity:** The strange ritual in Numbers 5 may seem harsh, but it shows that God values truth and takes relationships seriously. Are you living in a way that reflects honesty and trust?

3. **Set Apart on Purpose:** In Numbers 6, the Nazirite vow was a special way to be set apart for God. What would it look like for you to live "set apart" in your school, your friend group, or your online presence?

Bottom Line

God calls us to live with clear eyes and devoted hearts. When we choose to stay focused on Him, we avoid the pain that comes from blurry, misled decisions.

Prayer

Heavenly Father, thank You for loving me enough to guide me away from the things that can harm me. Help me recognize the things that blur my vision and distract me from You. Teach me to live with honesty, focus, and a heart fully set apart for You. Give me the courage to make wise choices, even when it's hard or unpopular. In Jesus' Name, Amen.

September 18

When You're Tempted to Fit In

3-Year-Bible Reading: Proverbs 24:1–2; Psalm 107; Numbers 7–8

"Be not envious of evil men, nor desire to be with them, for their hearts devise violence, and their lips talk of trouble." — Proverbs 24:1–2

"Let the redeemed of the Lord say so, whom he has redeemed from trouble." — Psalm 107:2

"Thus did Moses; according to all that the Lord commanded him, so he did." — Numbers 8:3

Ever feel like doing the right thing makes you stand out in the worst way? Maybe your friends are all about shortcuts, gossip, or just pushing boundaries, and there's pressure to go along so you don't seem weird or left out. **Proverbs 24:1–2** reminds us not to envy people who seem to get away with bad behavior. Their way might look fun or easy now, but it leads to trouble.

Meanwhile, **Psalm 107** celebrates people who've experienced God's rescue—they know how sweet it is to be set free. And in **Numbers 8**, we see Moses obeying God's commands exactly as instructed. No shortcuts. No compromise. Just faithful action. That kind of consistency matters—even when it's hard.

Think About It

1. **What Are You Looking At?** It's easy to admire people who seem powerful, popular, or untouchable. But Proverbs says to *not* envy them. Why? What do their hearts and words reveal about their true direction?

2. **Your Story Matters:** Psalm 107 says "Let the redeemed of the Lord say so." Has God helped you through something? Your story could be the hope someone else needs to hear. Are you bold enough to share it?

3. **Faithful Obedience:** Moses followed God's instructions exactly. Would people say the same about you? Do you follow God's way even when no one's watching?

Bottom Line

Fitting in isn't worth losing your footing. Stay faithful to God—even when it's unpopular—because His way leads to real peace, purpose, and freedom.

Prayer

Heavenly Father, help me to see clearly when I'm tempted to follow the wrong crowd. Give me the courage to stand for what's right and the wisdom to recognize when I'm being pulled away from You. Thank You for redeeming me and giving me a story worth telling. Help me live it out with bold faith. In Jesus' Name, Amen.

September 19

Built to Last

3-Year-Bible Reading: Proverbs 24:3–4; Psalm 108; Numbers 9–10

By wisdom a house is built, and by understanding it is established; by knowledge the rooms are filled with all precious and pleasant riches. —Proverbs 24:3–4

With God we shall do valiantly; it is he who will tread down our foes. —Psalm 108:13

At the command of the Lord they camped, and at the command of the Lord they set out. They kept the charge of the Lord, at the command of the Lord by Moses. —Numbers 9:23

Life can feel like a construction zone. You're building friendships, character, dreams for the future—but sometimes it's hard to know what tools to use or which way to go. In **Proverbs 24**, we learn that wisdom and understanding are the foundation of any strong life. In **Psalm 108**, David reminds us that God is the one who gives us strength to face anything.

And in **Numbers 9–10**, the Israelites didn't make a move without God's direction. These verses together teach us something huge: success isn't about having everything figured out—it's about trusting God to guide the process and being willing to follow Him, even when the next step feels uncertain.

Think About It

1. **Build Smart:** Are you building your life with God's wisdom or just going with what seems popular? Take time to check your "blueprints." Are you letting God's Word shape your goals, your friendships, your decisions?

2. **Don't Go Without God:** Like the Israelites followed God's cloud and fire, are you seeking His direction in your everyday decisions—school, relationships, activities? Ask yourself, "Am I moving because God is leading me, or just because I feel like it?"

3. **Victory Starts with Trust:** Psalm 108 says God brings the victory. What challenges are you facing right now? Remember, you don't have to be strong enough—you just have to trust the One who is.

Bottom Line

A life built on God's wisdom and led by His guidance is a life that stands strong—no matter what comes.

Prayer

Heavenly Father, thank You for being the foundation I can build my life on. Help me to seek Your wisdom and trust Your timing. When I'm tempted to rush ahead or figure things out on my own, remind me to wait for Your direction. I know that when I follow You, I won't be lost. In Jesus' Name, Amen.

SEPTEMBER 20

Power in Wisdom and Humility

3-Year-Bible Reading: Proverbs 24:5–6; Numbers 11–12

"A wise man is full of strength, and a man of knowledge enhances his might, for by wise guidance you can wage your war, and in abundance of counselors there is victory." — Proverbs 24:5–6

"Now the man Moses was very meek, more than all people who were on the face of the earth." — Numbers 12:3

"Would that all the Lord's people were prophets, that the Lord would put his Spirit on them!" — Numbers 11:29

We live in a world that often celebrates loud voices, bold opinions, and instant reactions. But God's way is different. In **Proverbs 24:5–6**, we're told that strength comes from wisdom—not just from muscles or being the loudest in the room.

In **Numbers 11–12**, Moses shows us what true leadership and strength look like: not pride or power-hunger, but humility and a deep reliance on God. When others questioned Moses' role, God defended him—not because Moses fought back, but because Moses trusted Him. This shows us that wisdom and meekness go hand in hand. You don't have to be the loudest to be strong in God's eyes.

Think About It

1. **What does real strength look like?** According to **Proverbs 24**, true strength isn't about physical power or popularity—it's about wisdom and seeking guidance. Who do you turn to when you need direction?

2. **God defends the humble:** When Moses was attacked verbally by his own family, he didn't fight back. He trusted God to handle it. How can we learn to respond with humility instead of anger when we're criticized?

3. **Celebrate others' gifts:** Moses wasn't jealous when others began to speak by the Spirit—he was excited! Instead of competing, he celebrated. Do you support and encourage the gifts of others, or do you feel threatened by them?

Bottom Line

God values wisdom and humility over noise and pride. Strength in His kingdom looks like trust, teachability, and encouragement toward others.

Prayer

Heavenly Father, help me to grow in true wisdom and strength. Teach me to be humble like Moses, even when it's hard. Help me to encourage others in their gifts and to trust You when I face challenges. May I always seek Your guidance and follow Your way over the world's way. In Jesus' Name, Amen.

September 21

When Fear Talks Louder Than Faith

3-Year-Bible Reading: Proverbs 24:7–9; Numbers 13–14

"Wisdom is too high for a fool; in the gate he does not open his mouth. Whoever plans to do evil will be called a schemer. The devising of folly is sin, and the scoffer is an abomination to mankind." — Proverbs 24:7–9

"We are not able to go up against the people, for they are stronger than we are." — Numbers 13:31

"But my servant Caleb, because he has a different spirit and has followed me fully, I will bring into the land into which he went." — Numbers 14:24

Have you ever wanted to try something new or bold—try out for a team, speak up for someone, or even share your faith—but then fear totally took over? In **Numbers 13–14**, God's people stood on the edge of the land He promised them. But instead of stepping in with courage, most of them freaked out. They saw the giants instead of God's promise. Only Joshua and Caleb held on to faith.

In **Proverbs 24**, we're reminded that foolishness and fear often come from ignoring God's wisdom. Caleb wasn't stronger than the others—he just trusted God more. What about you?

Think About It

1. **Fear or Faith?** Are you listening more to your fears or to God's promises? What "giants" in your life seem bigger than God right now?

2. **The Company You Keep:** The other spies spread fear, and the whole crowd followed. Who are the voices you let influence you most—friends, social media, or God's truth?

3. **Be Like Caleb:** Caleb had a "different spirit." What does it look like for you to follow God fully even when others don't?

Bottom Line

Faith doesn't ignore fear—it just trusts God more than it listens to fear. Be the one who chooses faith even when it's unpopular or uncomfortable.

Prayer

Heavenly Father, thank You for showing me that faith is stronger than fear. Help me to be like Caleb and trust You fully, even when the world feels scary or uncertain. Give me courage to follow You when others don't. Let my faith in You be louder than any fear in me. In Jesus' Name, Amen.

SEPTEMBER 22

Standing Strong When It's Hard

3-Year-Bible Reading: Proverbs 24; Psalm 109; Numbers 15–16

If you faint in the day of adversity, your strength is small. — Proverbs 24:10

But you, O GOD my Lord, deal on my behalf for your name's sake; because your steadfast love is good, deliver me! — Psalm 109:21

And the Lord said to Moses, "Get away from the midst of this congregation, that I may consume them in a moment." And they fell on their faces. — Numbers 16:45

Life throws curveballs. Maybe a friend betrayed you, school is overwhelming, or you're dealing with stuff at home no one knows about. In moments like these, it's easy to feel like giving up. But **Proverbs 24:10** reminds us that how we respond in tough times shows the real strength of our faith. **Psalm 109** shows us what to do with that pain—cry out to God, not just for rescue, but because His love never fails. And **Numbers 15–16** shows what happens when people rebel against God's authority and try to take control on their own. Spoiler alert: it doesn't end well.

God wants us to stand firm when life gets tough—not in our own power, but in His. Instead of running or rebelling, we fall on our faces before Him like Moses and Aaron did, trusting God to lead, even when we don't understand.

THINK ABOUT IT

1. **Check Your Strength:** When life gets hard, do you give up or lean into God's strength? How can you train your heart now to trust Him when life isn't easy?

2. **Turn Pain into Prayer:** Psalm 109 teaches us that we don't have to hide our hurt—we can bring it to God. What's something tough you're facing right now that you need to pray about honestly?

3. **Rebellion vs. Surrender:** In Numbers 16, people tried to take control instead of following God's leaders. Are there areas in your life where you're fighting God's plan instead of trusting Him?

BOTTOM LINE

Hard times don't mean God is absent—they're opportunities to show real faith. Trust Him, even when it hurts. That's where true strength is found.

PRAYER

Heavenly Father, Thank You for being my strength when I feel weak and overwhelmed. Help me to trust You in the middle of the chaos, to bring my pain to You, and to surrender instead of rebel. Teach me to stand strong in You, especially when life gets hard. In Jesus' Name, Amen.

SEPTEMBER 23

Stand Up and Speak Out

3-Year-Bible Reading: Proverbs 24:11–12; Numbers 17–19

Rescue those who are being taken away to death; hold back those who are stumbling to the slaughter. If you say, "Behold, we did not know this," does not he who weighs the heart perceive it? — Proverbs 24:11–12

And the staff of the man whom I choose shall sprout. Thus I will make to cease from me the grumblings of the people of Israel, which they grumble against you. — Numbers 17:5

Whoever touches the dead body of any person shall be unclean seven days. — Numbers 19:11

It's easy to think, "That's not my problem," when we see someone going down a destructive path—whether it's bullying, cheating, or walking away from faith. But **Proverbs 24:11–12** challenges that mindset. It reminds us that God sees not only what we do but also what we ignore. In **Numbers 17**, God confirms Aaron's leadership by making his staff miraculously grow. It was a clear sign to stop complaining and trust God's chosen plan.

Later in **Numbers 19**, we see how God set rules about purity, showing how seriously He takes sin and its consequences. When we put all this together, we get a powerful message: God wants us to care enough about others to step in and speak truth—because walking away in silence isn't love; it's indifference.

THINK ABOUT IT

1. **Speak Up With Courage:** Who around you might be "stumbling to the slaughter"? It could be a friend making risky choices or someone hurting emotionally. Ask God for boldness to say what needs to be said—with love.

2. **Trust God's Confirmation:** Just like God made Aaron's staff sprout to show His will, God often gives us signs or nudges when we're on the right path. Are you listening for His direction? Are you open to what He might ask you to do, even if it's hard?

3. **Take Sin Seriously:** God gave the Israelites strict rules about what made them unclean—not to punish them, but to show how much they needed His help to stay holy. Do you view sin as something serious, or something casual? What would it look like to pursue spiritual "cleanness" today?

BOTTOM LINE

God calls us not just to follow Him, but to help others follow too—even when it's uncomfortable. He sees our hearts and wants us to be bold, compassionate, and obedient.

PRAYER

Heavenly Father, Thank You for caring so deeply about each of us. Help me to see the people around me through Your eyes and give me the courage to speak up when someone is headed toward harm. Teach me to trust Your direction and to take my walk with You seriously. I want to honor You not just with my words, but with my actions and choices. In Jesus' Name, Amen.

September 24

Sweet Like Honey

3-Year-Bible Reading: Proverbs 24:13–14; Numbers 20–21

"My son, eat honey, for it is good, and the drippings of the honeycomb are sweet to your taste. Know that wisdom is such to your soul; if you find it, there will be a future, and your hope will not be cut off." — Proverbs 24:13–14

"And the Lord said to Moses and Aaron, 'Because you did not believe in me, to uphold me as holy in the eyes of the people of Israel, therefore you shall not bring this assembly into the land that I have given them.'" — Numbers 20:12

"And the Lord said to Moses, 'Make a fiery serpent and set it on a pole, and everyone who is bitten, when he sees it, shall live.'" — Numbers 21:8

Wisdom is sweet like honey. That sounds nice and cozy—until we realize that learning wisdom often happens in hard, uncomfortable situations. In **Proverbs 24**, we're reminded that finding wisdom gives us a future and fills us with hope.

But in **Numbers 20–21**, we watch as Moses makes a costly mistake by disobeying God. Even someone as faithful as Moses wasn't above consequences. Then in the next chapter, God brings healing through something unexpected—a bronze serpent lifted high for all to see. These chapters remind us that God's wisdom leads to life, even in our biggest mess-ups. The path might sting like a snake bite, but healing and hope are still possible when we look to Him.

Think About It

1. **What's Your Honey?** What are some "sweet" things you turn to for comfort or satisfaction? Do they actually fill your soul—or just your cravings?

2. **Even Leaders Fail:** Moses lost his chance to enter the Promised Land because of one act of disobedience. What does this teach you about taking God seriously, even when others are watching you?

3. **Look Up to Live:** When the Israelites were bitten by snakes, their healing came from looking up at the bronze serpent. How does this foreshadow Jesus? Are there areas in your life where you need to "look up" for healing?

Bottom Line

Wisdom may come through failure, but God's grace still leads us toward hope, healing, and a future.

Prayer

Heavenly Father, thank You for being patient with us, even when we mess up. Help us to learn wisdom through Your Word and through the tough lessons of life. Teach us to trust You fully, to take You seriously, and to always look to You for healing and hope. In Jesus' Name, Amen.

September 25

Bounce Back

3-Year-Bible Reading: Proverbs 24:15–16; Psalm 110; Numbers 22–24

"For the righteous falls seven times and rises again, but the wicked stumble in times of calamity." — Proverbs 24:16

"The LORD says to my Lord: 'Sit at my right hand, until I make your enemies your footstool.'" — Psalm 110:1

"Behold, I received a command to bless: he has blessed, and I cannot revoke it." — Numbers 23:20

Life can feel like a rollercoaster sometimes. You try to do the right thing, but then you mess up. You want to follow God, but distractions pull you off course. Maybe you've had a bad day, or a bad week—or you're just feeling like a failure. The good news? **Proverbs 24:16** says that even when you fall—again and again—God gives you the strength to rise back up.

In **Psalm 110**, God's power and authority are bigger than anything coming against you. And in **Numbers 22–24**, even when a prophet named Balaam tried to curse God's people, he couldn't. Why? Because when God says you're blessed, that blessing sticks.

Think About It

1. **Failure Isn't the End:** Have you fallen lately—maybe in your faith, with friends, or in a situation where you knew better? Falling doesn't mean you're finished. God's people fall but get back up. That's what makes them strong.

2. **God Has the Final Word:** Balaam couldn't curse what God had blessed. When you belong to God, no label, rumor, or bad opinion can change what God says about you. His voice is louder than any hate or failure.

3. **You're Sitting in a Strong Place:** Psalm 110 paints a picture of Jesus sitting at the right hand of God—total power and victory. As a follower of Jesus, you're on the winning side. That means you don't fight alone.

Bottom Line

You might fall, but in Christ, you're never out of the fight. God's blessing on your life can't be canceled—even when you mess up. Get up, keep going, and remember who's got your back.

Prayer

Heavenly Father, thank You for lifting me up every time I fall. Help me to keep rising, trusting in Your strength and blessing over my life. Remind me that nothing and no one can undo what You've spoken over me. Keep my eyes on You when life gets hard, and give me boldness to walk in Your victory. In Jesus' Name, Amen.

SEPTEMBER 26

Don't Cheer Too Soon

3-Year-Bible Reading: Proverbs 24:17–18; Numbers 25–27

"Do not rejoice when your enemy falls, and let not your heart be glad when he stumbles, lest the Lord see it and be displeased, and turn away his anger from him." — Proverbs 24:17–18

"While Israel lived in Shittim, the people began to whore with the daughters of Moab... And the Lord said to Moses, 'Take all the chiefs of the people and hang them in the sun before the Lord...'" — Numbers 25:1, 4

"Moses said to the Lord, 'Let the Lord, the God of the spirits of all flesh, appoint a man over the congregation...'" — Numbers 27:15–16

Sometimes it feels good when someone who wronged us gets what's coming to them. Maybe the bully at school gets in trouble, or a friend who betrayed you ends up embarrassed. But **Proverbs 24:17–18** reminds us that gloating over someone else's fall can actually pull us further from God's heart.

In **Numbers 25–27**, we see God's anger burn against sin, but we also see His mercy, His justice, and the need for godly leadership. These passages all point to one key truth: our reactions, especially to others' mistakes, matter deeply to God.

THINK ABOUT IT

1. **Don't Celebrate the Fall:** When someone messes up or faces consequences, it's not an excuse for us to feel superior. God calls us to humility and compassion—even for people we don't like.

2. **Sin is Serious:** The events in Numbers 25 show how quickly turning from God can lead to disaster. God doesn't take sin lightly, and neither should we. But rather than pointing fingers, we should focus on keeping our own hearts pure.

3. **Who's Leading Your Heart?** In Numbers 27, Moses asks God to appoint a new leader. Good leadership matters, but so does allowing God to lead *your* heart. Are you letting Him direct how you respond to others?

BOTTOM LINE

Don't cheer when others stumble. God is more interested in your humility than your sense of justice. Let His mercy guide your response to the failures of others.

PRAYER

Heavenly Father, help me to have a heart that reflects Your grace. Teach me not to gloat when others fall, but to respond with humility, compassion, and love. Keep my heart clean, my thoughts kind, and my actions led by You. I want to follow You, even when it's hard. In Jesus' Name, Amen.

SEPTEMBER 27

Don't Envy the Wrong Crowd

3-Year-Bible Reading: Proverbs 24:19–20; Numbers 28–30

"Fret not yourself because of evildoers, and be not envious of the wicked, for the evil man has no future; the lamp of the wicked will be put out."
— Proverbs 24:19–20

"You shall offer them before the LORD at their appointed time." — Numbers 28:2

"If a man vows a vow to the LORD, or swears an oath to bind himself by a pledge, he shall not break his word. He shall do according to all that proceeds out of his mouth." — Numbers 30:2

Have you ever felt left out because you're trying to follow God while others seem to be having more fun doing whatever they want? It can be hard not to get jealous when people who don't care about God seem to be winning. But **Proverbs 24:19–20** reminds us that what looks like success without God won't last. It might shine for a while, but it burns out in the end.

Meanwhile, in **Numbers 28–30**, we're reminded that God values faithfulness—daily offerings, keeping promises, and showing up for Him matter more than flashy moments. God sees your quiet obedience. You might not get a spotlight for being faithful, but God honors it in powerful ways.

Think About It

1. **Who are you watching?** It's easy to get distracted by people who seem to be winning without God. But where are their choices really leading them? Are they headed toward something lasting—or something empty?

2. **Faithfulness matters:** In **Numbers 28**, God calls for regular offerings. Why? Because He values consistency. It's not about grand gestures but small, steady steps of obedience.

3. **Your word counts:** Numbers 30:2 shows how much God values our promises. What you say and commit to—especially when it comes to God—matters deeply. Are you someone others (and God) can trust?

Bottom Line

Don't chase the spotlight the world offers when God is inviting you to a life that actually lasts. Stay faithful, keep your word, and trust that God sees you—even when no one else does.

Prayer

Heavenly Father, help me not to envy those who seem to succeed without You. Teach me to value faithfulness over flashiness and to keep my word even when it's hard. Strengthen me to walk with You daily, knowing that You see and honor every step. In Jesus' Name, Amen.

September 28

Living Wisely in a Loud World

3-Year-Bible Reading: Proverbs 24:21-22; Psalm 111; Numbers 31–32

"My son, fear the Lord and the king, and do not join with those who do otherwise, for disaster will arise suddenly from them, and who knows the ruin that will come from them both?" — Proverbs 24:21-22

"The fear of the Lord is the beginning of wisdom; all those who practice it have a good understanding. His praise endures forever!" — Psalm 111:10

"But if you will not do so, behold, you have sinned against the Lord, and be sure your sin will find you out." — Numbers 32:23

It's not always easy to do the right thing—especially when it feels like everyone around you is doing the opposite. Peer pressure is real. Whether it's gossip, cheating, or just going along with the crowd, the temptation to blend in can be strong. But **Proverbs 24:21-22** gives us a strong reminder: following God and honoring authority is the wise and safe path, even when others rebel.

In **Psalm 111**, we're reminded that real wisdom begins with respecting God. And in **Numbers 32**, we see that even when people think they can make their own plans, ignoring God's commands always comes with consequences.

Think About It

1. **Fear God First:** Who are you listening to more—God, or the people around you? Respect for God isn't about being scared; it's about trusting His way above all others.

2. **Wisdom in Action:** Psalm 111 says those who "practice" the fear of the Lord have understanding. Are your daily choices showing that you want to live wisely?

3. **Choices Have Consequences:** In Numbers 32, the tribes who wanted to settle outside the promised land had to promise to still fight with the rest of Israel. Moses reminded them that if they didn't, their sin would catch up with them. What choices are you making now that could affect your future?

Bottom Line

Living wisely means respecting God first, even when the world shouts something different. God sees your heart, your choices, and your loyalty. Choosing His way is always worth it.

Prayer

Heavenly Father, thank You for showing me what it means to live wisely. Help me not to follow the crowd, but to follow You. Give me courage to make the right choices, even when it's hard. I want my life to reflect Your wisdom and truth. In Jesus' Name, Amen.

September 29

Check Your Compass

3-Year-Bible Reading: Proverbs 24:23–25; Numbers 33–34

"These also are sayings of the wise. Partiality in judging is not good. Whoever says to the wicked, 'You are in the right,' will be cursed by peoples, abhorred by nations, but those who rebuke the wicked will have delight, and a good blessing will come upon them." — Proverbs 24:23–25

"And the Lord spoke to Moses in the plains of Moab by the Jordan at Jericho, saying, 'Command the people of Israel, and say to them, When you pass over the Jordan into the land of Canaan, then you shall drive out all the inhabitants of the land from before you…'" — Numbers 33:50–52

"This shall be your land as defined by its borders all around." — Numbers 34:12

It's easy to lose your way when you don't know where you're going—or when the path seems unclear. Whether it's making choices about friends, school, or what's right and wrong, we all need something solid to guide us. In **Proverbs 24:23–25**, we're reminded that being fair and standing up for what's right matters deeply to God.

And in **Numbers 33–34**, God gives Israel clear instructions for where they're supposed to go and what boundaries they should live within. God wasn't trying to limit them—He was setting them up for freedom and blessing inside the borders of His will. Just like them, we need a spiritual compass to keep us on the right path.

Think About It

1. **No Favorites:** Are you fair with people, or do you treat some better just because it benefits you? God calls us to be just—even when it's unpopular.

2. **Clear Directions:** God gave Israel specific boundaries for a reason. Are you listening to God's voice about the boundaries in your life—like the friendships you keep or the habits you're forming?

3. **Stand for Right:** Rebuking wrong isn't about being rude—it's about courage. Are you willing to speak truth and live it, even when others don't?

Bottom Line

God sets boundaries not to restrict us but to protect us. When we stay within His will and walk in justice, we find blessing, purpose, and clarity.

Prayer

Heavenly Father, thank You for being a God of order and justice. Help me to live with integrity and treat others fairly, even when it's hard. Show me the boundaries You've set for my life and give me the courage to stay inside them. Guide my steps, and let my choices reflect Your truth and love. In Jesus' Name, Amen.

September 30

Say It Straight

3-Year-Bible Reading: Proverbs 24:26; Psalm 112; Numbers 35–36

Whoever gives an honest answer kisses the lips. — Proverbs 24:26

He is not afraid of bad news; his heart is firm, trusting in the Lord. —Psalm 112:7

You shall not pollute the land in which you live, for blood pollutes the land, and no atonement can be made for the land for the blood that is shed in it, except by the blood of the one who shed it. — Numbers 35:33

Have you ever had a moment when you knew the truth, but you were afraid to speak it? Maybe you didn't want to hurt someone's feelings, or maybe you were just scared of how people would react. But **Proverbs 24:26** says that giving an honest answer is like a kiss—it may feel awkward or risky, but it's actually a sign of love and respect. Honesty, especially when it's hard, shows real courage.

Psalm 112 reminds us that when we trust God, we don't have to fear bad news or outcomes. Even in tough conversations, we can have peace. And **Numbers 35–36** shows how seriously God takes justice and fairness—truth matters deeply to Him. When we live truthfully, we reflect His character.

Think About It

1. **Truth is Love:** When you speak honestly, even if it's uncomfortable, you're actually showing kindness. How can you be lovingly honest in your friendships and family relationships?

2. **Trust Over Fear:** Psalm 112 says the person who trusts God isn't afraid of bad news. Are you letting fear stop you from doing what's right? What would it look like to trust God more with the outcome?

3. **Justice Matters to God:** In **Numbers 35–36**, God set up systems for fairness and safety. How can you stand up for what's right in your everyday life—at school, in your community, or online?

Bottom Line

Living with honesty and courage reflects God's heart. When you speak the truth in love and trust Him with the results, you walk in wisdom, strength, and real integrity.

Prayer

Heavenly Father, Help me to be someone who speaks the truth with love. Give me the courage to be honest, even when it's hard, and the trust to believe You're with me in every situation. Make me brave enough to stand for what's right and kind enough to care how I do it. Let my life reflect Your justice and peace. In Jesus' Name, Amen.

October 1

Prepare Before You Shine

3-Year-Bible Reading: Proverbs 24:27; John 1

"Prepare your work outside; get everything ready for yourself in the field, and after that build your house." — Proverbs 24:27

"In the beginning was the Word, and the Word was with God, and the Word was God." — John 1:1

"The true light, which gives light to everyone, was coming into the world." — John 1:9

Ever feel like you're stuck waiting for your real life to begin? Like you're in a holding pattern, waiting for your moment to shine? Whether it's the dream job, the big game, or the right friends to come along, it's easy to think *"I'll start living for God when __ happens."* But **Proverbs 24:27** reminds us that preparation is part of God's plan.

Even Jesus, the *Word who was God*, spent thirty quiet years before stepping into public ministry. His light was always there, but He waited for the right time to shine. That doesn't mean those years were wasted—they were part of the preparation.

Think About It

1. **Preparation Matters:** Are you making space now for what God might want to do in your life later? Whether it's building good habits, practicing honesty, or spending time in Scripture, your current choices are laying the foundation for what comes next.

2. **Jesus Is the Light:** How can you reflect His light where you are right now? You don't need a stage to shine. You can bring Jesus' light to your family, your friends, or even your school—just by being kind, honest, and willing to serve.

3. **Small Steps Count:** Don't overlook the "field work." The unseen moments—studying, praying, listening, growing—are what make you strong enough to handle the spotlight later. Even Jesus had a season of preparation.

Bottom Line

God prepares us before He positions us. Don't rush the process. Even in the quiet seasons, He's doing something powerful. Let His light grow in you now, so when the moment comes, you're ready to shine.

Prayer

Heavenly Father, Thank You for reminding me that preparation has a purpose. Help me not to waste the time You've given me, even when it feels slow or unnoticed. Teach me to seek You in the everyday moments and to reflect Your light wherever I go. I want to be ready for whatever You've planned for me. In Jesus' Name, Amen.

October 2

Revenge or Redemption?

3-Year-Bible Reading: Proverbs 24:28–29; Psalm 113; John 2

"Be not a witness against your neighbor without cause, and do not deceive with your lips. Do not say, 'I will do to him as he has done to me; I will pay the man back for what he has done.'" — Proverbs 24:28–29

"He raises the poor from the dust and lifts the needy from the ash heap, to make them sit with princes, with the princes of his people." — Psalm 113:7–8

"Jesus said to her, 'Woman, what does this have to do with me? My hour has not yet come.' His mother said to the servants, 'Do whatever he tells you.'" — John 2:4–5

It's easy to want payback when someone hurts you. Maybe a friend betrayed your trust, someone spread a rumor, or a classmate made you feel small in front of others. Our natural response is often, *"They'll get what's coming to them."* But the wisdom of **Proverbs 24:29** challenges that. God invites us to break the cycle of revenge and instead trust Him with justice.

Meanwhile, **Psalm 113** shows us a different side of God—the one who lifts up the broken and forgotten. Instead of fighting for payback, we're called to be like Him: lifting others, not dragging them down.

And in **John 2**, we see Jesus at a wedding in Cana. Even though His "hour" hadn't come, He still turned water into wine out of love and compassion. He didn't respond with, *"It's not my problem."* He responded with grace.

Think About It

1. **Choose Redemption Over Revenge:** When you feel wronged, do you try to "even the score," or do you look for a way to respond with grace? How could choosing mercy change the outcome?

2. **God Lifts the Lowly:** Psalm 113 reminds us that God sees those who are hurting and lifts them up. Could God be calling you to be that kind of person for someone else today?

3. **"Do Whatever He Tells You":** Mary's words in John 2 are simple but powerful. What is Jesus telling you to do in a tough situation right now—even if it's not easy?

Bottom Line

God calls us to respond to hurt with humility and grace, not revenge. When we follow Jesus' example, we bring peace and healing into situations where others expect conflict.

Prayer

Heavenly Father, thank You for being a God who lifts us up and sees our pain. Help me not to seek revenge but to trust You with justice. Teach me to respond with grace, like Jesus, even when it's hard. Let my life reflect Your mercy and love. In Jesus' Name, Amen.

October 3

Don't Sleep on It

3-Year-Bible Reading: Proverbs 24:30–34; John 3

"I passed by the field of a sluggard, by the vineyard of a man lacking sense… and behold, it was all overgrown with thorns; the ground was covered with nettles, and its stone wall was broken down." — Proverbs 24:30–31

"Little by little, poverty will come upon you like a robber, and want like an armed man." — Proverbs 24:34

"Truly, truly, I say to you, unless one is born again he cannot see the kingdom of God." — John 3:3

Have you ever put something off until the last minute? Maybe a school project, cleaning your room, or texting someone back—and before you know it, things were way messier than they needed to be. **Proverbs 24:30–34** paints a picture of a field left unattended, slowly falling apart. The owner didn't destroy it on purpose. They just didn't act.

Likewise, in **John 3**, Jesus tells Nicodemus about a spiritual reality that requires intentional change—being born again. It's not something we drift into. It's a decision. A lot of things in life won't take care of themselves, especially your spiritual life. The longer you wait, the harder it gets. But the good news? You can start right now.

Think About It

1. **The Danger of Delay:** Are there areas in your life—habits, relationships, or your time with God—that you've been neglecting? Like the field in Proverbs, those areas can get overgrown fast if we're not paying attention.

2. **Born Again?** Jesus says we need a new start, a spiritual rebirth, to enter God's kingdom. That isn't about trying harder—it's about surrendering to Him. Have you made that decision, or are you waiting for "a better time"?

3. **Small Steps, Big Impact:** Laziness isn't always obvious. Sometimes it looks like "I'll do it tomorrow." But change happens little by little. What small step can you take today to grow in your faith?

Bottom Line

Don't wait for things to fix themselves. Your heart, like a garden, needs attention. Jesus offers a new life—but it starts with saying "yes" to Him now, not later.

Prayer

Heavenly Father, Thank You for reminding me that my choices matter, even the small ones. Help me not to drift through life but to live with purpose. I want to grow closer to You and not let my spiritual life get overgrown with distractions or excuses. Teach me to be alert and ready to respond to Your love. In Jesus' Name, Amen.

October 4

Live Higher

3-Year-Bible Reading: Proverbs 25:1–7; Psalm 114; John 4

"Do not put yourself forward in the king's presence or stand in the place of the great, for it is better to be told, 'Come up here,' than to be put lower in the presence of a noble." — Proverbs 25:6–7

"Tremble, O earth, at the presence of the Lord, at the presence of the God of Jacob." — Psalm 114:7

"But whoever drinks of the water that I will give him will never be thirsty again. The water that I will give him will become in him a spring of water welling up to eternal life." — John 4:14

Have you ever tried really hard to impress someone—maybe by showing off your talents or trying to fit in with the "cool" crowd—only to feel like it backfired? In **Proverbs 25**, we're reminded that humility is more powerful than self-promotion. In **Psalm 114**, we see a picture of how awesome and powerful God is—so powerful even the earth shakes in His presence! And in **John 4**, Jesus meets a woman at a well who thought she was forgotten and unworthy. Instead of judging her, He offers her living water—hope, purpose, and eternal life.

These three passages may seem different at first, but they're all connected by a bigger idea: living a life that's not centered on ourselves, but on God. When we humble ourselves, recognize His power, and receive what only He can give, our lives begin to overflow with something so much better than popularity, status, or approval—we overflow with His presence.

Think About It

1. **True Confidence Comes from God:** Are you trying to prove your worth to others, or are you trusting that God has already given you value? Proverbs reminds us that we don't need to fight for attention. God sees us, and His invitation to "come up here" is far more meaningful.

2. **Be Amazed Again:** Psalm 114 reminds us how incredible God is. When was the last time you were truly in awe of Him? If the earth trembles at His presence, how much more should our hearts be moved by who He is?

3. **Jesus Fills What the World Can't:** In John 4, Jesus tells the woman He can give her living water. What are you trying to fill your heart with? Friends, success, likes, or achievements? Only Jesus satisfies completely.

Bottom Line

You don't have to push your way to the top or chase what doesn't last. Let Jesus fill you with living water, walk humbly, and live higher by staying close to Him.

Prayer

Heavenly Father, thank You for reminding me that I don't have to prove myself to the world. Help me to walk humbly, stay in awe of You, and receive the living water Jesus offers. Fill me with Your presence so that my life overflows with Your love. In Jesus' Name, Amen.

October 5

Handle It with Humility

3-Year-Bible Reading: Proverbs 25:8–10; John 5

"Do not hastily bring into court, for what will you do in the end, when your neighbor puts you to shame? Argue your case with your neighbor himself, and do not reveal another's secret." — Proverbs 25:8–9

"The man went away and told the Jews that it was Jesus who had healed him." — John 5:15

Have you ever been so sure you were right that you rushed to call someone out—only to realize later you didn't have the full picture? In **Proverbs 25:8–10**, we're reminded not to act impulsively when we feel wronged or want to prove a point. Jesus' encounter in **John 5** shows a different kind of caution: after healing a man on the Sabbath, Jesus is quickly judged by the religious leaders. They were more focused on catching Him breaking a rule than on the miracle that just changed someone's life.

Both moments speak to how quickly we can jump to conclusions or speak out without wisdom. Whether it's drama at school, something on social media, or a misunderstanding with a friend, the Bible calls us to pause, think, and act with humility.

Think About It

1. **Don't Rush to Judge:** Before you call someone out, check your heart. Are you seeking peace or just trying to be "right"?
2. **Handle Conflict Privately:** Proverbs reminds us not to blast someone's secret or mistake publicly. Talk it out one-on-one first.
3. **See the Bigger Picture:** Like the Pharisees who missed the miracle because of their rules, we can miss what God is doing when we're too focused on being in control.

Bottom Line

Real wisdom means slowing down, thinking things through, and handling others with respect—even when it's hard. Let God lead your heart, not your pride.

Prayer

Heavenly Father, help me to act with wisdom and humility. When I feel wronged or frustrated, remind me to pause and respond in a way that honors You. Teach me to handle conflict with grace and to look for what You're doing in every situation. In Jesus' Name, Amen.

October 6

Words That Stick

3-Year-Bible Reading: Proverbs 25:11–12; Psalm 115; John 6

"A word fitly spoken is like apples of gold in a setting of silver. Like a gold ring or an ornament of gold is a wise reprover to a listening ear." — Proverbs 25:11–12

"Not to us, O Lord, not to us, but to your name give glory, for the sake of your steadfast love and your faithfulness!" — Psalm 115:1

"Jesus said to them, 'I am the bread of life; whoever comes to me shall not hunger, and whoever believes in me shall never thirst.'" — John 6:35

Words can do a lot. They can lift someone up or tear someone down in seconds. A compliment at the right moment can make someone's day, and a harsh word can stick longer than we ever intended. **Proverbs 25:11–12** reminds us that the right words at the right time are like treasure. Not only that, but being willing to listen to truth—especially when it's hard—shows wisdom. In **Psalm 115**, we're reminded that our lives should point to God's glory, not our own.

Then **John 6** takes it deeper: Jesus doesn't just speak life—He *is* life. He satisfies our deepest needs in ways no friend, trend, or social media "like" ever could.

Think About It

1. **Words That Matter:** Are the things you say helping others, or hurting them? What does it look like to speak "apples of gold" in your daily life?

2. **The Right Kind of Glory:** When you succeed or get recognition, do you give God credit? How can you point people to His love and faithfulness instead of seeking all the spotlight?

3. **Soul Satisfaction:** Jesus said He's the "bread of life." That means He's what truly satisfies. Are you filling up on Him through prayer, scripture, and community—or trying to fill the void with temporary things?

Bottom Line

The words you speak and the words you listen to shape who you become. Choose to use your voice for encouragement, live for God's glory, and find your satisfaction in Jesus—He's the only one who never runs dry.

Prayer

Heavenly Father, thank You for the power of words and for being the ultimate Word who gives life. Help me speak truth and kindness, listen with wisdom, and live in a way that points back to You. Satisfy my heart in ways nothing else can. In Jesus' Name, Amen.

October 7

Cool Under Pressure

3-Year-Bible Reading: Proverbs 25:13–14; John 7

"Like the cold of snow in the time of harvest is a faithful messenger to those who send him, he refreshes the soul of his masters. Like clouds and wind without rain is a man who boasts of a gift he does not give." — Proverbs 25:13–14

"So Jesus proclaimed, as he taught in the temple, 'You know me, and you know where I come from. But I have not come of my own accord. He who sent me is true, and him you do not know. I know him, for I come from him, and he sent me.'" — John 7:28–29

Have you ever had someone totally let you down—like a friend who promised to help but ghosted when it really mattered? That kind of disappointment sticks with you. Proverbs talks about this when it describes someone who *boasts* but doesn't *deliver* (**Proverbs 25:14**). On the flip side, there's something powerful and refreshing about someone who shows up, does what they say, and stays true—even when it's tough.

That's exactly what Jesus did in **John 7**. Even with people questioning Him and pressure rising, He stayed focused on His mission and trusted God. He didn't boast or try to impress; He simply lived the truth.

Think About It

1. **Faithfulness Refreshes:** Are you the kind of friend who follows through? Like a cold drink on a hot day, your reliability can actually encourage and lift up those around you.

2. **Don't Fake the Rain:** Proverbs warns about pretending to be something you're not. What are you tempted to *boast* about to seem important or cool? What would it look like to just be honest and real instead?

3. **Jesus Under Pressure:** Even when people doubted or misunderstood Him, Jesus didn't cave. What's one way you can stand strong in your faith, even when others don't get it?

Bottom Line

Being faithful—whether to a friend, a promise, or your relationship with God—is rare and powerful. Jesus shows us what it looks like to stay true under pressure. Let your actions speak louder than words.

Prayer

Heavenly Father, Help me to be someone who is faithful and real. Teach me to follow through on my word, to be honest about who I am, and to trust You even when things get hard. I want to live like Jesus—bold, truthful, and focused on You. In Jesus' Name, Amen.

October 8

Sweet and Steady

3-Year-Bible Reading: Proverbs 25:15–16; Psalm 116; John 8

With patience a ruler may be persuaded, and a soft tongue will break a bone. If you have found honey, eat only enough for you, lest you have your fill of it and vomit it. —Proverbs 25:15–16

I love the Lord, because he has heard my voice and my pleas for mercy. Because he inclined his ear to me, therefore I will call on him as long as I live. —Psalm 116:1–2

So if the Son sets you free, you will be free indeed. —John 8:36

Sometimes life feels like it's all about extremes. You're either drowning in stress or bored out of your mind. You're either all-in with God or you're struggling and feel far away. These passages remind us that God isn't looking for extremes—He's looking for steadiness, honesty, and freedom. In **Proverbs 25**, there's wisdom in knowing your limits. Don't overdo even the good stuff, like honey.

In **Psalm 116**, we're reminded that God listens to us with compassion, even when we're at our lowest. And in **John 8**, Jesus makes this bold promise: true freedom comes through Him. He doesn't expect perfection—He offers grace that sets us free.

Think About It

1. **Patience Wins:** Have you ever tried to force something to happen—like changing someone's mind, proving your point, or fixing something fast? Proverbs says that patience and gentle words can be more powerful than pressure or anger. How can you practice patience this week?

2. **Know Your Limits:** The honey metaphor is about self-control. What are things in your life (even good ones) that can become "too much"? Is God inviting you to find balance?

3. **Freedom in Christ:** Jesus said, *"You will be free indeed."* What kind of freedom are you craving—freedom from guilt, fear, pressure to fit in? Real freedom starts when we lean into who Jesus says we are: loved, heard, and free.

Bottom Line

True strength is steady, not extreme. God calls us to live wisely, walk in freedom, and trust Him with every step.

Prayer

Heavenly Father, thank You for hearing me even when I don't have all the right words. Teach me to live with patience, balance, and freedom in You. Help me recognize when I'm overdoing things and remind me that true peace comes from trusting You. I want to walk in the freedom Jesus gives—free from fear, free to follow You. In Jesus' Name, Amen.

October 9

Handle with Care

3-Year-Bible Reading: Proverbs 25:17–18; John 9

Let your foot be seldom in your neighbor's house, lest he have his fill of you and hate you. A man who bears false witness against his neighbor is like a war club, or a sword, or a sharp arrow. — Proverbs 25:17–18

Jesus answered, "It was not that this man sinned, or his parents, but that the works of God might be displayed in him." — John 9:3

Have you ever had a friend who just... doesn't know boundaries? Maybe they text you non-stop, or show up at your place uninvited a little too often. At first, it's fine. But over time, it gets exhausting. That's kind of what **Proverbs 25:17–18** is talking about. Respect and truth go hand-in-hand when it comes to our relationships.

Meanwhile, in **John 9**, Jesus heals a blind man—not to gain attention, but to show God's power. The people around the man are quick to assume and judge, but Jesus sees a deeper purpose. These two passages may seem totally different, but both teach us how to treat others with wisdom, grace, and intention.

Think About It

1. **Respect Boundaries:** Do you give people space, or do you sometimes push past their comfort zones without realizing it? Relationships thrive when we respect others' time, space, and emotional energy.

2. **Words Have Power:** Proverbs says lying about someone is like swinging a weapon at them. Are your words building people up or cutting them down?

3. **See with Compassion:** In **John 9**, people assumed the blind man's condition was a punishment. Jesus corrected them. Do you make quick judgments, or do you pause to see people as God does?

Bottom Line

Be the kind of person who respects others, speaks truth, and sees people through the lens of God's love—not assumptions.

Prayer

Heavenly Father, thank You for showing us how to treat others with wisdom and love. Help us to be thoughtful in how we speak and act, respecting others' boundaries and seeing them as You do. Teach us to lead with compassion and truth. In Jesus' Name, Amen.

October 10

Unbreakable Trust

3-Year-Bible Reading: Proverbs 25:19–20; Psalm 117; John 10

"Trusting in a treacherous man in time of trouble is like a bad tooth or a foot that slips. Whoever sings songs to a heavy heart is like one who takes off a garment on a cold day."— Proverbs 25:19–20

"Praise the Lord, all nations! Extol him, all peoples! For great is his steadfast love toward us, and the faithfulness of the Lord endures forever. Praise the Lord!"— Psalm 117:1–2

"My sheep hear my voice, and I know them, and they follow me. I give them eternal life, and they will never perish, and no one will snatch them out of my hand."— John 10:27–28

Have you ever leaned on someone in a hard time, only to realize they weren't really there for you? Maybe a friend said they'd have your back but disappeared when things got tough. That's exactly what **Proverbs 25** is talking about—trusting the wrong person can leave you hurting, like stepping on a twisted ankle or biting down on a sore tooth.

But there's a big contrast in **John 10**, where Jesus says that His followers—His sheep—can hear His voice and trust Him completely. His grip on your life is so strong, nothing can break it. And when we remember His love and faithfulness like **Psalm 117** describes, we're reminded that He's worthy of our full trust.

Think About It

1. **Who Are You Trusting?** Not everyone who says they're your friend will be reliable when life gets messy. Are you putting your trust in people who build you up—or break you down?

2. **Listen for the Shepherd's Voice:** Jesus says His sheep know His voice. Are you spending time in His Word, learning to recognize when He's speaking to your heart?

3. **God's Love Is Forever:** Psalm 117 says God's love and faithfulness never end. What difference would it make in your day if you really believed that God is always steady—even when everything else shifts?

Bottom Line

People will fail you sometimes—but Jesus never will. He knows you, He speaks to you, and He will never let you go.

Prayer

Heavenly Father, thank You for being a God I can count on, even when people let me down. Help me to hear Your voice more clearly and trust You more deeply. Teach me how to be a trustworthy friend to others too. Your love and faithfulness are the anchor I need every day. In Jesus' Name, Amen.

October 11

Unlikely Kindness

3-Year-Bible Reading: Proverbs 25:21–22; John 11

"If your enemy is hungry, give him bread to eat, and if he is thirsty, give him water to drink, for you will heap burning coals on his head, and the Lord will reward you." — Proverbs 25:21–22

"Jesus wept." — John 11:35

Have you ever been angry with someone—like, really angry—and then heard someone say, "Be kind to them anyway"? It feels impossible, right? Being kind to someone who hurt you isn't usually our first instinct. And yet, in **Proverbs 25:21–22**, we're told to care for even our enemies. That sounds backwards until you see it in action.

Jesus shows us this in **John 11**, when His friend Lazarus dies. Even though the people around Him are doubting and accusing Him, Jesus still shows deep compassion. He cries with them. He loves them. That kind of kindness doesn't come from us—it comes from God.

Think About It

1. **Kindness as a Weapon?** Why do you think Proverbs describes kindness to enemies as "heaping burning coals on their head"? How does choosing kindness challenge or surprise those who expect anger in return?

2. **Jesus Wept:** In **John 11**, Jesus knew He would raise Lazarus, yet He still cried. What does that tell you about how much He cares about our pain—even when He knows the ending will be good?

3. **React or Reflect:** When someone hurts you, do you react with anger or take time to reflect and respond with grace? How might praying before reacting help you love like Jesus?

Bottom Line

Loving like Jesus means showing compassion—even when it's hard. Kindness to those who hurt us doesn't make us weak; it shows the power of God's love working in us.

Prayer

Heavenly Father, Help me love people the way You love me—even when it's hard. Teach me to respond to hurt with kindness, to choose grace instead of revenge, and to be a light in a world that often chooses hate. Thank You for showing me compassion, even when I fall short. Help me be more like Jesus every day. In Jesus' Name, Amen.

October 12

Peace Over Drama

3-Year-Bible Reading: Proverbs 25:23–24; Psalm 118; John 12

"The north wind brings forth rain, and a backbiting tongue, angry looks. It is better to live in a corner of the housetop than in a house shared with a quarrelsome wife."— Proverbs 25:23–24

"The Lord is on my side; I will not fear. What can man do to me?... This is the day that the Lord has made; let us rejoice and be glad in it." — Psalm 118:6, 24

"Whoever loves his life loses it, and whoever hates his life in this world will keep it for eternal life. If anyone serves me, he must follow me..." — John 12:25–26

Drama. You know it when you see it—and sometimes, it's hard to avoid. Whether it's in your friend group, at school, or even at home, conflict can pop up fast. Proverbs warns us that it's better to live on the roof than in a house full of tension (**Proverbs 25:24**). Yikes! But here's the thing—God doesn't want us stuck in cycles of drama and negativity. **Psalm 118** reminds us that even in the middle of stress or fear, God is with us. He's on our side.

And in **John 12**, Jesus calls us to a higher way of living: not chasing popularity or always being "right," but following Him and living for something bigger than the moment.

Think About It

1. **Drama Detour:** Are there areas in your life where conflict is stealing your peace? What would it look like to step back and let God guide your response?

2. **God's Got You:** Psalm 118 says God is on your side. Do you truly believe that? How can that confidence change the way you handle tough situations?

3. **Follow the Leader:** Jesus says to follow Him, even when it means letting go of what the world values. What's one thing you might need to surrender to follow Jesus more closely?

Bottom Line

True peace doesn't come from winning arguments or avoiding problems—it comes from trusting God, choosing kindness, and following Jesus through it all.

Prayer

Heavenly Father, Help me to choose peace over drama and trust You when things get tough. Teach me to follow Jesus, even when it's hard or unpopular. Remind me that You are with me and that I can let go of fear. Make me someone who brings calm, not chaos, into the world around me. In Jesus' Name, Amen.

October 13

Fresh Water in a Dry Place

3-Year-Bible Reading: Proverbs 25:25–26; John 13

"Like cold water to a thirsty soul, so is good news from a far country. Like a muddied spring or a polluted fountain is a righteous man who gives way before the wicked." — Proverbs 25:25–26

"If I then, your Lord and Teacher, have washed your feet, you also ought to wash one another's feet." — John 13:14

Have you ever been outside on a hot day, totally parched, and then someone hands you an ice-cold drink? Instant relief, right? That's what **Proverbs 25:25** is talking about—how powerful and refreshing good news can be. But then, **verse 26** flips it: when someone who should stand strong gives in to what's wrong, it's like their influence becomes dirty and unhelpful, like muddy water.

In **John 13**, Jesus sets an example that flips the script too—not with weakness, but with humility. He does something unexpected: He washes His disciples' feet. It wasn't just a kind gesture—it was a challenge to love and serve others, no matter our position. What does all this mean for us as young people trying to live out our faith? It means we're called to be the refreshing kind of people, not the muddy kind.

Think About It

1. **Be the Good News:** Are your words and actions like cold water to the people around you? Think about the way you talk to your friends or the attitude you bring to school or your team. Is it refreshing and kind, or does it drain people?

2. **Stand Strong:** It's easy to go along with the crowd, especially when standing out could make you feel alone or awkward. But Proverbs says when we don't stand up for what's right, we're like polluted water—people can't trust what comes from us.

3. **Lead by Serving:** Jesus was the most powerful person in the room, yet He chose to kneel down and wash feet. That's next-level humility. What would it look like for you to serve others at home, at school, or online?

Bottom Line

You were made to be a refreshing presence in a dry and broken world. When you live with courage, kindness, and humility like Jesus, you don't just blend in—you bring life.

Prayer

Heavenly Father, Thank You for showing me what real love looks like through Jesus. Help me be like cold water to thirsty people—encouraging, bold, and kind. Give me the strength to stand for what's right, even when it's hard, and the humility to serve others like Jesus did. I want to live in a way that brings You glory and shows others who You are. In Jesus' Name, Amen.

October 14

Too Much of Me

3-Year-Bible Reading: Proverbs 25:27; Psalm 119:1–32; John 14

"It is not good to eat much honey, nor is it glorious to seek one's own glory." — Proverbs 25:27

"Blessed are those whose way is blameless, who walk in the law of the Lord!" — Psalm 119:1

"Jesus said to him, 'I am the way, and the truth, and the life. No one comes to the Father except through me.'" — John 14:6

We live in a world that tells us to "put ourselves first," "be our own truth," and "chase the glory." But sometimes, the more we focus on ourselves, the emptier we feel. Proverbs warns us that seeking our own glory is like eating too much honey—it might taste good at first, but too much will make you sick (**Proverbs 25:27**).

In contrast, **Psalm 119** shows us a different path: the person who walks in God's ways is *blessed*—truly happy and fulfilled. And **John 14** brings it all together: Jesus Himself is *the way, the truth, and the life*. If we're looking for purpose, confidence, and peace, He's the answer—not our own success or fame.

Think About It

1. **Check Your Glory Diet:** Are you craving the "sweetness" of attention or praise more than seeking God's presence? Like honey, a little encouragement is good—but it can't replace God.

2. **The Better Path:** Psalm 119 reminds us that living by God's Word leads to a full life. What would it look like for you to choose obedience over popularity today?

3. **Following the Way:** Jesus didn't say He *shows* the way—He *is* the way. What areas of your life are you still trying to lead instead of letting Jesus guide?

Bottom Line

When we stop chasing our own glory and start walking in God's way, we find the real peace and purpose we've been searching for. Jesus isn't just a part of life—He *is* life.

Prayer

Heavenly Father, thank You for reminding me that I don't need to make life all about me. Help me to stop craving attention and start craving more of You. Teach me to walk in Your truth and trust that following Jesus is the best way to live. Fill me with Your peace and guide my steps every day. In Jesus' Name, Amen.

October 15

Guardrails for Your Soul

3-Year-Bible Reading: Proverbs 25:28; Psalm 119:33–64; John 15

"A man without self-control is like a city broken into and left without walls." — Proverbs 25:28

"Teach me, O Lord, the way of your statutes; and I will keep it to the end." — Psalm 119:33

"Abide in me, and I in you. As the branch cannot bear fruit by itself, unless it abides in the vine, neither can you, unless you abide in me." — John 15:4

Ever seen a video of a car speeding down a winding mountain road with no guardrails? It's stressful, right? That's kind of what life looks like without God's Word and guidance. In **Proverbs 25:28**, we're told that lacking self-control is like a city with broken walls—totally vulnerable and open to attack. But **Psalm 119** shows us that God's commands aren't rules to ruin our fun—they're the guardrails that keep us safe and growing.

And in **John 15**, Jesus says we need to stay connected to Him like a branch to a vine if we want to bear fruit in our lives. Together, these verses remind us that when we live with purpose, rooted in Jesus, we become strong, protected, and fruitful.

Think About It

1. **Guardrails or Chains?** Do you ever feel like God's commands are just a bunch of restrictions? What if instead, they're boundaries meant to protect your joy and peace?

2. **Staying Connected:** Jesus said we need to "abide" in Him. What are practical ways you can stay close to Jesus in your daily life—especially when you're busy or feeling distracted?

3. **Self-Control Starts with Surrender:** Where in your life do you struggle with self-control? How could leaning into God's Word help you build strength in that area?

Bottom Line

Living with self-control and staying rooted in God's truth isn't about being perfect—it's about trusting God's design for your life, staying close to Jesus, and letting Him shape who you're becoming.

Prayer

Heavenly Father, thank You for loving me enough to give me Your Word and guidance. Sometimes I want to do life my own way, but I know Your ways lead to real life and peace. Help me to stay close to You, like a branch connected to the vine. Teach me self-control and help me trust Your boundaries as protection, not punishment. I want to grow strong and fruitful in You. In Jesus' Name, Amen.

October 16

Wisdom, Discipline, and Peace

3-Year-Bible Reading: Proverbs 26:1,3; Psalm 119:65–96; John 16

"Like snow in summer or rain in harvest, so honor is not fitting for a fool... A whip for the horse, a bridle for the donkey, and a rod for the back of fools." — Proverbs 26:1,3

"You have dealt well with your servant, O Lord, according to your word... If your law had not been my delight, I would have perished in my affliction." — Psalm 119:65,92

"I have said these things to you, that in me you may have peace. In the world you will have tribulation. But take heart; I have overcome the world." — John 16:33

Sometimes life feels totally upside down—like snow falling in July or rain ruining a long-awaited game day. That's how **Proverbs 26** describes the chaos that comes from foolishness and the consequences it brings. On the flip side, **Psalm 119** reminds us that even when things are hard, delighting in God's Word gives us stability and purpose.

Jesus takes it even further in **John 16**, promising peace in the middle of all the crazy. Not because everything is perfect, but because He has already won. As a teen, it's easy to feel the pressure of school, friends, and figuring out life—but God offers wisdom, discipline, and deep peace in the middle of it all.

Think About It

1. **Foolish or Faithful?** Proverbs points out how foolishness leads to destruction. Are there any areas in your life where you're resisting wisdom—maybe in relationships, school habits, or attitude?

2. **Delight in God's Word**: Psalm 119 talks about loving God's commands even in hard times. What helps you *enjoy* God's Word instead of seeing it as just another thing on your to-do list?

3. **Jesus Has Overcome**: In John 16, Jesus doesn't promise an easy life—He promises victory through Him. What's one stress or challenge you can give to Jesus today, trusting that He's already overcome it?

Bottom Line

Life might not always make sense, but when you walk in God's wisdom, love His Word, and trust Jesus, you'll find peace that can't be shaken.

Prayer

Heavenly Father, thank You for offering me wisdom when life is confusing and peace when the world feels overwhelming. Help me to treasure Your Word and live with purpose. Even when things are hard, remind me that Jesus has already overcome everything I face. In Jesus' Name, Amen.

October 17

Unshakable Truth

3-Year-Bible Reading: Proverbs 26:2; Psalm 119:97–136; John 17

"Like a sparrow in its flitting, like a swallow in its flying, a curse that is causeless does not alight." — Proverbs 26:2

"Oh how I love your law! It is my meditation all the day." — Psalm 119:97

"Sanctify them in the truth; your word is truth." — John 17:17

Sometimes it feels like the world throws labels, insults, and expectations at you like darts. People say things that sting or try to define who you are. But God's Word says that empty words don't have to stick—just like a bird flying aimlessly, a curse without cause won't land (**Proverbs 26:2**). When you root yourself in truth, the lies lose power. That's why the psalmist says he *loves* God's Word—it gives life, wisdom, and direction (**Psalm 119:97**).

And in **John 17**, Jesus prays for His followers (that includes you!) to be made holy and strong through the truth—God's Word.

Think About It

1. **Words That Don't Stick:** Have you ever felt weighed down by something someone said about you? God's Word says not every word has power—only truth does. What labels have you believed that God wants to free you from?

2. **Love the Word:** The psalmist didn't just read the Bible—he *loved* it. What would it look like to enjoy God's Word like your favorite song or series? How can you start making it part of your everyday life?

3. **Set Apart by Truth:** Jesus prayed that we would be "sanctified" in the truth. That means being set apart—shaped by God's reality, not the world's noise. What areas of your life need God's truth to shine brighter?

Bottom Line

God's Word is your anchor when the world tries to shake your identity. His truth is unchanging, powerful, and personal—and it's what sets you free.

Prayer

Heavenly Father, thank You for giving me Your Word to guide, protect, and strengthen me. When people speak things that don't line up with Your truth, help me to remember who I am in You. Give me a heart that loves Your Word and a mind that is shaped by it. Keep me close to You and set me apart for Your purposes. In Jesus' Name, Amen.

October 18

Walk the Line

3-Year-Bible Reading: Proverbs 26:4–5; Psalm 119:137–176; John 18

Answer not a fool according to his folly, lest you be like him yourself. Answer a fool according to his folly, lest he be wise in his own eyes. — Proverbs 26:4–5

Righteous are you, O Lord, and right are your rules… I am small and despised, yet I do not forget your precepts. — Psalm 119:137, 141

Then Pilate said to him, "So you are a king?" Jesus answered, "You say that I am a king. For this purpose I was born and for this purpose I have come into the world—to bear witness to the truth." — John 18:37

Have you ever been caught in a situation where you didn't know whether to speak up or stay quiet? Proverbs **26:4–5** seems confusing at first glance—should you answer a fool or not? The reality is, sometimes wisdom means knowing *how* and *when* to respond. In **John 18**, Jesus stands before Pilate. He doesn't argue or panic. He doesn't dodge the truth. He simply speaks with calm authority, knowing who He is and why He came.

Meanwhile, **Psalm 119** reminds us that God's word can guide us through situations that seem impossible to navigate. Even when we feel small or misunderstood, we're called to stay anchored in God's truth.

Think About It

1. **Wisdom in Timing:** Proverbs shows us that responding to foolishness is complicated. How can you tell when it's wise to speak up and when it's better to stay silent?

2. **Rooted in Truth:** Jesus didn't need to prove Himself to Pilate—He already knew His identity. What does it look like for you to live confidently in the truth of who God says you are?

3. **Standing Strong:** Psalm 119 speaks of feeling small and despised, yet holding tightly to God's Word. How can you stay faithful to God even when it feels like no one else gets it?

Bottom Line

Being wise isn't about having all the answers—it's about knowing when to speak, when to listen, and always staying grounded in the truth of God's Word, like Jesus did.

Prayer

Heavenly Father, thank You for Your Word that gives me direction when things feel confusing. Help me know when to speak up and when to stay quiet. Teach me to live with the confidence of Jesus, even when others question me. Help me stay rooted in Your truth no matter what. In Jesus' Name, Amen.

October 19

Walking with Wisdom and Wounds

3-Year-Bible Reading: Proverbs 26:6–7; John 19

"Whoever sends a message by the hand of a fool cuts off his own feet and drinks violence. Like a lame man's legs, which hang useless, is a proverb in the mouth of fools." — Proverbs 26:6–7

"So Jesus came out, wearing the crown of thorns and the purple robe. Pilate said to them, 'Behold the man!' ... When Jesus had received the sour wine, he said, 'It is finished,' and he bowed his head and gave up his spirit." — John 19:5, 30

Let's be real—sometimes it feels like the world is full of noise. Opinions flying around, people talking big but saying little. Proverbs warns us that wisdom in the wrong hands is useless—it's like giving deep truth to someone who's not ready to live it (**Proverbs 26:6–7**).

On the flip side, we see Jesus in **John 19**, silent in the face of injustice, but full of strength. He didn't just talk about love—He proved it by giving His life. Jesus shows us what true wisdom and sacrifice look like. Not flashy. Not foolish. But powerful, even when it hurts.

Think About It

1. **Words Matter:** Have you ever said something that sounded wise, but you weren't really living it out? Proverbs reminds us that wisdom without action is empty. Ask yourself: Do my actions back up my words?

2. **Behold the Man:** In **John 19:5**, Pilate says, "Behold the man." Take a moment to really look at Jesus—beaten, mocked, crowned with thorns. What does His suffering say about His love for you?

3. **Finished, Not Failed:** Jesus' last words, "It is finished," weren't words of defeat—they were a declaration of victory. Everything needed for your forgiveness and future was completed at the cross. How does that change the way you see your mistakes or struggles?

Bottom Line

Real wisdom isn't just about saying the right thing—it's about living like Jesus, who showed the ultimate wisdom through His love and sacrifice.

Prayer

Heavenly Father, help me live with real wisdom—the kind that looks like Jesus. Teach me not just to speak truth, but to walk it out in love, even when it's hard. Thank You for finishing the work on the cross so I can walk in freedom. Help me reflect Your heart today. In Jesus' Name, Amen.

October 20

Wisdom, Wounds, and Wonder

3-Year-Bible Reading: Proverbs 26:8–9; John 20

"Like one who binds the stone in the sling is one who gives honor to a fool. Like a thorn that goes up into the hand of a drunkard is a proverb in the mouth of fools." — Proverbs 26:8–9

"Then he said to Thomas, 'Put your finger here, and see my hands; and put out your hand, and place it in my side. Do not disbelieve, but believe.'" — John 20:27

We all know what it's like to hear advice from someone who clearly doesn't live it out. It feels empty, or worse—like a slap in the face. **Proverbs 26:8–9** warns against honoring fools and letting truth fall into the wrong hands.

In contrast, **John 20** gives us a powerful picture of Jesus meeting Thomas in his doubt—not with judgment, but with proof and presence. Jesus' wounds spoke louder than words. When people see that our faith is real—rooted in both truth and love—they'll believe it's worth something.

Think About It

1. **Truth in the Right Hands:** How are you using the wisdom you know? Are you applying it to your life, or just repeating it to others without living it?

2. **Wounds that Witness:** Jesus showed Thomas His scars to prove His resurrection. What "scars" or experiences in your life can God use to show others He's real?

3. **Belief and Doubt:** Thomas didn't hide his doubt, and Jesus didn't shame him for it. Are you honest with God about your questions? What would it look like to bring your doubts to Him in faith?

Bottom Line

Wisdom without love is empty, but real faith—shown through your life and even your struggles—can point others to Jesus.

Prayer

Heavenly Father, thank You for showing us the difference between empty words and real wisdom. Help me live what I believe, and let my life reflect the truth of who You are. Use even my doubts and scars to bring others closer to You. Strengthen my faith like You did for Thomas, and make me a witness of Your love. In Jesus' Name, Amen.

October 21

Don't Go Back to the Vomit

3-Year-Bible Reading: Proverbs 26:10–11; John 21

"Like a dog that returns to his vomit is a fool who repeats his folly." — Proverbs 26:11

"Simon Peter said to them, 'I am going fishing.' ... Just as day was breaking, Jesus stood on the shore; yet the disciples did not know that it was Jesus." — John 21:3–4

Sometimes we go back to old habits, even when we know they're bad for us. It's like binge-watching that show that always leaves you drained, or hanging out with that group that pulls you down. In **Proverbs 26:11**, God compares going back to foolish ways to a dog eating its own vomit—gross, but it makes the point.

In **John 21**, Peter returns to fishing after denying Jesus, like he's falling back into the life he had before Jesus changed everything. But Jesus doesn't leave him there. He meets Peter right where he is—tired, disappointed, and probably feeling like a failure—and invites him back into purpose.

Think About It

1. **The Cycle of Old Habits:** What's one "vomit" (bad habit, toxic thought, unwise decision) you tend to return to, even though you know it's harmful?

2. **Jesus Meets You in the Middle:** Jesus found Peter in the middle of his return to the old life—not to shame him, but to restore him. Are you open to letting Jesus speak to you, even in your lowest or most disappointing moments?

3. **God's Calling Stays the Same:** Even when Peter messed up, Jesus still had plans for him. What is one area where you need to believe that God's calling on your life hasn't changed, even after failure?

Bottom Line

Jesus doesn't define you by your worst mistake. He calls you forward, not backward—into grace, purpose, and real change.

Prayer

Heavenly Father, thank You for loving me even when I fall back into old patterns. Help me to recognize the things that pull me away from You and give me the courage to walk forward instead of turning back. Remind me that Your grace is bigger than my mistakes, and that You still have a purpose for me. In Jesus' Name, Amen.

October 22

Too Smart for Your Own Good

3-Year-Bible Reading: Proverbs 26:12; Revelation 1–3

"Do you see a man who is wise in his own eyes? There is more hope for a fool than for him." — Proverbs 26:12

"Blessed is the one who reads aloud the words of this prophecy, and blessed are those who hear, and who keep what is written in it, for the time is near." — Revelation 1:3

"I know your works: you are neither cold nor hot. Would that you were either cold or hot!" — Revelation 3:15

Have you ever had someone call you a "know-it-all"? Maybe you didn't mean to come across that way—you were just confident. But confidence without humility can get us in trouble fast. **Proverbs 26:12** warns us that thinking we've got all the answers is actually more dangerous than being foolish. That's wild, right?

When we read **Revelation 1–3**, we see Jesus speaking to churches full of people who thought they were doing just fine—but they were missing the point. Some were lukewarm, spiritually sleepy, or living off their reputation instead of truly following Jesus. God loves us too much to let us stay stuck in pride or complacency. He calls us to listen, wake up, and really follow Him.

Think About It

1. **Check Your Confidence:** Is your confidence based on your own knowledge, or on God's truth? It's okay to be smart or sure of yourself—but God calls us to stay humble, always learning from Him.

2. **Lukewarm or On Fire?** Jesus tells the church in Laodicea that being "lukewarm" isn't good enough. Are you just going through the motions of faith, or are you really pursuing Jesus with your heart?

3. **Listen Up:** Each letter to the churches in Revelation ends with, "He who has an ear, let him hear." Are you really listening when God speaks through His Word, or do you tune out what's uncomfortable?

Bottom Line

Being "wise in your own eyes" might feel good in the moment, but God calls us to a deeper wisdom—one that starts with humility and a heart that listens. Don't settle for a lukewarm faith. Stay teachable, stay close to Jesus, and keep your fire burning.

Prayer

Heavenly Father, Thank You for loving me enough to tell me the truth. Help me not to be prideful or think I've got it all figured out. Teach me to stay humble, to listen to Your Word, and to follow You fully. I don't want to be lukewarm—I want to be on fire for You. Show me where I need to grow and give me the courage to change. In Jesus' Name, Amen.

October 23

Hit Snooze or Wake Up?

3-Year-Bible Reading: Proverbs 26:13–14; Revelation 4–5

"The sluggard says, 'There is a lion in the road! There is a lion in the streets!' As a door turns on its hinges, so does a sluggard on his bed." — Proverbs 26:13–14

"Holy, holy, holy, is the Lord God Almighty, who was and is and is to come!" — Revelation 4:8

"Worthy are you to take the scroll and to open its seals, for you were slain, and by your blood you ransomed people for God from every tribe and language and people and nation." — Revelation 5:9

Have you ever made up an excuse just to stay in bed a little longer? Maybe it wasn't a "lion in the street," but it might've been something like, "I'm too tired," "It's just one class," or "I'll do that later." In **Proverbs 26**, we meet a sluggard—someone so full of excuses that they let opportunities pass them by.

Fast forward to **Revelation 4 and 5**, and we get a glimpse of something mind-blowingly opposite: heaven bursting with worship, honor, and purpose. No hesitation, no excuses—just praise for a Savior who gave everything. These passages together challenge us: are we snoozing through our lives, or are we awake to the glory of God?

Think About It

1. **Excuses vs. Purpose:** What "lions" have you imagined that keep you from doing what matters? How can you trade excuses for action?

2. **Wake Up to Worship:** The scenes in Revelation show non-stop worship and awe in heaven. How can you bring some of that same heart of worship into your daily routine?

3. **What Do You Think Jesus Is Worth?** The Lamb who was slain is declared "worthy" because He gave His life for us. What would it look like if your everyday choices reflected His worth?

Bottom Line

Don't sleep through your calling. Wake up to the beauty of worship and the worth of Jesus—and live like He matters.

Prayer

Heavenly Father, help me recognize when I'm making excuses and choosing comfort over calling. Open my eyes to Your worth, and stir my heart to respond with passion, not laziness. Let my life reflect the worship You deserve. In Jesus' Name, Amen.

October 24

Too Tired to Try

3-Year-Bible Reading: Proverbs 26:15–16; Revelation 6–7

"The sluggard buries his hand in the dish; it wears him out to bring it back to his mouth. The sluggard is wiser in his own eyes than seven men who can answer sensibly." — Proverbs 26:15–16

"For the great day of their wrath has come, and who can stand?" — Revelation 6:17

"They shall hunger no more, neither thirst anymore... For the Lamb in the midst of the throne will be their shepherd, and he will guide them to springs of living water." — Revelation 7:16–17

Ever feel like doing *literally anything* is just too much? Like you're so tired, you can't even be bothered to scroll through your phone, let alone finish your homework or spend time with God? In **Proverbs 26**, the sluggard is so lazy, he can't even feed himself. It sounds extreme, but the point is this: laziness can sneak in and rob us of purpose, action, and even truth.

Meanwhile, in **Revelation 6**, we're reminded of how serious life is—judgment is coming. But then Revelation 7 gives hope. For those who follow Jesus, He promises rest, care, and satisfaction that goes beyond physical hunger or thirst. When you feel tired of trying, remember this: God offers a life worth the effort.

Think About It

1. **Too Tired or Just Unmotivated?** Laziness doesn't always look like lying around—it can be avoidance, procrastination, or making excuses. Is there something you've been avoiding that you know God wants you to face?

2. **Eternal Perspective:** Revelation 6 is intense, showing God's judgment. How does remembering that Jesus will return someday change the way you live today?

3. **God's Rest is Real:** Revelation 7 shows the reward of those who follow Jesus—they are taken care of forever. Are you finding your strength and purpose in Him, or trying to do life your own way?

Bottom Line

God calls us to live with purpose—not passivity. When life feels heavy or hard, He gives us the strength to press on and promises eternal rest in His presence.

Prayer

Heavenly Father, sometimes I feel tired, unmotivated, or stuck in a loop of doing nothing. Help me not to waste the life You've given me. Give me strength to move, wisdom to act, and a heart that seeks You first. Thank You for the promise of Your rest and presence. In Jesus' Name, Amen.

October 25

Mind Your Own Drama

3-Year-Bible Reading: Proverbs 26:17; Psalm 120; Revelation 8–9

"Whoever meddles in a quarrel not his own is like one who takes a passing dog by the ears." — Proverbs 26:17

"Deliver me, O LORD, from lying lips, from a deceitful tongue." — Psalm 120:2

"The rest of mankind, who were not killed by these plagues, did not repent of the works of their hands..." — Revelation 9:20

Ever been tempted to jump into someone else's drama? Maybe your friends are arguing, or someone posted something wild online, and suddenly you feel the urge to pick a side or throw in your opinion. But **Proverbs 26:17** compares meddling in a fight that's not yours to grabbing a stray dog by the ears—basically, a really bad idea. In **Psalm 120**, we hear someone crying out to God for peace in the middle of lies and conflict.

And in **Revelation 8–9**, things get intense: God's judgment is unfolding, but people still refuse to change. Put all that together, and the message is loud and clear—be careful about what you get involved in and pay attention to your own heart first.

Think About It

1. **Mind Your Boundaries:** Are you getting involved in things that aren't your responsibility? Proverbs warns that meddling can lead to unnecessary trouble. Think before you speak or post—are you helping, or just stirring the pot?

2. **Pray for Peace:** Psalm 120 reminds us that we can call out to God when lies and drama surround us. Instead of trying to fix everything yourself, what would it look like to hand it over to Him?

3. **Change Starts with You:** Revelation 9 shows us that even after major warnings, people refused to repent. Is there anything in your life that God might be asking you to change—but you're ignoring it?

Bottom Line

Not every battle is yours to fight. Focus on keeping peace, staying out of unnecessary drama, and letting God work on your heart.

Prayer

Heavenly Father, help me know when to speak and when to stay out of things. Give me wisdom to avoid getting caught up in drama that doesn't involve me. Teach me to be a peacemaker and to listen when You call me to change. I want to follow You more closely every day. In Jesus' Name, Amen.

OCTOBER 26

Words That Hit Different

3-Year-Bible Reading: Proverbs 26:18–19; Psalm 121; Revelation 10–11

"Like a madman who throws firebrands, arrows, and death is the man who deceives his neighbor and says, 'I am only joking!'"— Proverbs 26:18–19

"I lift up my eyes to the hills. From where does my help come? My help comes from the Lord, who made heaven and earth." — Psalm 121:1–2

"And he said to me, 'You must again prophesy about many peoples and nations and languages and kings.'" — Revelation 10:11

Have you ever had someone say something hurtful and then try to play it off with, "Just kidding!"? Maybe it was a joke that cut too deep or sarcasm that didn't feel so funny. **Proverbs 26:18–19** calls out that behavior—it's like throwing weapons around without caring who gets hit. In contrast, **Psalm 121** reminds us that when life gets confusing or painful, our true help doesn't come from people trying to be funny or cool—it comes from God, who never lets us down.

And in **Revelation 10–11**, we see John being told to speak truth again, even when it's hard. That's because God's truth, spoken with love, has real power to change lives.

THINK ABOUT IT

1. **Jokes Can Hurt:** Have you ever said something "as a joke" that actually hurt someone? What does Proverbs 26 teach us about taking responsibility for our words?

2. **Look Up for Help:** Psalm 121 reminds us where to look when life feels overwhelming. What are some ways you can "lift your eyes" to God in your daily routine?

3. **Speak Truth with Courage:** John was told to speak God's truth again. How can you be bold about your faith without being harsh? Where is God asking you to speak up?

BOTTOM LINE

Words carry weight. Be someone whose words heal, not hurt—and look to God for the strength to speak truth with love.

PRAYER

Heavenly Father, thank You for being my constant help and for teaching me to be careful with my words. Help me to speak truth with kindness and courage. When life gets messy, remind me to look up and lean on You. Use my voice to encourage and build up others. In Jesus' Name, Amen.

October 27

Fuel or Fire?

3-Year-Bible Reading: Proverbs 26:20–21; Psalm 122; Revelation 12–13

For lack of wood the fire goes out, and where there is no whisperer, quarreling ceases. As charcoal to hot embers and wood to fire, so is a quarrelsome man for kindling strife — Proverbs 26:20–21

Pray for the peace of Jerusalem! "May they be secure who love you!" — Psalm 122:6

And they have conquered him by the blood of the Lamb and by the word of their testimony, for they loved not their lives even unto death — Revelation 12:11

Have you ever noticed how quickly drama spreads—especially at school, in group chats, or even within families? It's like a tiny spark that suddenly becomes a wildfire. Proverbs warns that gossip and conflict are like fuel to a fire (**Proverbs 26:20–21**). But what happens if we stop adding fuel? The fire dies out. Meanwhile, **Psalm 122** reminds us that God values peace. And **Revelation 12** shows us the kind of victory that comes when we live boldly for Jesus, trusting His power more than our own lives. These verses together call us to be peacemakers and truth-speakers in a world that thrives on conflict and confusion.

Think About It

1. **Are You Fuel or Water?** Do your words stir up drama or settle things down? The way you respond to rumors, gossip, or arguments can either add to the chaos or help bring peace.

2. **Where's Your Loyalty?** Revelation talks about those who overcame the enemy by their testimony and by trusting Jesus more than their own lives. What does your life say about what matters most to you?

3. **Peace is Powerful:** Psalm 122 encourages us to pray for peace. Are you praying for peace in your home, school, and heart? Peace isn't weakness—it's a powerful weapon against division and fear.

Bottom Line

You have a choice every day: to be someone who fuels conflict or someone who reflects the peace and victory of Jesus. Even small choices—like not passing along a rumor or standing firm in your faith—can make a big impact.

Prayer

Heavenly Father, Thank You for reminding me that peace is powerful and that my words and actions matter. Help me to be someone who brings calm instead of chaos, truth instead of gossip, and love instead of drama. Give me the courage to stand strong in my faith and to be a light for You even when it's hard. In Jesus' Name, Amen.

October 28

Words That Burn or Build

3-Year-Bible Reading: Proverbs 26:22–23; Psalm 123; Revelation 14

"The words of a whisperer are like delicious morsels; they go down into the inner parts of the body. Like the glaze covering an earthen vessel are fervent lips with an evil heart." — Proverbs 26:22–23

"Behold, as the eyes of servants look to the hand of their master… so our eyes look to the Lord our God, till he has mercy upon us." — Psalm 123:2

"Then I looked, and behold, on Mount Zion stood the Lamb… It is these who follow the Lamb wherever he goes." — Revelation 14:1, 4

Have you ever said something and instantly regretted it? Maybe it was a rumor, a sarcastic joke, or a comment you thought was harmless but ended up hurting someone deeply. **Proverbs 26** reminds us that words can go deep, and once they're spoken, they don't just disappear. Like sweets that taste good at first but sit heavy in your stomach later, gossip and fake flattery can do more damage than we realize. But **Psalm 123** turns our eyes upward, reminding us that while people may fail us, we can always look to God with hope and trust.

And then **Revelation 14** paints a powerful picture of those who follow Jesus closely—people marked by truth, faithfulness, and worship. So the real question is: Do our words and actions show we follow the Lamb?

Think About It

1. **Words Have Weight:** Do you think before you speak—or post? Proverbs warns us that whispers and flattery can mask a heart that isn't right with God. How are you using your voice?

2. **Eyes on Jesus:** Psalm 123 reminds us to fix our eyes on God like a servant watching their master. What would it look like to depend on God that completely in your daily life?

3. **Marked by the Lamb:** Revelation 14 describes those who follow Jesus closely—they speak the truth, worship Him alone, and don't compromise. Would someone know you follow Jesus just by listening to your words?

Bottom Line

Our words reflect our hearts. Whether we build others up or tear them down shows who we're really following. Let your mouth—and your life—show that you're following the Lamb wherever He goes.

Prayer

Heavenly Father, help me to guard my words and use them to build others up, not tear them down. When I'm tempted to gossip or fake kindness, remind me of the deep impact my words can have. Teach me to fix my eyes on You and follow Jesus faithfully in both what I say and how I live. Make me someone marked by truth and love. In Jesus' Name, Amen.

October 29

Behind the Smile

3-Year-Bible Reading: Proverbs 26:24–26; Psalm 124; Revelation 15–16

"Whoever hates disguises himself with his lips and harbors deceit in his heart… though his hatred be covered with deception, his wickedness will be exposed in the assembly." — Proverbs 26:24,26

"If it had not been the Lord who was on our side… then the flood would have swept us away." — Psalm 124:1,4

"Who will not fear, O Lord, and glorify your name? For you alone are holy. All nations will come and worship you, for your righteous acts have been revealed." — Revelation 15:4

Ever had someone smile to your face but tear you down behind your back? It hurts—deep. **Proverbs 26** reminds us that not all smiles are sincere; some people hide hate behind kind words. But no matter how good someone is at faking it, God sees their heart and brings truth to light. In **Psalm 124**, David praises God for being on his side—saving him when life felt like a flood threatening to drown him.

And in **Revelation 15–16**, we see God's justice clearly poured out. He doesn't ignore evil; He deals with it fully and righteously. While people might pretend and manipulate, God is always real, always just, and always on the side of truth. As young people navigating friendships, social pressures, and online drama, it's comforting to know that God isn't fooled by appearances—and we don't need to be either.

Think About It

1. **Real vs. Fake:** Are there people in your life who act one way to your face but another behind your back? How can you protect your heart while still showing love?

2. **God Sees All:** Even when others don't see the truth, God does. Are there situations where you need to trust Him to bring justice or healing?

3. **You Reflect Him:** When you speak, are your words real and kind—or do you sometimes hide your true feelings? Ask God to help you be honest and loving like He is.

Bottom Line

People can fake it, but God never does. He sees the heart, defends the innocent, and calls us to live with real love and truth.

Prayer

Heavenly Father, thank You for being on my side when life gets messy and people aren't always real. Help me to trust You when I feel betrayed or hurt, and teach me to reflect Your honesty and love in how I treat others. I want to be real—not just on the outside, but in my heart. In Jesus' Name, Amen.

October 30

Falling Into Your Own Trap

3-Year-Bible Reading: Proverbs 26:27–28; Revelation 17–18

"Whoever digs a pit will fall into it, and a stone will come back on him who starts it rolling. A lying tongue hates its victims, and a flattering mouth works ruin." — Proverbs 26:27–28

"For this reason her plagues will come in a single day, death and mourning and famine, and she will be burned up with fire; for mighty is the Lord God who has judged her." — Revelation 18:8

Have you ever seen someone try to mess with others only for it to backfire? Maybe they spread a rumor and ended up losing trust themselves. That's the kind of thing Proverbs warns about—digging a trap for someone else and falling into it yourself. In **Proverbs 26:27–28**, it's a reminder that deception and manipulation often hurt the one who started them.

In **Revelation 17–18**, we see the fall of Babylon—a powerful symbol of pride, greed, and rebellion against God. Even though Babylon looked strong, God brought justice and exposed her corruption. These verses show us a powerful truth: evil might look like it's winning for a while, but it never ends well.

Think About It

1. **Check your motives:** Are you tempted to manipulate a situation to get what you want? Proverbs warns that when we do things out of selfish ambition, it often backfires. God honors honesty and humility.

2. **The danger of "Babylon living":** Revelation shows us what happens when a society puts wealth, power, and pleasure above God. What are some "Babylon-like" temptations in your world? How can you stay faithful to God in the middle of them?

3. **God's justice is real:** Babylon seemed untouchable—but God's judgment came swiftly. Don't be fooled by how things look on the outside. Trust that God sees everything, and He will make things right in His time.

Bottom Line

Trying to win by doing wrong will never truly work. God calls us to live with integrity, even when it's hard, because He sees the heart and always brings justice in the end.

Prayer

Heavenly Father, Thank You for showing me that Your justice is real and that evil never wins in the end. Help me to choose honesty and humility, even when I'm tempted to take shortcuts. Keep me from falling into the traps of pride, lies, or selfishness. I want to live in a way that honors You. In Jesus' Name, Amen.

October 31

Words That Win or Wound

3-Year-Bible Reading: Proverbs 26:28; Psalm 125; Revelation 19–20

"A lying tongue hates its victims, and a flattering mouth works ruin."— Proverbs 26:28

"Those who trust in the Lord are like Mount Zion, which cannot be moved, but abides forever."— Psalm 125:1

"Then I saw heaven opened, and behold, a white horse! The one sitting on it is called Faithful and True..."— Revelation 19:11

Words are powerful. You've probably heard that before—maybe when someone reminded you to think before you speak, or after you said something you wish you could take back. In **Proverbs 26:28**, we're warned about two misuses of words: lies and fake flattery. Both can hurt people, even if they sound nice on the surface. But **Psalm 125** gives us a picture of the kind of life we can have when we trust God—steady, unshakable, like a mountain.

And in **Revelation 19**, we're reminded that Jesus is called "Faithful and True." His words are never fake, and He always keeps His promises.

So how do we live like that? How do we move from wounding words to words that reflect faithfulness and truth?

Think About It

1. **What's behind your words?** Are you saying things just to be liked, to fit in, or to control a situation? Lies and insincere compliments can seem harmless but end up hurting others and damaging trust. God calls us to speak truth with love.

2. **Unshakable trust:** Psalm 125 says those who trust in the Lord are like Mount Zion—immovable. When you base your life on God's truth, you don't have to play games with your words. You can be real, honest, and strong, even when it's hard.

3. **Look to Jesus:** Jesus is called "Faithful and True" for a reason. He always speaks truth—even when it's tough—and always in love. When you're unsure how to respond to a situation, ask yourself: "What would Jesus say?" Not just in tone, but in truth and love.

Bottom Line

Your words have the power to hurt or to heal. Be someone who speaks like Jesus—faithfully, truthfully, and with love.

Prayer

Heavenly Father, Help me use my words to build others up and not tear them down. Teach me to be honest, kind, and full of truth like Jesus. When I feel pressure to lie or pretend, remind me of Your strength and the security I have in You. Make me steady like Mount Zion and help me speak life in every situation. In Jesus' Name, Amen.

NOVEMBER 1

Don't Wait for "Someday"

3-Year-Bible Reading: Proverbs 27:1; Deuteronomy 1–2

"Do not boast about tomorrow, for you do not know what a day may bring." — Proverbs 27:1

"Yet you would not go up, but rebelled against the command of the Lord your God." — Deuteronomy 1:26

"You have circled this mountain long enough. Turn northward." — Deuteronomy 2:3

Have you ever put something off because you thought you'd have time "later"? Maybe it was saying sorry to someone, trying out for something, or just doing what you knew God wanted you to do. We've all been there.

The Israelites in **Deuteronomy 1** were right at the edge of the Promised Land—so close to something amazing God had planned—but fear and doubt made them hesitate. And that hesitation turned into rebellion. Instead of walking into God's promise, they walked in circles for 40 years.

Proverbs **27:1** reminds us we're not guaranteed tomorrow. That doesn't mean we should panic—but it does mean we shouldn't waste today.

THINK ABOUT IT

1. **Today > Someday:** What's something you feel God nudging you to do that you've been putting off for "later"?

2. **Fear Isn't the Boss:** Like the Israelites, do you ever let fear talk you out of trusting God? What could happen if you chose faith instead?

3. **Time to Move:** Deuteronomy 2:3 is like God saying, "Enough waiting—let's go." Is there an area in your life where God might be saying it's time to stop going in circles?

BOTTOM LINE

You don't need to wait for the perfect moment—God is ready to move now. Trust Him and take the next step today.

PRAYER

Heavenly Father, thank You for reminding me that today is a gift. Help me not to waste it by putting things off or letting fear lead the way. Show me where I need to trust You and take that next step, even if it feels scary. I don't want to wander—I want to walk in Your promises. In Jesus' Name, Amen.

November 2

Bragging Rights or God's Glory?

3-Year-Bible Reading: Proverbs 27:2; Psalm 126; Deuteronomy 3–4

"Let another praise you, and not your own mouth; a stranger, and not your own lips." — Proverbs 27:2

"The Lord has done great things for us; we are glad." — Psalm 126:3

"For what great nation is there that has a god so near to it as the Lord our God is to us, whenever we call upon him?" — Deuteronomy 4:7

We all want to be noticed—whether it's getting the highest score in a game, being complimented for how we look, or getting recognized for our talents. But sometimes, the line between confidence and bragging gets blurry. In **Proverbs 27:2**, God reminds us not to seek attention for ourselves. Instead, like the people in **Psalm 126**, we should be quick to point to what *God* has done.

And in **Deuteronomy 4**, Moses reminds Israel—and us—that our greatest strength isn't what we achieve, but the fact that God is close to us, listening, guiding, and loving. When we realize how amazing God is, our praise shifts from ourselves to Him.

Think About It

1. **Who's getting the credit?** When something good happens—like a win, a compliment, or an opportunity—do you give God the glory, or do you try to keep the spotlight?

2. **God is near:** Deuteronomy 4:7 reminds us that God isn't distant. He's right here, ready to listen when we call. Are you taking time to talk with Him, or trying to do things all on your own?

3. **Joy worth sharing:** Psalm 126 speaks of joy that overflows because of what God has done. Do you share your joy with others in a way that points them to God, or just to yourself?

Bottom Line

Real joy and confidence come not from bragging about ourselves, but from recognizing and sharing what God has done in our lives. Let your life be a spotlight that points to Him.

Prayer

Heavenly Father, thank You for being close to me and always listening when I call. Help me to remember that every good thing in my life comes from You. Teach me to celebrate wins and blessings without making it all about me. Let my words, actions, and attitude bring You glory, not just attention to myself. In Jesus' Name, Amen.

NOVEMBER 3

Fire or Fuel?

3-Year-Bible Reading: Proverbs 27:3–4; Deuteronomy 5

"A stone is heavy, and sand is weighty, but a fool's provocation is heavier than both. Wrath is cruel, anger is overwhelming, but who can stand before jealousy?" — Proverbs 27:3–4

"You shall have no other gods before me." — Deuteronomy 5:7

"Know therefore that the Lord your God is God, the faithful God who keeps covenant and steadfast love with those who love him and keep his commandments." — Deuteronomy 5:9b–10

We all know what it's like to feel mad. Maybe someone betrayed you. Maybe your sibling got away with something—again. Anger flares up fast, and if we're not careful, it can take control. But **Proverbs 27:4** says anger is overwhelming and jealousy is even more dangerous. That's wild to think about—God's Word warns us that jealousy can be more destructive than rage.

Then in **Deuteronomy 5**, we're reminded of the Ten Commandments, where God calls us to love Him first, above all else. The truth is, when we let anger or envy take the lead in our hearts, we start pushing God out of first place. And that never ends well.

THINK ABOUT IT

1. **What's weighing you down?** Are there grudges, comparisons, or jealous thoughts you've been carrying? God wants to help you lay those down.

2. **Who or what comes first in your life?** The first commandment in **Deuteronomy 5** says to put no other gods before Him. Sometimes, emotions like anger or envy become "gods" when we let them control us.

3. **God's faithfulness is fuel:** Even when we fall short, God stays true. His love and faithfulness can help us choose peace, forgiveness, and contentment over jealousy and rage.

BOTTOM LINE

Anger and jealousy can feel powerful, but they're not meant to control you. God wants your heart—and when you put Him first, everything else finds its place.

PRAYER

Heavenly Father, thank You for loving me even when I get overwhelmed with emotions. Help me recognize when anger or jealousy is creeping in and give me the strength to choose peace and trust in You. I want You to be first in my heart, always. In Jesus' Name, Amen.

NOVEMBER 4

Better Wounds

3-Year-Bible Reading: Proverbs 27:5–6; Psalm 127; Deuteronomy 6

"Better is open rebuke than hidden love. Faithful are the wounds of a friend; profuse are the kisses of an enemy." — Proverbs 27:5–6

"Unless the Lord builds the house, those who build it labor in vain. Unless the Lord watches over the city, the watchman stays awake in vain." — Psalm 127:1

"You shall love the Lord your God with all your heart and with all your soul and with all your might." — Deuteronomy 6:5

Ever had a friend call you out on something you didn't want to hear—but deep down, you knew they were right? Yeah, it stings. But that kind of honesty is actually a gift. In **Proverbs 27:5–6**, we're reminded that tough love from a real friend is way better than fake flattery from someone who doesn't truly care.

Psalm 127 teaches us that doing life without God is like building a house with no foundation—it might look okay for a bit, but it won't stand. And **Deuteronomy 6** brings it all together by pointing us to the heart of it all: loving God with everything we've got.

THINK ABOUT IT

1. **Truth Hurts (But Heals):** Are there people in your life who speak truth to you, even when it's hard? Do you let God use them to help you grow?

2. **God at the Center:** What are you building your life on—your own plans or God's? Psalm 127 reminds us that without Him, our efforts are empty.

3. **All-In Faith:** Loving God with "all your heart, soul, and might" isn't about being perfect—it's about being committed. What's one way you can show that love today?

BOTTOM LINE

Real love speaks truth. Real life is built on God. And real faith is all in. Don't settle for surface-level living when God invites you to build something lasting with Him.

PRAYER

Heavenly Father, thank You for friends who love me enough to tell me the truth. Help me not to push them away but to learn and grow from their honesty. Teach me to build my life on You, not just my own ideas or dreams. Help me love You with all my heart, soul, and strength every single day. In Jesus' Name, Amen.

November 5

Restless and Full?

3-Year-Bible Reading: Proverbs 27:7–8; Deuteronomy 7–8

One who is full loathes honey, but to one who is hungry everything bitter is sweet. Like a bird that strays from its nest is a man who strays from his home. — Proverbs 27:7–8

For you are a people holy to the Lord your God. The Lord your God has chosen you to be a people for his treasured possession... — Deuteronomy 7:6

And you shall remember the whole way that the Lord your God has led you these forty years in the wilderness... that he might humble you, testing you to know what was in your heart... — Deuteronomy 8:2

Ever felt empty even when you have everything you thought you needed? Like you're full of stuff—friends, music, social media, even snacks—but still not satisfied? **Proverbs 27:7** hits on that: when we're full, even sweet things lose their flavor. And when we're empty, we'll chase anything to fill the hunger—even if it's bitter.

Deuteronomy 7–8 reminds us that we are chosen, loved, and led by God—even through dry or difficult seasons. But when we forget that, we can wander, like a bird leaving its nest too soon. Maybe you've felt that pull to leave God's way for something more exciting, or something that just feels more "now." But those feelings of restlessness are actually an invitation back—to the One who calls you His treasure and wants to satisfy your deepest hunger.

Think About It

1. **What Are You Chasing?** Are you hungry for attention, purpose, or peace? What "bitter" things are you settling for when you feel spiritually empty?

2. **God's Wilderness Lessons:** Like the Israelites in the wilderness, has God been teaching you something in a tough or quiet season? What could He be showing you about your heart?

3. **Stay Close to Home:** The bird that strays from the nest loses protection and purpose. What would it look like for you to stay rooted in God's truth this week?

Bottom Line

When life feels restless or empty, don't run after anything that looks sweet—run back to the One who truly satisfies. God has chosen you, leads you, and wants to fill you with what's real.

Prayer

Heavenly Father, Thank You for choosing me and calling me Your treasure. Sometimes I feel restless and chase things that don't really satisfy me. Help me to remember who I am in You and to stay close to You—even in the quiet or hard times. Teach me to trust that You're enough and that You're always leading me with purpose. In Jesus' Name, Amen.

November 6

True Friends and a Faithful God

3-Year-Bible Reading: Proverbs 27:9; Psalm 128; Deuteronomy 9–10

Oil and perfume make the heart glad, and the sweetness of a friend comes from his earnest counsel. — Proverbs 27:9

Blessed is everyone who fears the Lord, who walks in his ways! — Psalm 128:1

And now, Israel, what does the Lord your God require of you, but to fear the Lord your God, to walk in all his ways, to love him, to serve the Lord your God with all your heart and with all your soul... — Deuteronomy 10:12

We all want to be seen, understood, and valued—especially during the rollercoaster years of being a teen. Friendships can be everything: the joy of a real conversation, someone who texts back with honesty, or just being able to laugh till you can't breathe. Proverbs reminds us that a true friend gives wise, heartfelt advice that brings real joy. But even the best friendships can let us down sometimes. That's why it's such good news that God is always steady, always faithful.

Deuteronomy 10 shows us that even when Israel messed up big time, God didn't give up on them. Instead, He reminded them of what matters: love, obedience, and awe for Him. And **Psalm 128** reminds us that when we walk in God's ways, blessings follow—not always flashy, but deeply satisfying. God wants our hearts, and He also wants to surround us with real community and meaningful friendships rooted in Him.

Think About It

1. **What kind of friend are you?** Do your words build others up, like perfume that makes the heart glad (Proverbs 27:9)? Are you pointing your friends toward God, or away from Him?

2. **God's Faithfulness, Even When You Mess Up:** In **Deuteronomy 9**, Israel made a golden calf right after God rescued them—yikes. But God didn't cancel them. He invited them back. What does that say about His love for you when you mess up?

3. **Walking with God Isn't Just Rules:** **Psalm 128** says blessings come when we "walk in His ways." That's not about being perfect—it's about daily choosing God's path, even in small ways. What's one step you can take today to walk with Him?

Bottom Line

God calls you to love and follow Him wholeheartedly—and He surrounds you with true friends and second chances along the way.

Prayer

Heavenly Father, thank You for being patient and faithful, even when I fail. Help me to be a true friend who speaks life, and help me walk in Your ways every day. Remind me that You are always with me and that You never give up on me. In Jesus' Name, Amen.

NOVEMBER 7

Stick With Wisdom

3-Year-Bible Reading: Proverbs 27:10–11; Deuteronomy 11–12

"Do not forsake your friend and your father's friend, and do not go to your brother's house in the day of your calamity. Better is a neighbor who is near than a brother who is far away. Be wise, my son, and make my heart glad, that I may answer him who reproaches me." —Proverbs 27:10–11

"You shall therefore lay up these words of mine in your heart and in your soul… You shall teach them to your children, talking of them when you are sitting in your house, and when you are walking by the way…" —Deuteronomy 11:18–19

"You shall not do according to all that we are doing here today, everyone doing whatever is right in his own eyes…" —Deuteronomy 12:8

Life throws choices at us constantly—who to trust, what to believe, and how to live. As a teen, the pressure to figure it all out can feel overwhelming. Friends come and go, social media sends all kinds of mixed messages, and the world around us often says, "Just do what feels right." But in **Deuteronomy 11** and **12**, God's people were reminded to follow *His* way—not just whatever seemed good in the moment.

And in **Proverbs 27**, we're challenged to make wise choices that reflect well on those who've invested in us. God's Word is clear: lasting peace and purpose come from sticking with Him and walking in wisdom, even when the world pulls in other directions.

Think About It

1. **Wise friends matter:** Proverbs says not to abandon the friendships that have stood the test of time. Who are the people in your life that point you toward God and wise decisions?

2. **Truth takes root:** Deuteronomy reminds us to plant God's words deep in our hearts. Are you spending time in His Word regularly, or are you relying on feelings and trends to guide your choices?

3. **Feelings vs. faith:** When culture says, "Just do what's right for you," it can sound freeing—but it often leads to confusion. How can you stay grounded in God's truth instead of following the crowd?

Bottom Line

God calls us to live wisely—not by chasing what feels right in the moment, but by sticking close to His Word and choosing faith-filled friendships and habits that help us grow.

Prayer

Heavenly Father, thank You for giving us Your Word to lead us in truth. Help me to hold tightly to what You say, even when it's hard or unpopular. Give me wisdom to choose friends and habits that build me up in faith. Teach me to live not by what feels right, but by what is right in Your eyes. In Jesus' Name, Amen.

November 8

Danger Ahead!

3-Year-Bible Reading: Proverbs 27:12; Deuteronomy 13–14

"The prudent sees danger and hides himself, but the simple go on and suffer for it." —Proverbs 27:12

"If a prophet or a dreamer of dreams arises among you...and says, 'Let us go after other gods,'...you shall not listen to the words of that prophet or that dreamer of dreams." —Deuteronomy 13:1–3

"You are the sons of the Lord your God...for you are a people holy to the Lord your God." —Deuteronomy 14:1–2

Ever seen a "DANGER" sign and just had to see what the fuss was about? Whether it's ignoring a "Wet Paint" sign or testing out a sketchy shortcut, we all sometimes choose curiosity over caution. But God reminds us in **Proverbs 27:12** that wise people pay attention to warnings and avoid trouble.

In **Deuteronomy 13–14**, God was warning Israel not to be misled by people—even seemingly "spiritual" leaders—who tried to pull them away from Him. Instead, they were to remember their identity as God's chosen people and live differently. That message still matters today, especially when we're faced with messages that sound good but lead us in the wrong direction.

Think About It

1. **Watch for Red Flags:** What are some "danger signs" in your life right now? Are there people, habits, or choices that are slowly pulling you away from your walk with God?

2. **Voices of Influence:** In a world full of influencers, how can you tell who's speaking truth and who's leading you off course? God's Word is the filter—if it doesn't match Scripture, it's not worth following.

3. **You Belong to God:** God called the Israelites His own—and if you follow Jesus, that's your identity too. How can remembering that help you make stronger choices today?

Bottom Line

God gives us warning signs for a reason—because He loves us and wants to protect us. Don't ignore the red flags. Choose wisdom, stay grounded in truth, and remember who you belong to.

Prayer

Heavenly Father, thank You for loving me enough to warn me when I'm headed the wrong way. Help me to be wise and alert, and to recognize the people or situations that could pull me away from You. Remind me daily that I belong to You and that I'm set apart for something greater. In Jesus' Name, Amen.

NOVEMBER 9

Wise Words and Open Hands

3-Year-Bible Reading: Proverbs 27:13–14; Deuteronomy 15–16

"Take a man's garment when he has put up security for a stranger, and hold it in pledge when he puts up security for an adulteress. Whoever blesses his neighbor with a loud voice, rising early in the morning, will be counted as cursing." — Proverbs 27:13–14

"But there will be no poor among you; for the Lord will bless you in the land that the Lord your God is giving you... You shall open wide your hand to your brother, to the needy and to the poor, in your land." — Deuteronomy 15:4, 11

"They shall not appear before the Lord empty-handed. Every man shall give as he is able, according to the blessing of the Lord your God that he has given you." — Deuteronomy 16:16–17

Have you ever had someone say something nice to you—but in the most awkward or annoying way possible? Like a way-too-early "GOOD MORNING!!" that feels more like a jump scare than a blessing? That's kind of what **Proverbs 27:14** is talking about. It reminds us that how we treat people—and *when* and *why*—matters. It's not just about saying the right words, but about being thoughtful, genuine, and wise.

And over in **Deuteronomy 15–16**, God calls His people to be openhanded—generous and compassionate—especially to those in need. He didn't want His people just following rules but living with hearts full of grace. These passages challenge us to live with both wisdom and generosity, not just for show, but because God has been so generous to us.

THINK ABOUT IT

1. **Motives Matter:** Why do you do good things? Is it for attention, or because you truly want to help and honor God? Proverbs reminds us that even a "blessing" can be annoying if it's not done with the right heart.

2. **Open Hands, Open Heart:** Deuteronomy teaches that God's people should be generous because He blesses us. Are you someone who gives freely—of your time, your attention, your stuff?

3. **Giving Isn't Just About Money:** God said, "Don't come to Me empty-handed," but He didn't say everyone had to give the same thing. What do you have that you *can* give—your encouragement, your skills, your listening ear?

BOTTOM LINE

God calls us to live wisely and give generously—not just out of obligation, but out of love. When we check our motives and choose to give with purpose, we reflect His heart to the world.

PRAYER

Heavenly Father, thank You for being so generous to me. Help me to be wise in how I treat others, and teach me to give with a cheerful heart. Show me ways I can serve the people around me today—not to impress anyone, but to honor You. In Jesus' Name, Amen.

November 10

Nagging, Noise, and God's Voice

3-Year-Bible Reading: Proverbs 27:15–16; Psalm 129; Deuteronomy 17–18

"A continual dripping on a rainy day and a quarrelsome wife are alike; to restrain her is to restrain the wind or to grasp oil in one's right hand." — Proverbs 27:15–16

"Greatly have they afflicted me from my youth—yet they have not prevailed against me." — Psalm 129:2

"The Lord your God will raise up for you a prophet like me from among you, from your brothers—it is to him you shall listen." — Deuteronomy 18:15

Sometimes life just feels loud. Not just the external stuff like buzzing phones, clashing opinions, or constant pressure—but the inner noise, too. The fear of not being enough. The drama at school. The stress of trying to get it all right. **Proverbs 27:15–16** compares a nagging voice to constant dripping—something that's hard to ignore and nearly impossible to stop. And just like grabbing oil or catching the wind, trying to control that kind of chaos feels pointless.

But **Psalm 129** reminds us that even when we're "afflicted" or weighed down, we don't have to be defeated. Why? Because God hasn't left us alone in the noise. **Deuteronomy 18** promises a prophet—Jesus—whose voice we can trust. In a world full of sound, He's the voice worth listening to.

Think About It

1. **What Voices Are Loudest?** Are there people or thoughts in your life that feel like "dripping rain"—negative, constant, draining? Take time to name them and ask God to help you tune them out.

2. **You Can Be Afflicted and Still Stand:** Life will come with challenges, but Psalm 129 reminds us that struggle doesn't equal defeat. Where have you seen God help you stand strong even when things were hard?

3. **Jesus Still Speaks:** In Deuteronomy, God promises to send someone we should listen to. That's Jesus. What does it look like for you to listen to Him today—through prayer, the Bible, or even wise people He places in your life?

Bottom Line

The world can be noisy, but God hasn't left you to figure it out alone. In the middle of nagging thoughts, stress, or drama, Jesus is the steady voice that brings peace and direction.

Prayer

Heavenly Father, thank You for being a calm voice in a loud world. Help me recognize when I'm listening to things that drain me or distract me from You. Teach me to hear You clearly and to trust that You're always speaking truth and peace over my life. In Jesus' Name, Amen.

November 11

Sharpened Together

3-Year-Bible Reading: Proverbs 27:17–18; Deuteronomy 19–20

"Iron sharpens iron, and one man sharpens another." — Proverbs 27:17

"Whoever keeps the fig tree will eat its fruit, and he who guards his master will be honored." — Proverbs 27:18

"Let not your heart faint. Do not fear or panic or be in dread of them, for the Lord your God is he who goes with you to fight for you against your enemies, to give you the victory." — Deuteronomy 20:3–4

You've probably heard the phrase "you become like the people you hang out with." Whether it's your best friend hyping you up before a test or a teammate pushing you to work harder, who we spend time with matters.

In **Proverbs 27:17**, we're reminded that just like iron sharpens iron, people are meant to help each other grow stronger—especially in our faith. And in **Deuteronomy 19–20**, God tells the Israelites not to be afraid, because He is with them in every battle. Whether you're navigating conflict or standing up for what's right, God wants you to stay sharp, stay faithful, and remember you're never alone.

Think About It

1. **Who Sharpens You?** Are you surrounding yourself with people who make your faith stronger, or people who wear you down? Real friends help you grow, not just laugh at your memes.

2. **Faith Over Fear:** When challenges hit—like drama, tests, or tough decisions—do you let fear lead, or do you trust God is fighting for you like He promised in **Deuteronomy 20**?

3. **Stay Faithful in the Small Stuff:** Just like guarding a fig tree brings fruit in **Proverbs 27:18**, showing up in little things—helping a friend, praying, being honest—builds a life that honors God.

Bottom Line

God places people in our lives to help sharpen our faith and remind us that we don't face life's battles alone. Choose friends who challenge you to grow, and keep trusting that God is with you, giving you strength and victory.

Prayer

Heavenly Father, thank You for putting people in my life who help me grow. Help me to be the kind of friend who sharpens others and to stay faithful, even in the little things. When I face challenges, remind me that You are with me and fighting for me. Help me choose courage over fear and faith over doubt. In Jesus' Name, Amen.

NOVEMBER 12

Mirror, Mirror

3-Year-Bible Reading: Proverbs 27:19–20; Psalm 130; Deuteronomy 21–22

As in water face reflects face, so the heart of man reflects the man. Sheol and Abaddon are never satisfied, and never satisfied are the eyes of man — Proverbs 27:19–20

Out of the depths I cry to you, O Lord! O Lord, hear my voice! Let your ears be attentive to the voice of my pleas for mercy! — Psalm 130:1–2

So you shall purge the evil from your midst, and all Israel shall hear, and fear. — Deuteronomy 21:21

Ever stood in front of a mirror and noticed something off—maybe your hair's wild or you've got something in your teeth? Mirrors don't lie; they show what's really there. Proverbs tells us that our hearts are like that mirror. What's in your heart reflects who you truly are. And if we're honest, sometimes we don't like what we see—selfishness, jealousy, guilt. The Psalmist gets it.

In **Psalm 130**, we see someone crying out from the depths, desperate for mercy. That's real. And in **Deuteronomy**, we see God's desire for His people to live in a way that brings justice, integrity, and purity into their communities. These scriptures together point us to one big truth: what's inside us matters—and God cares deeply about helping us get our hearts right.

THINK ABOUT IT

1. **The Heart Reflects the Real You:** What's going on in your heart right now? Are you harboring envy, pride, or unforgiveness? Remember, just like a mirror shows your face, your actions reflect your heart.

2. **Crying Out Is OK:** Feeling overwhelmed? Like the writer of **Psalm 130**, it's okay to cry out to God. He hears you. You don't need to be perfect to approach Him—just honest.

3. **God Wants You to Choose Right:** The laws in **Deuteronomy 21–22** might feel intense, but they show how seriously God takes justice and purity. He wants you to make choices that reflect His character—choices that stand out in a world that often goes the opposite way.

BOTTOM LINE

Your heart is the real mirror of who you are. Let God shape it so that what's reflected points back to Him.

PRAYER

Heavenly Father, thank You for loving me even when my heart is messy. Help me to see myself clearly and to be honest about where I need to grow. Teach me to cry out to You and trust that You hear me. Shape my heart so my actions reflect You more and more each day. In Jesus' Name, Amen.

November 13

Refined by the Fire

3-Year-Bible Reading: Proverbs 27:21; Deuteronomy 23–24

"The crucible is for silver, and the furnace is for gold, and a man is tested by his praise." — Proverbs 27:21

"You shall not pervert the justice due to the sojourner or to the fatherless, or take a widow's garment in pledge." — Deuteronomy 24:17

"You shall not give up to his master a slave who has escaped from his master to you. He shall dwell with you, in your midst, in the place that he shall choose." — Deuteronomy 23:15–16

Ever been complimented and felt like you were on top of the world? Maybe someone said you were talented, good-looking, or just really kind—and it felt awesome. But sometimes, that praise can make us crave more attention, or start comparing ourselves to others. **Proverbs 27:21** reminds us that praise is like a furnace—it reveals what's inside us. Will we become prideful, or stay humble and grounded in God?

In **Deuteronomy 23–24**, God gives laws about justice, fairness, and protecting the vulnerable. These chapters remind us that God cares deeply about how we treat others, especially those who are often ignored. Together, these verses challenge us to think about how we respond when we're in the spotlight—and how we treat people when no one's watching.

Think About It

1. **The Test of Praise:** When someone compliments you, do you let it go to your head or thank God for how He's working in you? Praise is a test—what's it revealing in your heart?

2. **Justice and Compassion:** God's laws in Deuteronomy protect those who are often overlooked. Are you standing up for those who are left out, bullied, or treated unfairly?

3. **What's Your True Value?** Silver and gold are refined by fire, but God refines your character through the choices you make—especially when no one's watching. Are you choosing integrity?

Bottom Line

Praise might feel great in the moment, but it's what's in your heart that matters most. God wants you to reflect Him—whether you're being cheered on or standing up for someone who's been forgotten.

Prayer

Heavenly Father, thank You for seeing my heart even when no one else does. Help me stay humble when I receive praise and to use my life to show Your love. Teach me to care for others, especially those who are hurting or left out. Refine my heart like gold so I can honor You in every part of my life. In Jesus' Name, Amen.

NOVEMBER 14

Stirring the Pot Won't Change It

3-Year-Bible Reading: Proverbs 27:22; Psalm 131; Deuteronomy 25–27

"Crush a fool in a mortar with a pestle along with crushed grain, yet his folly will not depart from him." —Proverbs 27:22

"O Lord, my heart is not lifted up; my eyes are not raised too high; I do not occupy myself with things too great and too marvelous for me." —Psalm 131:1

"Cursed be anyone who does not confirm the words of this law by doing them." —Deuteronomy 27:26

Sometimes it's hard to admit when we're wrong—or even just when we're not in control. We want to figure everything out, prove ourselves, or even fix other people. But **Proverbs 27:22** reminds us that no matter how much you try to force wisdom into someone who refuses it, it won't stick. That can be frustrating, especially when the person is *you*.

In **Psalm 131**, we see a heart that's learned to chill—to stop striving for answers that belong to God alone. Then in **Deuteronomy 25–27**, we see a clear pattern: God lays out blessings for obedience and consequences for turning away. He's not just giving rules—He's showing what leads to life and what doesn't.

THINK ABOUT IT

1. **You can't force growth:** Have you ever tried to help someone who didn't want help? Proverbs 27:22 is a reminder that forcing change on someone who refuses to grow is like trying to pound wisdom into stone. God calls us to love people, not fix them.

2. **A quiet heart is powerful:** Psalm 131 is only three verses long, but it hits deep. It's about trusting God instead of stressing over stuff beyond our control. Are you carrying burdens that God never asked you to carry?

3. **Obedience is about relationship:** In Deuteronomy 27, God's laws aren't random. They're like guardrails on a mountain road—meant to protect, not restrict. Choosing to follow His way isn't about perfection; it's about love and trust.

BOTTOM LINE

Trying to control everything—yourself, others, outcomes—only leads to frustration. Let go of pride, lean into God's wisdom, and choose trust over stress. Real growth starts when we surrender.

PRAYER

Heavenly Father, Sometimes I try to fix things that aren't mine to fix, or I stress over things I can't control. Teach me to have a quiet heart, like in Psalm 131. Help me to obey You not just because I "should," but because I trust that Your way leads to life. Show me how to let go and lean on You. In Jesus' Name, Amen.

NOVEMBER 15

Watch What You're Tending

3-Year-Bible Reading: Proverbs 27:23–25; Deuteronomy 28

"Know well the condition of your flocks, and give attention to your herds, for riches do not last forever; and does a crown endure to all generations? When the grass is gone and the new growth appears and the vegetation of the mountains is gathered…" — Proverbs 27:23–25

"And if you faithfully obey the voice of the Lord your God… all these blessings shall come upon you and overtake you…" — Deuteronomy 28:1–2

"But if you will not obey the voice of the Lord your God… then all these curses shall come upon you and overtake you." — Deuteronomy 28:15

Ever tried to grow something, like a plant or even a friendship, and then watched it slowly fall apart because you stopped paying attention? That's exactly what Proverbs is getting at. God tells us to "know well" what we're responsible for—whether that's your friendships, your time, your habits, or your relationship with Him. Just like you wouldn't expect a garden to grow if you never watered it, you can't expect your life to thrive without intentional care.

In **Deuteronomy 28**, God makes it clear that blessings come when we listen to Him and live according to His ways. But when we stop listening, things unravel. God isn't being harsh—He's being real. He knows that what you focus on grows… and what you neglect fades.

THINK ABOUT IT

1. **What Are You Tending?** Are you paying more attention to your phone than your faith? More to your image than your integrity? Take stock of what you've been giving your time and energy to.

2. **Blessings or Burdens?** Deuteronomy 28 lays out two paths: one of blessing and one of burden. Which direction are your choices taking you today?

3. **Start With Small Steps:** You don't have to fix everything overnight. What's one area of your life you can be more intentional with this week—maybe prayer, Scripture, or even just how you treat people?

BOTTOM LINE

A thriving life takes attention. When you consistently listen to God and tend to what matters, blessings will grow—and so will you.

PRAYER

Heavenly Father, thank You for trusting me with things that matter—my life, my time, my relationships. Help me to stay focused and faithful with what You've given me. Teach me to listen to Your voice, even when distractions are loud. I want to choose the path of blessing and grow closer to You every day. In Jesus' Name, Amen.

November 16

Bold Like a Lion

3-Year-Bible Reading: Proverbs 28:1–3; Deuteronomy 29–30

"The wicked flee when no one pursues, but the righteous are bold as a lion." — Proverbs 28:1

"Beware lest there be among you a root bearing poisonous and bitter fruit." — Deuteronomy 29:18

"I have set before you life and death, blessing and curse. Therefore choose life, that you and your offspring may live." — Deuteronomy 30:19

Have you ever made a mistake and tried to hide it, hoping no one would find out? It's like living with a shadow always creeping behind you. Guilt and fear tend to do that. But **Proverbs 28:1** paints a different picture—one of boldness, confidence, and peace that comes when we're living in the light, not hiding in the shadows.

In **Deuteronomy 29–30**, God reminded Israel of the choice before them: obey and live with blessing, or turn away and face the consequences. That message still hits today—our choices shape our lives, and God wants us to choose Him, every time.

Think About It

1. **What does boldness look like?** When you live with integrity and stay close to God, you don't have to live in fear. Being bold like a lion isn't about being loud or fearless—it's about being grounded in truth and knowing who you belong to.

2. **Check the roots:** God warns about a "root" that produces bitterness. Sometimes, small sins or toxic attitudes grow silently. Are you letting anything take root in your heart that could poison your faith or relationships?

3. **Choose life:** Life with God isn't about following rules just to stay out of trouble. It's about choosing what leads to joy, peace, and purpose. Every choice to obey Him leads to more freedom, not less.

Bottom Line

When we walk with God, we don't have to hide. His way leads to boldness, blessing, and real life. Choose Him every day—and live like someone who has nothing to fear.

Prayer

Heavenly Father, thank You for offering me life and blessing through Your Word. Help me to recognize the little things that pull me away from You and to choose what's right, even when it's hard. Make me bold like a lion, not because I'm perfect, but because I walk with You. In Jesus' Name, Amen.

NOVEMBER 17

Stand Firm, Even When It's Hard

3-Year-Bible Reading: Proverbs 28:4–5; Deuteronomy 31–32

Those who forsake the law praise the wicked, but those who keep the law strive against them. Evil men do not understand justice, but those who seek the Lord understand it completely. — Proverbs 28:4–5

Be strong and courageous. Do not fear or be in dread of them, for it is the Lord your God who goes with you. He will not leave you or forsake you. — Deuteronomy 31:6

For the Lord will vindicate his people and have compassion on his servants, when he sees that their power is gone and there is none remaining, bond or free. — Deuteronomy 32:36

Let's be real—standing up for what's right isn't always easy. Sometimes it feels like everyone else is going the opposite direction, and following Jesus makes you stick out. Whether it's choosing not to gossip, walking away from drama, or saying no to something you know isn't right, it can feel lonely.

But in **Deuteronomy 31**, God reminds us that He *never* leaves us—He walks with us through the tough stuff. And **Proverbs 28** makes it clear: when you follow God, you'll see things differently. You'll understand truth and justice in a way the world can't. That kind of wisdom doesn't come from just knowing the rules—it comes from knowing God.

THINK ABOUT IT

1. **Courage Over Comfort:** Are you willing to stand firm for God even when it's uncomfortable or unpopular? Remember, God is with you, and He never expects you to do it alone.

2. **Truth Gives You Vision:** Proverbs says those who seek the Lord understand justice. How can seeking God through prayer, His Word, and community help you see right from wrong more clearly?

3. **God Has Your Back:** When you feel weak or alone, remember Deuteronomy 32:36—God sees you, He cares, and He steps in when you need Him. Do you trust Him to fight for you?

BOTTOM LINE

God calls you to stand for truth, even when it's hard—but you're never standing alone. He gives you the courage, the wisdom, and the strength to walk His way, and He promises He's not going anywhere.

PRAYER

Heavenly Father, Thank You for always being with me, even when things get tough. Give me courage to stand for what's right and help me see things the way You do. When I feel alone or misunderstood, remind me that You've got my back and You're never leaving me. Help me trust You more every day. In Jesus' Name, Amen.

November 18

Stay True, Stand Tall

3-Year-Bible Reading: Proverbs 28:6–7; Psalm 132; Deuteronomy 33–34

"Better is a poor man who walks in his integrity than a rich man who is crooked in his ways. The one who keeps the law is a son with understanding, but a companion of gluttons shames his father." — Proverbs 28:6–7

"For the LORD has chosen Zion; he has desired it for his dwelling place: 'This is my resting place forever; here I will dwell, for I have desired it.'" — Psalm 132:13–14

"So Moses the servant of the LORD died there in the land of Moab, according to the word of the LORD… And there has not arisen a prophet since in Israel like Moses, whom the LORD knew face to face." — Deuteronomy 34:5,10

Every day, you face pressure to fit in, to chase popularity, or to do whatever it takes to "get ahead." But God's Word tells a different story. **Proverbs 28:6** says it's better to be broke but honest than to be rich and shady. **Psalm 132** reminds us that God chooses where He wants to dwell—and He chooses hearts that are loyal.

And in **Deuteronomy 34**, we see the legacy of Moses, a man who didn't have it all together but stayed close to God to the very end. His story wasn't about perfection—it was about integrity, obedience, and deep friendship with God. You don't need to be famous or flawless to make a difference. You just need to stay true to God.

Think About It

1. **Integrity Matters:** Are you making choices that honor God, even when no one is watching? Remember, God values integrity more than success.

2. **God's Presence is Personal:** Psalm 132 shows us that God desires a place to dwell. Is your heart a place He'd want to live?

3. **Leave a Legacy:** Moses didn't enter the Promised Land, but he left behind a life of deep impact. What kind of legacy are you building right now?

Bottom Line

You don't need to have it all to walk tall. Live with integrity, invite God into your daily life, and trust that your faithfulness will leave a legacy.

Prayer

Heavenly Father, thank You for showing me that character matters more than status. Help me to walk in integrity, to honor You in my choices, and to build a life that reflects Your presence. I want to know You like Moses did and make You at home in my heart. In Jesus' Name, Amen.

NOVEMBER 19

Faith Over Fear

3-Year-Bible Reading: Proverbs 28:8–9; Joshua 1–2

"Whoever multiplies his wealth by interest and profit gathers it for him who is generous to the poor. If one turns away his ear from hearing the law, even his prayer is an abomination." — Proverbs 28:8–9

"Have I not commanded you? Be strong and courageous. Do not be frightened, and do not be dismayed, for the Lord your God is with you wherever you go." — Joshua 1:9

"And as soon as we heard it, our hearts melted, and there was no spirit left in any man because of you, for the Lord your God, he is God in the heavens above and on the earth beneath." — Joshua 2:11

Have you ever faced something that felt way too big for you to handle—like a huge exam, a big move, or a tough conversation? In **Joshua 1**, Joshua is stepping into some enormous shoes—taking over for Moses and leading an entire nation into a land filled with enemies. Scary stuff. But God tells him three times in one chapter to *"be strong and courageous."* Why? Because Joshua wasn't doing it alone. In **Joshua 2**, even Rahab, a woman from Jericho, believed that Israel's God was powerful—and because of her faith, she risked everything to help God's people.

And over in **Proverbs 28**, we're reminded that true strength and blessing come from living wisely and walking closely with God—not from taking shortcuts or ignoring His Word. All of this points to one truth: when you listen to God and trust Him, He gives you the courage to do hard things.

THINK ABOUT IT

1. **Courage Comes from God:** Joshua wasn't told to be fearless on his own—God said, *"I am with you."* Are you relying on God's strength when you're afraid?

2. **Faith Can Come from Unexpected Places:** Rahab wasn't an Israelite, but she believed in God more than many of His own people. What does her story show you about God's grace and your own potential to make a difference?

3. **Listening to God Matters:** Proverbs says if we ignore God's Word, even our prayers can be affected. How can you stay tuned in to what God is saying through Scripture?

BOTTOM LINE

Real courage doesn't mean you're never scared—it means you trust God more than your fear.

PRAYER

Heavenly Father, thank You for being with me in every situation, no matter how overwhelming it feels. Help me to listen to Your Word and trust You like Joshua and Rahab did. Give me the strength to be courageous and to live boldly for You today. In Jesus' Name, Amen.

November 20

Stepping Stones and Standing Strong

3-Year-Bible Reading: Proverbs 28:10–11; Psalm 133; Joshua 3–4

Whoever misleads the upright into an evil way will fall into his own pit, but the blameless will have a goodly inheritance. A rich man is wise in his own eyes, but a poor man who has understanding will find him out. — Proverbs 28:10–11

Behold, how good and pleasant it is when brothers dwell in unity! — Psalm 133:1

And Joshua said to them, "Pass on before the ark of the Lord your God into the midst of the Jordan, and take up each of you a stone upon his shoulder... that this may be a sign among you. When your children ask in time to come, 'What do those stones mean to you?' then you shall tell them..." — Joshua 4:5–6

Have you ever gone through something tough—like moving to a new school, facing a challenge, or stepping out of your comfort zone—and then looked back and thought, "Wow, I made it through that"? That's kind of what's happening in **Joshua 3–4**. The Israelites were about to enter the Promised Land, but they had to cross a river at flood stage first. God stopped the waters so they could walk through—and He told them to take stones from the riverbed to remember the miracle. Like personal trophies of God's power, these stones told a story of trust, unity, and obedience.

In **Psalm 133**, we're reminded of how good it is when people live in unity. That kind of teamwork and shared faith helped the Israelites cross together. And **Proverbs 28** warns us not to follow people who lead us away from truth, but instead to stay wise and walk with understanding.

Think About It

1. **What Are Your Stones?** What moments in your life remind you of God's faithfulness? Think of times He helped you through something big or small—those are your "stones."

2. **Unity Matters:** Are you someone who helps create peace and unity in your group, family, or friend circle? God sees that kind of heart as "good and pleasant."

3. **Choose Your Guides Carefully:** Are you following people who are wise in God's eyes or just in their own? Proverbs challenges us to be careful about who we let influence our path.

Bottom Line

God often leads us through challenges so we can remember His faithfulness, walk in unity, and grow in wisdom. Look for the "stones" in your story—and keep moving forward with a blameless heart.

Prayer

Heavenly Father, Thank You for leading me through both the easy and the hard moments. Help me to recognize Your hand in my life and remember Your goodness. Teach me to walk in wisdom, stay away from harmful influences, and be someone who brings peace and unity to those around me. Help me trust You, even when the river in front of me looks too deep. In Jesus' Name, Amen.

NOVEMBER 21

Victory Starts with Surrender

3-Year-Bible Reading: Proverbs 28:12-13; Joshua 5–6

When the righteous triumph, there is great glory, but when the wicked rise, people hide themselves. Whoever conceals his transgressions will not prosper, but he who confesses and forsakes them will obtain mercy. — Proverbs 28:12-13

And the Lord said to Joshua, "Today I have rolled away the reproach of Egypt from you." — Joshua 5:9

On the seventh day they rose early… And at the seventh time, when the priests had blown the trumpets, Joshua said to the people, "Shout, for the Lord has given you the city." — Joshua 6:15a, 16

Ever felt like you're facing a wall too high to climb? Maybe it's anxiety, peer pressure, a habit you want to break, or just the stress of life piling up. In **Joshua 6**, God's people faced the massive, fortified walls of Jericho. But they didn't win with swords or strength. They obeyed God's unusual instructions—march, wait, blow trumpets, and shout. The wall fell when they fully surrendered and trusted God's way.

Similarly, **Proverbs 28** reminds us that hiding sin or pretending everything's okay never leads to real success. Healing and mercy come when we confess, surrender, and follow God's lead—just like the Israelites did before Jericho. In **Joshua 5**, they prepared spiritually before the battle. Surrender came *before* victory.

THINK ABOUT IT

1. **God's Plans Don't Always Make Sense:** Marching in circles probably seemed silly, but God's strategy for Jericho wasn't about logic—it was about obedience. Are you willing to trust Him even when it doesn't seem to "make sense"?

2. **Surrender Leads to Freedom:** The Israelites had to deal with their past (like in Joshua 5) before they could move forward. What walls in your life need to come down through confession or surrender?

3. **Obedience Opens Doors:** The walls fell *after* they obeyed. Is there something God's been nudging you to do that you've been putting off?

BOTTOM LINE

Sometimes, the biggest victories in life start with quiet surrender to God. Trusting Him, obeying even when it's hard, and being honest about your struggles are the keys to breakthrough.

PRAYER

Heavenly Father, help me trust Your ways, even when they don't make sense to me. Teach me to surrender the things I've been holding onto and to confess the areas I've been hiding. I want to walk in freedom and see Your victory in my life. Thank You for Your mercy and love. In Jesus' Name, Amen.

November 22

Stay Awake and Worship

3-Year-Bible Reading: Proverbs 28:14; Psalm 134; Joshua 7–8

"Blessed is the one who fears the Lord always, but whoever hardens his heart will fall into calamity." — Proverbs 28:14

"Come, bless the Lord, all you servants of the Lord, who stand by night in the house of the Lord!" — Psalm 134:1

"Then Joshua said to Achan, 'My son, give glory to the Lord God of Israel and give praise to him. And tell me now what you have done; do not hide it from me.'" — Joshua 7:19

Have you ever kept something hidden, hoping no one would find out? Maybe it was something small that felt harmless at the time. But like in **Joshua 7**, even one wrong choice can affect more than just you. Achan thought he could get away with disobedience, but his hidden sin led to defeat and heartbreak. When he finally confessed, healing could begin.

Proverbs 28:14 reminds us that a heart that stays sensitive to God is blessed—but when we grow cold or stubborn, things fall apart. And **Psalm 134** encourages us to keep worshiping God, even in the late hours or hard seasons. God wants our hearts—honest, humble, and awake to His presence.

Think About It

1. **Hidden things matter:** What we keep in the dark can grow stronger and cause more harm. Is there anything in your life you need to bring into the light and give to God?

2. **A soft heart is a strong heart:** Fearing God doesn't mean being scared—it means caring deeply about what He says and being quick to listen and change when needed.

3. **Worship in the dark:** Even when things feel tough or quiet, like the night shift mentioned in Psalm 134, we're called to worship. Praise shifts our focus back to God.

Bottom Line

God blesses those who stay honest, humble, and open to Him. Don't hide your struggles—bring them to God, and choose worship no matter the hour.

Prayer

Heavenly Father, Thank You for seeing me completely and loving me anyway. Help me to keep my heart soft and my life honest before You. I don't want to hide—I want to live in Your light and walk in Your truth. Teach me to worship You even when things are hard. In Jesus' Name, Amen.

November 23

Wolves in the Hallway

3-Year-Bible Reading: Proverbs 28:15–16; Joshua 9–10

"Like a roaring lion or a charging bear is a wicked ruler over a poor people. A ruler who lacks understanding is a cruel oppressor, but he who hates unjust gain will prolong his days." — Proverbs 28:15–16

"So the men took some of their provisions, but did not ask counsel from the Lord." — Joshua 9:14

"And the Lord threw them into a panic before Israel, who struck them with a great blow at Gibeon…" — Joshua 10:10

Have you ever trusted someone and then realized they weren't who they said they were? Maybe it was a friend who turned out to be fake, or someone online who seemed cool but wasn't real with you. In **Joshua 9**, the Israelites get tricked by a group pretending to be travelers from far away—but they were actually neighbors trying to sneak into a peace treaty. Why did it work? Because Israel *did not ask counsel from the Lord* (**Joshua 9:14**).

In **Proverbs 28**, we're warned about leaders who hurt others when they lack wisdom or act out of selfish ambition. Whether it's in leadership, friendships, or decisions, not checking in with God can lead to big regrets. But even when we mess up, like Israel did, God still steps in when we call out to Him, just like He helped them in battle in **Joshua 10**.

Think About It

1. **Ask First:** Are you making choices based on your own judgment, or are you inviting God into your decisions? Israel assumed they knew what was going on, but a quick prayer could've changed everything.

2. **Recognize the Wolves:** Not everyone who sounds wise or friendly is looking out for your best. How can you grow in wisdom to tell the difference?

3. **God Still Shows Up:** Even when we make mistakes, God can redeem the situation. Are you trusting Him to help you clean up the mess, or are you trying to handle it alone?

Bottom Line

Trusting God's wisdom over your own instincts can protect you from being misled. Don't skip the step of seeking His direction—He sees what you can't.

Prayer

Heavenly Father, thank You for always being available to guide me. Help me to remember to ask You first when I'm facing decisions, even when they seem small. Give me wisdom to see through lies and courage to follow what's right. Thank You for Your mercy, even when I mess up. In Jesus' Name, Amen.

November 24

Walking Straight in a Twisted World

3-Year-Bible Reading: Proverbs 28:17–18; Joshua 11–12

"If one is burdened with the blood of another, he will be a fugitive until death; let no one help him. Whoever walks in integrity will be delivered, but he who is crooked in his ways will suddenly fall."
—Proverbs 28:17–18

"And Joshua captured all these kings and their land at one time, because the Lord God of Israel fought for Israel."—Joshua 10:42

"And these are the kings of the land whom Joshua and the people of Israel defeated… in all, thirty-one kings."—Joshua 12:24

Life can feel like a never-ending maze of decisions—some big, some small, and some that seem to sneak up on us. Whether it's dealing with drama at school, choosing who we hang out with, or standing up for what's right, we're constantly being tested.

In **Proverbs 28**, we're reminded that walking in integrity—doing what's right even when no one's watching—leads to safety and deliverance. But those who live a double life? Eventually, it catches up with them. Joshua's story in **Joshua 11–12** shows what it looks like when we follow God with courage and trust: victory after victory, even against overwhelming odds. The common thread? God honors those who walk in obedience and integrity.

Think About It

1. **Integrity Matters:** What does walking in integrity look like in your everyday life—at school, with your friends, or online?

2. **God Fights for You:** In Joshua 11–12, the Israelites didn't win battles because they were the strongest—they won because God was with them. Are you trying to fight battles on your own, or are you trusting God to lead you?

3. **The Consequences of a Crooked Path:** Proverbs warns us about the dangers of living a secret life filled with sin or guilt. Is there anything you need to bring into the light today?

Bottom Line

Living with integrity may not always be the easiest path, but it's the one that leads to peace, protection, and God's power working in your life. Like Joshua, you can face any challenge when you walk closely with God.

Prayer

Heavenly Father, thank You for reminding me that walking in integrity matters. Help me to make wise choices even when it's hard, and give me courage to trust You like Joshua did. I want to live a life that reflects You, not just when people are watching, but all the time. Thank You for being my strength and my guide. In Jesus' Name, Amen.

NOVEMBER 25

Staying Planted in the Right Soil

3-Year-Bible Reading: Proverbs 28:19-20; Psalm 135; Joshua 13–14

"Whoever works his land will have plenty of bread, but he who follows worthless pursuits will have plenty of poverty. A faithful man will abound with blessings, but whoever hastens to be rich will not go unpunished." — Proverbs 28:19–20

"For I know that the Lord is great, and that our Lord is above all gods." — Psalm 135:5

"So now, give me this hill country of which the Lord spoke on that day… It may be that the Lord will be with me, and I shall drive them out just as the Lord said." — Joshua 14:12

There's something powerful about someone who stays faithful through the long haul. In **Joshua 14**, Caleb is 85 years old, yet he's still as bold and faithful as he was when he first spied out the promised land. He reminds Joshua of the promise God made to him and says, "Give me that hill country." He's not chasing fame or fortune—he's pursuing the purpose God gave him.

That same theme shows up in **Proverbs 28**, where we're reminded to "work our land," stay faithful, and not be swayed by quick fixes or shallow pursuits. And in **Psalm 135**, we're reminded why we can trust this path: because our God is above all others—strong, sovereign, and worthy of praise. The question is: are we staying planted in God's soil, trusting His timing, or chasing after "worthless pursuits"?

THINK ABOUT IT

1. **Faith Over Flash:** What does it mean to "work your land" today? Maybe it's studying hard, practicing kindness, or sticking with a goal God has given you, even when it's tough. Where in your life are you tempted to take shortcuts?

2. **God Is Worthy:** Psalm 135 reminds us that God is above all. What would change in your life if you truly believed God is greater than everything you're facing—your fears, your goals, or even your dreams?

3. **Be Like Caleb:** Caleb didn't let age, obstacles, or the opinions of others stop him from holding on to God's promises. What promises has God made in His Word that you need to hold on to more tightly today?

BOTTOM LINE

Faithfulness may not always feel flashy, but it always leads to blessing. When we trust God's timing, stay rooted in His purpose, and believe He is above all, we position ourselves to live boldly—just like Caleb.

PRAYER

Heavenly Father, thank You for being greater than anything I face. Help me to be faithful like Caleb, to work the land You've given me, and to stay rooted in Your purpose for my life. I don't want to chase worthless things—I want to live for what really matters. Strengthen me to trust You day by day. In Jesus' Name, Amen.

November 26

No Shortcuts

3-Year-Bible Reading: Proverbs 28:21–22; Joshua 15–16

To show partiality is not good, but for a piece of bread a man will do wrong. A stingy man hastens after wealth and does not know that poverty will come upon him. — Proverbs 28:21–22

This was the inheritance of the tribe of the people of Judah according to their clans. — Joshua 15:20

The people of Joseph, Manasseh and Ephraim, received their inheritance. — Joshua 16:4

Have you ever been tempted to cut corners—maybe sneak a peek at someone else's test, exaggerate a story to look good, or take a shortcut that no one will notice? In **Proverbs 28:21–22**, we're warned that chasing quick rewards or being unfair just to gain something small can lead to bigger problems.

Meanwhile, **Joshua 15–16** shows how God carefully and fairly distributed land to His people. Each tribe received their share—not because they rushed ahead or cheated, but because they trusted God's process. There's something powerful about waiting for what's yours and not trying to grab what isn't.

Think About It

1. **What's the rush?** Are you tempted to speed ahead or grab more than you need? Proverbs reminds us that shortcuts often lead to setbacks. Why do you think it's hard to wait on God's timing?

2. **Inheritance isn't just land:** In Joshua, the land wasn't random—it was God's promise coming true. What has God promised you? How can you stay focused on His plan rather than what others seem to be getting?

3. **Check your heart:** Greed and impatience can sneak in subtly. Is there a situation where you're tempted to take more than your share or bend the truth to get ahead?

Bottom Line

God's way may take longer, but it leads to lasting peace. Trust the process and resist the urge to grab what isn't yours. His promises are worth the wait.

Prayer

Heavenly Father, thank You for being fair and faithful. Help me to trust Your timing and stay away from shortcuts that lead to trouble. Teach me to be content, honest, and patient as I wait for what You've promised. In Jesus' Name, Amen.

NOVEMBER 27

Real Love Tells the Truth

3-Year-Bible Reading: Proverbs 28:23–24; Psalm 136; Joshua 17–18

Whoever rebukes a man will afterward find more favor than he who flatters with his tongue. Whoever robs his father or his mother and says, "That is no transgression," is a companion to a man who destroys. — Proverbs 28:23–24

Give thanks to the Lord, for he is good, for his steadfast love endures forever. — Psalm 136:1

The people of Joseph said, "The hill country is not enough for us," ... Then Joshua said ... "You are numerous and very powerful. You will have not only one allotment but the forested hill country as well." — Joshua 17:14,17–18

Let's be real—no one *loves* being corrected. Whether it's a parent calling you out for an attitude or a friend pointing out you crossed a line, it can feel harsh or embarrassing. But Proverbs **28:23** reminds us that loving correction is better than fake flattery. Real love isn't afraid to speak the truth.

Psalm **136** repeats one powerful truth 26 times: God's love *never* runs out. And in **Joshua 17–18**, we see the people of Joseph wanting more land, but Joshua doesn't give them an easy pass—he challenges them to rise up and claim what God has already given them. That's what love does. It calls us to more, not less.

Think About It

1. **Truth Over Flattery:** Do you surround yourself with people who tell you what you want to hear, or what you *need* to hear? Godly friends and mentors are willing to be honest with you—even when it's uncomfortable.

2. **Forever Love:** Psalm 136 reminds us again and again that God's love *endures forever*. Why do you think that truth is repeated so often? How does knowing that God's love never gives up help you receive correction better?

3. **Step Into It:** The tribes in Joshua were hesitant to take all God had given them. Are you sitting back in fear or frustration when God is calling you to step out in faith and effort?

Bottom Line

God's love is real, honest, and forever. It doesn't flatter—it builds. Through correction, challenge, and truth, God is shaping us to step into all He's planned for us.

Prayer

Heavenly Father, Thank You that Your love never gives up on me. Help me to receive correction with a humble heart and recognize it as an act of love. Surround me with people who speak truth and push me toward Your best. Give me the courage to step forward when You call me to more. In Jesus' Name, Amen.

November 28

Trust the Safe Place

3-Year-Bible Reading: Proverbs 28:25; Joshua 19–20

"A greedy man stirs up strife, but the one who trusts in the Lord will be enriched." — Proverbs 28:25

"These were the cities designated for all the people of Israel and for the stranger sojourning among them, that anyone who killed a person without intent could flee there, so that he might not die by the hand of the avenger of blood, till he stood before the congregation." — Joshua 20:9

Have you ever messed up big time—like, seriously regretted something you did? Maybe it wasn't on purpose, but it still hurt someone, and now you're dealing with the fallout. In **Joshua 20**, God set up "cities of refuge" for people who accidentally hurt someone so they wouldn't be punished without a fair trial. It was a way of saying, "There's still hope. There's still safety."

In **Proverbs 28:25**, we're reminded that when we trust in God—not in ourselves, or what we can get, or how we can fix things on our own—He brings peace and blessing. God is our safe place, not just when we do everything right, but especially when we don't.

Think About It

1. **Where's your trust?** Are you trying to handle life all on your own—your reputation, your mistakes, your future? What would it look like to actually trust God with those things?

2. **God provides refuge:** Just like the cities of refuge in Joshua, God still offers a place of safety today—not always physical, but emotional and spiritual safety in His presence.

3. **Be someone's safe place:** God's people were told to make room for others—even outsiders—to find safety. How can you be a friend who offers grace and understanding to someone who's messed up?

Bottom Line

God is a safe place when life gets messy. Trust Him, run to Him, and let Him be your refuge—no matter what.

Prayer

Heavenly Father, thank You for being my refuge and strength, even when I make mistakes. Help me to trust You more than myself or the things around me. Show me how to run to You first, and how to offer that same grace to others. In Jesus' Name, Amen.

November 29

Trust Issues

3-Year-Bible Reading: Proverbs 28:26; Psalm 137; Joshua 21–22

Whoever trusts in his own mind is a fool, but he who walks in wisdom will be delivered. —Proverbs 28:26

How shall we sing the Lord's song in a foreign land? —Psalm 137:4

Not one word of all the good promises that the Lord had made to the house of Israel had failed; all came to pass. —Joshua 21:45

Life gets complicated. You have decisions to make, emotions to navigate, people to deal with—and sometimes it feels like your own brain is your only GPS. But **Proverbs 28:26** warns us: leaning only on your own understanding isn't just risky—it's foolish. Why? Because feelings can be misleading, thoughts can be clouded, and we don't see the full picture like God does.

Psalm 137 shows us what it's like to be in a dark place, struggling to stay hopeful. The Israelites were grieving in exile, far from home, wondering if they'd ever feel joy again. And yet, in **Joshua 21**, we're reminded that *not one* of God's promises failed. Even when it felt like everything was falling apart, He was still working things out—perfectly, faithfully.

Think About It

1. **Who are you trusting?** When life gets confusing or emotional, do you automatically go with your gut—or do you pause and ask God for wisdom? Trusting your own heart over God's Word can lead you into trouble.

2. **How do you respond in hard times?** Like the people in **Psalm 137**, there may be seasons when joy feels far away. But even in sadness, God invites us to draw near to Him, not pull away.

3. **God keeps His word:** Joshua 21:45 is a major reminder that God never breaks a promise. Even if the timeline feels slow, His faithfulness never fails.

Bottom Line

Feelings change, circumstances shift, and our own minds can trick us—but God's wisdom is solid, and His promises never miss. Don't rely on yourself. Lean on the One who always comes through.

Prayer

Heavenly Father, Sometimes I think I know best, and I act without asking You for guidance. Help me to trust You more than my feelings, more than my instincts. Thank You for keeping every promise and never giving up on me, even when things feel confusing or heavy. Help me to lean into Your wisdom and walk in Your truth. In Jesus' Name, Amen.

November 30

All In or All Out

3-Year-Bible Reading: Proverbs 28:27–28; Joshua 23–24

Whoever gives to the poor will not want, but he who hides his eyes will get many a curse. — Proverbs 28:27

You know in your hearts and souls, all of you, that not one word has failed of all the good things that the Lord your God promised concerning you; all have come to pass for you, not one of them has failed. —Joshua 23:14

And if it is evil in your eyes to serve the Lord, choose this day whom you will serve… But as for me and my house, we will serve the Lord. —Joshua 24:15

It's easy to get stuck somewhere in the middle. You want to follow God, but life gets distracting. Friends, school, sports, phones—everything competes for your attention. In **Joshua 23–24**, Joshua challenges the Israelites to make a clear choice: be "all in" for God or not. No halfway, no just-on-Sundays kind of faith.

Meanwhile, **Proverbs 28** reminds us that our actions reflect our hearts—whether we choose to help others or ignore those in need. God sees it all. When life feels chaotic or uncertain, He hasn't failed—**Joshua 23:14** says *not one* of His promises has fallen through. The question is: will you stay committed to Him?

THINK ABOUT IT

1. **Make the Choice:** Are you fully committed to following Jesus, or just doing the bare minimum to look Christian from the outside? Joshua calls us to take a stand.

2. **Faith in Action:** According to Proverbs, helping those in need is one way our faith shows up in real life. Are you open to seeing others' needs, or are you turning a blind eye?

3. **God is Always Faithful:** Even when life doesn't go as planned, God hasn't failed you. Can you look back and see how He's been working things out for your good?

BOTTOM LINE

God has never let you down—and He never will. So make the choice to follow Him with your whole heart, not just when it's convenient.

PRAYER

Heavenly Father, thank You for always being faithful, even when I get distracted or forget to put You first. Help me choose You every day, to live boldly for You and love others like You do. Make me someone who sees needs and responds with compassion. I want to be all in, not halfway. In Jesus' Name, Amen.

December 1

Warning Signs

3-Year-Bible Reading: Proverbs 29:1; Genesis 3; Romans 8:18–23

He who is often reproved, yet stiffens his neck, will suddenly be broken beyond healing. — Proverbs 29:1

So when the woman saw that the tree was good for food... she took of its fruit and ate, and she also gave some to her husband who was with her, and he ate. — Genesis 3:6

For the creation waits with eager longing for the revealing of the sons of God... in hope that the creation itself will be set free from its bondage to corruption. — Romans 8:19–21

Have you ever ignored a warning—like your phone dying at 1% or your gas tank being on empty—and thought, "I'll be fine"? We all have moments where we think we know better, but ignoring warnings can lead to serious consequences.

In **Proverbs 29:1**, we see that consistently refusing correction leads to a sudden fall. That's exactly what happened in **Genesis 3** when Adam and Eve ignored God's clear instructions. Because of their choice, all of creation was impacted. But the story doesn't end there. In **Romans 8**, we're reminded that even in the middle of this broken world, God is working on a plan to restore everything—and that includes us.

Think About It

1. **Heed the Warnings:** Are there areas in your life where you're ignoring God's correction or advice from wise people around you? Take a moment to reflect on what God's been trying to show you.

2. **Choices Matter:** Adam and Eve's decision didn't just affect them—it affected all of creation. What kind of influence do your choices have on those around you?

3. **Hope Isn't Lost:** Even though things are broken, **Romans 8** reminds us there's hope. How does knowing that God will restore everything give you strength today?

Bottom Line

Ignoring God's warnings leads to pain, but He hasn't given up on us. He offers hope, healing, and a future—so pay attention when He speaks and trust in His plan to make all things new.

Prayer

Heavenly Father, Thank You for loving me enough to warn me when I'm heading in the wrong direction. Help me to listen when You speak—through Your Word, through others, or through that nudge in my heart. When I mess up, remind me that You haven't given up on me. Thank You for the hope I have in Jesus and the promise that one day everything broken will be made whole again. In Jesus' Name, Amen.

December 2

When the World Gets Loud

3-Year-Bible Reading: Proverbs 29:2–3; Psalm 2; Hebrews 1–2

"When the righteous increase, the people rejoice, but when the wicked rule, the people groan. He who loves wisdom makes his father glad, but a companion of prostitutes squanders his wealth." — Proverbs 29:2–3

Why do the nations rage and the peoples plot in vain? He who sits in the heavens laughs; the Lord holds them in derision." — Psalm 2:1, 4

"Long ago, at many times and in many ways, God spoke to our fathers by the prophets, but in these last days he has spoken to us by his Son... Therefore we must pay much closer attention to what we have heard, lest we drift away from it." — Hebrews 1:1–2, 2:1

Life can feel chaotic. News, social media, and opinions fly around like confetti, and it's hard to know what to believe or how to feel. Sometimes it seems like the world is out of control—people choosing what's wrong over what's right, leaders making decisions that cause pain, and influencers promoting empty lifestyles.

Proverbs reminds us that when the wrong people lead, everyone feels it (**Proverbs 29:2**). But God isn't shaken. **Psalm 2** shows that even when the world rebels, God sits in heaven with full authority. He's not panicked. And **Hebrews 1–2** points us back to Jesus—the One God speaks through now. He is steady, strong, and worth listening to when everything else gets loud.

Think About It

1. **Who's Leading Your Heart?** Are you being influenced more by people and culture, or by God's wisdom? What voices are shaping your thinking?

2. **God Isn't Nervous:** The world might look like it's spinning out of control, but Psalm 2 reminds us that God is still in charge. Do you trust that He sees and knows everything—even when life feels overwhelming?

3. **Don't Drift:** Hebrews 2:1 warns us not to drift away. Drifting happens slowly, almost without noticing. Are there areas in your life where you've stopped paying attention to God's voice?

Bottom Line

When the world gets loud and confusing, God's voice cuts through the noise. He speaks through Jesus—our anchor and hope. Stay close to Him, and you won't drift.

Prayer

Heavenly Father, thank You for being in control, even when the world feels crazy. Help me not to follow the noise around me but to listen closely to You. Teach me to love Your wisdom, trust Your plan, and stay close to Jesus. In Jesus' Name, Amen.

December 3

The Kind of King We Need

3-Year-Bible Reading: Proverbs 29:4–5; Psalm 110; Genesis 14:8–20; Hebrews 7–8:2

"By justice a king builds up the land, but he who exacts gifts tears it down." —Proverbs 29:4

"The LORD says to my Lord: 'Sit at my right hand, until I make your enemies your footstool.'" —Psalm 110:1

"And Melchizedek king of Salem brought out bread and wine. (He was priest of God Most High.)" —Genesis 14:18

"He is without father or mother or genealogy, having neither beginning of days nor end of life… but resembling the Son of God he continues a priest forever." —Hebrews 7:3

We live in a world full of leaders—some good, some… not so much. Maybe you've seen people in power make selfish decisions or use others to get ahead. It's frustrating, especially when you want to believe someone will do what's right. In **Proverbs 29:4**, we're reminded that true leadership is built on justice, not on greed.

Psalm 110 talks about a different kind of king—one who rules with God's authority and doesn't abuse power. And then, there's this guy Melchizedek in **Genesis 14**, a king and priest who blesses Abraham and points forward to Jesus. In **Hebrews 7**, the writer shows how Jesus is a forever kind of priest and king—righteous, holy, and never changing. That's the kind of leader we actually need.

Think About It

1. **Justice Over Power:** How do you respond when you see unfairness or selfish leadership around you? Are you seeking to build others up with your actions like the just king in Proverbs?

2. **Jesus is Better:** Hebrews tells us Jesus is both king and priest. That means He rules with authority *and* speaks to God on your behalf. How does it change your view of Jesus knowing He always stands for you?

3. **Kingdom Living:** If Jesus is your King, how should that affect your choices—at school, with friends, or online? Are you following His lead in how you treat others?

Bottom Line

The world offers flawed leaders, but Jesus is the perfect King and Priest who reigns with justice, mercy, and forever love. He's the one you can fully trust.

Prayer

Heavenly Father, thank You for giving us Jesus, the perfect King who rules with justice and love. Help me to follow His example in how I live, lead, and love others. Remind me that He always intercedes for me, even when I mess up. I want to live in a way that honors Him. In Jesus' Name, Amen.

December 4

Freed to Follow

3-Year-Bible Reading: Proverbs 29:6; Psalm 138; Genesis 12:1–3; Galatians 3

"An evil man is ensnared in his transgression, but a righteous man sings and rejoices." — Proverbs 29:6

"The Lord will fulfill his purpose for me; your steadfast love, O Lord, endures forever." — Psalm 138:8

"Now the Lord said to Abram, 'Go from your country and your kindred and your father's house to the land that I will show you. And I will make of you a great nation… and in you all the families of the earth shall be blessed.'" — Genesis 12:1–3

"And if you are Christ's, then you are Abraham's offspring, heirs according to promise." — Galatians 3:29

Have you ever been stuck doing something you knew wasn't good, but it was hard to break free? That's kind of what **Proverbs 29:6** is getting at—the trap of sin. It holds us back. But when we live rightly, there's freedom and joy, like a song we can't help but sing. Abraham experienced this firsthand in **Genesis 12**, when God called him to leave everything familiar and follow Him into the unknown. That sounds scary, but Abraham trusted God and walked into a life of purpose and blessing.

The amazing part? **Galatians 3** says that if we belong to Jesus, we're part of that same promise—called out, blessed, and sent to bless others. God isn't just freeing us from something; He's freeing us *for* something.

Think About It

1. **Trapped or Free?** What things in your life feel like they're trapping you or holding you back? Are there habits, friendships, or fears that are keeping you from fully following God?

2. **Purpose in the Unknown:** Abraham didn't know where he was going—he just trusted God's promise. What step of faith might God be asking you to take, even if the destination isn't clear?

3. **You're in the Story:** Galatians reminds us that we're part of God's bigger plan. Do you believe that God wants to use *you* to bless others? How could your life point others to Him?

Bottom Line

God sets us free not just to leave sin behind, but to live with joy, trust His promises, and walk boldly into the purpose He's planned for us.

Prayer

Heavenly Father, thank You for calling me to something bigger than myself. Help me recognize the things that trap me and give me the courage to step into the freedom You offer. Remind me that I am part of Your promise and that my life has purpose in You. Use me to be a blessing to others, even when the path ahead seems unclear. In Jesus' Name, Amen.

DECEMBER 5

Counted as Righteous

3-Year-Bible Reading: Proverbs 29:9–10; Psalm 32; Genesis 15:1–6; Romans 4

"If a wise man has an argument with a fool, the fool only rages and laughs, and there is no quiet." —Proverbs 29:9

"Blessed is the one whose transgression is forgiven, whose sin is covered." —Psalm 32:1

"And he believed the Lord, and he counted it to him as righteousness." —Genesis 15:6

"For what does the Scripture say? 'Abraham believed God, and it was counted to him as righteousness.'" —Romans 4:3

Arguments. Mistakes. Insecurities. If you've ever felt like you couldn't do enough to be "good enough" for God, you're not alone. Abraham, known as a father of faith, didn't always get it right either. But in **Genesis 15**, God makes Abraham a huge promise—descendants as countless as the stars. And Abraham? He simply believed. That faith, not his performance, was what made him right with God.

Later in **Romans 4**, Paul reminds us that the same is true for us: we are made right not by our perfect actions, but by believing in the One who forgives and saves. **Psalm 32** celebrates that joy—being forgiven, cleaned up, and loved. And in **Proverbs 29**, we're reminded that trying to argue with foolishness (even our own) often just brings chaos. Sometimes, the wisest thing we can do is trust God and walk away from the noise.

THINK ABOUT IT

1. **Faith Over Performance:** Are you trusting more in your ability to "be good" or in God's grace? Abraham's righteousness came from faith, not perfection.

2. **Freedom in Forgiveness:** Psalm 32 says we are *blessed* when we are forgiven. Are you holding on to guilt that God is ready to forgive?

3. **Pick Your Battles:** Proverbs reminds us that arguing with foolishness can lead to more drama. Where in your life do you need to choose peace instead of trying to win an argument?

BOTTOM LINE

God isn't looking for perfection—He's looking for trust. Like Abraham, when we believe Him, He counts us as righteous. That's grace.

PRAYER

Heavenly Father, thank You for loving me even when I mess up. Help me trust in Your promises like Abraham did, and remind me that I don't have to earn Your love—I just need to believe. Teach me to walk in forgiveness and choose peace over pride. In Jesus' Name, Amen.

December 6

When Trust Gets Real

3-Year-Bible Reading: Proverbs 29:11–12; Psalm 139; Genesis 22:1–18; Hebrews 11:17–19

"A fool gives full vent to his spirit, but a wise man quietly holds it back." — Proverbs 29:11

"Search me, O God, and know my heart! Try me and know my thoughts!" — Psalm 139:23

"By faith Abraham, when he was tested, offered up Isaac…considering that God was able even to raise him from the dead." — Hebrews 11:17, 19

Ever had one of those moments when everything in you wanted to scream, "This doesn't make sense!"—but you had to trust someone anyway? That's kind of what Abraham faced in **Genesis 22**. God asked him to do something that seemed impossible and even cruel. Give up his son? Yet Abraham obeyed, believing somehow God would still keep His promise. That's a level of trust most of us can't even imagine.

But what if faith like that isn't just for ancient heroes? What if God wants us to learn to trust Him that deeply—even when life is confusing or hard? It starts with knowing that God sees every part of us (like in **Psalm 139**) and teaches us to respond with wisdom and self-control (see **Proverbs 29:11**) instead of letting fear or frustration rule us.

Think About It

1. **Faith When It's Hard:** Abraham trusted God even when the command seemed crazy. What would it look like for you to trust God in a situation where you don't understand what He's doing?

2. **God Knows You Fully:** Psalm 139 reminds us that God sees our thoughts, our fears, and our hearts. Do you believe that God understands what you're going through better than anyone else?

3. **Control vs. Chaos:** Proverbs 29:11 talks about the difference between reacting emotionally and responding wisely. How can you practice pausing and praying before reacting in a tough moment?

Bottom Line

Real trust in God shows up when life doesn't make sense. He sees you, He knows your heart, and He's working even when you don't understand. Faith means choosing His way—even when it's hard.

Prayer

Heavenly Father, sometimes life feels confusing, and trusting You isn't easy. Help me remember that You see me, know me, and love me. Teach me to trust You like Abraham did and to respond with faith, not fear. Shape my heart to follow You, even when the road isn't clear. In Jesus' Name, Amen.

December 7

When Life Doesn't Make Sense

3-Year-Bible Reading: Proverbs 29:13–14; Genesis 41–45

"The poor man and the oppressor meet together; the Lord gives light to the eyes of both. If a king faithfully judges the poor, his throne will be established forever." — Proverbs 29:13–14

"And Pharaoh said to Joseph, 'See, I have set you over all the land of Egypt.'" — Genesis 41:41

"And Joseph said to his brothers, 'Come near to me, please.' And they came near. And he said, 'I am your brother, Joseph, whom you sold into Egypt.'" — Genesis 45:4

Have you ever felt like your life was way off track? Like things weren't just unfair—they were totally upside down? Joseph probably felt that way too. He was sold into slavery by his own brothers, falsely accused, and thrown in prison. But through all of it, God was working.

In **Genesis 41–45**, we see Joseph rise from prisoner to second-in-command in Egypt. And instead of getting revenge on his brothers, he forgives them. Why? Because he saw that God had a bigger plan. Even when things didn't make sense, God was still in control. That's also what **Proverbs 29:13–14** reminds us: whether you're struggling or in power, God is the one who gives light and sees it all.

Think About It

1. **God sees both sides:** Whether you're going through a hard time or doing well, **Proverbs 29:13** says God gives light to both the poor and the powerful. How does that change the way you see others—or your own situation?

2. **Purpose in the pain:** Joseph could have given up in the pit or in prison. But he trusted God. What hard things in your life might God be using for something bigger?

3. **Forgiveness is powerful:** Joseph didn't hold a grudge. He saw how God used even his brothers' betrayal for good. Is there someone you need to forgive, trusting God to work in the situation?

Bottom Line

Even when life feels confusing or unfair, God is working behind the scenes. He sees you, He's with you, and He has a plan that's bigger than what you can see right now.

Prayer

Heavenly Father, thank You for seeing me, even when life doesn't make sense. Help me trust that You are in control, just like You were with Joseph. Give me courage to forgive, to wait on Your timing, and to believe that You are working everything out for good. In Jesus' Name, Amen.

December 8

Listening Matters

3-Year-Bible Reading: Proverbs 29:15,17; Psalm 140; Deuteronomy 18:15–19; Acts 3

"The rod and reproof give wisdom, but a child left to himself brings shame to his mother… Discipline your son, and he will give you rest; he will give delight to your heart." — Proverbs 29:15,17

"I know that the Lord will maintain the cause of the afflicted, and will execute justice for the needy." — Psalm 140:12

"The Lord your God will raise up for you a prophet like me from among you, from your brothers—it is to him you shall listen." — Deuteronomy 18:15

"You are the sons of the prophets and of the covenant that God made with your fathers… God, having raised up his servant, sent him to you first, to bless you by turning every one of you from your wickedness." — Acts 3:25–26

It's easy to tune out advice, especially when it comes from parents, teachers, or anyone who seems like they're just trying to control your life. But the truth is, God often speaks through those voices to guide you toward what's best.

In **Deuteronomy 18**, God promised to send a prophet we should listen to. That prophet is Jesus, and He's not just someone to admire—He's someone to *listen to*. When we ignore His voice, we miss out on healing, wisdom, and real life change. In **Acts 3**, Peter calls people to turn from their ways and listen to Jesus, the one sent to bless them. And in **Proverbs 29**, we're reminded that discipline—though it might not feel great—actually leads to wisdom and peace.

Think About It

1. **Who Are You Listening To?** Are the voices influencing your life pointing you toward Jesus, or away from Him? It's worth checking whose opinions you value most.

2. **Discipline = Love:** What if correction isn't rejection, but actually God's way of loving you? Proverbs reminds us that loving discipline leads to rest, not stress.

3. **Jesus Speaks—Do You Hear Him?** In a noisy world full of distractions, make time to listen to the voice of the one sent to bless and lead you.

Bottom Line

God uses discipline, His Word, and even others to help us grow in wisdom. Jesus is the promised one we're called to listen to—and when we do, He leads us into blessing, not burden.

Prayer

Heavenly Father, thank You for loving me enough to guide me—even when it comes through correction. Help me not to tune out Your voice, but to truly listen to Jesus and follow His way. Teach me to recognize Your wisdom in the people You've placed in my life. Give me a heart that welcomes truth and a desire to walk in it. In Jesus' Name, Amen.

December 9

Freedom Starts with Vision

3-Year-Bible Reading: Proverbs 29:16,18; Exodus 12; 1 Corinthians 5:7–8

"When the wicked increase, transgression increases, but the righteous will look upon their downfall. Where there is no prophetic vision the people cast off restraint, but blessed is he who keeps the law." — Proverbs 29:16,18

"It is the Lord's Passover… The blood shall be a sign for you, on the houses where you are. And when I see the blood, I will pass over you." — Exodus 12:11b,13

"Cleanse out the old leaven that you may be a new lump, as you really are unleavened. For Christ, our Passover lamb, has been sacrificed. Let us therefore celebrate the festival… with the unleavened bread of sincerity and truth." — 1 Corinthians 5:7–8

Have you ever felt like your life was running on autopilot, just reacting to things instead of living with purpose? That's what **Proverbs 29:18** is getting at—when people don't have vision, they end up going wherever the crowd leads.

In **Exodus 12**, God gave Israel a new beginning with the first Passover. They were leaving behind a life of slavery and stepping into freedom. But they couldn't just walk away—they had to follow God's instructions and trust His plan. Fast forward to **1 Corinthians 5**, and Paul reminds us that Jesus is *our* Passover Lamb. He's the reason we can live differently. If you're a follower of Jesus, you're not meant to blend in or stay stuck in the past. You've been set free—for real purpose.

Think About It

1. **Where's Your Vision?** Are you just surviving, or are you living with purpose? God's Word gives you vision, direction, and clarity. Without it, it's easy to fall into things that hold you back.

2. **Passover Points to Jesus:** Just like the Israelites marked their doors with lamb's blood to be protected, Jesus' sacrifice marks us as His. His blood means we're covered, forgiven, and free.

3. **Clean Out the Old Stuff:** Paul talks about getting rid of "old leaven," which represents sin and bad habits. What's something you need to let go of so you can live in "sincerity and truth"?

Bottom Line

Jesus, our Passover Lamb, has set us free—not just from sin, but for a life with vision, purpose, and truth.

Prayer

Heavenly Father, thank You for giving me a new start through Jesus. Help me live with purpose, guided by Your Word. Show me what I need to let go of so I can fully walk in the freedom You've given me. I want to live a life that's sincere, honest, and pleasing to You. In Jesus' Name, Amen.

December 10

Fire, Freedom, and Faith

3-Year-Bible Reading: Proverbs 29:19, 21; Exodus 19–20; Hebrews 12:18–29; Romans 8:1–4

"By mere words a servant is not disciplined, for though he understands, he will not respond." — Proverbs 29:19

"Now therefore, if you will indeed obey my voice and keep my covenant, you shall be my treasured possession among all peoples." — Exodus 19:5

"Indeed, so terrifying was the sight that Moses said, 'I tremble with fear.'" — Hebrews 12:21

"There is therefore now no condemnation for those who are in Christ Jesus." — Romans 8:1

Ever been in trouble but didn't really understand *why* until someone actually showed you, not just told you? That's what Proverbs is getting at—sometimes words aren't enough. We need more than rules—we need relationship, truth, and transformation. In **Exodus 19–20**, God's people were terrified at His power on Mount Sinai, where He gave them the Ten Commandments. The scene was intense—fire, smoke, thunder. But it wasn't just for show. God was revealing His holiness and His desire for His people to live differently.

Fast forward to **Hebrews 12**, and we see how things have changed because of Jesus. We're no longer standing at a mountain of fear—we've been invited to one of grace and joy. And thanks to Jesus, **Romans 8** says we don't have to live in fear of condemnation anymore. Instead, we walk in the Spirit, with freedom and peace.

Think About It

1. **Fear vs. Freedom:** In Exodus, people feared God's presence. In Jesus, we're invited into it. Are you living like God is someone to run from or run to?

2. **Rules or Relationship?** God didn't just give commandments—He wanted a covenant, a relationship. Are you more focused on "being good" or being close to God?

3. **No Condemnation:** Romans 8:1 is a game-changer. If you're in Christ, guilt doesn't get the last word. Do you believe you're free, or are you still carrying shame Jesus already paid for?

Bottom Line

God is holy and powerful, but through Jesus, we are invited into His presence without fear. You're not stuck in the rules—you're free to live by the Spirit, with purpose, confidence, and peace.

Prayer

Heavenly Father, thank You for showing me that Your holiness isn't meant to scare me but to draw me into something greater. Thank You for sending Jesus to take away my condemnation and invite me into freedom. Help me to live in step with Your Spirit and remember that I am fully loved, fully forgiven, and fully Yours. In Jesus' Name, Amen.

December 11

Watch Your Words

3-Year-Bible Reading: Proverbs 29:20; Exodus 40:18–30; Hebrews 8–9; Revelation 21:1–4

Do you see a man who is hasty in his words? There is more hope for a fool than for him. — Proverbs 29:20

Moses erected the tabernacle... just as the Lord had commanded Moses. — Exodus 40:18, 30

He entered once for all into the holy places... by means of his own blood, thus securing an eternal redemption. — Hebrews 9:12

He will wipe away every tear from their eyes, and death shall be no more... for the former things have passed away. — Revelation 21:4

Ever said something and instantly regretted it? Maybe it was a harsh word in an argument, or a snap judgment on social media. Proverbs **29:20** warns us that quick words can lead to foolish outcomes. But today's readings remind us that God has a better plan—not just for our words, but for our whole lives.

In **Exodus 40**, Moses follows God's instructions to set up the tabernacle exactly as he was told. It wasn't rushed. It was thoughtful, obedient, and holy. Then in **Hebrews 9**, we're reminded that Jesus went into the heavenly tabernacle once and for all, offering His own blood to redeem us forever. And finally, in **Revelation 21**, we get a glimpse of the future—no more pain, no more crying, just God living with us in perfect peace.

Think About It

1. **Slow Down:** When you feel like blurting something out, pause and ask, "Will this help or hurt?" Proverbs warns that hasty words can make us look foolish—and worse, they can wound others.

2. **Obey Fully:** Moses didn't set up the tabernacle halfway or his own way—he did it *just as the Lord commanded.* How are you doing with following God's instructions in your daily life?

3. **Live with Hope:** Hebrews reminds us that Jesus already paid the price for our mistakes. Revelation gives us a picture of our future with Him. How does knowing your future is secure change how you live today?

Bottom Line

God calls us to live with purpose, speak with wisdom, and trust in the hope Jesus gives us—because He's already done the hard work of making a way for us to live forever with Him.

Prayer

Heavenly Father, thank You for giving me wisdom through Your Word. Help me to pause and think before I speak, to obey You even in the small things, and to hold tightly to the hope of eternity with You. Teach me to walk each day knowing You are with me now and forever. In Jesus' Name, Amen.

December 12

Check Your Heart Before You Speak

3-Year-Bible Reading: Proverbs 29:22; Psalm 89:1–37; 2 Samuel 7

"A man of wrath stirs up strife, and one given to anger causes much transgression." — Proverbs 29:22

"I will sing of the steadfast love of the Lord, forever; with my mouth I will make known your faithfulness to all generations." — Psalm 89:1

"And your house and your kingdom shall be made sure forever before me. Your throne shall be established forever." — 2 Samuel 7:16

Have you ever said something in the heat of the moment and immediately regretted it? Maybe it was during an argument with a friend, a parent, or even just venting online. We've all been there. Proverbs reminds us that uncontrolled anger doesn't just hurt others—it leads us into sin. But there's good news: God doesn't give up on us when we mess up.

In **Psalm 89**, we're reminded that God's love is steady and faithful, no matter what. And in **2 Samuel 7**, we see God making a lasting promise to David, even though David was far from perfect. God isn't looking for perfection—He's looking for hearts that trust Him, even in the mess.

Think About It

1. **Anger Isn't Always Worth It:** Proverbs 29:22 warns us about letting anger control our actions. What situations usually trigger your temper? What can you do to pause and respond differently?

2. **Remember God's Faithfulness:** Psalm 89 talks about singing of God's love forever. When has God shown you His faithfulness—even when you didn't deserve it?

3. **God's Promises Are Stronger Than Our Mistakes:** In 2 Samuel 7, God promised David a forever kingdom. That promise was fulfilled in Jesus! How does knowing God keeps His promises give you confidence in your own journey?

Bottom Line

When you feel overwhelmed by anger or frustration, remember that God offers peace, love, and promises that never fail. Trust Him more than your emotions.

Prayer

Heavenly Father, thank You for being patient with me, even when I lose control of my emotions. Help me to pause, breathe, and seek Your wisdom instead of reacting in anger. Thank You for Your faithfulness and for keeping Your promises, even when I fall short. Fill my heart with Your peace and love so I can reflect You to others. In Jesus' Name, Amen.

December 13

The Upside-Down Crown

3-Year-Bible Reading: Proverbs 29:23; Psalm 141; Isaiah 7:14; Isaiah 9:1–7; Isaiah 11:1–10

One's pride will bring him low, but he who is lowly in spirit will obtain honor. — Proverbs 29:23

Set a guard, O Lord, over my mouth; keep watch over the door of my lips! — Psalm 141:3

Behold, the virgin shall conceive and bear a son, and shall call his name Immanuel. — Isaiah 7:14

For to us a child is born, to us a son is given… and his name shall be called Wonderful Counselor, Mighty God, Everlasting Father, Prince of Peace. — Isaiah 9:6

There shall come forth a shoot from the stump of Jesse, and a branch from his roots shall bear fruit. — Isaiah 11:1

We usually think of power, popularity, and confidence as signs of success. But **Proverbs 29:23** flips that idea upside down: it says that pride actually brings people low, while humility leads to honor. That's not just a good quote—it's God's truth. And the most powerful example? Jesus.

Isaiah 7:14 tells us Jesus was born in the most unexpected way—not in a palace but through a virgin, in a tiny town. The King of Kings didn't arrive with loud fanfare or military power. He came as a baby—weak, quiet, and humble. But that baby would change the world.

Isaiah 9 paints Jesus as our "Prince of Peace," and **Isaiah 11** describes Him as a new shoot growing from what looked like a dead tree—bringing life, hope, and justice. That's God's way: not through hype or ego, but through humility, wisdom, and love.

Think About It

1. **Pride vs. Honor:** Where in your life do you feel tempted to show off or act like you've got it all together? How might humility actually lead to something greater?

2. **Watch Your Words:** Psalm 141 reminds us that our mouths matter. Are your words building others up or tearing them down?

3. **Jesus' Example:** How does Jesus' humble birth and life challenge the world's idea of what it means to be "great"?

Bottom Line

True greatness isn't about being the loudest, the coolest, or the most followed—it's about living like Jesus: humble, loving, and full of peace.

Prayer

Heavenly Father, help me not to chase pride or popularity, but to follow the example of Jesus. Teach me to speak with kindness, to live with humility, and to trust that Your way leads to true honor. Remind me that greatness in Your Kingdom looks different—and better—than the world's version. In Jesus' Name, Amen.

DECEMBER 14

Fear or Freedom?

3-Year-Bible Reading: Proverbs 29:24–25; Psalm 142; Jeremiah 23:1–5; Jeremiah 30:1–9; Jeremiah 33:14–26

"The fear of man lays a snare, but whoever trusts in the Lord is safe." — Proverbs 29:25

"I cry to you, O Lord; I say, 'You are my refuge, my portion in the land of the living.'" — Psalm 142:5

"Behold, the days are coming, declares the Lord, when I will raise up for David a righteous Branch, and he shall reign as king and deal wisely..." — Jeremiah 23:5

"It shall come to pass in that day, declares the Lord of hosts, that I will break his yoke from off your neck..." — Jeremiah 30:8

"I will restore the fortunes of Jacob and have mercy on his dwellings..." — Jeremiah 33:26

Ever feel like you're stuck trying to please people—parents, teachers, friends, or even just your social media followers? It's like there's this invisible pressure to be perfect, cool, or always right. **Proverbs 29:25** calls that trap "the fear of man." It's real—and it can take over your thoughts, your choices, and your sense of who you are. But God's Word doesn't leave us there. Instead, it points us to something better: freedom that comes from trusting Him.

King David knew what it felt like to be overwhelmed by fear and pressure. In **Psalm 142**, he's hiding in a cave, running for his life. But even there, he cries out to God, calling Him his *refuge* and *portion*. He chose to trust God when everything felt dark.

Jeremiah's writings might seem distant at first glance, but they're all about hope and restoration. In a time when God's people were broken and exiled, He promised a King—the Righteous Branch—who would reign with wisdom (**Jeremiah 23:5**). That King is Jesus. Through Him, the chains of fear, sin, and shame are broken. When we follow Him, we're not stuck in fear—we're walking in freedom.

THINK ABOUT IT

1. **Who are you trying to please?** Is fear of what others think keeping you from living boldly for Jesus? God wants to set you free from that snare.
2. **Where do you run when life gets hard?** Like David in the cave, do you go to God as your refuge, or try to fix everything on your own?
3. **Jesus is your freedom:** Jeremiah's promise of a righteous King is fulfilled in Jesus. Are you letting Him lead your life with wisdom and love?

BOTTOM LINE

You don't have to live in fear of what others think. True safety and freedom come when you trust in Jesus, your refuge and King.

PRAYER

Heavenly Father, thank You for being my refuge and the One I can always trust. Help me to stop living for the approval of others and start living in the freedom You offer through Jesus. Thank You for breaking every chain and calling me to walk with You. Give me boldness to follow You today. In Jesus' Name, Amen.

DECEMBER 15

The Unexpected King

3-Year-Bible Reading: Proverbs 29:26–27; Psalm 143; Hosea 3:4–5; Micah 5:2–5a; Zechariah 9:9; John 12:12–16

"Many seek the face of a ruler, but it is from the Lord that a man gets justice." — Proverbs 29:26

"For the children of Israel shall dwell many days without king or prince… Afterward the children of Israel shall return and seek the Lord their God, and David their king, and they shall come in fear to the Lord and to his goodness in the latter days." — Hosea 3:4–5

"Rejoice greatly, O daughter of Zion! Shout aloud, O daughter of Jerusalem! Behold, your king is coming to you; righteous and having salvation is he, humble and mounted on a donkey." — Zechariah 9:9

"And Jesus found a young donkey and sat on it, just as it is written, 'Fear not, daughter of Zion; behold, your king is coming, sitting on a donkey's colt!'" — John 12:14–15

When you think of a king or a hero, what comes to mind? Probably someone powerful, impressive, maybe even a bit intimidating. In today's readings, though, we're reminded that God often flips our expectations.

While people seek justice from rulers (**Proverbs 29:26**), real justice and hope come from the Lord. Israel waited a long time for a king—not just any king, but *the* King. And when He came, He didn't roll up in a chariot with a sword. He rode in on a donkey, humble and peaceful (**Zechariah 9:9, John 12:14–15**). This is the unexpected beauty of Jesus: He came not to crush enemies but to save us, not to rule with fear but with love.

Think About It

1. **Who are you trusting for justice?** It's easy to put our hope in leaders, influencers, or systems to make things right. But how often do we look to God first?

2. **Jesus doesn't fit the mold:** The King of kings came riding a donkey. Are you open to God working in your life in ways you don't expect?

3. **Peace in the middle of the storm: Psalm 143** shows someone crying out in distress. Are you inviting Jesus—the peaceful King—into your hardest moments?

Bottom Line

Jesus is the King we didn't expect but exactly the one we need—humble, loving, and just. Trust Him to lead your heart, especially when the world feels confusing or unfair.

Prayer

Heavenly Father, thank You for sending Jesus, our humble King. Help me trust You when things don't make sense and follow You even when the path looks different than I imagined. Remind me that real hope and justice come from You, not from the world around me. In Jesus' Name, Amen.

December 16

Chosen to Shine

3-Year-Bible Reading: Proverbs 30:1–4; Isaiah 42:1–7; Isaiah 49:5–6; Matthew 12:14–21

"Who has ascended to heaven and come down? Who has gathered the wind in his fists? Who has wrapped up the waters in a garment? Who has established all the ends of the earth? What is his name, and what is his son's name? Surely you know!" — Proverbs 30:4

"Behold my servant, whom I uphold, my chosen, in whom my soul delights; I have put my Spirit upon him; he will bring forth justice to the nations." — Isaiah 42:1

"I will make you as a light for the nations, that my salvation may reach to the end of the earth." — Isaiah 49:6

"And in his name the Gentiles will hope." — Matthew 12:21

Ever feel like the world is too messed up for one person to make a difference? Like, what can one teen really do with all the injustice, hurt, and confusion around us? You're not alone. The Bible reminds us over and over that we're not just here to survive life—we're here to shine light into it.

In **Proverbs 30**, we see a glimpse of God's majesty and power—a reminder that the Creator of the universe isn't distant. He has a Son, Jesus, who brings hope to the world. In **Isaiah 42** and **Isaiah 49**, God talks about His chosen servant, filled with His Spirit, sent to bring justice and light. And in **Matthew 12**, Jesus is revealed as that servant—the hope for everyone. What's crazy amazing? If we follow Jesus, we get to reflect that same light.

Think About It

1. **God's Power, Your Purpose:** If God, who holds the wind and the seas, chose Jesus to bring hope—what does that say about what He can do through you?

2. **You Were Made to Shine:** Isaiah says God's servant is a "light to the nations." Jesus fulfilled that—but He also calls *you* to be a light (see **Matthew 5:14–16**). How are you shining right now?

3. **Hope Has a Name:** The world is craving hope. In **Matthew 12**, we're reminded that hope is found in Jesus' name. How can you share that hope with someone this week?

Bottom Line

God chose Jesus to bring light and justice to the world—and if you belong to Him, you're chosen to reflect that light. You don't need to be perfect or powerful. You just need to be willing to shine where you are.

Prayer

Heavenly Father, Thank You for sending Jesus to be the light and hope for the world. Sometimes it's hard to believe You can use someone like me to make a difference, but I trust that You've chosen me for a purpose. Help me to shine Your light in my school, my family, and my friendships. Fill me with Your Spirit so I can be a reflection of Your love and justice wherever I go. In Jesus' Name, Amen.

December 17

Faith in the Desert

3-Year-Bible Reading: Proverbs 30:5–6; Psalm 144; Isaiah 35:1–6; Matthew 11:1–6

Every word of God proves true; he is a shield to those who take refuge in him. — Proverbs 30:5

The wilderness and the dry land shall be glad; the desert shall rejoice and blossom like the crocus... they shall see the glory of the Lord, the majesty of our God. — Isaiah 35:1–2

And Jesus answered them, "Go and tell John what you hear and see: the blind receive their sight and the lame walk... and the poor have good news preached to them." — Matthew 11:4–5

Have you ever felt stuck in a "dry season" where everything seems hard, hope feels far away, and God seems silent? It might be a tough class, family drama, or just feeling overwhelmed and alone. But God hasn't forgotten you. The Bible paints a powerful picture in **Isaiah 35**—even the driest desert can bloom with life again when God steps in.

And in **Matthew 11**, Jesus reminds John the Baptist (who was stuck in prison and probably doubting everything) that God's power is real, and His promises are being fulfilled—even if it doesn't look like we expected. When we're struggling, these scriptures remind us that God's word is true (**Proverbs 30**) and His goodness shows up even in hard places.

Think About It

1. **God's Word Never Fails:** Do you believe that *every word of God proves true* (Proverbs 30:5)? What would it look like to take refuge in His promises today?

2. **Hope in Hard Places:** Isaiah talks about deserts blooming. Where in your life does it feel like a desert? How can you invite God into that space and trust Him to bring beauty out of the struggle?

3. **Jesus Sees You:** John needed reassurance, and Jesus didn't shame him—He reminded him of the truth. If you're feeling doubt or fear, don't hide it. Bring it to Jesus. He can handle your questions.

Bottom Line

God's promises are real, His presence shows up in our hardest seasons, and He's working—even when we can't see it.

Prayer

Heavenly Father, thank You for being with me, even when life feels dry or confusing. Help me trust Your promises and remember that You are always working for good, even when things are tough. Help me to see the beauty You're growing, even in my deserts. In Jesus' Name, Amen.

December 18

Not Too Much, Not Too Little

3-Year-Bible Reading: Proverbs 30:7–9; Psalm 118:22–23; Matthew 21:33–46

"Two things I ask of you; deny them not to me before I die: Remove far from me falsehood and lying; give me neither poverty nor riches; feed me with the food that is needful for me."— Proverbs 30:7–8

"The stone that the builders rejected has become the cornerstone. This is the Lord's doing; it is marvelous in our eyes."— Psalm 118:22–23

"Have you never read in the Scriptures: 'The stone that the builders rejected has become the cornerstone; this was the Lord's doing, and it is marvelous in our eyes?'"— Matthew 21:42

Sometimes we dream of having it all—more money, more popularity, more success. But Proverbs 30 reminds us of a different kind of wisdom: asking God for just enough, not too much or too little. Why? Because too much can make us forget God, and too little might tempt us to dishonor Him. It's all about staying in a place of trust and dependence on Him.

In **Psalm 118**, we see that what the world rejects, God can turn into the most important thing—the cornerstone. Jesus refers to this in **Matthew 21**, showing how He was rejected by many but became the foundation of salvation. These verses together call us to trust God with our needs, our identity, and even the moments when we feel overlooked or underestimated.

THINK ABOUT IT

1. **What Are You Asking For?** Are you more focused on asking God for stuff, or for the strength to trust Him daily? Proverbs reminds us that the best prayers aren't always for more, but for what's *right*.

2. **Feeling Rejected?** Just like Jesus was rejected, sometimes we feel left out or not chosen. But remember: rejection isn't the end of your story. God can turn what seems like failure into something powerful.

3. **Who's the Cornerstone in Your Life?** A cornerstone is the first stone laid in a building—the one everything else is built on. Is Jesus the foundation of your decisions, dreams, and identity?

BOTTOM LINE

God doesn't always give us everything we want, but He always gives us what we *need*—including purpose in rejection, strength in simplicity, and Jesus as the foundation for our lives.

PRAYER

Heavenly Father, help me to be content with what You give and to trust You whether I have a lot or a little. Teach me to see value in Your plan, even when others don't see it. Make Jesus the foundation of my life and guide my heart to depend fully on You. In Jesus' Name, Amen.

December 19

Betrayed for a Price

3-Year-Bible Reading: Proverbs 30:10; Psalm 145; Psalm 41:9; Zechariah 11:12–13; Matthew 26:14–15

"Even my close friend in whom I trusted, who ate my bread, has lifted his heel against me." — Psalm 41:9

"Then I said to them, 'If it seems good to you, give me my wages; but if not, keep them.' And they weighed out as my wages thirty pieces of silver. Then the Lord said to me, 'Throw it to the potter'—the lordly price at which I was priced by them." — Zechariah 11:12–13

"Then one of the twelve, whose name was Judas Iscariot, went to the chief priests and said, 'What will you give me if I deliver him over to you?' And they paid him thirty pieces of silver." — Matthew 26:14–15

Have you ever had someone betray your trust—maybe a friend who turned their back on you or said something behind your back? It stings, right? In **Psalm 41:9**, David talks about this pain, and it points ahead to the ultimate betrayal of Jesus by Judas. The price? Thirty pieces of silver—just like the symbolic amount in **Zechariah 11**.

Jesus, the one who healed the sick, loved the outcasts, and never sinned, was sold out by a close friend in **Matthew 26**. And yet, through all of this, God's plan of redemption was unfolding. When betrayal enters our lives, it's easy to feel crushed, but the story of Jesus shows us that even betrayal can be part of a bigger story—one of love, grace, and ultimate victory.

Think About It

1. **Recognizing Betrayal Hurts:** Jesus knows what it's like to be betrayed. If you're dealing with that pain, you're not alone. How does knowing Jesus experienced betrayal help you deal with your own?

2. **God's Plan is Bigger:** Judas saw a quick reward; God saw redemption. How might God be using a difficult situation in your life for something bigger?

3. **Faithfulness Over Fame:** In a world where popularity can tempt us to trade loyalty for likes, what would it look like to be a faithful friend like Jesus?

Bottom Line

Even when people fail us, God never does. He sees the hurt, knows the whole story, and can turn betrayal into a breakthrough.

Prayer

Heavenly Father, thank You for understanding what it's like to be hurt by someone close. Help me to forgive like You do and to stay faithful even when others aren't. Remind me that You never leave me and that Your plans are always greater than the pain. In Jesus' Name, Amen.

December 20

No Respect, No Rest

3-Year-Bible Reading: Proverbs 30:11–14; Psalm 22; Isaiah 53

"There are those who curse their fathers and do not bless their mothers. There are those who are clean in their own eyes but are not washed of their filth." —Proverbs 30:11–12

"But I am a worm and not a man, scorned by mankind and despised by the people." —Psalm 22:6

"He was despised and rejected by men; a man of sorrows and acquainted with grief... he has borne our griefs and carried our sorrows." —Isaiah 53:3–4

Ever felt like no one gets you? Like people don't really see what you're going through—or worse, they just write you off? In **Psalm 22**, we hear someone crying out, "Why have you forsaken me?" It's raw, honest, and painfully familiar. When you're going through stuff—family drama, pressure at school, feeling invisible—it's easy to think no one cares.

Isaiah 53 shows us that Jesus *knows* what rejection feels like. He was misunderstood, judged unfairly, and pushed aside—just like we sometimes are. **Proverbs 30** reminds us how broken this world is, with people who dishonor parents, act like they're flawless, and treat others with arrogance. But in the middle of all that mess, God sees us, carries our pain, and offers a better way.

Think About It

1. **Respect Starts With the Heart:** Proverbs talks about dishonor in families. How do you treat your parents or people in authority, even when it's hard? Our attitude toward others reflects what's really in our hearts.

2. **Jesus Gets It:** Isaiah 53 reminds us that Jesus didn't just suffer physically—He went through emotional pain and rejection. When you feel alone, remember He's been there. He's not distant; He's deeply personal.

3. **It's Not Just About You:** The people described in Proverbs 30 think they're clean, but they're not. Sometimes we ignore our own faults and focus on others. What's one area where you need to be real with God today?

Bottom Line

Even when people let you down or make you feel invisible, Jesus sees you, knows your pain, and chose to carry it for you. Respect isn't just about behavior—it's about reflecting the heart of the One who loved us even when we were at our worst.

Prayer

Heavenly Father, thank You for seeing me when I feel overlooked. Thank You, Jesus, for choosing to carry my pain and not turning away from my struggles. Help me to respect others, even when it's tough, and to be honest with You about where I fall short. Teach me to love like You do. In Jesus' Name, Amen.

December 21

Unshakable Hope

3-Year-Bible Reading: Proverbs 30:15–17; Psalm 146; Psalm 16:8–11; Acts 2:22–39

"The leech has two daughters: Give and Give. Three things are never satisfied; four never say, 'Enough.'" — Proverbs 30:15

"Put not your trust in princes, in a son of man, in whom there is no salvation… Blessed is he whose help is the God of Jacob, whose hope is in the Lord his God." — Psalm 146:3, 5

"I have set the Lord always before me; because he is at my right hand, I shall not be shaken." — Psalm 16:8

"Let all the house of Israel therefore know for certain that God has made him both Lord and Christ, this Jesus whom you crucified… Repent and be baptized every one of you in the name of Jesus Christ for the forgiveness of your sins." — Acts 2:36, 38

Have you ever wanted something so badly you couldn't stop thinking about it? A new phone, popularity, the perfect grades, or the approval of someone you admire? We live in a world that constantly tells us we need more to be happy. But **Proverbs 30:15** reminds us that the desire for more—like the leech—never says "enough."

In contrast, **Psalm 146** and **Psalm 16** show us where real security and satisfaction come from: putting our trust in God. **Acts 2** reveals how that trust becomes real through Jesus—our Savior, our unshakable hope.

Think About It

1. **What Are You Chasing?** The world screams "more!" but God whispers "I'm enough." Are there things you're chasing that will never satisfy you? Take a moment to reflect on whether your priorities are helping you grow closer to Jesus.

2. **God Doesn't Change:** People, trends, and even your feelings can be unreliable. Psalm 146 reminds us not to put our ultimate trust in people, but in God—who is always faithful and never fails.

3. **Real Life Starts With Jesus:** In **Acts 2**, Peter tells the crowd they need to repent and be baptized because Jesus is Lord. When we choose Jesus, we receive more than momentary satisfaction—we get forgiveness, purpose, and eternal life.

Bottom Line

Chasing the things of this world will always leave you empty. But when you set the Lord always before you, like David did in **Psalm 16**, you can live with confidence and joy that can't be shaken.

Prayer

Heavenly Father, help me recognize the things in my life that are never enough. Teach me to stop chasing what can't satisfy and to place my hope fully in You. Thank You for giving me Jesus—the only One who can save, satisfy, and give me true life. I want to trust You more every day. In Jesus' Name, Amen.

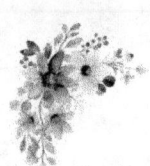

December 22

Mystery, Fire, and the Messenger

3-Year-Bible Reading: Proverbs 30:18–20; Isaiah 40:1–8; Malachi 3:1–5; Malachi 4:1–6; Matthew 11:7–15

"Three things are too wonderful for me; four I do not understand: the way of an eagle in the sky, the way of a serpent on a rock, the way of a ship on the high seas, and the way of a man with a virgin." — Proverbs 30:18–19

"A voice cries: 'In the wilderness prepare the way of the Lord; make straight in the desert a highway for our God.'" — Isaiah 40:3

"Behold, I send my messenger, and he will prepare the way before me." — Malachi 3:1

"Truly, I say to you, among those born of women there has arisen no one greater than John the Baptist." — Matthew 11:11

There's something captivating about a good mystery—whether it's a plot twist in your favorite show or trying to understand why people act the way they do. **Proverbs 30** talks about the wonder of things we don't fully get, like how love works or why certain things move us deeply. **Isaiah 40** and **Malachi 3** bring up another kind of mystery: the arrival of God's messenger, preparing the way for something huge.

Fast forward to **Matthew 11**, and we find out that John the Baptist was *that* messenger—bold, gritty, a little wild, and completely focused on getting people ready for Jesus. But even John had doubts sometimes. So, what does it mean to prepare for Jesus—and to recognize Him when He shows up?

Think About It

1. **Preparation Takes Action:** John the Baptist wasn't just talking—he lived differently to help people wake up spiritually. What are some ways you can "prepare the way" for God in your life today?

2. **God Works Through Messengers:** John had a purpose: to point people to Jesus. You don't have to be famous to do the same. Who in your life might need hope, comfort, or truth—and could *you* be the one to share it?

3. **Not Always What We Expect:** People expected a flashy king, but Jesus came quietly, healing and teaching. Are you open to seeing God work in unexpected ways—in your school, your friendships, or even your struggles?

Bottom Line

God sends messengers to prepare us—but we have to be willing to listen, even when the message challenges us. Like John the Baptist, we're invited to live lives that point people to Jesus.

Prayer

Heavenly Father, help me to recognize Your voice and Your messengers in my life. Give me courage to live in a way that prepares the way for others to know You. Even when I don't understand everything, help me trust that You are moving. In Jesus' Name, Amen.

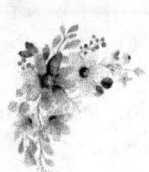

December 23

Small but Mighty

3-Year-Bible Reading: Proverbs 30:21–28; Psalm 147; Luke 1

"Four things on earth are small, but they are exceedingly wise: the ants are a people not strong, yet they provide their food in the summer." — Proverbs 30:24–25

"His delight is not in the strength of the horse, nor his pleasure in the legs of a man, but the Lord takes pleasure in those who fear him, in those who hope in his steadfast love." — Psalm 147:10–11

"For he who is mighty has done great things for me, and holy is his name." — Luke 1:49

Have you ever felt small, unnoticed, or like your voice doesn't carry much weight? Whether it's being overlooked at school, feeling awkward in your friend group, or wondering if God even sees you—know this: in the Bible, God constantly shows us how He uses the "small" things to make a big impact.

Proverbs 30 points out tiny creatures like ants and lizards that survive and thrive using wisdom and persistence. **Psalm 147** reminds us that God isn't impressed by outward strength, but by those who trust in Him. And in **Luke 1**, Mary, a young, humble girl, becomes the mother of Jesus—the Savior of the world—simply because she believed and said yes to God.

Think About It

1. **Small Doesn't Mean Powerless:** Like ants and lizards, even if you feel small, God can give you the wisdom and courage to do great things. What small choices can you make today that honor God?

2. **God Sees What Really Matters:** The world values strength, popularity, and appearance. But God values your heart. Are you putting more effort into how you look or into trusting and obeying God?

3. **Say Yes Like Mary:** Mary didn't have status or power, but she was willing. What's something God might be asking you to do—even if it feels scary or uncertain?

Bottom Line

God uses small, humble, and faithful people to do big things. You don't have to be the loudest, strongest, or most popular—just willing.

Prayer

Heavenly Father, thank You for reminding me that You see me, even when I feel small. Help me to trust You, to be wise in the little things, and to say yes when You call me. I want to live a life that brings You joy, even when no one else notices. In Jesus' Name, Amen.

December 24

God With Us

3-Year-Bible Reading: Matthew 1:18–25; Luke 2:1–20

"She will bear a son, and you shall call his name Jesus, for he will save his people from their sins." — Matthew 1:21

"And she gave birth to her firstborn son and wrapped him in swaddling cloths and laid him in a manger, because there was no place for them in the inn." — Luke 2:7

"And the angel said to them, 'Fear not, for behold, I bring you good news of great joy that will be for all the people.'" — Luke 2:10

Have you ever felt like things weren't going according to plan? Maybe your expectations got flipped upside down, or you were asked to do something way outside your comfort zone. Joseph and Mary definitely knew that feeling. Joseph didn't expect his fiancée to be pregnant by the Holy Spirit (**Matthew 1:18**), and Mary surely didn't picture giving birth in a stable. Yet, in the middle of this chaos, God was doing something amazing. He was sending Jesus, Emmanuel— *God with us*—to the world. And not just for kings or religious people, but for *everyone*. The first to hear the news were shepherds—ordinary, overlooked people—yet God invited them into the most important birth announcement in history.

Think About It

1. **God's Plans > Our Plans:** Joseph had to change his plans when God called him to raise Jesus. Are you open to God's direction, even when it's unexpected or challenging?

2. **No One Is Left Out:** The shepherds weren't the "important" people, yet they were the first to hear about Jesus' birth. What does that tell you about who God values?

3. **Real Joy:** The angel said Jesus' birth was "good news of great joy." What brings you joy right now? How can Jesus bring you a deeper, lasting joy?

Bottom Line

Even in the middle of uncertainty or messy situations, God is with you. Jesus came to be close, not distant—and He invites everyone, including you, to be part of His story.

Prayer

Heavenly Father, thank You for sending Jesus to be with us, even in our chaos and confusion. Help me trust You, even when life doesn't go the way I expect. Remind me that You are near and that I matter to You. Let the joy of Jesus fill my heart and guide my steps. In Jesus' Name, Amen.

December 25

Growing Up with Purpose

3-Year-Bible Reading: Matthew 2; Luke 2:21–52

"And going into the house they saw the child with Mary his mother, and they fell down and worshiped him." — Matthew 2:11

"And at the end of eight days, when he was circumcised, he was called Jesus, the name given by the angel before he was conceived in the womb." — Luke 2:21

"And Jesus increased in wisdom and in stature and in favor with God and man." — Luke 2:52

Ever feel like life is just one big "waiting to grow up" moment? Whether it's waiting to drive, finish school, or finally figure out who you are, the in-between years can feel confusing and frustrating. In **Luke 2**, we catch a glimpse of Jesus as a child and teenager. Even though He was the Son of God, He still went through the slow, steady process of growing up—learning, obeying His parents, and waiting for the right time to begin His mission.

In **Matthew 2**, we see how the wise men worshiped Jesus even as a small child, showing that God had big plans for Him from the start. Your life might feel ordinary, but like Jesus, God is growing something amazing in you too.

Think About It

1. **God Works in the Ordinary:** Jesus' early life included diaper changes, chores, and following His parents. What parts of your everyday life might God be using to shape your future?

2. **Obedience Builds Character:** Luke 2:51 says Jesus was obedient to His parents. How can respecting authority and making wise choices now prepare you for what's ahead?

3. **Jesus Understands You:** He didn't skip the teen years—He lived them. How does it help to know that Jesus understands what it feels like to grow up?

Bottom Line

Even in the slow, ordinary moments of life, God is doing something extraordinary in you—just like He did with Jesus.

Prayer

Heavenly Father, thank You for showing us that even Jesus had to grow up step by step. Help me be patient in the process and trust that You're shaping me into who You created me to be. Give me wisdom, courage, and obedience in the everyday. In Jesus' Name, Amen.

December 26

Courage in the Chaos

3-Year-Bible Reading: Proverbs 30:29–31; Daniel 7:9–14; Daniel 9:24–27; Mark 13

"Three things are stately in their tread; four are stately in their stride: the lion, which is mightiest among beasts and does not turn back before any…" — Proverbs 30:29–30

"And behold, with the clouds of heaven there came one like a son of man, and he came to the Ancient of Days and was presented before him. And to him was given dominion and glory and a kingdom…" — Daniel 7:13–14

"But when you see the abomination of desolation standing where he ought not to be… then let those who are in Judea flee to the mountains." — Mark 13:14

When you look at the world today, it might feel a little chaotic. Headlines can be scary, people argue about the future, and sometimes you might wonder what's really going on behind the scenes. In **Mark 13**, Jesus speaks honestly about hard times ahead, but He also points to hope. **Daniel 7** shows us a powerful vision of God's throne and the final victory of "one like a son of man"—a title Jesus used for Himself.

Meanwhile, **Proverbs 30** highlights bold, fearless creatures that carry themselves with purpose. These verses remind us that we're not meant to live in fear, but to walk with confidence because Jesus reigns. He's not surprised by anything happening now or in the future. And He's coming back.

Think About It

1. **Who's in control?** Daniel's visions may sound intense, but they all point to this truth: God sits on the throne. Even when the world feels upside down, Jesus has already won the ultimate victory.

2. **Live bold like the lion:** Proverbs describes the lion as "not turning back before any." What would it look like for you to face your fears with that kind of courage—trusting that God's got your back?

3. **Jesus prepares us, not scares us:** Mark 13 isn't about freaking out. It's about staying alert, focused, and faithful. Jesus is giving us a heads-up so we're not caught off guard—and so we can help others find hope in Him.

Bottom Line

Jesus is King over everything. Even when the world looks dark, we can stand firm, knowing He is with us and will return in power and glory.

Prayer

Heavenly Father, thank You for being on the throne even when life feels uncertain. Help me to trust that Jesus is in control, no matter what. Teach me to walk with boldness, like the lion, and to live with faith and focus. Give me courage when I'm afraid, and help me point others to Your love and truth. In Jesus' Name, Amen.

December 27

Check Yourself Before You Wreck Yourself

3-Year-Bible Reading: Proverbs 30:32–33; 1 John 4:1–4; 1 Thessalonians 1–2; Revelation 13

"If you have been foolish, exalting yourself, or if you have been devising evil, put your hand on your mouth. For pressing milk produces curds, pressing the nose produces blood, and pressing anger produces strife." — Proverbs 30:32–33

"Beloved, do not believe every spirit, but test the spirits to see whether they are from God, for many false prophets have gone out into the world." — 1 John 4:1

"For our gospel came to you not only in word, but also in power and in the Holy Spirit and with full conviction." — 1 Thessalonians 1:5

"It performs great signs… and by the signs that it is allowed to work… it deceives those who dwell on earth." — Revelation 13:13–14

Have you ever been tricked by something that *looked* good on the outside but turned out to be bad news? Like a flashy ad for something that ends up being a scam, or someone who seemed super nice but had shady motives? Life's full of voices trying to lead us—some to truth, some to lies.

The Bible warns us that not everything spiritual or powerful is from God (**1 John 4:1**). Sometimes it's just noise—or worse, deception. Whether it's pride bubbling up inside us (**Proverbs 30:32**), pressure from people around us (**1 Thessalonians 2:4–6**), or even supernatural signs (**Revelation 13:13**), we've got to stay grounded in truth. God doesn't want us to fall for what looks impressive—He wants us to know *Him* and live from His Spirit.

Think About It

1. **Test the Source:** Not every "spiritual" thing is from God. How can you tell what's true? Use God's Word as your filter. If something contradicts the Bible or glorifies anything more than Jesus, it's not from Him.

2. **Watch Your Heart:** Pride and anger can be subtle traps. Are you acting from a place of humility or just trying to prove something? Proverbs reminds us that unchecked emotions lead to destruction.

3. **Be Rooted in the Real:** Paul told the Thessalonians that the gospel didn't come with just words, but with *power and the Holy Spirit*. When you truly walk with God, there's a depth and conviction that fake faith can't imitate.

Bottom Line

Stay sharp—just because something looks spiritual or powerful doesn't mean it's from God. Anchor yourself in His Word, stay humble, and let His Spirit lead you.

Prayer

Heavenly Father, help me to recognize Your voice in a world full of noise. Teach me to test what I hear and see through the lens of Your truth. Keep my heart humble, my spirit grounded, and my eyes focused on Jesus. In Jesus' Name, Amen.

December 28

Speak Up and Shine Bright

3-Year-Bible Reading: Proverbs 31:1–9; Psalm 148; 1 Thessalonians 4–5

"Open your mouth for the mute, for the rights of all who are destitute." — Proverbs 31:8

"Praise the Lord! Praise the Lord from the heavens; praise him in the heights!" — Psalm 148:1

"For God has not destined us for wrath, but to obtain salvation through our Lord Jesus Christ, who died for us so that whether we are awake or asleep we might live with him." — 1 Thessalonians 5:9–10

Have you ever seen something wrong happening and stayed silent because speaking up felt too risky? Maybe you saw someone getting bullied, or a friend making a bad decision, and you weren't sure what to do. **Proverbs 31** encourages us to stand up for others, especially those who don't have a voice.

Meanwhile, **Psalm 148** reminds us that all of creation—yes, even YOU—exists to praise God. And in **1 Thessalonians 4–5**, we're reminded that Jesus gave everything for us, so we can live with purpose, hope, and courage. When we speak out with love and live with bold faith, we not only honor others, but we also shine the light of Jesus into a dark world.

THINK ABOUT IT

1. **Use Your Voice for Good:** Who around you needs help, encouragement, or someone to speak up for them? Ask God to show you how to be brave and loving in those moments.

2. **Created to Praise:** Psalm 148 says everything should praise God—stars, animals, people...even teens! How can your daily actions, words, or even your social media reflect God's greatness?

3. **Live Awake:** In 1 Thessalonians, Paul encourages believers to live alert and self-controlled. Are there areas of your life where you've been "asleep" to what God wants for you? What would it look like to "wake up" spiritually?

BOTTOM LINE

You were made to shine, speak truth, and praise God—right where you are. Don't underestimate the power of your voice and your life when it's rooted in Jesus.

PRAYER

Heavenly Father, thank You for giving me a voice, a purpose, and the hope of salvation through Jesus. Help me to be brave in standing up for others, to live a life that praises You, and to stay spiritually awake and ready to follow You each day. Fill me with Your love and courage. In Jesus' Name, Amen.

December 29

Radiant in the Dark

3-Year-Bible Reading: Proverbs 31:10–31; 2 Peter 3:1–13; Revelation 19

"Charm is deceitful, and beauty is vain, but a woman who fears the Lord is to be praised." — Proverbs 31:30

"But the day of the Lord will come like a thief, and then the heavens will pass away with a roar... and the earth and the works that are done on it will be exposed." — 2 Peter 3:10

"Let us rejoice and exult and give him the glory, for the marriage of the Lamb has come, and his Bride has made herself ready." — Revelation 19:7

Have you ever tried to get ready in the dark? Maybe your power went out, or it was early and you didn't want to wake anyone up. It's frustrating, right? You can't see clearly, you make mistakes, and things feel uncertain. Spiritually speaking, we're living in a world that feels a lot like darkness. But God calls us to get ready anyway—not with perfect hair or the latest trends, but with hearts that are full of love for Him.

In **Proverbs 31**, we see a picture of someone who is valuable not because of appearance, but because she fears the Lord. In **2 Peter 3**, we're reminded that this world won't last forever. And in **Revelation 19**, we see the celebration that's coming when Jesus returns for His Bride—the Church. That's us. Are we getting ready?

Think About It

1. **What Really Matters:** The Proverbs 31 woman isn't praised for her looks or popularity—she's praised for her character and faith. What are you focusing on in your daily life? Is it helping you grow in your relationship with God?

2. **Live with Purpose:** 2 Peter 3 tells us everything in this world will eventually fade. So how should that change the way you live right now? Are you building your life on things that last?

3. **Ready for the Party?** Revelation 19 talks about a great wedding feast for Jesus and His people. Imagine the biggest celebration ever—and it's for you if you're part of His Church. Are you living like someone invited to that celebration?

Bottom Line

God is preparing a glorious future for those who love Him. In the middle of a dark and distracted world, we're called to live with purpose, character, and deep love for Jesus—because He's coming back, and we want to be ready.

Prayer

Heavenly Father, thank You for reminding me that real beauty comes from knowing and following You. Help me not to get distracted by things that won't last, but to live with purpose and hope. Teach me to be ready, full of love, and walking in Your light—even when the world feels dark. In Jesus' Name, Amen.

December 30

Shaped for Glory

3-Year-Bible Reading: Psalms 149; 1 John 3:2–3; 1 Corinthians 15; Romans 12:1–2

"Praise the Lord! Sing to the Lord a new song, his praise in the assembly of the godly!" — Psalms 149:1

"Beloved, we are God's children now, and what we will be has not yet appeared; but we know that when he appears we shall be like him, because we shall see him as he is. And everyone who thus hopes in him purifies himself as he is pure." — 1 John 3:2–3

"Do not be conformed to this world, but be transformed by the renewal of your mind, that by testing you may discern what is the will of God, what is good and acceptable and perfect." — Romans 12:2

Ever feel like you don't quite fit in—or that you're constantly trying to live up to other people's expectations? Whether it's pressure from social media, school, or even your own fears, it's easy to feel like you're supposed to mold yourself into someone you're not. But here's the truth: **1 John 3:2** tells us we are already God's children, and there's more—God is shaping us to be like Jesus!

That process isn't about pretending to be someone else. It's about transformation, the kind that begins deep inside your heart and mind (**Romans 12:2**). And as we're transformed, we're invited to praise, not just with songs but with lives that reflect His goodness (**Psalms 149:1**). You're not stuck being who the world says you are. You're becoming who God made you to be.

Think About It

1. **Who Are You Becoming?** When you think about your future, do you picture someone shaped by God's truth—or by the trends around you? Ask God to show you who He sees when He looks at you.

2. **Worship as a Lifestyle:** Psalm 149 talks about praising God in the assembly, but what if your everyday choices were worship too? How can you reflect God's love in how you live, think, and treat others?

3. **Don't Conform, Transform:** The world shouts a lot about what you should look like, want, and chase. But God calls you to a different path—one that transforms your mind and heart. What's one way you can renew your mind this week?

Bottom Line

God isn't asking you to be perfect—He's inviting you to be transformed. As His child, you are becoming more like Jesus, not by trying harder, but by letting Him renew your heart, mind, and life.

Prayer

Heavenly Father, thank You for calling me Your child and loving me as I am. Help me not to be shaped by the world around me, but by Your truth. I want to worship You with my life, not just my words. Keep transforming me so I can live in a way that reflects who You are. In Jesus' Name, Amen.

December 31

Praise that Never Ends

3-Year-Bible Reading: Psalms 150; Revelation 21–22

"Let everything that has breath praise the Lord! Praise the Lord!" — Psalm 150:6

"And I saw no temple in the city, for its temple is the Lord God the Almighty and the Lamb." — Revelation 21:22

"They will see his face, and his name will be on their foreheads. And night will be no more." — Revelation 22:4–5

Ever been to a concert where the music was so powerful you could feel it in your chest? Or a moment in worship where you felt totally connected to God, like time stopped? Those glimpses of beauty, joy, and awe are just a taste of what God has planned for us. In **Psalm 150**, we're invited to praise God with everything we've got—voices, instruments, breath.

And in **Revelation 21–22**, we get a stunning picture of our future: a place with no more pain, no more night, and no more distance from God. Heaven isn't just about harps and clouds—it's about full-on life with the One who made us, knows us, and loves us completely.

Think About It

1. **What's Your Praise Style?** Psalm 150 is like a playlist of praise, calling for every instrument and every breath to be used in worship. How do you express your love for God? Through music? Art? Acts of kindness? Your praise doesn't have to look like someone else's—just make sure it's real.

2. **No Temple, No Problem:** Revelation tells us there's no temple in the new city because God *is* the temple. That means God won't be confined to a building. How does that change the way you think about worship or being close to God in your daily life?

3. **Face to Face with God:** Imagine seeing God's face and living in a place where there's no more darkness. This isn't fantasy—it's your future in Christ. How does knowing that shape the way you face tough times right now?

Bottom Line

Our lives were made for praise—not just now, but forever. Whether through music, serving others, or just being real with God, we get to start living heaven's rhythm today.

Prayer

Heavenly Father, Thank You for the promise of a future with You where there's no more pain, darkness, or distance. Help me to live a life of praise right now, with every breath and every moment pointing back to You. Teach me to worship You not just with my words, but with my whole life. Let my heart reflect heaven, even here on earth. In Jesus' Name, Amen.

CONTINUE THE JOURNEY: YEAR TWO AWAITS

Loved your journey through Year One? Keep going! *Bible Chat 3-Year Chronological Daily Devotional: Year Two* is now available—ready to walk with you through Job, the Psalms, and the wisdom of Solomon, all while continuing your daily time in the New Testament and Proverbs. With the same short, meaningful devotions, reflection questions, and heartfelt prayers, Year Two deepens your understanding of God's Word in fresh and powerful ways. Don't stop here—scan the QR code to order your copy on Amazon and continue growing one day at a time!